DECADENCE AND THE SENSES

LEGENDA

LEGENDA is the Modern Humanities Research Association's book imprint for new research in the Humanities. Founded in 1995 by Malcolm Bowie and others within the University of Oxford, Legenda has always been a collaborative publishing enterprise, directly governed by scholars. The Modern Humanities Research Association (MHRA) joined this collaboration in 1998, became half-owner in 2004, in partnership with Maney Publishing and then Routledge, and has since 2016 been sole owner. Titles range from medieval texts to contemporary cinema and form a widely comparative view of the modern humanities, including works on Arabic, Catalan, English, French, German, Greek, Italian, Portuguese, Russian, Spanish, and Yiddish literature. Editorial boards and committees of more than 60 leading academic specialists work in collaboration with bodies such as the Society for French Studies, the British Comparative Literature Association and the Association of Hispanists of Great Britain & Ireland.

The MHRA encourages and promotes advanced study and research in the field of the modern humanities, especially modern European languages and literature, including English, and also cinema. It aims to break down the barriers between scholars working in different disciplines and to maintain the unity of humanistic scholarship. The Association fulfils this purpose through the publication of journals, bibliographies, monographs, critical editions, and the MHRA Style Guide, and by making grants in support of research. Membership is open to all who work in the Humanities, whether independent or in a University post, and the participation of younger colleagues entering the field is especially welcomed.

ALSO PUBLISHED BY THE ASSOCIATION

Critical Texts
Tudor and Stuart Translations • New Translations • European Translations
MHRA Library of Medieval Welsh Literature

MHRA Bibliographies
Publications of the Modern Humanities Research Association

The Annual Bibliography of English Language & Literature
Austrian Studies
Modern Language Review
Portuguese Studies
The Slavonic and East European Review
Working Papers in the Humanities
The Yearbook of English Studies

www.mhra.org.uk
www.legendabooks.com

EDITORIAL BOARD

Chair: Professor Jonathan Long, University of Durham
For *Germanic Literatures*: Ritchie Robertson (University of Oxford)
For *Italian Perspectives*: Simon Gilson (University of Warwick)
For *Moving Image*: Emma Wilson (University of Cambridge)
For *Research Monographs in French Studies*:
Diana Knight (University of Nottingham)
For *Selected Essays*: Susan Harrow (University of Bristol)
For *Studies in Comparative Literature*: Duncan Large
(British Centre for Literary Translation, University of East Anglia)
For *Studies in Hispanic and Lusophone Cultures*:
Trevor Dadson (Queen Mary, University of London)
For *Studies in Yiddish*: Gennady Estraikh (New York University)
For *Transcript*: Matthew Reynolds (University of Oxford)

Managing Editor
Dr Graham Nelson
41 Wellington Square, Oxford OX1 2JF, UK

www.legendabooks.com

Decadence and the Senses

Edited by Jane Desmarais and Alice Condé

Modern Humanities Research Association
2017

Published by Legenda
an imprint of the Modern Humanities Research Association
Salisbury House, Station Road, Cambridge CB1 2LA

ISBN 978-1-78188-481-2 (HB)
ISBN 978-1-78188-482-9 (PB)

First published 2017

All rights reserved. No part of this publication may be reproduced or disseminated or transmitted in any form or by any means, electronic, mechanical, photocopying, recording or otherwise, or stored in any retrieval system, or otherwise used in any manner whatsoever without written permission of the copyright owner, except in accordance with the provisions of the Copyright, Designs and Patents Act 1988, or under the terms of a licence permitting restricted copying issued in the UK by the Copyright Licensing Agency Ltd, Saffron House, 6–10 Kirby Street, London EC1N 8TS, England, or in the USA by the Copyright Clearance Center, 222 Rosewood Drive, Danvers MA 01923. Application for the written permission of the copyright owner to reproduce any part of this publication must be made by email to legenda@mhra.org.uk.

Disclaimer: Statements of fact and opinion contained in this book are those of the author and not of the editors or the Modern Humanities Research Association. The publisher makes no representation, express or implied, in respect of the accuracy of the material in this book and cannot accept any legal responsibility or liability for any errors or omissions that may be made.

Trademark notice: Product or corporate names may be trademarks or registered trademarks, and are used only for identification and explanation without intent to infringe.

© Modern Humanities Research Association 2017

Copy-Editor: Dr Susan Wharton

CONTENTS

	Acknowledgements	ix
	Notes on the Contributors	x
	List of Illustrations	xiii
	Introduction JANE DESMARAIS AND ALICE CONDÉ	1
1	Symons and Whistler: The Art of Seeing NICK FREEMAN	15
2	Carnal Flowers, Charnel Flowers: Perfume in the Decadent Literary Imagination CATHERINE MAXWELL	32
3	Decadent Sensuality in Rachilde and Wilde PETRA DIERKES-THRUN	51
4	'Things worldly and things spiritual': Huysmans's *À rebours* and the House at Fontenay JESSICA GOSSLING	66
5	'All the senses would melt into one': Theodore Watts-Dunton's *Aylwin* and the Decadent Pleasures of the *Roman-à-clef* ANGELA DUNSTAN	83
6	'Use my body like the pages of a book': Decadence and the Eroticized Text KOSTAS BOYIOPOULOS	101
7	Bittersweet: Michael Field's Sapphic Palate SARAH PARKER	121
8	Dancing the Image: Sensoriality and Kinesthetics in the Poetry of Stéphane Mallarmé and Arthur Symons KATHARINA HEROLD	141
9	Decadent Sensations: Art, the Body and Sensuality in the 'Little Magazines' (1885–1897) MATTHEW BRINTON TILDESLEY	162
10	'Selecting, transforming, recombining': John Singer Sargent's *Madame X* and the Aesthetics of Sculptural Corporeality LIZ RENES	182

11 Sensory Nullification in the Poetry of Ernest Dowson
    ALICE CONDÉ   200
12 Afterword: Decadent Taste
    DAVID WEIR   219

    Appendix   229
    Select Bibliography   236
    Index   238

ACKNOWLEDGEMENTS

We would like to express our thanks to all who helped to organize the *Decadence and the Senses* conference at Goldsmiths on 10–11 April 2014. Thank you to the Modern Humanities Research Association for generously awarding us a Conference Grant. We are grateful to our co-organizers Angie Dunstan and Jessica Gossling, and the students and colleagues in the Department of English and Comparative Literature who helped us during the event, especially Magdalena Dyczkowska, Johanna O'Shea, Priya Shemar, Jasmine Tompkins and Maxwell Wassmann. Richard Bolley and Maria MacDonald provided invaluable administrative support, and we would like to thank Shivi Hotwani and Caroline Rondel from the Goldsmiths Conference Centre. Thanks to Gary Howells, Karl Hatton and Stephan Barrett for providing the post-conference Black Feast, cocktails, and music respectively. We are grateful to Graham Nelson, Managing Editor at Legenda, for his support and advice throughout the publication process, and to Professor Martha Vicinus of the University of Michigan for reading through the volume and offering such positive and constructive feedback.

For permission to reproduce the images included in this volume we are grateful to the following institutions: the Science and Society Picture Library, the Bibliothèque nationale de France, the National Portrait Gallery, the Metropolitan Museum of Art, Durham University Library, the National Gallery of Art, Washington D.C., and the British Library. We are grateful to Peter Greenaway for permission to reproduce stills from his film *The Pillow Book*. Finally we would like to thank everyone who attended and contributed to the *Decadence and the Senses* conference for two days of fascinating discussion that inspired this collection of essays.

J.D., A.C., August 2016

NOTES ON THE CONTRIBUTORS

KOSTAS BOYIOPOULOS is a Teaching Associate in the Department of English Studies at Durham University. His main research interests include *fin-de-siècle* Decadence and Aestheticism, comparative poetics, and currently science fiction. He is the author of *The Decadent Image: The Poetry of Wilde, Symons, and Dowson* (Edinburgh University Press, 2015); he was awarded the Friends of Princeton University Library Research Grant in connection with this project. He co-edited the essay collection *Decadent Romanticism: 1780–1914* (Ashgate, 2015) with Mark Sandy, and *The Decadent Short Story: An Annotated Anthology* (Edinburgh University Press, 2014) with Matthew Brinton Tildesley and Yoonjoung Choi.

ALICE CONDÉ is a Postdoctoral Research Associate in the Department of English and Comparative Literature at Goldsmiths, University of London. She completed her PhD, 'Incorporeal Punishment: Writing Masochism and the Cruel Woman in English Decadence, 1860–1900', at Goldsmiths in 2014. She co-organized the *Decadence and the Senses* conference in April 2014 and the *Ernest Dowson: Poet, translator, novelist* symposium at Goldsmiths in April 2016.

JANE DESMARAIS is Senior Lecturer in English in the Department of English and Comparative Literature at Goldsmiths, University of London. With Chris Baldick, she co-edited *Decadence: An Annotated Anthology* (Manchester University Press, 2012) and their edition for MHRA's 'Critical Texts' series, *Arthur Symons: Selected Early Poetry*, is forthcoming in 2017. Her monograph *Hothouse Flowers: A Cultural History, 1850–1950* is due to be published by Reaktion Books in 2018.

PETRA DIERKES-THRUN's research and teaching interests include the European and transatlantic *fin de siècle* and modernism; feminist and queer history and theory; LGBTQ literary and cultural studies; and digital pedagogy as well as pedagogically smart uses of technology in teaching and learning in the humanities. At Stanford University, Petra is a Lecturer in Comparative Literature and also serves as the Director of Interdisciplinary Teaching and Learning for the Office of the Vice Provost for Teaching and Learning. She is also an Advisory Editor for Gender and Sexuality Studies at *boundary 2.org* (Duke University Press) and was the Founding Editor of *The Latchkey: Journal of New Woman Studies*, a peer-reviewed, international scholarly online journal dedicated to the figure of the New Woman in *fin-de-siècle* and modernist society and culture (Rivendale Press).

ANGELA DUNSTAN is a London-based Postdoctoral Researcher for the Australian National University, and an Honorary Research Fellow at Birkbeck, University of London, and has taught at Oxford (University College), the University of London

(Goldsmiths) and the University of Sydney. She has published on Victorian literature and visual cultures, nineteenth-century literary lectures, and global communities of reading in *Modern Language Quarterly*, *The British Art Journal*, *Burlington Magazine*, *19: Interdisciplinary Studies in the Long Nineteenth Century*, the *Dictionary of Nineteenth-Century Journalism* and in collections such as *William Morris and the Art of Everyday Life* (2010). Angie is currently completing a monograph on Victorian literature, sculpture and the idea of authenticity, and recently guest-edited the 'Victorian Sculpture' special issue of *19: Interdisciplinary Studies in the Long Nineteenth Century* (Summer 2016).

NICK FREEMAN is Reader in Late Victorian Literature at Loughborough University. He has published essays on a number of decadent writers, including Wilde, Swinburne, Dowson, and Arthur Machen, as well as two monographs, *Conceiving the City: London, Literature and Art, 1870–1914* (Oxford University Press, 2007), and *1895: Drama, Disaster and Disgrace in Late Victorian Britain* (Edinburgh University Press, 2011, paperback 2013). He has a particular interest in the work of Arthur Symons, and edited his *Spiritual Adventures* for the MHRA's 'Critical Texts' series (2017).

JESSICA GOSSLING is a PhD student in the Department of English and Comparative Literature at Goldsmiths, University of London, and was co-organizer of the *Decadence and the Senses* conference in 2014. Her research interests are interdisciplinary, concentrating on the literature and the visual arts of the nineteenth century in England and France. Her thesis is a study of Decadent literature between 1884 and 1900, and examines the role and significance of 'threshold' space in selected works of Charles Baudelaire, Joris-Karl Huysmans, Arthur Symons, and Ernest Dowson.

KATHARINA HEROLD is studying for a DPhil in English Literature at the University of Oxford supported by an AHRC grant. Previously, she trained and worked as a theatre director in Germany, before embarking on a BA degree in English and Comparative Literature at Goldsmiths, University of London, followed by an MSt in English Literature (1830–1914) at Oxford. Her research focuses on interdisciplinary projects involving the European *fin de siècle*, Aestheticism, Drama and Performance Theory, Orientalism, and Translation Studies. Her DPhil thesis investigates the ways in which the East shaped English and German Decadent writing between 1880 and 1920.

CATHERINE MAXWELL is Professor of Victorian Literature at Queen Mary, University of London. Her publications include the monographs *The Female Sublime from Milton to Swinburne: Bearing Blindness* (Manchester University Press, 2001), *Swinburne* in the British Council series Writers and Their Work (Northcote House, 2006), and *Second Sight: The Visionary Imagination in Late Victorian Literature* (Manchester University Press, 2008). Her most recent book is the essay collection *Algernon Charles Swinburne: Unofficial Laureate*, co-edited with Stefano Evangelista (Manchester University Press, 2013). She has published essays on Shelley, Browning, Christina and Dante Gabriel Rossetti, George Eliot, Ruskin, Swinburne, Thomas Hardy, Theodore Watts-Dunton, Oscar Wilde, Arthur Symons, John Addington

Symonds, and Vernon Lee. She has recently completed a monograph, *Scents and Sensibility: Perfume in Victorian Literary Culture*, for publication by Oxford University Press in late 2017.

SARAH PARKER is Lecturer in English at Loughborough University. Her first monograph is *The Lesbian Muse and Poetic Identity, 1889–1930* (Routledge, 2013). Her other publications include articles on Michael Field, Olive Custance and a chapter in *Algernon Charles Swinburne: Unofficial Laureate* (Manchester University Press, 2013). She is currently working on her second monograph project, provisionally entitled 'Picturing the Poetess: Women Poets and Photography, 1850–1930'. An article, 'Publicity, Celebrity, Fashion: Photographing Edna St. Vincent Millay', is forthcoming in *Women's Studies*, based on AHRC-funded research into Millay's papers in the Library of Congress.

LIZ RENES completed her PhD in History of Art at the University of York in 2015. Her previous educational background includes an MA in Fine and Decorative Art from Sotheby's Institute of Art, London and a BA in Art History from New College of Florida. She is currently the Visual Arts Convenor for the Bath Royal Literary and Scientific Institution (BRLSI), and the Visual Arts editor for the postgraduate journal *HARTS & Minds*. She is co-organizer of the recent conference *Sargentology: New Perspectives on the Works of John Singer Sargent*, and is currently working on launching sargentology.com, a new web thinkspace for Sargent studies, news and events. Publication-wise, she is currently working on a book chapter exploring Sargent's Modernist status for the proceedings from the *Beyond the Victorian and Modernist Divide* conference held in Rouen in 2014, as well as co-editing a selection of papers from *Sargentology* for *Visual Culture in Britain*, forthcoming in 2018.

MATTHEW BRINTON TILDESLEY is an Associate Professor of English Literature at Hankuk University of Foreign Studies, Seoul, South Korea. Since completing his postgraduate career at Durham University in 2008, Matthew's main field of research has been periodical culture of the 1880s and 1890s, Aestheticism, Decadence and Modernism. He has published various articles on authors such as Oscar Wilde, Ernest Dowson, Joseph Conrad, Émile Zola and Virginia Woolf, and his work on *The Savoy* magazine in particular has enjoyed worldwide success online. In 2008, he contributed 19 entries to the British Library's *Dictionary of Nineteenth-Century Journalism*, and co-edited *The Decadent Short Story: An Annotated Anthology* with Kostas Boyiopoulos and Yoonjoung Choi (Edinburgh University Press, 2014).

DAVID WEIR is Professor Emeritus of Comparative Literature at Cooper Union in New York City. He is the author of eight books, including two on the topic of decadence: *Decadence and the Making of Modernism* (1995) and *Decadent Culture in the United States* (2009). More recently, he has written the 'Decadence' entry for the second edition of *The Oxford Encyclopedia of Aesthetics* and the entry on American decadence for *Le Dictionnaire de la décadence* to be published by Éditions Honoré Champion. His current project, with Oxford University Press, is *Decadence: A Very Short Introduction*.

LIST OF ILLUSTRATIONS

FIG. 1.1. Alvin Langdon Coburn, Fountain Court, photograph, c. 1907. With thanks to the Science and Society Picture Library.

FIG. 4.1. Joris-Karl Huysmans in his study. Dornac, *Nos contemporains chez eux*, fol. 1, photograph. Bibliothèque nationale de France, Département des Estampes et de la photographie.

FIG. 5.1. May Morris, *Kelmscott Manor*, n.d., watercolour on paper. Distributed under a CC-BY 2.0 licence.

FIG. 5.2. Henry Treffry Dunn, *Dante Gabriel Rossetti; Theodore Watts-Dunton*, 1882, gouache and watercolour on paper, 54.3 × 81.9 cm. © National Portrait Gallery, London.

FIG. 6.1. Still from *The Pillow Book* (dir. Peter Greenaway, 1996), at 00:47:06.

FIG. 6.2. Still from *The Pillow Book* (dir. Peter Greenaway, 1996), at 00:56:44.

FIG. 6.3. Still from *The Pillow Book* (dir. Peter Greenaway, 1996), at 01:00:06.

FIG. 6.4. Still from *The Pillow Book* (dir. Peter Greenaway, 1996), at 01:33:12.

FIG. 8.1. Samuel Joshua Beckett, *Loie Fuller Dancing*, 1900, gelatin silver print. Metropolitan Museum of Art, New York.

FIG. 8.2. Double page 9 from Stéphane Mallarmé's *Un coup de Dés*. Bibliothèque nationale de France.

FIG. 8.3. Double page 3 from Stéphane Mallarmé's *Un coup de Dés*. Bibliothèque nationale de France.

FIG. 8.4. John Singer Sargent, *Heads and Faces of Javanese Dancers* (from *Sketchbook of Javanese Dancers*), 1889, graphite on off-white wove paper. Metropolitan Museum of Art, New York.

FIG. 8.5. John Singer Sargent, *Heads and Faces of Javanese Dancers* (from *Sketchbook of Javanese Dancers*), 1889, graphite on off-white wove paper. Metropolitan Museum of Art, New York.

FIG. 9.1. Charles Ricketts, initial piece to 'Maurice de Guérin', c. 1892, *The Dial*, 2, p. 11. Reproduced by permission of Durham University Library.

FIG. 9.2. Charles Shannon, *The Queen of Sheba*, 1889, *The Dial*, 1, AD. Reproduced by permission of Durham University Library.

FIG. 10.1. John Singer Sargent, *Madame X*, 1883–84, oil on canvas, 208.6 × 109.9 cm. Metropolitan Museum of Art, New York.

FIG. 10.2. John Singer Sargent, *Margaret Stuyvesant Rutherfurd White, or Mrs. Henry White*, 1883, oil on canvas, 225.1 × 143.8 cm. Courtesy of the National Gallery of Art, Washington D.C.

FIG. 11.1. Front cover of Ernest Dowson's *Verses* (1896) with design by Aubrey Beardsley. © The British Library Board, K.T.C.26.a.11 (front cover).

INTRODUCTION

Jane Desmarais and Alice Condé

From the perfumed verse of Charles Baudelaire and the 'fleshly' poetry of A. C. Swinburne, to the extravagant and perverse tastes of Des Esseintes in *À rebours*, the sensual aesthetics of Oscar Wilde's *The Picture of Dorian Gray*, and the cold cloistered spaces of Ernest Dowson's poetry, the tradition of literary Decadence in the nineteenth century stands out for its preoccupation, even obsession, with extreme sensations. Indeed, this obsession is a defining feature of the tradition. Almost without exception, Decadent writers aimed to bring the reader's senses alive, sometimes in a pleasurable way, sometimes in a way that turns the stomach, and sometimes both. To the visual spectacle of modern life documented by Realist writers like Charles Dickens and Émile Zola, Decadent writers added a range of smells, tastes, and textures that had never been written about before. Many critics looking back at the decadent *fin de siècle* evoke the period in terms of this intoxicating yet exhausting sensory indulgence: 'Draw the curtains, kindle a joss-stick in a dark corner, settle down on a sofa by the fire, light an Egyptian cigarette and sip a brandy and soda,' fantasized John Betjeman in 1948, 'as you think yourself back to the world which ended in prison and disgrace for Wilde, suicide for Crackanthorpe and John Davidson, premature death for Beardsley, Dowson, Lionel Johnson, religion for some, drink and drugs for others, temporary or permanent oblivion for many more ...'.[1]

With their highly developed senses and refined intellectual tastes, Decadent writers were both fascinated and repulsed by the human body and its functions, and they were particularly attracted to physical states and conditions that were intensified by nervous or pathological psychological states. Joris-Karl Huysmans's Des Esseintes is the Decadent synaesthete *ne plus ultra*. In retreating to a suburb outside Paris to escape the urban humdrum, he renounces the notion of normal physical well-being and luxuriates in the alternating conditions of self-indulgence and self-denial. He suffers from recognizably anorexic tendencies, and is careful and obsessive with what enters his home and his ailing body. He organizes a Black Feast to celebrate his sexual impotence, and later, when unable to take food orally, embarks on a new method of nourishment via a peptone enema. To appreciate Decadence is to indulge in voluptuous pleasures, but it is also to experience (sometimes simultaneously) pain and violent disgust. In the work of late nineteenth-century Decadents, like Huysmans, Rachilde, and Wilde, the senses are yoked to a realm of oriental fantasy and in the aesthetic preferences of Des Esseintes, Raoule de Vénérande, and Dorian Gray, the reader is invited to sample exotic tastes, smells and sounds, and to envisage states of mind in highly sensual terms. 'For each emotion', as Wilde imagined for his drama, *Salomé* (1894), 'a new perfume'.²

At a time when political, cultural and scientific revolutions had swept across Europe, when social change seemed to be accelerating towards a state of affairs of which no one could be fully certain, late nineteenth-century Decadent writers — much like their Roman forebears — envisaged history in biological terms, as a series of life cycles, where youth and maturity ultimately fade and decline. In their work we repeatedly encounter highly sensual images of beauty and rot, decrepitude and disease, cruelty and sterility. Disgusted by metropolitan landscapes of overcrowding and poverty, and revolted by the impact of industrialization and the new commercial culture, Aesthetes and Decadents found in sensory experience an escape from the evil of banality, and in acts of private sensual indulgence they identified a way of shocking the complacent and culturally deodorized middle classes. They were connoisseurs of the opium pipe and passing cloud. Flux, filth and all manner of sensual excitements were their obsessions.

In the work of Decadent writers there is a significant preoccupation with intersensoriality and synaesthesia.³ The opening paragraphs of Wilde's *The Picture of Dorian Gray*, for example, wilfully confuse the natural and the artificial and we, like the feminine and aestheticized Dorian, are meant to appreciate the scene as 'a kind of momentary Japanese effect'. In an unnatural synthesis of the visual, olfactory, and aural, Wilde endows language with the sensuality of paint on canvas. Our attention is directed by a series of natural scents and artificial perfumes from the garden exterior, with its 'rich odour of roses', 'the heavy scent of the lilac' and 'the more delicate perfume of the pink-flowering thorn', to the interior of the studio and the perfume of Lord Wotton's 'innumerable cigarettes'.⁴

Like an unstoppered perfume bottle, the Decadent imaginary has all the provocative and vertiginous expansiveness of scent. Baudelaire describes this well in his poem 'Le Flacon' [The Flask] from *Les Fleurs du mal* (1857):

> Mille pensers dormaient, chrysalides funèbres,
> Frémissant doucement dans les lourdes ténèbres,
> Qui dégagent leur aile et prennent leur essor,
> Teintés d'azur, glacés de rose, lamés d'or.
>
> [A thousand thoughts, tombed chrysalises, slept here
> Quietly quivering in the heavy shade
> Who now, shaking their wings, take to the air
> Azure-tinted, rose-glazed, gold-inlaid.]⁵

To imagine Decadence is to conjure up hedonism, dissipation and material extravagance — lakes filled with wine, ceilings freighted with rose petals, sandal-wearing catamites administering culinary delicacies to feasting emperors. The long and rich tradition of cultural and historical imagination about Decadence owes much to eighteenth-century historical accounts of the luxurious tastes and cruel whims of Emperors such as Nero and Tiberius, and to circulating notions of linguistic and literary decline. The decline of the Roman Empire 'was the inescapable point of historical reference for all the extended and enriched meanings of the Decadent idea in the nineteenth century and beyond.'⁶ By 1892, when Wilde left his lecture tour in the United States for Paris to get an à la mode haircut in the style of Nero,[7] Decadents were trading fairly liberally and parodically on notions of Roman licence and style. The confidences and anxieties that accompanied ideas of progress and technological advance at the *fin de siècle* were all prefigured in the debauched sensory excesses of the Romans at the end of empire.

Classical scholars, like Désiré Nisard (1806–88) in his *Études de mœurs et de critique sur les poètes latins de la décadence* [Cultural-Critical Studies] (1834), argued that in comparison to true classical Latin of the periods of the late republic and early (i.e. Augustan) empire — approximately 80BCE to 14CE — later Latin writings were inferior and unworthy of study. In his critique of the Romantics, and Victor Hugo's subversive handling of alexandrine verse form, Nisard used a gustatory metaphor and compared aspects of decadent style to culinary confection. In much the same way as an appetite can be weakened by the consumption of sweets and trifles, he protested, so the writer's creative talent is impoverished (and made effeminate and decadent) by over-attention to description and literary flourishes. Too much, he complained, was in the detail, but attention to detail, especially detail in dress and manner, becomes a trademark of the Decadent writer, many of whom adopted natural emblems and floral motifs that signified the idea of metamorphosis or the triumph of art over nature.

This volume of essays contains a selection of contributions to an international conference on *Decadence and the Senses* held at Goldsmiths, University of London, in April 2014, the aim of which was to explore the Decadent sensorium and its ubiquitous representation in Decadent literature and visual culture from antiquity to the present day. At the heart of the discussion was a preoccupation with paradox and perversion, a 'delight in disgust', as David Weir describes it. All classic nineteenth-century texts of Decadence, he concluded, share a common taste for 'delight in disgust, an attraction to things that people who have normal taste react to with revulsion' (see p. 221). The essays collected here constitute the first book-length study of Decadent obsessions in relation to the senses and the Decadent preoccupation with extreme forms of sensuality. The contributors explore a number of rich and varied perspectives on the five senses and Decadent intersensoriality. Focusing on the work of both prominent and less well-known figures in the Decadent tradition, established and emergent scholars trace sensual motifs and figures, examine the significance of the (sexual and textual) body as a locus of sensual pleasure and pain, and ponder the Decadent preoccupation with synaesthesia and synecdoche.

To a large extent, recent research on Decadence and the senses emerges from wider cultural-historical investigations into the role and significance of the human senses. The pioneering work of Mark M. Smith (*Sensing the Past*, 2008) in the rapidly developing field of sensory history and the extensive cultural-historical research of David Howes, Alain Corbin, and Constance Classen, among others, in recent decades have led to a greater understanding of the social and cultural significance of the senses and their relationship to biology (particularly neurology), psychology, the environment and the human imagination.[8] The work of Corbin perhaps stands out here, because as Frank Kermode commented in 1994, 'no respected historian had ever before written so much, and so explicitly, about shit, which, as more sanitized historians had omitted to specify, occupied in former times the worry-space now claimed by nuclear waste.'[9] Corbin's historical study of the 'malodorous effluvia'[10] of human life created a fresh field of scholarship, and contributions of American scholars to forums in the *Journal of American History* and *American Historical Review* stimulated intellectual debate about the Decadent sensorium and how it changes over time and place. Classen's *The Deepest Sense: A Cultural History of Touch* (2012), one of the early volumes in the ongoing series *Studies in Sensory History* (University of Illinois Press), explores the tactile foundations of Western culture, focusing on the lived experiences of embodiment in the Middle Ages, and the six-volume series, *A Cultural History of the Senses* (ed. by Classen, 2014), significantly expands the terrain. In the course of sixty essays, with broad geographical scope from Europe to North America, we are given an historical overview of the role of sensations and sensory interest in social life, particularly its significance in relation to urbanism, religion, philosophy, science, medicine, literature, and art.

The radiating phenomenon of sensory studies has generated new interdisciplinary research areas that focus on a single sense in relation to the creative literary imagination. One such area is scholarly research into olfaction, or 'smell studies', as Clare Brant has described,[11] which has been developing since the late 1980s when Corbin published his influential book, *The Foul and the Fragrant: Odour and the Social Imagination* (1986). This was followed by a number of cultural-historical studies on smell, including Constance Classen, David Howes and Anthony Synnott, *Aroma: The Cultural History of Smell* (1994), and works on olfaction in literature and the visual arts: Hans Rindisbacher, *The Smell of Books* (1992) and Janice Carlisle, *Common Scents: Comparative Encounters in High-Victorian Fiction* (2004). In 2006 two edited collections were published: *The Smell Culture Reader* (ed. by Jim Drobnick) and *Nosegay: A Literary Journey from the Fragrant to the Fetid* (ed. by Lara Fiegel), and over the last few years, scholarly attention has focused on late nineteenth-century fiction and painting, with particular emphasis on the traditions of Aestheticism and Decadence. Christina Bradstreet considers nineteenth-century debates surrounding the role of smell in aesthetics,[12] and in her essay '"Wicked with Roses": Floral Femininity and the Erotics of Scent' (2007), she offers a detailed visual analysis of smell in Charles Courtney Curran's painting *Scent of the Rose* (1890) and John William Waterhouse's *The Soul of the Rose* (1908).[13] A woman smelling flowers was a familiar image in paintings and perfume advertisements, and many artists used the image to endorse conservative notions about femininity. The association of women with roses was a way of promoting an idealized view of womanhood that emphasized innocence, purity, and devotion. In Waterhouse's *The Soul of the Rose*, for example, a Pre-Raphaelite beauty is depicted in the throes of imagining some romantic encounter, her thoughts triggered, the image suggests, by the sweet odour of a rose she holds to her nose and lips. But the juxtaposition of woman and flowers could be interpreted in a variety of ways. As Bradstreet argues, 'Whether the female figure is shown daintily tilting the rose to her face, presenting the blossom to her lover, or lustily burying her nose into a lavish bloom, the simple gesture of smelling flowers can present a number of different meanings including eligibility for polite courtship, sexual impropriety, and the fantasy of sexual abandon.'[14]

Leading the field of research into olfactory Decadence is Catherine Maxwell, whose Leverhulme Major Research Fellowship (2014–16) has supported an in-depth study of the role and significance of perfume in Victorian literary culture. In 'Scents and Sensibility: The Fragrance of Decadence' (a pre-published part of this longer study), Maxwell suggests that a 'poetics of perfume' directs our attention to the 'strongly symbolic or figurative dimension' of relatively unodiferous English Decadent writing, 'providing a powerful set of connections between the material and immaterial, the body and the spirit'.[15] Maxwell focuses on the work of Wilde and two poems by Arthur Symons, 'White Heliotrope' and 'Peau d'Espagne', which evoke past erotic encounters through fragrances that were popular in the late Victorian period. Drawing attention to the poems' modernity in two important ways, Maxwell argues that the visual impressionism of the poems shares some techniques of modern advertising copy (blurring, layering, close-ups, fade-outs), and she concludes that in both poems we find pre-Proustian associations between perfume and memory.

A preoccupation among the themes in this collection of essays is the anatomization and fetishization of the human body in Decadent writing, and the ventriloquial mode of discourse adopted by various writers, including Theodore Watts-Dunton, Arthur Symons and Ernest Dowson, in order to explore radical reconfigurations of gender and sexuality. Because the senses are by definition physical and bodily, we see examples of Decadent sensory writing around the locus of bodies — and female bodies in particular — in the work of both male and female writers. A number of essays in this volume focus on women writers, such as Michael Field, Agnes Mary Frances Robinson, and Rachilde. As Maxwell, Petra Dierkes-Thrun, and Sarah Parker demonstrate, there are fruitful lines of investigation to be pursued in terms of female writers in the Decadent tradition. The sculptural body and the Pygmalion myth are recurring themes in many of the chapters here. As George L. Hersey argues in *Falling in Love with Statues: Artificial Humans form Pygmalion to the Present* (2009), statues are representations of ideals, beautiful or divine images, and replicas of real life. Statuary appeals primarily to the sense of touch, and Hersey considers the capacity of sculpted stone and marble to evoke a physical reaction in the viewer. He argues that 'Tactility is a work's ability to make the viewer feel in his or her own body what the portrayed figure would be feeling if it were real.'[16]

Of all the senses, it is perhaps the provocations of touch that appealed most to late nineteenth-century Decadent writers, and their handling of this sense differentiates them from the previous generation of poets and writers. The wonders of skin, the primary organ of sense, were admired in both aesthetic and scientific terms in mid nineteenth-century popular-science books. In *The Toilet and Cosmetic Arts and Ancient and Modern Times* (1866), for instance, Arnold J. Cooley rhapsodizes that 'while [skin] possesses the softness of velvet and exhibits the delicate hues of the lily, the carnation, and the rose, it is nevertheless gifted with extraordinary strength and power of resisting injury'.[17] But in Decadent writing, touching the body is a boundary-crossing experience, one that confuses the ideas of attraction and repulsion and inverts the religious notion of touch as part of a process that is beneficent and healing. Surfaces and skins were a source of fascination to Decadent writers seeking to evoke strong bodily sensations in the reader, and in the catalogues of collectible items that we find in both Decadent poetry and prose fiction the sensation of touch is foregrounded; the text becomes textural. The layered and sumptuous piling on of references to multi-sensory objects such as food, fur, flowers, fragrances, fine fabrics, feathers and marble, overwhelm and stun the reader who is temporarily forced to surrender any desire for narrative progression. Sometimes this surrender has a strangely erotic, fetishistic appeal, as in Huysmans's *À rebours*, but sometimes the eroticism is combined with a strong feeling of disgust. Nowhere is this more explicit than in Octave Mirbeau's decadent horror novel, *Le Jardin des supplices* [*Torture Garden*] (1899), in which Clara leads the narrator (and thereby the reader) through an anti-Eden where human remains — blood, internal organs, flecks of skin and muscle — both nourish and decorate a garden of outstanding natural beauty. In this realm of horti-torture the fingers of the gardener are not so much green as vermillion.

In Decadent literature the senses are a gateway to both physical and metaphysical experiences. While Decadent writers generally invoke the senses of sight and hearing in both naturalistic and synaesthetic ways, they focus particularly on smell, taste and touch, perhaps because these senses stimulate and correspond to the phenomenon of appetite, a popular theme in Decadent literature. In the late nineteenth century bourgeois appetites were proliferating, not just for food and drink, but for powerful currencies like sex and money. Decadents were spellbound by the dangerous and illimitable desire generated by idealization, a preoccupation that we find in its most intense form in Baudelaire's *Les Fleurs du mal*. In 'Chanson d'après-midi' [Afternoon Song], the poet expresses his desire through highly sensual images that simultaneously suggest religious devotion and sexual submission:

> Tu me déchires, ma brune,
> Avec un rire moqueur,
> Et puis tu mets sur mon cœur
> Ton œil doux comme la lune.
>
> Sous tes souliers de satin,
> Sous tes charmants pieds de soie,
> Moi, je mets ma grande joie,
> Mon génie et mon destin,
>
> Mon âme par toi guérie,
> Par toi, lumière et couleur!
> Explosion de chaleur
> Dans ma noire Sibérie!
>
> [Tearing at hip and thigh
> With a primaeval giggle;
> And then my frantic goggle
> Rests in your lunar eye.
>
> Beneath your satin heel
> And silken toe I set
> My genius, my delight,
> My fate and my dark soul –

> A soul given new light
> And colour by this bright
> Explosion of white heat
> In my Siberian night!][18]

The correspondences that we find in *Les Fleurs du mal* between the material and immaterial realms inspired a range of Decadent writers in the second half of the nineteenth century keen to disassociate themselves from the Realist and Naturalist traditions. Recalling his reading of Baudelaire as a heady fusion of scent, music and text, Huysmans's Des Esseintes 'used to roam haphazardly through the dreams conjured up for him by these aromatic stanzas, until he was suddenly brought back to his starting point, to the motif of his meditation, by the recurrence of the initial theme, reappearing at fixed intervals in the fragrant orchestration of the poem'.[19] The Decadent preoccupation with synaesthesia and the interrelationship of different art forms, which Pater termed *Anders-streben*, motivates many discussions in the present volume. Katharina Herold examines words as sensual objects in relation to the poetry of Stéphane Mallarmé and Arthur Symons, while Jessica Gossling, Petra Dierkes-Thrun, and Kostas Boyiopoulos explore the relationship between the sensual and the textual, and the potential of words to cause moral and physical degeneration. Featuring in their discussions is perhaps the most well-known instance of sexual/textual corruption: Wilde's Dorian Gray and the 'fatal book'.

Visual and textual imagery are brought together in Chapter 1 as Nick Freeman demonstrates how Whistler's painterly technique is converted to literary style in Symons's poetry and prose. Freeman observes that Symons's poetic vocabulary shares the qualities of Whistler's limited colour palette. The two artists are united by their way of seeing and presenting the world. Though Symons disliked the term 'impressionism', his work displays its qualities. In his story 'The Death of Peter Waydelin' (1904) the eponymous Waydelin emphasizes, in a Whistlerian sense, the importance of impressionistic vision: not seeing objects or scenes, but shades and nuances of colour in what Whistler called 'arrangements'. These arrangements can be interpreted in both a visual and musical sense, and Freeman argues that, even though Symons claimed each form of art should be considered distinct from one another, he allows the visual to dominate in his works by 'painting in music'. Reappraising Symons's work through a 'Whistlerian lens' allows us to consider their artistic dialogue in Decadent terms. As Freeman demonstrates, Symons uses the techniques that gained Whistler fame and notoriety in order to indulge his decadent self-absorption and disconnection from the masses.

Moving from the sense of sight and its correspondent quality *in*sight to the sense of smell in Chapter 2, Catherine Maxwell explores the Decadent preoccupation with floral fragrances. She acknowledges that the orchid is the focus of much Decadent work, owing to its sexually suggestive appearance and exotic origin, but she argues that the tuberose should be considered another decadent 'carnal flower' because of the sensual qualities of its fragrance. Maxwell analyses the depiction of tuberoses in the lyrical poetry of Mark André Raffalovich, Agnes Mary Frances Robinson, and Theodore Wratislaw. Tuberose perfume is described by Victorian and modern commentators as having floral, fleshly, bloody and medicinal qualities.

Maxwell notes that within the Victorian 'language of flowers', the tuberose is exceptional for its consistent description as dangerously pleasurable, or 'voluptuous'. This is reflected in the Decadent preoccupation with the flower, exemplified in Wratislaw's erotic poem 'Tuberose' from *Orchids* (1896), in which the scent recalls a sexual encounter in the mind of the speaker but is also compared to a toxic poison. In Raffalovich's collection *Tuberose and Meadowsweet* (1885), the tuberose is similarly celebrated for its exotic sensuality. It is an intoxicating, almost deadly, perfume. Maxwell reveals the hints of homosexual passion in Raffalovich's poetry in which the tuberose symbolizes the hidden and dangerous desire (homosexuality was then illegal), and has the power to stimulate fleshly sensations thereby reigniting the desire. The tuberose is likewise a signifier of lesbian desire in Robinson's 'Tuberoses', which evokes the melancholy, funereal qualities of the scent; an ending love affair is compared to the fading and dying bouquet of cut flowers. Maxwell concludes her chapter with an inventory of twentieth- and twenty-first-century perfumes that draw on the sensational, sexual connotations of the flower.

À rebours has long been cited as the mysterious yellow book that influences or poisons Dorian Gray, but in Chapter 3 Petra Dierkes-Thrun offers a reading of the potential reciprocities between Rachilde's and Wilde's Decadent and Symbolist works, suggesting that Rachilde's *Monsieur Vénus* (1884) may have influenced *The Picture of Dorian Gray* both in terms of the novel itself and the character of Dorian. With reference to the original manuscript of *Dorian Gray*, in which the famous 'little yellow book' is given the suggestive title 'Le Secret de Raoul' by 'Catulle Sarazzin', Dierkes-Thrun argues that we might read Gray's corruption differently if we consider this an allusion to *Monsieur Vénus*. It brings out the homoeroticism of Wilde's novel, and implies that Gray might have been reading about Raoule's transgendered sexual adventures rather than Des Esseintes's experiments in Decadent seclusion. It opens up new possibilities for reading Wilde's novel, and Dierkes-Thrun comments on other striking similarities between Wilde's work and Rachilde's in terms of shared themes of queer love triangles, art and criminality. These reappear in Wilde's *Salomé*, which Dierkes-Thrun suggests may in turn have influenced Rachilde's Symbolist play *L'Araignée de cristal*, pointing out shared motifs of the moon, mirrors, the danger of the gaze, and decapitation. *Dorian Gray* becomes a potentially more decadent text through association with *Monsieur Vénus*, a homoerotic and gender-bending novel that includes sadistic and masochistic sexuality, and culminates in the creation of a 'sex puppet'. In *Monsieur Vénus* this perverse collector's item brings together the sculptural body and erotic sensuality in a grotesque reversal of the Pygmalion myth. Jacques's body becomes an item in Raoule's boudoir; a corpse and a corpus that has been written on and symbolically rewritten according to the author/creator's desire.

As Matthew Potolsky argues in *The Decadent Republic of Letters* (2014), Decadents 'adopt[ed] the libertine association of canon building and perverse connoisseurship' and spent their time constructing countercanons that 'challenge[d] the authority and singularity of national canons by offering a cosmopolitan alternative to national literary traditions, and by showing how such alternatives can be imagined.'[20] In Chapter 4 Jessica Gossling focuses on the perverse connoisseur-protagonist of

Huysmans's *À rebours*, a novel that challenges traditional notions of the form, functioning more as a catalogue of Decadent sensations than a plot-driven narrative. Des Esseintes is a Decadent collector, perfumer, bibliophile, and horticulturalist. He leads a secluded life in his retreat at Fontenay-aux-Roses, cloistered away like a secular monk worshipping Baudelaire's writing in place of a crucifix. His is a religion of the material and sensual, and this divide is replicated in the structure of two sides of the villa — one sensory, one utilitarian. Gossling notes the chapters of the novel are structured around different Decadent sensory pleasures, each contained within a different room of the house. However, she resists interpretations that read the villa's contents as a simple museum inventory, and argues that the rooms are not as separate as they seem. Des Esseintes's senses form a dynamic interaction with the surroundings as he carries his impressions from room to room, creating Baudelairean 'correspondances'. This creates a claustrophobic environment, in which Des Esseintes's body is affected by his own collections. He is trapped by and within his own neuroses like one of his hothouse plants. Memories and synaesthetic impressions intrude upon him randomly, and living in the villa intensifies his nervous disorder that is 'brought on' like a plant under hothouse glass.

As Angela Dunstan argues in her chapter on the Decadent sensorium in the work of Theodore Watts-Dunton, Decadent characters are often trapped in 'mausoleums of scholarship'. The sensorium can be a pleasure palace but can also be a prison. Dunstan offers an examination of the *roman-à-clef* that allows readers the fantasy of a real life written into fiction. Watts-Dunton's *Aylwin* (1898) is a multi-sensual novel, and within the narrative Aylwin experiences a 'Nature-ecstasy', in which the senses are blended and unified ('all the senses ... melt into one') and so strong that they exceed expression. Dunstan explores *Aylwin* as a 'celebrity sensorium' in her conceptualization of the minor character D'Arcy as a ventriloquization of the recently deceased poet-painter Dante Gabriel Rossetti. Contemporary readers would have been keen participants in the fantasy of engaging with this celebrity, a fantasy acted out by the characters in the novel. D'Arcy/Rossetti possesses a mystical spiritual or demonic power and animal magnetism, particularly for Aylwin himself. In Aylwin's description of the androgynous D'Arcy, Watts-Dunton foregrounds homoerotic sensuality. D'Arcy's male body is anatomized, and Dunstan focuses on a particularly evocative passage that centres upon the feminized description of his mouth. She concludes that *Aylwin* is affective in more ways than one, and functions as a consumable novel that invites its readers into the sensorium. Dunstan explains that the 1914 illustrated edition of *Aylwin* was a prized collector's object, a physical artifact that united the senses; one could touch the object, look at the illustrations, and experience the musicality of the written vignettes.

While Dunstan focuses on the anatomized erotic description of D'Arcy's androgynous facial features, in Chapter 6 Kostas Boyiopoulos describes the Decadent practice of synecdoche and fragmentation, but focuses on the female body in a comparative study of Arthur Machen and Peter Greenaway. Boyiopoulos extends the theme of Decadent bodies to include the body as text. He considers Susan Sontag's 'erotics of art', examining a duality, 'the text as erotic body and, inversely, the body as erotic text', in two works from the previous *fins de siècle*: Machen's *The*

Hill of Dreams (written 1895–97, published 1907), and Greenaway's film *The Pillow Book* (1996), in which both living and dead bodies symbolically become books. In *The Pillow Book* text is visually imprinted on the skin of the actors, and calligraphic writing on the body is an act of sensual pleasure. The body of a lover is compared, through simile, to writing materials. In *The Hill of Dreams*, Lucian's writings are Pygmalionic; he shapes words to his desires, forming a kind of Galatea. His beloved Annie Morgan's body becomes like an erotic idol, while the text — an erotic manuscript Lucian treasures — comes to replace her. Lucian also torments himself physically while reading the manuscript, making his own body into a fleshly palimpsest in an interplay of body and book. The reader becomes a participant in these Decadent fantasies as they engage with the text.

The suggestive sensuality of the female mouth — or more specifically, the tongue — is the focus of Chapter 7, in which Sarah Parker brings together two often overlooked aspects of Decadent scholarship: lesbian sexuality in the work of female writers, and the sense of taste. Parker observes the common nineteenth-century association between synaesthesia and sexual degeneracy or 'inversion' in men (according to Max Nordau and Havelock Ellis respectively), pointing out a lack of consideration of female homoeroticism and the senses. She explores the 'flavours' of eroticism in Michael Field's poetry, in which Sappho is invoked as the model for a sexually ambiguous female poet who writes of her own desire in sensory terms. Parker concentrates on the shared language of taste and flavour, in what she calls a 'Sapphic palate'. The juxtaposition of sweetness (honey and bee imagery) and bitterness (salt, sweat, tears and sea water), recalls Sappho's 'bittersweet' eros of Fragment 130. The consumption of these bitter and sweet substances in poems from Michael Field's *Long Ago* (1889) and *Wild Honey from Various Thyme* (1908), is linked by Parker to the desire to consume the beloved, reminiscent of Swinburne's Sappho-inspired poem 'Anactoria' with its imagery of the broken tongue, which represents both lyrical speech and oral eroticism.

The associations between taste, flavour, and the female body that are evoked by language in Michael Field's poetry are counterpointed by the next chapter's exploration of poetry and movement. In Chapter 8 Katharina Herold shows how the movement of the female body is suggested by linguistic patterns and arrangement of words in the Symbolist and Decadent poetry of Stéphane Mallarmé and Arthur Symons. Herold examines the 'dance of signs' in Mallarmé's *Un coup de Dés jamais n'abolira le Hasard* (1897) in terms of the arrangement of the poem on the page, and the dance and dancer as subject matter in Symons's *fin-de-siècle* poetry collections. *Un coup de Dés* is a poem crafted as an image of dance. The layout prompts the reader to become a collaborative artist, navigating the words and the space on the page. The words become sensory objects with material quality. Herold argues that the reader interacts with the typography and the shape of the poem and thereby participates in the dance. In Symons's poems, however, the reader is not invited to participate but to witness a spectacle. In contrast to Mallarmé's free use of language and space, Symons's verse is more formally constrained, deploying rhyme to convey movement, a visual impression of twirling dancers. Symons's 'The Dance of the Daughters of Herodias' (1899) signals a transformation of dance from Decadent to

Symbolist trope, while maintaining (in contrast to Mallarmé's abstracted woman in his earlier Symbolist work, *Hérodiade*) a focus on the sensuality of the female body, its eroticism and transgression.

In Chapter 9 Matthew Brinton Tildesley explores the negative reaction to bodily sensuousness in the work of contributors to Decadent Little Magazines in conservative Purity campaigns at the end of the nineteenth century in Britain. These included the fraught discussion surrounding the infamous 'British Matron' letters in *The Times*, calling for a ban on nudes in galleries. Tildesley explores the responses of contributors to *The Dial* and *The Pageant* to such campaigns. These publications and their contributors (most notably Charles Ricketts, Charles Shannon, and John Gray), are presented as figureheads of the 'new hedonism' who celebrate bodily sensations within their essays and artwork. In *The Dial*, for example, the female form is depicted in a number of works with a mirror, symbolic of voyeurism and narcissism. In Thomas Sturge Moore's poem 'Danaë', the female body is anatomized, shaping and firing the reader's imagination in a titillating way, and in Shannon's artwork *The Queen of Sheba* the image of the nude female form is presented in a setting that stimulates all the senses. These hetero-normative expressions of bodily sensuality are juxtaposed with the homoerotic overtones of Gray's Catholic poetry, in which sensual and scandalous subject matter is hidden behind a veil of religious themes. Parker observes similarly veiled glimpses of female homoeroticism in Michael Field's poetry, and Tildesley reveals here how sensation and sensuality work in harmony with the poets' adherence to the Catholic faith.

In Chapter 10 Liz Renes revisits the theme of Decadent vision and imagery, turning to a common Decadent obsession touched upon by other scholars in this volume: the whiteness and sculptural form of the female body. She explores the controversy surrounding the exhibition of John Singer Sargent's *Madame X*, submitted to the Paris Salon in 1884, and re-evaluates the painting's significance in terms of another of Sargent's paintings, *Mrs. Henry White* (1883), which was intended as a companion portrait. Renes draws on the aesthetic works of Pater, with whom Sargent was personally acquainted, in order to demonstrate the ways in which the sculptural body evokes a kinetic duality between life (the fleshliness of the living corporeal form) and art (classical statuary). This duality, she argues, is enacted in the portrait of Virginie Gautreau (Madame X), whose pose suggests both classical sculpture and the allure of a contemporary 'professional beauty'. In an examination of selected literary works by Sargent's friend Vernon Lee, and Henry James, Renes asserts that the sculptural body also functions as a metaphor for non-normative passions. In 'The Last of the Valerii' (1874), for example, James alludes to the Pygmalion myth, telling the story of a Juno statue worshipped by Count Marco Valerio, which leads him to neglect his wife Martha. The kinetic duality in James's story — the relationship between the eternal sensuality and sexuality embodied by the Juno statue and the innocence and ephemerality of the living Martha — echoes and resonates in a Decadent way, Renes argues, with the duality of Sargent's *Madame X* and *Mrs. Henry White*.

In Chapter 11 Alice Condé also explores the white, female sculptural form as it appears in Ernest Dowson's two published poetry collections, *Verses* (1896) and

Decorations: In Verse and Prose (1899). In Decadent poetry, such as Swinburne's or Baudelaire's, sexual desire is conceptualized in masochistic terms as both painful and pleasurable. This dynamic is often depicted in imagery of men genuflecting before female idols who hold the promise of sensory and sexual stimulation. Similarly, in Dowson's poetry the female body is frequently imagined as a cold, distant, inaccessible aesthetic ideal of perfection. However, his poems lack the same emphasis on fleshly sensations. Dowson idolized youth, and in particular young girls. In the poem 'Epigram', the speaker conceptualizes himself as a reverse Pygmalion, whose living ideal is turned to stone before him. This is a reflection of Dowson's own frustrated desire for Adelaide Foltinowicz, the teenage daughter of a restaurant-owner, who refused his romantic advances. Dowson does not revel in bodily sensation; rather his work engages with the paradox of amorous desire for the purity of childhood, resulting in an impulse (both personal and poetic) towards the nullification of the senses and retreat from all bodily pleasures and pains. Dowson's work, Condé argues, represents a diminuendo for Decadence in England.

By way of bringing the volume to a close, David Weir conflates the physical and metaphorical questions that circulate around the notion of Decadent taste. Relating the idea of aesthetic taste to the physical sense of taste, he describes Decadence as an 'uncommon sense' that evidences a taste for the distasteful, but does not evoke the quality of poor taste. Weir points out that the cultivation of perverse tastes is in fact paradoxically a mark of education and civilization, a reaction against our own instincts in favour of artifice and outsider taste:

> Decadent taste, then, involves a paradox that does not attach to the taste for beauty, since the sense of taste in that typical aesthetic case is truly like the taste of sense. Just as we know instantly whether the taste of food delights or disgusts, so we know immediately whether a work of art or the face of one's friend is beautiful or ugly. But the uncommon sense of decadent taste seems to be something that requires cultivation. The senses, in short, need to be educated. (p. 224)

The Decadent sensorium is clearly built upon old and new foundations, and we find in Decadent literature a number of sense-pairings that go back to antiquity. The association between seeing and hearing, for example, can be traced back to poetry as spoken word and to Horace's dictum, 'Ut pictura poesis' [As in painting so in poetry], but in many instances, as shown in the following chapters, the synaesthetic blendings are modern and draw upon new scientific discoveries and technological advances. As Maxwell, Gossling and Parker demonstrate, the Decadent preoccupation with smell and taste, for example, is as much rooted in new perfume technologies, in advances in fields as diverse as botany, medicine and sexology, as it is in the Decadent writer's desire to shock. Given the potent sensuality of Decadent literature, it is no surprise therefore that at the *fin de siècle* we encounter exhaustion and faint disgust. As we hope to have shown by the order of the essays in the collection, there is a significant attenuation in Decadent sensoriality by the 1890s. In English Decadent poetry, represented here principally by the work of Wilde, Symons and Dowson, there is a whitening of imagery, a thinning of passion, and a sense of depletion and failure overall. As Dowson expresses it in his poem, 'Non sum qualis eram bonae sub regno Cynarae', 'the feast is finished, and the lamps expire'.[21]

The empty banqueting hall is a poignant image of Decadence at the *fin de siècle* and an appropriate one to finish on. However, the tradition does not expire at the century's close but continues to delight and disgust (sometimes both) in unequal measure. The sensory excesses that define nineteenth-century Decadent texts find their corollary in all manner of modern obsessions, none perhaps more striking than the contemporary fascination with the body, its functions and flavours, appetites and desires, boundaries and processes, particularly ageing and degeneration. Decadent texts beckon seductively from the past, promising sense and sensationalism for the modern reader.

Notes to the Introduction

1. *The 1890s: A Period Anthology in Prose and Verse*, ed. by J. Betjeman and M. Secker (London: The Richards Press, 1948), pp. xii-xiii.
2. Richard Ellmann, *Oscar Wilde* (London: Penguin, 1987), p. 351.
3. See Steven Connor, 'Intersensoriality' (talk given at the Conference of the Senses, Thames Valley University, 6 February 2004, <www.stevenconnor.com/intersensoriality> (accessed 1 November 2016)).
4. 'These opening sentences fairly reek', claims John Sutherland in *Is Heathcliff a Murderer? Puzzles in 19th-century Fiction* (Oxford: Oxford University Press, 1997, p. 196), and he goes on to state that for Anglo-Saxon literature 'smells are indelicate' (p. 197). In regard to the horticultural references in *The Picture of Dorian Gray*, Sutherland underlines their unnatural coincidence: 'It is not inconceivable that the flowers, blooms and blossoms which Wilde describes (lilac, rose, laburnum, thorn) might just coincide on the branch in mid-June — but not in the full odiferousness about which the first chapter is eloquent' (pp. 196–97).
5. Translation by Derek Mahon, August 2012.
6. *Decadence: An Annotated Anthology*, ed. by Jane Desmarais and Chris Baldick (Manchester: Manchester University Press, 2012), p. 40.
7. See Karl Beckson, *London in the 1890s: A Cultural History* (New York and London: W. W. Norton, 1992), p. 43.
8. In 2005, *Empire of the Senses: The Sensual Culture Reader*, ed. by David Howes (Oxford: Berg, 2005) was published, followed in 2014 by *Ways of Sensing: Understanding Senses in Society*, ed. by David Howes and Constance Classen (Oxford: Routledge, 2014).
9. Frank Kermode, 'With the Aid of a Lorgnette', *London Review of Books*, 16.8 (28 April 1994), 14–15 (p. 14).
10. Ibid.
11. Clare Brant, 'Fume and Perfume: Some Eighteenth-Century Uses of Smell', *Journal of British Studies*, 40 (2004), 441. It is worth noting, however, that Frank Kermode, in his review of Corbin's *The Foul and the Fragrant* (*LRB*, 28 April 1994), identified this new field ten years earlier when he described it as 'modified smell discourse' (p. 14).
12. Christina Bradstreet, 'Scented Visions: The Nineteenth-century Olfactory Imagination' (unpublished PhD thesis, Birkbeck, University of London, 2008).
13. See Christina Bradstreet, '"Wicked with Roses": Floral Femininity and the Erotics of Scent', *Nineteenth-century Art Worldwide*, 6 (Spring 2007) <http://www.19thc-artworldwide.org/index.php/spring07/144-qwicked-with-rosesq-floral-femininity-and-the-erotics-of-scent>.
14. Ibid.
15. Catherine Maxwell, 'Scents and Sensibility: The Fragrance of Decadence', in *Decadent Poetics: Literature and Form at the British Fin de Siècle*, ed. by Jason David Hall and Alex Murray (Basingstoke: Palgrave, 2013), pp. 201–25 (pp. 202 and 222).
16. George L. Hersey, *Falling in Love with Statues: Artificial Humans form Pygmalion to the Present* (Chicago: University of Chicago Press, 2009), p. 19.

17. Arnold J. Cooley, *The Toilet and Cosmetic Arts in Ancient and Modern Times* (London: Robert Hardwicke, 1866), p. 197.
18. Charles Baudelaire, 'Chanson d'après-midi' [Afternoon Song], in *Les Fleurs du mal*, 1861; translated by Derek Mahon, 2011, in *Decadence: An Annotated Anthology*, pp. 95–96 (p. 96).
19. Joris-Karl Huysmans, *À rebours* [*Against Nature*], trans. by Robert Baldick (1884; London: Penguin, 2003), p. 109.
20. Matthew Potolsky, *The Decadent Republic of Letters: Taste, Politics, and Cosmopolitan Community from Baudelaire to Beardsley* (Philadelphia: University of Pennsylvania Press, 2013), pp. 78 and 77 respectively.
21. Ernest Dowson, 'Non sum qualis eram bonae sub regno Cynarae', *Verses* (London: Leonard Smithers, 1896), p. 17.

CHAPTER 1

Symons and Whistler: The Art of Seeing

Nick Freeman

> Things are because we see them, and what we see, and how we see it, depends on the arts that have influenced us.
> OSCAR WILDE, 'The Decay of Lying: An Observation' (1889)

Between the early 1890s and his calamitous mental collapse in the autumn of 1908, Arthur Symons was a key figure in the English literary avant-garde. A poet, critic, translator, reviewer, editor, travel journalist, and occasional writer of fiction, he was at once a feverishly industrious man of letters and a courageous advocate of new art. In essays such as 'The Decadent Movement in Literature' (1893), in his editorship of *The Savoy* (1896), in the ground-breaking poems of *Silhouettes* (1892) and *London Nights* (1895), and in critical explorations of French poetry and prose in *The Symbolist Movement in Literature* (1899) and elsewhere, Symons built bridges not only between English and continental culture but also between the Victorian and the modern. He wrote on Rodin's sculptures, the dramatic performances of Sarah Bernhardt and Eleonora Duse, and the cabaret singing of Yvette Guilbert. He discovered episodes of Casanova's memoirs, offered vivid accounts of his visits to Venice, Constantinople, Moscow, and Madrid, and could list among his friends Stéphane Mallarmé, Paul Verlaine, W. B. Yeats, Joseph Conrad, Toulouse-Lautrec, and Vladimir de Pachmann. He belonged to the Rhymers' Club, contributed to the *Yellow Book*, offered vital early encouragement to James Joyce, and helped introduce English readers to figures as diverse as Gabriele d'Annunzio, J.-K. Huysmans and Jules Laforgue. Had he not fallen ill when he did, one can only wonder what role he might have played in the evolution and appreciation of later forms of Modernism.

For all these accomplishments, however, Symons is usually considered to be a decadent writer, a louche celebrant of artificiality, dancing girls, foggy gas-lit streets and transient sexual encounters, whose recurrent delineations of his finely tuned consciousness made him at last a relic of 'Yellow Bookery' and the subject of T. S. Eliot's 'The Perfect Critic', an essay in which his 'sensitive and cultivated mind' is said to produce only a superior version of 'a common type of popular literary lecture'.[1] In his essays and prefaces, Symons advocated the independence of art from morality and didacticism, dismissed attempts to judge art on anything other than aesthetic terms, and studied the ways in which, in the hyper-sophisticated society of *fin-de-siècle* Europe, 'artificiality is a way of being true to nature'.[2] Fairly or otherwise, however, it is his decadent associations which have endured rather than his critical writing; it is often forgotten that Symons was a theorist of decadent aesthetics as well as a practitioner. Indeed, Holbrook Jackson identified him as the one critic of the 1890s who was 'sufficiently intimate with the modern movement to hold, and sufficiently removed from it in his later attitude to express, an opinion which should be at once sympathetic and reasonably balanced.'[3]

Symons was undoubtedly a cultured man of widely diverse interests, and he moved in a rich artistic milieu: he seems to have been equally at home at a lute recital by Arnold Dolmetsch, a poetry reading at Ye Olde Cheshire Cheese or a ballet at the Alhambra music hall. However, although he was a passable pianist who wrote perceptively about Chopin, Wagner and Richard Strauss, and although he was able to dramatize the mnemonic stimulus of olfactory sensation in poems such as 'White Heliotrope' (1895) and 'Peau d'Espagne' (written 1896, published 1913), his primary mode of engagement with the world was through its appearances.[4] Largely self-taught, he proved to be a perceptive critic of painting and its audiences, attending exhibitions in London and Paris and discussing them in essays such as 'Art and the Royal Academy' (1903).[5] He regularly quoted Théophile Gautier's remark, 'Je suis un homme pour qui le monde visible existe' [I am a man for whom the visible world exists], clarifying his position in a poem of 1907, 'The Brother of a Weed', which summed up his subjective and primarily visual relationship with the world:

> I have delighted in all visible things
> And built the world of my imaginings
> Out of the splendour of the day and night,
> And I have never wondered that my sight
> Should serve me for my pleasure, or that aught
> Beyond the lonely mirror of my thought
> Lived, and desired me.[6]

If Conrad aimed to use 'the power of the written word [...] to make you *see*', Symons aimed first and foremost, 'to make you *look*'.[7] In 'The Decadent Movement', he argued that Impressionism and Symbolism, two strains of that 'interesting disease', both sought 'not general truth merely, but *la vérité vraie*, the very essence of truth — the truth of appearances to the senses, of the visible world to the eyes that see it'. The essay also hailed the Goncourt brothers' 'morbid intensity in seeing and seizing things.'[8] *Silhouettes* had shown Symons experimenting with an impressionist perspective, capturing fleeting moods and urban vistas in poems such as 'On the Bridge' and relishing the freedom of apparently direct and unmediated engagement with the world. Like many of the artists associated with the movement, Symons disliked the term 'impressionism' — it had, after all, pejorative origins — but it allowed him to 'render' rather than to 'narrate,' as well as exalting the personal, subjective aspects of experience above the ostensible objectivity associated with earlier modes of realist practice.[9] Lionel Johnson may have jibed that Symons offered 'Parisian impressionism' instead of intellectual discipline in producing three dexterous stanzas of 'London fog, blurred tawny lamplight, red omnibuses, dreary trains, depressing mud, glaring gin-shops and slatternly shivering women', but his criticism misrepresents Symons's approach even as it appears to pastiche it.[10] Johnson's judgemental modifiers play little part in Symons's most successful poems.

Had Symons been born in the 1830s, he would probably have grown up in thrall to the Pre-Raphaelites, but born in the 1860s and possessed of Gallic sympathies, it was to be impressionist art which represented his break with Victorian convention. By the early 1890s, he was resident in London, regularly visiting Paris, and pursuing an artistic education that saw him studying Monet, Manet, and Degas, whose paintings of ballerinas he aspired to imitate in his prose. Clive Scott has observed how 'all Impressionist paintings imply that they are one of a series', and as metropolitan life became ever more rapid, impressionism seemed the form of art best suited to the types of fleeting experiences and vistas that caught Symons's eye.[11] He explicitly linked the pictorial and the written word in 'The Decadent Movement', where he claimed that 'The Impressionist, in literature as in painting, would flash upon you in a new, sudden way so exact an image of what you have just seen, just as you have seen it.'[12] Twenty years later, Ford Madox Ford would advance a similar thesis, arguing that impressionism was 'the accord of the impression of a moment' rather than being 'a sort of rounded, annotated set of circumstances.'[13] The absence of 'annotation', that is to say subsequent reflection on and analysis of an experience rather than the conveying of its immediacy, was central to Symons's poetic practice in his early poetry, but its inspiration at this point came less from Monet or Degas than from a painter whose relationship with any notion of impressionism was elusive and uncertain. 'The Decadent Movement' instead singled out an artist who 'seems to think his picture upon every canvas' without giving any hint of the discipline and effort such accomplishment demanded. This figure was James McNeill Whistler, a man whose influence upon Symons would continue long after his innovations had been overshadowed by more aggressive forms of artistic radicalism, and about whom Symons published essays from October 1890, when he discussed *The Gentle Art of Making Enemies* in the *Chicago Tribune*, to October 1929, when 'Whistler and Manet' appeared in *From Toulouse-Lautrec to Rodin*, his final volume of art criticism.[14] It is the artistic and intellectual influence of Whistler on Symons that is explored in what follows, notably the extent to which Whistler's version of an impressionist aesthetic might be recalibrated in the context of the writer's 'decadent' sympathies.

Born in 1834, Whistler embodied much of what Symons aspired to be. 'I am not an Englishman', he said proudly, though as Stanley Weintraub adds, 'Nor was he recognisably an American, a Russian, a Frenchman, although he was born in Massachusetts, was raised in Russia, and had learned his art in France.'[15] Cosmopolitan, rootless, bohemian, Francophile (and Francophone), Whistler's ambivalent relationship with various forms of national identity anticipated Symons's own sense of vagabondage.[16] 'I have never known what it was to have a home, as most children know it', Symons wrote in 1913.[17] Born in Wales, raised in Cornwall but spending almost all his adult life in London and Kent, Symons always regarded himself as

Celtic rather than English, this elective allegiance allowing him to slip out of the moral and creative handcuffs that he associated with Victorianism. He and Whistler both brought an outsider's perspective to what they regarded as a provincial and constrained artistic culture, Symons later borrowing something of Whistler's cool panache in his idealized self-portrait, Daniel Roserra, the protagonist of 'An Autumn City' (1905) and a man who 'respected nature, for what might be cunningly extracted from nature'.[18] He was certainly drawn to Whistler's forceful personality, remarking that he had never seen 'any one so feverishly alive' and admiring the spontaneity and precision of his witticisms.[19]

When Whistler fought his epochal libel battle with John Ruskin in 1878, taking issue with the critic's claim that he was 'a coxcomb' who 'ask[ed] two hundred guineas for throwing a pot of paint in the public's face', Symons was a precocious schoolboy living in a Cornish backwater with his staunchly Methodist parents and reading about the case, if he read about it at all, only in the attenuated coverage provided by *The Times*.[20] He probably learned the details from Whistler's own edited account — the trial records themselves were destroyed when there was no appeal against the verdict — and therefore acquired a misleading sense of Whistler's individualism and daring. Tellingly, the version included in *The Gentle Art of Making Enemies* (1890) omits the supporting testimony of William Michael Rossetti, Albert Moore, and the playwright W. G. Wills, and unscrupulously polishes up the plaintiff's repartee to produce what Linda Merrill calls a 'quasifictional account' that is annotated 'like a scholarly treatise'.[21] Whistler won his libel action, though he was awarded only token (and insulting) damages of a farthing rather than the £1000 he had sought, a verdict which left him bankrupt. However harrowing this must have been — he was forced to leave England for Venice as a consequence — his retrospective account portrayed his suit as a daring tilt at the Victorian artistic establishment, rather than the piece of self-advertisement conservatives considered it to be. Developments in art have, to a considerable extent, vindicated Whistler's arguments, but his views were certainly not uncontroversial in 1890, when Symons read *The Gentle Art* and when Ruskin was still living. It is hardly surprising that a rebelliously inclined young man, whose father was a Methodist minister, should have opted for Whistler's glamour rather than the evangelicalism of his antagonist. 'Ruskin by much preaching had brought the public to its knees', Symons wrote in 1905. '[I]t was not convinced that it liked Pre-Raphaelite pictures, but it was certain that its duty to its higher self condemned it to accept them as what it ought to like.'[22]

Whistler's persona appealed strongly to Symons, though being essentially shy and serious in character, he was unable to replicate the artist's charismatic dynamism. Dandified but heterosexual, Whistler was acceptably scandalous, a gadfly (or rather, butterfly) who, unlike his dissident disciple, Oscar Wilde, brought libel actions about art rather than life. Stage-managing his appearance down to a needless monocle and an affected and rarely genuine laugh, Whistler was an exuberant self-publicist, ever ready to share his quips with the newspapers and erecting monuments to his wit through the publication of his letters and telegrams. He argued for the autonomy of art, suggesting that only artists (not, by any means, *all* artists) were able to discuss it intelligently and, as Symons only belatedly realized, 'deceiv[ing] the public into believing that he was a frivolous dandy [...] when, in fact, he was intent on directing the academic art of his time to a new sense of painting's visionary possibilities.'[23] 'Art should be independent of all clap-trap', Whistler announced in 1878, and 'the artistic sense of eye' should not be 'confound[ed]' 'with emotions entirely foreign to it, as devotion, pity, love, patriotism, and the like. All of these have no concern with it.'[24]

In his libel action against Ruskin, Whistler said he was waging a war 'between the brush and the pen', and perhaps the arrogance and flippancy of his derisive writings on art critics helped inspire Symons when composing uncharacteristically arch responses to those who found fault with *Silhouettes, London Nights*, and the opening number of *The Savoy*.[25] The *Pall Mall Gazette* had infuriated (and deeply hurt) Symons with a dismissive verdict on *London Nights* in September 1895, making him instruct his solicitor to demand an apology, but while he seethed in private and resented the inadequate income which debarred him from bringing legal action against a newspaper owned by William Waldorf Astor, his later public face was altogether more insouciant.[26] 'Art may be served by morality', he wrote in the Preface to the second edition of the book a year later, 'it can never be its servant. For the principles of art are eternal, while the principles of morality fluctuate with the spiritual ebb and flow of the ages.'[27] The 'Editorial Note' to the second number of *The Savoy* went further in ironically applauding the critics who had given its predecessor such a 'flattering reception', one which was 'none the less flattering because it has been for the most part unfavourable.' Warming to his theme, he concluded:

> I confess cheerfully that I have learnt much from the newspaper criticisms of the first number of 'The Savoy'. It is with confidence that I anticipate no less instruction from the criticisms which I shall have the pleasure of reading on the number now issued.

Karl Beckson sees this as 'revealing a capacity for wit and irony' rarely acknowledged in Symons, adding that Aubrey Beardsley considered the riposte 'extraordinarily witty and brilliant'.[28]

Whistler was hardly the first to argue for art's independence from morality, but he did so from a position of chic cosmopolitanism, flamboyant celebrity and technical virtuosity far outside Symons's own expertise. This made him very different from English aesthetes such as Swinburne, then living under genteel house arrest in Putney with Theodore Watts-Dunton, or Pater, the retiring Oxford don. Thirty years older than Symons, Whistler could also claim veteran status when it came to fighting artistic philistinism. As early as 1867, W. M. Rossetti had recognized his refusal to 'reproduce facts, or present a story of any kind'.[29] His well-publicized disdain for moralizing anecdotalism saw him exhibiting paintings of his mistresses as arrangements of colour rather than as didactic narratives, for instance in his rendering of Joanna Hiffernan as the subject of *Caprice in Purple and Gold: The Golden Screen* (1864). Symons much preferred this approach to that of earlier Victorian art, remarking in 1905 that Holman Hunt's *The Awakening Conscience* (1853), the famous image of a 'kept' woman suddenly realizing the perils of seduction, was 'futile and repulsive' and essayed a realism that 'tortures the eyes'.[30] Whistler deplored those 'people who have acquired the habit of looking [...] not *at* a picture but *through* it, at some human fact, that shall, or shall not, from a social point of view, better their mental or moral state'.[31] Paintings were not to be confused with novels, any more than 'nobility' was to be confused with technique; labels were merely academic conveniences and invariably misleading. Symons would, in time, concur, proclaiming in the opening number of *The Savoy*:

> All we ask from our contributors is good work, and good work is all we offer our readers. [...] We have no formulas, and desire no false unity of form and matter. We have not invented a new point of view. We are not Realists, or Romanticists, or Decadents. For us, all art is good which is good art.[32]

'Great critics like Ruskin and great artists like Watts have done infinite harm by taking the side of the sentimentalists', he wrote in 1903, noting an unfortunate tendency to attach 'moral values to lines and colours'.[33]

It was not only Whistler's attitudes that Symons sought to imitate. Technically too, the painter had many lessons to impart, not least in deploying a subtle chromatic minimalism that made him the visual counterpart to Symons's poetic mentor, Paul Verlaine, who sought only nuance and fine shades and exhorted his followers to 'Take Eloquence, and wring the neck of him!'[34] Verlaine's poetry, wrote Symons in 1892, 'is an art of impressionism — sometimes as delicate, as pastoral, as Watteau, sometimes as sensitively modern as Whistler, sometimes as brutally modern as Degas.'[35] That year, *Silhouettes* showed how Symons had begun to exploit impressionist concerns with the fixing of the fleeting moment, splicing together literature and art. Browning's notion of 'the instant made eternity', a line from 'The Last Ride Together' (1855) Symons often quoted, and the exaltation of the momentary from the Conclusion to Pater's *Studies in the History of The Renaissance* (1873) mixed with Verlaine's technical and linguistic restraint and the muted tones of Whistler's nocturnes in a series of quatrain-based 'colour studies' of Dieppe. Ford's 'annotation' was replaced by the embodied immediacy of the impressionist sketch in 'Pastel: Masks and Faces', a poem in which the beloved is illuminated by the momentary flare of the match that lights her cigarette. Such a blending of Anglo-French literature and art had rich aesthetic possibilities. Symons's poetic vocabulary echoes the visual austerity and insinuation of Whistler's paintings, and is deliberately sparse, rarely extending beyond two-syllable words: pink, white, black, grey, and gold are his preferred colours in his early poetry.[36]

Whistler may have seen his spat with Ruskin as a war between different forms of expression, but Symons was concerned with harmony (a suitably Whistlerian word) between the arts, and sought a coherent aesthetic discourse that would allow him to move between them, 'to paint in music, perhaps' as he wrote in *London: A Book of Aspects* (1909).[37] His search was informed by Whistler's fondness for musical titles, the painter's nocturnes infusing older traditions of the 'night piece' with the Chopinesque. As a disciple of Chopin and Pater, it was inevitable that Symons would insist that 'music could hardly have failed to represent the type of all that [Whistler's] own art was aiming at, in its not always fully understood or recognized way.'[38] John M. Munro has shown how Symons's use of musical analogies could be problematic, particularly when he praised the 'purity of tone' in paintings that 'blurr[ed] outlines and tones until they all but melt into one indefinable vapor', but they were consistent with the contradictory elements of Whistler's own aesthetic: one wonders if he might have inspired Wilde's quip, 'The well-bred contradict others. The wise contradict themselves.'[39]

Whistler experimented continually with the physical resources available to him, thinning his paints with linseed oil or turpentine to produce his characteristically subtle tones. His brushwork was slow and delicate — Symons noted that he had 'the most sensitive fingers I have ever seen', resembling those of a mesmerist — and he gently bleached his canvases by leaving them to dry in the sun.[40] Such experiments had no clear literary parallel, unless one sees analogies between the 'thinned' paint and a consciously sparse poetic vocabulary, but other aspects of Whistler's practice did find echoes in Symons's work. His nocturnes, paintings which Symons especially admired, were studies in subjective observation, beginning as black and white chalk sketches on brown paper and a corresponding series of what might be called 'mental photographs' — thinking the picture onto canvas, perhaps. Back in the studio, the drawings informed the basic relationships of bridges, buildings, lights and shorelines, but Whistler derived and prioritized colour, mood and even perspective from his own memories of the scene. He had learned these techniques from his friend Henri Fantin-Latour, whose teacher, Lecoq de Boisbaudran, author of *Éducation de la mémoire pittoresque* (1848) had encouraged him to work from recollection rather than directly from life, and to study the moonlight effects in the Bois de Boulogne. Symons advised something similar in 'Impressionistic Writing' (1923), instructing would-be authors to 'see with an eye that sees all' before writing 'from a selecting memory'.[41] Such methods imbue the travel essays of *Cities* (1903) and *Cities of Italy* (1907) with a particularly idiosyncratic flavour, insisting as they do on the distinction between things seen 'unconsciously' and those which comprise the 'essential part of my memory of the scene afterward'.[42] Symons's Venice is not Byron's, or Wagner's, or Henry James's, any more than it is the city inhabited by thousands of Venetians. It is instead 'lonely, discriminating, exquisite' and, as Derek Stanford adds, 'one man's record — that of one man hardly aware of the social ties which bind him to the body of mankind within a common culture.'[43]

As naturalist techniques began to gain ground in English fiction, aesthetes recoiled from what Wilde called 'that great and daily increasing school of novelists, for whom the sun always rises in the East-End', figures who 'find life crude, and leave it raw'.[44] For Symons and Whistler alike, subjective perception and its transformation into art supplanted the more apparently objective realism which, as it ventured ever further into topics previously held taboo in, say, its increasingly frank depictions of sexuality, became a central pillar of the late Victorian literary aesthetic. Yet as the controversy surrounding the 1893 London exhibition of Degas's *L'Absinthe* showed, and the critical reception of *London Nights* tended to confirm, impressionism's intellectual detachment did not necessarily inoculate it against the sordid.[45] Whistler was not immune to such charges either; in 1884, his portrait of Lady Archibald Campbell, *Arrangement in Black: The Lady in the Yellow Buskin*, was rejected by the Campbell family on the grounds that its subject resembled 'a street-walker encouraging a shy follower with a backward glance'.[46] Symons had courted controversy with depictions of prostitutes in poems such as 'Stella Maris' (1894) and 'Leves Amores' (1895), and his ears were well-tuned to the baying of moralist mobs. For him, Whistler's infallible 'taste' allowed him to sidestep such concerns and develop an art wholly independent of them. Whistler, he wrote, 'carried [taste] to the point of genius [...] He touched nothing, possessed nothing, that he did not remake or assimilate in some faultless and always personal way'.[47] Such gifts were an invaluable bulwark when faced with 'the devouring mouths of the common virtues' against which modern art was so much on the defensive at the *fin de siècle*.[48]

Whistler's relationship with impressionism was complex, and Symons made careful distinctions between the moods and methods he shared with it and the distinctive aspects of his individual genius.[49] Sometimes, Symons wrote, impressionism of the Monet variety is too sketchy, resembling 'a shorthand note, which the reporter has not even troubled to copy out.' Whistler, by contrast:

> begins by building his world after nature's, with supports as solid and as visible. Gradually, he knocks away support after support, expecting the structure to support itself by its own consciousness, so to speak. At the perfect moment he gives to the eye just enough to catch in the outlines of things that it may be able to complete them by that imaginative sympathy which is part of the seeing of works of art.[50]

Symons may be thinking of the *Nocturne — Blue and Gold — Old Battersea Bridge* (1872–73), which transforms a metropolitan landmark into a cluster of shadowy tangrams, the frame audaciously divided by the T-shaped pillar that holds the bridge aloft. The picture's mimetic accuracy was challenged by Ruskin's counsel, with Whistler informing a seemingly bewildered audience that he 'did not intend it to be a "correct" picture of the bridge' but 'only a moonlight scene [...] a certain harmony of colour'.[51] Such 'knocking away' of precise or identifying detail was central to Whistler's methods. He maintained that 'a picture is finished when all traces of the means used to bring about the end has disappeared' adding that 'the work of the master reeks not of the sweat of the brow'.[52] A picture that betrayed the effort of its composition was therefore not yet complete. Symons appropriated this idea, reprinting individual works with minimal or no alteration rather than opting for the laborious perpetual revision of Henry James. This changed only after his breakdown, when his revisiting and reordering of earlier work would have such disastrous consequences for his reputation.

It is clear that Whistler had a substantial influence on the ways in which Symons saw the world, but his response to the painter was not merely uncritical homage. In 'The Death of Peter Waydelin', the fifth story in Symons's collection of Paterian 'imaginary portraits', *Spiritual Adventures* (1905), Whistler's views are placed in dialogue with Symons's own practice and with the work of Aubrey Beardsley, the *enfant terrible* of English art who had died from tuberculosis in 1898 aged only twenty-five. Waydelin, like Beardsley, produces 'mysterious, brutal pictures' and dies young and largely misunderstood.[53] Such a triangulation is notably problematic. Symons and Beardsley may have collaborated on *The Savoy* and been caught up in the intrigues of its publisher, Leonard Smithers, but they were never close friends.

Beardsley mocked Symons's credentials as a Don Juan, while Symons, though often in awe of Beardsley's drawings and skill as a designer, dismissed the artist's literary pretensions. Beardsley in turn admired Whistler, frequently caricatured him, and offended him with a spiteful drawing of his wife, *The Fat Woman*, in May 1894.[54] When Whistler at last acknowledged Beardsley's worth after seeing his illustrations for *The Rape of the Lock* in 1896, and telling him he was a great artist, Beardsley apparently burst into tears.[55] 'The Death of Peter Waydelin' is therefore at once a story and a debate about aesthetics, one through which Symons is able to address his own artistic credo and the allegorical opposition of Art and Life: tellingly, at the beginning of the piece, the narrator comments that Waydelin never speaks of himself, 'only of his ideas'.[56] By 1905, Symons was no longer the controversial decadent he had been perceived as being ten years earlier, and *Spiritual Adventures* was greeted with polite critical nods rather than outrage. *The Dial* adjudged its component stories 'thoroughly subjective and tantalizingly incomplete', which might imply a lingering Whistlerian influence, though its reviewer doubted that the subjects of its portraiture were worthy of Symons's effort.[57]

Originally entitled 'Peter Waydelin's Experiment', the story first appeared in *Lippincott's Monthly Magazine* in February 1904, six months after the lengthy consideration of Whistler that would be reprinted in *Studies in Seven Arts*, and only a few weeks after another of his essays, 'Beardsley as Man of Letters', had featured in the *Saturday Review*. Waydelin is initially encountered sitting on the beach at Bognor Regis, throwing stones into the sea and disdaining the natural environment. The narrator makes his Whistlerian sympathies clear from the outset, admiring 'the colour-sense of those arrangements of sand, water, and sky' of the Sussex coast, but Waydelin is not so easily categorized. 'All art, of course [...] is a way of seeing', he says:

> Like everybody else, I began by seeing too much. Gradually I gave up seeing things in shades, in subdivisions; I saw them in masses, each single. It takes more choice than you think, and more technical skill, to set one plain colour against another, unshaded [...] (p. 150)

Waydelin seems for a moment to be anticipating the later work of Mark Rothko, but any suggestions of proto-abstract expressionism are short-lived. 'The art of the painter', he goes on, 'consists in seeing in a new summarizing way, getting rid of everything but the essentials; in seeing by patterns' (p. 150). This approach seems more akin to Beardsley's tendency in his prints of the early 1890s to use blocks of black and to reject shading in favour of starkly stylized images, and it is immediately contrasted with Whistler's mistiness. 'You have to train your eye not to see', says Waydelin:

> Whistler sees nothing but the fine shades, which unite into a picture in an almost bodiless way, as Verlaine writes songs almost literally 'without words'. You can see, if you like, in just the opposite way: leaving in only the hard outlines, leaving out everything that lies between. To me that is the best way of summarizing, the most abbreviated way. (pp. 150–51)

In training the eye 'not to see', Waydelin is emphasizing the importance of subjective apprehension and perception, that is, the maintenance of an individual vision rather than a seeming objective response to external detail that is inevitably overwhelmed by minutiae, the horses, cabs, trees and kiosks that the 'true impressionist' of 'Impressionistic Writing' would never think to include in his painting of the Luxembourg Gardens.[58] Only the finest artists ever overcome the importunate solicitation of the real, the story suggests, and only 'abbreviated art' can properly be said to see 'square' and 'hit from the shoulder' (p. 150).

In this passage, Beardsley and Whistler offer different models of adversarial aesthetics, paintings which assault the viewer like blows. Waydelin refuses to turn out the 'pretty' pictures he dismisses as 'confectionaries' (p. 151), working instead on a portrait of his wife, 'crueller even than usual in its insistence on the brutality of facts: the crude contrasts of bone and fat, the vulgar jaw, the brassy eyes' (p. 157). Recalling Beardsley's mocking image of Beatrice Whistler, the painting is fashioned with 'hatred' (p. 158), though its subject dismisses it as a 'horrid thing' as well as a poor likeness (p. 158). The unenlightened Clara Waydelin insists on judging the worth of a portrait in purely mimetic terms, an approach which allows her the comfort of perceiving the representation as inaccurate, whereas the narrator is able to appreciate how her husband has harmonized her appearance with his perception of it. She is, Waydelin says, 'a very nice woman' (p. 158), suggesting perhaps that his 'hatred' is a Baudelairean opposition to the tyranny of the corporeal rather than a reflection of his true feelings towards his wife. Echoing Beardsley's quip that 'even my lungs are affected', Waydelin pronounces himself 'dead, relatively speaking' — he could not be more of a contrast with the elderly Whistler, who was so 'feverishly alive' in Symons's 1903 essay. This may be what leads him to make such agonized assaults upon the flesh, and may indicate too how Symons had moved away from his initial enthusiasm for impressionism and towards a symbolist aesthetic of interiority. Whistler, as he noted, painted the world from a subjective position which displaced actuality in order to insist on the primacy of the perceiving consciousness.

Symons had not rejected Whistler, of course, but his friendship with Yeats and his research for the books that became *The Symbolist Movement* and *William Blake* (1907) had left him increasingly dissatisfied with what Wilde called in *The Importance of Being Earnest* (1895) 'an age of surfaces'.[59] Whistler had imbued these surfaces with his own perceptions of them — to borrow Wilde's formulation, he was creating the world rather than simply recording it. Whether he was imbuing it with symbolic depth was, however, a separate issue. Whistler had told the libel jury that his paintings were simply 'arrangements' — Waydelin's 'patterns' — that refused moral interpretation. But did that mean that they refused *any* interpretation beyond the analysis of their colour and composition, and if they did, would it compromise their achievement? The poems Symons was writing during the late 1890s and early 1900s, which were to comprise *Images of Good and Evil* (1900), *The Fool of the World* (1906), and *Knave of Hearts* (1913) offered a hybridity that insisted that the 'seeing eye' worked alongside the imagination's reservoir of symbols and allusions in works such as 'The Dogs' (1896), 'The Chimaera' (1897–98), and the lavish masque, 'The Dance of the Seven Sins' (1896–97). Such works were radically different from the impressionism of *Silhouettes* — Tom Gibbons has even argued for Symons's 'expressionist' phase — but their impatient pursuit of new methods led to unsatisfactory results and, in poetry at least, the loss of much of Symons's former subtlety.[60]

In his critical writing, Symons foregrounded his debt to Pater, beginning the Acknowledgements page of *Studies in Seven Arts* addressed to his wife with a lengthy quotation from 'The School of Giorgione'. Pater here warned against neglecting 'the sensuous element in art' and rebuked a tendency 'of popular criticism' to assume that all art was merely a 'translation into different languages' of 'the same fixed quantity of imaginative thought'. He insisted that poetry, painting, and music each had their specific 'sensuous material' and 'a special phase or quality of beauty untranslatable into the forms of any other'.[61] Symons claimed to be studying every art 'from its own point of view' but feared 'slipping [...] into tempting and easy confusions'. This was exactly what happened in his discussion of Whistler later in the book, when he drifted into inaccurate music analogy when trying to compare paintings with the tone of differing violinists: similar 'slippages' can be found throughout his critical essays. For all that he claimed to agree with Pater concerning the uniqueness of differing forms of art, Symons seemed unable to resist 'painting in music' and allowing the visual to override other considerations. This approach had many positive aspects, but it could encourage imprecision or an 'appreciation' — another Paterian word — that merely euphemized less critical enthusiasms.

Painterly influences were present in Symons's work almost from the beginning, deployed first in poetry, then in a creative criticism in which he wrote poems and critical essays on the same topic, then in fiction such as 'Peter Waydelin', and finally in the literary and photographic collaboration of 1906–07 that he entitled *London: A Book of Aspects*. Though one could make a case for Degas influencing his approach to certain subjects, notably ballet, it was Whistler who remained the dominant artistic deity in Symons's pantheon, encouraging and even licensing his immersion in the visible world and governing how it might best be manipulated and understood.

His partner in this ultimately unsuccessful enterprise was the young American photographer, Alvin Langdon Coburn, a man who idolized Whistler to such an extent that he even wore the same style of silk hat. Coburn believed Whistler to have been 'photographic', not in the sense of 'hard lens work' but in terms of his skill in rendering diffused light. 'It's a pity, by the way, that he didn't live long enough to use a camera', he ingenuously remarked, 'it would have saved him so much time'.[62] At a sitting in St John's Wood in September 1906, Coburn photographed Symons using a special lens to give a blurred, impressionistic effect which, while quite different from Whistler's own style of portraiture, succeeded in capturing the subject's dreamy inwardness. It was not published until Coburn collected it in *Men of Mark* (1913), by which time Symons had fallen ill and their relationship had ended. Coburn's frustratingly uninformative autobiography has nothing to say of the collaboration, and many of its details remain to be discovered. It is clear however that the two were excited about Symons's strikingly original idea for a folio in which his Whistler-inflected accounts of London would be paired with Coburn's tributes to the painter, the two agreeing that 'Whistler has created the Thames, for most people'.[63] Drawing on Whistler's prose account of the misty river in 'The Ten O'Clock Lecture', in which 'the evening mist clothes the river-side with poetry', and the lecture's wider claim that nature contained all the necessary materials for art but that only the artist could select them properly, they spent several months amassing literary and photographic images of the capital.[64] They took long walks beside the Thames and through the gas-lit streets of the nocturnal metropolis armed with notebook and camera, recording their responses to places such as Leicester Square, Chelsea Embankment, and Ludgate Circus.[65] Coburn even took a particularly beautiful picture from the window of Symons's former rooms in Fountain Court in The Temple (Fig. 1.1).

Coburn's pictures were far more than simply imitations of Whistler's nocturnes, though individual images such as *Wapping*, later Plate X of his folio, *London* (1909), recalled him through their titles as well as their composition. Coburn had studied the same Japanese painters who had interested Whistler, and their influence lingered in his framing and his unusual mixture of close-up detail and stark simplicity. At the same time, Symons made the prose text of the book far more than a descriptive counterpart or cue for Coburn's images. *London: A Book of Aspects* encompassed memoir, topography, cultural history, literary criticism, a trenchant opposition to mechanization, and a series of provocative comparisons between London and other European cities. A century later, it still seems strikingly modern in recognizing the radical possibilities of a collaboration between prose and photography, in its mixture of genres, the unselfconscious ease with which Symons navigates between observation, reminiscence and more general discussion, and the claim that London is itself 'a form of creative literature' (p. 165). It is little wonder that such an original volume should have proved impossible to place with publishers, and only a handful of properly integrated copies was ever produced. Coburn's proposed pictures were incorporated into his later books about London, notably one with G. K. Chesterton in 1914, while Symons had to wait until 1918 to see his sections become commercially available as part of *Cities and Sea-Coasts and Islands*.[66]

Whistler's influence allowed Symons to indulge in evocative word-painting that revisited 'The Ten O'Clock Lecture' as well as evoking the world of the nocturnes. Mist and smoke transformed London, he said, into 'a picture continually changing, a continual sequence of pictures'. 'When the mist collaborates with night and rain', he added, 'the masterpiece is created' (p. 162). Looking at the Thames from Hungerford Bridge, Symons observes how:

> The river seems to have become a lake; under the black arches of Waterloo Bridge there are reflections of golden fire, multiplying arch beyond arch in a lovely tangle. The Surrey side is dark, with tall vague buildings rising out of the mud on which a little water crawls: is it the water that moves or the shadows? A few empty barges or steamers lie in solid patches on the water near the bank [...] (p. 163)

Recalling the collaboration in 1913, Coburn judged this 'a passage Whistler would have revelled in'.[67] Whatever revolutions might have been taking place in Symons's poetry at this time, his topographical writing was still able to respond to Whistler's prompting in addressing 'my constant challenge to myself [...] to be content with nothing short of that *vraie vérité* which one imagines to exist somewhere on this side

FIG. 1.1. Alvin Langdon Coburn, Fountain Court, photograph, c. 1907. With thanks to the Science and Society Picture Library.

of ultimate attainment.'[68] One might have thought that the camera's instantaneous recording would counteract Whistler's 'memory method', but Coburn's completed works were photogravures, prints ingeniously treated in his studio so as to recreate what he felt he had seen rather than what he had actually committed to his plates; appropriate levels of mist and shadow were conjured up by caressing the negative with a soft wire brush. The book refused to match images to text in any bluntly illustrative or obvious way, leaving the reader to puzzle out or dream over the evocative juxtapositions of poetic pictures and prose. It remains a striking and too little-known achievement.

Is the artistic dialogue between Symons and Whistler *decadent*? There would seem to be precious little concern with such decadent characteristics as rarefied or elitist language, or transgressive or perverse subject matter, though its fascination with artificiality and the superior perceptions of the artist reaffirm its credentials to some extent. If however one considers what is viewed through the Whistlerian lens, or who the viewer of it might be, the situation changes. To judge from another 'spiritual adventure', the autobiographical 'A Prelude to Life', Symons was, by his own admission, given to solipsism even in childhood, and his fascination with his own impressions and sensations, as he habitually called them, was absolute. While other decadent writers cut themselves off from the multitude by the sheer difficulty of their work, their contempt for the mass, or their recondite preoccupations and linguistic over-refinement, Symons consciously or otherwise used the methods that had won Whistler success and notoriety to license self-absorption, or, if one were unsympathetic to him, to fuel a narcissism that would have terrible consequences in the autumn of 1908 and the years that followed.

Notes to Chapter 1

1. 'The Aesthetic Fallacy' (review of Arthur Symons's *Cities and Sea-Coasts and Islands*), *Times Literary Supplement*, 3 October 1918, p. 465; T. S. Eliot, *The Sacred Wood: Essays on Poetry and Criticism* (1920; London: Faber, 1997), pp. 2, 4.
2. Arthur Symons, 'The Decadent Movement in Literature', *Harper's New Monthly Magazine*, 87 (November 1893): 858–67 (p. 859).
3. Holbrook Jackson, *The Eighteen Nineties: A Review of Art and Ideas at the Close of the Nineteenth Century* (London: Grant Richards, 1913), p. 50.
4. See Catherine Maxwell, 'Scents and Sensibility: The Fragrance of Decadence', in *Decadent Poetics: Literature and Form at the British Fin de Siècle*, ed. by Jason David Hall and Alex Murray (Basingstoke: Palgrave Macmillan, 2013), pp. 201–25, and my '"Mad music rising": Chopin, Sex, and Secret Language in Arthur Symons's "Christian Trevalga"', *Victoriographies*, 1 (2011), 157–76.
5. Arthur Symons, 'Art and the Royal Academy', *Weekly Critical Review*, 1 (14 and 28 May 1903), 1–2, 10–11.
6. Arthur Symons, 'The Brother of a Weed: I', ll. 5–11 from his *Knave of Hearts, 1894–1908* (1913), in *The Collected Works of Arthur Symons, Volume Three: Poems* (London: Martin Secker, 1924), p. 7. Symons dates the poem 'June 4-7—14, 1907'.
7. Joseph Conrad, Preface to *The Nigger of the 'Narcissus': A Tale of the Sea* (1897; Harmondsworth: Penguin, 1977), p. 13.
8. Symons, 'The Decadent Movement in Literature', pp. 859, 860.
9. Taking his cue from Monet's *Impression, soleil levant* [*Impression: Sunrise*] (1872), the journalist Louis Leroy dubbed Pissarro, Monet, Renoir, Cézanne, and Sisley, the 'Société anonyme des artistes peintres, sculpteurs, graveurs', 'Impressionists' in a derisive review in *Le Charivari* in

April 1874. As Bernard Denvir points out, although the Society hosted seven further exhibitions under that name, the public now considered them to be 'impressionists', a label which the artists came to partially acknowledge. It did, after all, give their diverse productions 'a coherence and an ideological unity' which would prove beneficial in the ensuing debates about the nature of 'modern art' (*The Impressionists at First Hand*, ed. by Bernard Denvir (London: Thames and Hudson, 1987), p. 11). In Ford Madox Ford's memoir of Joseph Conrad, he remarks that 'Life did not narrate, but made impressions on our brains. We in turn, if we wished to produce on you an effect of life, must not narrate but render impressions' (*Joseph Conrad: A Personal Remembrance* (London: Duckworth, 1924), pp. 194–95).

10. W. B. Yeats, 'The Tragic Generation', in *Autobiographies* (London: Macmillan, 1955), p. 378.
11. Clive Scott, 'Symbolism, Decadence and Impressionism', in *Modernism: A Guide to European Literature 1890–1930*, ed. by Malcolm Bradbury and James McFarlane (1976; London: Penguin, 1991), p. 222.
12. Symons, 'The Decadent Movement in Literature', p. 859.
13. Ford Madox Ford, 'On Impressionism' (1914), *Critical Writings of Ford Madox Ford*, ed. by Frank MacShane (Lincoln, NE: University of Nebraska, 1965), p. 41.
14. For a wider contextualization of Symons's work as an art critic, see Lawrence W. Markert, *Arthur Symons, Critic of the Seven Arts* (Ann Arbor, MI: UMI Research Press, 1988), pp. 87–126.
15. Stanley Weintraub, *Whistler: A Biography* (London: Collins, 1974), p. 3.
16. Symons noted how Whistler 'part tuned' his 'strange accent, part American, part deliberately French' to 'the key of his wit'. 'Whistler' (1903) in *Studies in Seven Arts* (London: Archibald Constable, 1907), p. 124. See also Andrew Stephenson's essay, 'Refashioning modern masculinity: Whistler, aestheticism and national identity', in *English Art 1860–1914: Modern Artists and Identity*, ed. by David Peters Corbett and Lara Perry (New Brunswick, NJ: Rutgers University Press, 2001), pp. 133–49.
17. Arthur Symons, 'Unspiritual Adventures in Paris', in *Wanderings* (London: J. M. Dent, 1931), p. 77.
18. Arthur Symons, 'An Autumn City', in *Spiritual Adventures* (London: Constable, 1905), p. 177.
19. Symons, 'Whistler', *Studies in Seven Arts*, pp. 124–25.
20. James McNeill Whistler, *The Gentle Art of Making Enemies* (London: William Heinemann, 1890), p. 1. Linda Merrill observes that although a number of London papers covered the trial in detail, 'perhaps because the case was of special interest to Londoners', the account in *The Times* is 'exceptionally brief (and apparently tempered with a Ruskinian bias)' (*A Pot of Paint: Aesthetics on Trial in Whistler v. Ruskin* (Washington: Smithsonian Institute Press, 1992), pp. 2–3).
21. Merrill, *A Pot of Paint*, p. 2.
22. Arthur Symons, 'On the Purchase of a Whistler for London', *Outlook*, 16 (5 August 1905), 158–59; reprinted in *Studies on Modern Painters* (New York: William Edwin Rudge, 1925), p. 44.
23. Karl Beckson, *London in the 1890s: A Cultural History* (New York: Norton, 1992), p. 256. With regard to his own profound artistic seriousness, Symons wrote, 'He deceived the public for many years; he probably deceived many of his acquaintances till the day of his death' ('Whistler', *Studies in Seven Arts*, p. 121).
24. James McNeill Whistler in *The World*, 22 May 1878, in *Whistler on Art: Selected Letters and Writings of James McNeill Whistler*, ed. by Nigel Thorp (Manchester: Carcanet, 1994), p. 52. Symons quoted this approvingly in 'Whistler', *Studies in Seven Arts*, pp. 132–33.
25. Whistler, 'Whistler vs. Ruskin: Art and Art Critics' (December 1878), in *The Gentle Art of Making Enemies*, p. 25.
26. The anonymous review was headed simply, 'Pah!' and began 'Mr Arthur Symons is a very dirty-minded man, and his mind is reflected in the puddle of his bad verses', *Pall Mall Gazette* (2 September 1895), 4. For Symons's ensuing correspondence with Henry Cust, the paper's editor, see his *Selected Letters, 1880–1935*, ed. by Karl Beckson and John M. Munro (Basingstoke: Macmillan, 1989), pp. 112–13.
27. Arthur Symons, Preface to the revised edition of *London Nights* (London: Leonard Smithers, 1897). The piece is dated 'Rosses Point, Sligo, September 2, 1896.'
28. Arthur Symons, 'Editorial Note' to *The Savoy*, No. 2 (London: Leonard Smithers, April 1896), p. 5; Beckson, *Arthur Symons: A Life* (Oxford: Clarendon Press, 1987), p. 136; *The Letters of Aubrey Beardsley*, ed. by Henry Maas, J. L. Duncan and W. G. Good (London: Cassell, 1970), p. 130.

29. W. M. Rossetti, 'Royal Academy Exhibition', *The Chronicle* (25 May 1867), 210.
30. Arthur Symons, 'The Pre-Raphaelites at Whitechapel', *Outlook*, 15 (1 April 1905), 451.
31. Whistler, 'The Ten O'Clock Lecture', in *The Gentle Art of Making Enemies*, pp. 137–38.
32. Arthur Symons, 'Editorial Note' to *The Savoy*, 1 (London: Leonard Smithers, January 1896), p. 5.
33. Symons, 'Whistler', in *Studies in Seven Arts*, p. 134.
34. Symons's faithful rendering of Verlaine's 'Art Poétique' from *Jadis et naguère* (1884), included in *Knave of Hearts*. The original reads, 'Prends l'éloquence et tords-lui son cou!'
35. Arthur Symons, 'Paul Verlaine', *National Review*, 19 (June 1892), 502.
36. For further discussion of this point, see Robert L. Peters, 'Whistler and the English Poets of the 1890s', *Modern Language Quarterly*, 18 (September 1957), 251–61, and my '"The Harem of Words": Attenuation and Excess in Decadent Poetry', in *Decadent Poetics*, ed. by Hall and Murray, pp. 83–99.
37. Symons, *Cities and Sea-Coasts and Islands* (London: W. Collins, 1918), p. 199. Further references to this text will be given parenthetically in the body of the essay.
38. Symons, 'Whistler', in *Studies in Seven Arts*, pp. 131–32. Whistler did not advertise the fact that the term 'nocturne' was actually coined by his sometime patron, F. R. Leyland. 'I can't thank you too much for the name "Nocturne" as a title for my moonlights!' he said in a letter of November 1872. 'You have no idea what an irritation it proves to the critics and consequently pleasure to me — besides it is really so charming and does so poetically say all I want to say and no more than I wish.' Quoted in Margaret F. MacDonald and Patricia de Montfort, *An American in London: Whistler and the Thames* (London: Dulwich Picture Gallery, 2013), p. 28.
39. John M. Munro, *Arthur Symons* (New York: Twayne, 1969), p. 91; Oscar Wilde, 'Phrases and Philosophies for the Use of the Young', *The Chameleon: A Bazaar of Dangerous and Smiling Chances*, No. 1 (December 1894).
40. Symons, 'Whistler', in *Studies in Seven Arts*, p. 124.
41. Symons, 'Impressionistic Writing', in *Critics of the 'Nineties*, ed. by Derek Stanford (London: John Baker, 1970), p. 116.
42. Ibid.
43. Stanford, *Critics of the 'Nineties*, p. 115.
44. Wilde, 'The Decay of Lying: An Observation' (1889), *Complete Works of Oscar Wilde* (London: HarperCollins, 1994), pp. 1074–75. Symons would later suggest that only Hubert Crackanthorpe's 'intellectual' and 'impersonal' approach allowed him to practise the 'deliberately unsympathetic record of sordid things' in his fiction. Symons, 'Hubert Crackanthorpe', *Saturday Review*, 1 (8 January 1898): 52–53 (p. 52).
45. For a useful compendium of responses to the painting, see Kate Flint, *Impressionists in England: The Critical Reception* (London: Routledge, 1984), pp. 8–11, 279–96.
46. Lisa N. Peters, *James McNeill Whistler* (New York: Todtri, 1996), p. 67. The picture was not sold until 1895.
47. Symons, 'Whistler', in *Studies in Seven Arts*, p. 127.
48. Ibid., p. 134.
49. Degas was the main target of *La Cigale*, a French comedy by Meilhac and Halévy, but when it was adapted for the English stage in December 1877 as *The Grasshopper*, its lead character, Marignan, became 'Pygmalion Flippit', a recognizable caricature of Whistler. See Weintraub, *Whistler*, pp. 192–93.
50. Arthur Symons, 'The Painting of the Nineteenth Century' (1903), in *Studies in Seven Arts*, pp. 44, 52.
51. Whistler, *The Gentle Art of Making Enemies*, p. 8.
52. Ibid., p. 115.
53. Symons, 'The Death of Peter Waydelin', *Spiritual Adventures*, p. 147. Subsequent references to this text are given parenthetically.
54. 'With Beardsley, the line between homage and subversion was seldom clearly marked,' observes Matthew Sturgis, *Aubrey Beardsley: A Biography* (London: HarperCollins, 1998), p. 127. The caricature of Beatrice 'Trixie' Whistler, initially given the Whistlerian title, 'A Study in Major Lines', was originally intended for the opening volume of the *Yellow Book* but was wisely

rejected by John Lane. It finally appeared in Jerome K. Jerome's *To-Day* (12 May 1894), p. 29. See Beardsley's letter to Lane, March 1894, *The Letters of Aubrey Beardsley*, pp. 65–66.
55. At least, so claimed Whistler's friend and biographer, Joseph Pennell, but though the story has often been repeated, it lacks corroboration.
56. Symons, 'The Death of Peter Waydelin', *Spiritual Adventures*, p. 149. Subsequent references to this text are given parenthetically.
57. Unsigned review of *Spiritual Adventures*, The Dial, 40 (1906), 201–02.
58. Symons, 'Impressionistic Writing', in *Critics of the 'Nineties*, p. 116.
59. 'We live, I regret to say, in an age of surfaces' (Lady Bracknell, *The Importance of Being Earnest*, Act III).
60. Tom Gibbons, *Rooms in the Darwin Hotel: Studies in English Literary Criticism and Ideas, 1880–1920* (Nedlands, WA: University of Western Australia Press, 1973), p. 69.
61. Walter Pater, *Studies in the History of the Renaissance*, quoted in Symons, 'To Rhoda', in *Studies in Seven Arts*, p. v.
62. Quoted in Mike Weaver, *Alvin Langdon Coburn: Symbolist Photographer* (New York: Aperture Foundation, 1986), p. 29.
63. Symons, *London: A Book of Aspects*, in *Cities and Sea-Coasts and Islands*, p. 187.
64. Whistler, *The Gentle Art of Making Enemies*, p. 144. For a discussion of how this passage influenced Symons and other writers of the 1890s, see my *Conceiving the City: London, Literature and Art 1870–1914* (Oxford: Oxford University Press, 2007), pp. 103–28. Whistler draws an ingenious analogy between nature and a piano — the latter contains all the notes of great music, but only an accomplished composer or performer can find or choose them. Symons and Coburn were both keen students of the piano, and Coburn owned hundreds of pianola rolls of his favourite pianists.
65. At the same time as he was exploring London with Symons, Coburn was collaborating with Henry James on the illustrative frontispieces for James's *New York Edition*.
66. The Minneapolis bookseller, Edmund D. Brooks, patron of Coburn, privately published a small number of copies of the illustrated *London: A Book of Aspects* for himself and his friends; Coburn's copy is now in Reading University Library. Brooks also printed the plain text in 1909 so as to establish Symons's US copyright.
67. A. L. Coburn, *Men of Mark* (London: Duckworth, 1913), p. 21.
68. Arthur Symons, 'Dedication' to *Cities* (London: J. M. Dent, 1903), pp. vi-vii.

CHAPTER 2

Carnal Flowers, Charnel Flowers: Perfume in the Decadent Literary Imagination

Catherine Maxwell

An orchid-collector purchases at auction a selection of plants belonging to a fellow collector found dead in a mangrove swamp, his body apparently sucked dry by leeches. Among the plants purchased is an unidentifiable rhizome that, once planted in his hothouse, quickly produces shoots and leaves. Entering his glasshouse the collector realizes his plant has flowered by 'a new odour in the air, a rich, intensely sweet scent, that overpowered every other', but on admiring the blooms that are the source of this scent, begins to find it 'insufferable', feels faint, and passes out. In the nick of time his housekeeper cousin, a woman suspicious of the strange and exotic, finds him in the hothouse where the orchid has begun to feed on him with its leech-like suckers. Resisting the faintness caused by the scent and having managed to drag him outside, she kills the predatory orchid by exposing it to the cold air, thus saving her cousin.

H. G. Wells's 'The Flowering of the Strange Orchid' of 1894 makes use of key decadent tropes and figures — the foreign invader, the 'strange flower', the dangerous artificial hothouse atmosphere, a poisonous perfume that overwhelms the senses. The story is a tongue-in-cheek cautionary tale about the dangers of a vampirical decadence, whose orchidaceous excesses can nonetheless be quickly quelled by the application of a brisk and breezy common sense. However, we might notice that the collector, recovered from his ordeal, seems curiously energized by it, appearing 'bright and garrulous [...] in the glory of his strange adventure'.[1]

One of the iconic flowers of decadence, the orchid's out-of-the ordinary, even peculiar, appearance reliably puts it in the category of 'strange flowers' that Walter Pater suggests should be sought out by the aspiring aesthete along with 'strange dyes' and 'curious odours'.[2] Unsurprisingly then orchids appear to greatest effect in *fin-de-siècle* texts where they are associated with monstrosity, perversity, and sin. Oscar Wilde's Lord Henry Wotton cuts for his buttonhole an orchid, which he says is 'a marvellous spotted thing, as effective as the seven deadly sins', while Dorian Gray is another man who mysteriously faints among the orchids in his own hothouse, although not, it should be said, on account of their overwhelming perfume.[3]

Rare, exotic, high-maintenance foreign beauties requiring a carefully controlled artificial environment at some considerable expense, orchids tick all the boxes when it comes to decadent credentials. These include the flowers' none-too-subtle, uncanny evocation of human sexuality. 'Orchid' derives from the Greek *orchis*, meaning testicle, which the tuber of the plant was thought to resemble, although most viewers find the flowers vulval in appearance. Moreover, the vanilla orchid, whose fruit produces the sweet essence used in perfume and cookery, takes its name from the diminutive of the Spanish *vaina*, meaning 'pod' or 'sheath', itself derived from the Latin word 'vagina'. Orchids thus have the characteristics of what we might call a 'carnal flower', a flower whose nature inevitably causes one to think of sex and sensuality.

Although the orchid nicely introduces us to the notion of dangerous intoxicating perfume and sensual pleasure, it is not the carnal flower I intend to explore in this essay. That distinction falls to the tuberose (*Polianthes tuberosa*), the inspiration for the contemporary fragrance *Carnal Flower* created by the perfumer Dominique Ropion for the niche perfume house Frédéric Malle. *Carnal Flower* contains more tuberose oil than any other contemporary perfume currently available, a fact reflected in its price at £150.00 for a 50ml bottle, as good quality tuberose absolute, at £5,500-£10,000 per kilo, is one of the most valuable substances in the world. Although tuberose does not have the immediate visual impact and graphic sexual suggestiveness of orchids, it is the carnal flower par excellence because of its fragrance, being called by the perfumer Roja Dove 'the harlot of perfumery'.[4]

In spite of the seeming connection, the tuberose is not related to the rose, its name deriving from its tuberous root. Its flower sprays of white blossoms, sometimes tipped with pale pink in the bud, look innocent enough, but emit a complex sweet fragrance often described as heady and narcotic and composed of several hundred different molecules with different scent properties. The artisan perfumer Alec Lawless describes tuberose as 'Sweet, heavy, floral and balsamic, with a slightly green, honey back note. Has been described as a "well stocked garden at eventide".'[5] Lawless apparently alludes to the Victorian perfume manual, *Piesse's Art of Perfumery*, first published in 1855, which says the scent is 'a nosegay in itself, and reminds one of a well-stocked flower-garden at evening close', and declares 'And oh, what a fragrance breathes from it! what a bouquet, snatching perfume from every flower with superb eclecticism!'[6] Among that bouquet initial notes may strike one as camphoraceous, a medicinal scent of wintergreen or Vicks vapo-rub induced by methyl salicylate, a natural compound found in the flower. Also present is eugenol, a spicy isolate of clove oil, more usually associated with carnations. And then there is a strange rubber note. The bio-physicist and perfume critic Luca Turin describes tuberose absolute as 'black rubber flower', observing: 'This is a natural oil, a complex mixture. This one's smell evolves. The rubber is kinky, dusted with talcum. Then an almost meaty blood-like smell reminiscent of carnations, and finally a "white flower" [...] Decorous but unquestionably poisonous.'[7]

Indeed, in common with other sensual white flowers, tuberose has an underlying animalic character, with fragrance notes that hint at the body and sex. Such white flower scents, including tuberose, are often described as indolic, as they contain an inky or tarry-smelling molecule called indole, also found in faeces and rotting corpses, that gives flowers like lilies, ylang ylang, orange blossom, lilac, and gardenia a putrid-sweet, sultry, intoxicating note. According to the perfume critic Denyse Beaulieu, 'tuberose is the white flower that contains the greatest quantity and variety of lactones', fatty or buttery-smelling molecules with 'coconut, hay and peach facets', which are also produced by the human scalp. Tuberose scent also contains a trace of skatol, a natural isolate found in animalic civet, and butyric acid, found in cheese and foot odour. This complex bouquet helps tuberose flowers achieve pollination. Beaulieu comments:

> Tuberose and her sisters jasmine, orange blossom, gardenia, honeysuckle are the vamps of the floral world, pallid creatures whose hypnotic, diffusive scents are potions for attracting nocturnal pollinating insects [...] Stick your nose in them. Go past the pretty. Zero in on the weird. Butter, Camembert, mushrooms, horse manure, bad breath, dirty feet, blood, meat, shit ... Despite their tiny size and pristine petals, white flowers bellow Nature's obscene secret through their outsized fragrance: flowers are sexual organs. And if those organs have ended up grafted David Cronenberg-style onto our skin, it is precisely *because* they also smell like the human body in all its extreme states, whether pleasure or death.[8]

As Beaulieu intimates, tuberose is a flower whose scent is stronger at night to attract pollinators, specifically moths. In India and Malaya, tuberose is called 'mistress of the night', another detail that hints at its after-hours harlotry. In darkness the white blossoms of the flower also have a luminescence that helps them attract insects. In his oriental poetic romance *Lalla Rookh* (1817), Thomas Moore writes of

> The tube-rose, with her silvery light,
>   That in the Gardens of MALAY
> Is call'd the Mistress of the Night,
> So like a bride, scented and bright,
>   She comes out when the sun's away.[9]

Although Moore's bridal imagery suggests something more virtuous, the vigorous night-life of the flower leads the early twentieth-century perfumer, William A. Poucher, to explain:

> The tuberose has for years been regarded as the symbol of voluptuousness, and the reasons for this may be traced to the beliefs of some of the older writers who generally considered the perfume to be slightly intoxicating. For instance, one writer recommends good girls not to breathe the odour of the tuberose on a fine evening, because its subtle perfume throws one into a voluptuous intoxication from which one does not easily become liberated.[10]

John Ingram, the Victorian author of a book on the symbolism of flowers, concurs, writing that the flower's 'white blossom exhales the most exquisite perfume — a perfume, however, it is alleged, so powerful, that to enjoy it without danger it is necessary to keep at some distance from the plant.'[11]

Contrary to popular belief, there is no one stable set of significations for the Victorian language of flowers, which varies considerably from authority to authority. However, tuberose is something of an exception, proving remarkably consistent across different flower dictionaries, where it reliably translates as 'dangerous pleasures' or, as Poucher specifies, 'voluptuousness'.[12] I would suggest that this rare consistency arises from consensus on the strong sensual scent of the tuberose.

Like jasmine, tuberose is too delicate to be subjected to the regular extraction processes of steam distillation, one of the factors that make tuberose absolute so extremely expensive. Although nowadays almost exclusively produced by solvent extraction, it was formerly obtained through the process known as 'enfleurage' in which the flowers are covered in a thin layer of highly refined, odourless fat, which they imbue with their odour. The resulting 'pomade' is melted, washed with alcohol, and the alcohol heated and evaporated leaving the rich, full-bodied absolute. Tuberose flowers have the unusual quality of producing essential oil for up to seventy-two hours after they are picked, which makes them ideal for enfleurage. Reminding us of the tuberose's night-time blandishments, its 'marked exhalation of odour after sundown', *Piesse's Art of Perfumery* observes that 'The *enfleurage* laboratory is always kept dark, an artificial inducement for the blossoms to "work hard"'.[13] This is an extended after-life that is also a slow death. Beaulieu remarks of the languorous demise of culled white flowers 'They are *dying*, not fading', citing her fellow perfume critic Octavian Coifan: 'The white flower is a flower that decomposes in sheer beauty!'[14]

The prolonged fragrant expiration of tuberose is not its only link with death, for if it is a carnal flower it is also a charnel flower. Originally found in Mexico, it was cultivated by the Aztecs who called it 'bone-flower' (*omixochitl*) on account of its white blossoms.[15] According to Beaulieu, it was one of those white flowers used in Aztec sacrificial rituals, where 'their smell blended with the stench of [the] sacrificial victim's blood — there is a bit of a blood note in the tuberose, and that hint of blood is, again, a bond between death and life, human sacrifice and female fertility'.[16] Like other indolic white flowers, tuberose has been also used as a funeral flower, its strong scent helping camouflage but also blending with the smell of human decay, an association possibly responsible for a not uncommon ambivalence or queasiness about white flower scents.

Something of that ambivalence can be found in the Romantic poet Percy Shelley, author of some of the most influential literary references to tuberose. In 'The Sensitive-Plant', he celebrates 'The jessamine faint, and the sweet tuberose, | The sweetest flower for scent that blows', while in 'The Woodman and the Nightingale', the nightingale's song is able to 'Satiate the hungry dark with melody | [...] as a tuberose | Peoples some Indian dell with scents which lie | Like clouds above the flower from which they rose'.[17] However, when referring to the classical bucolic poets in his *A Defence of Poetry* (1821), Shelley finds

> Their poetry is intensely melodious; like the odour of the tuberose, it overcomes and sickens the spirit with excess of sweetness; whilst the poetry of the preceding age was as a meadow-gale of June which mingles the fragrance of all the flowers of the field, and adds a quickening and harmonizing spirit of its own which endows the sense with a power of sustaining its extreme delight.[18]

The classicist John Addington Symonds endorses this assessment in his *Studies of the Greek Poets* (1873):

> Over the waning day of Greek poetry Theocritus, Bion, and Moschus cast the sunset hues of their excessive beauty. Genuine and exquisite is their inspiration; pure, sincere, and true is their execution. Yet we agree with Shelley, who compares their perfume to 'the odour of the tuberose, which overcomes and sickens the spirit with excess of sweetness.'[19]

Picking up on that note of cloying sweetness, Symonds goes on to draw out a more explicit comparison with decay in contemporary literary decadence:

> In the same way the erotic epigrammatists, though many of them genuine poets, especially the exquisite Meleager of Gadara, in the very perfection of their peculiar quality of genius offer an unmistakable sign of decay. It is the fashion among a certain class of modern critics to rave about the art of Decadence, to praise the hectic hues of consumption and even the strange livors of corruption, more than the roses and the lilies of health. Let them peruse the epigrams of Meleager and of Straton. Of beauty in decay sufficient splendours may be found there.[20]

The phrase 'livors of corruption' references the Latin term 'livor mortis', alluding to the lividity, or purplish red discoloration of the skin that can set in after death. Shelley's sickly tuberose seems inevitably to lead Symonds to thoughts of decadent death and decay, perhaps something not surprising in a writer whose own favourite scent was the airy fragrance of cut grass and hay, closer to the June 'meadow-gale' or breeze that Shelley himself seems to prefer.

Yet Walter Pater, whose own perfume tastes tend mainly towards light florals, calls upon the tuberose to represent an exotic style of writing that can be accomplished within one's native English.[21] In his unfinished imaginary portrait, 'An English Poet', a story probably written in the late 1870s but not published till 1931, Pater's Anglo-French protagonist grows up in Cumberland. Out of sympathy with his immediate surroundings and filled with a Baudelairean 'sensuous longing for that warmer soil out of which exotic flowers [...] would naturally grow', he nonetheless finds sanctuary in a species of literary English:

> the English tongue had revealed itself to him as a living spirit of mysterious strength and sweetness and he had elected to be an artist in that. [...] the boy required from words, and not in vain, in books, the picture, the tuberose, the marble face, the fading light on ancient cities, all that was not actually there for ear and eye, above all the genius of refinement; and this not as the new subject of writing, its more obvious and immediate presentations, but by a subtler operation from the style, the ether-like manner of the thing. So written language came to be form and colour as well as sound to him, exotic perfume almost.[22]

Here the exotic or 'strange flower', the tuberose, again represents a highly refined, nuanced, or rarefied style, such an exquisite style as characterizes Pater's own aesthetic prose, imitated by his decadent successors.

One of those decadent successors is the poet Mark André Raffalovich (1864–1934), a Russian Jewish emigré, whose wealthy, cultured family moved from Odessa to Paris in 1863 where Marie, his brilliant multilingual mother, became a noted *salonnière*. In 1882 the eighteen-year-old Raffalovich, accompanied by his former governess, settled in London, where he began writing poetry, fiction, and drama in English. His first collection of poetry, *Cyril and Lionel*, was published in 1884, his second, *Tuberose and Meadowsweet* in 1885. *Tuberose and Meadowsweet* is best known not for its content, but for a somewhat feline notice by Oscar Wilde, who reviewed it anonymously for the *Pall Mall Gazette* of 27 March 1885.

Wilde undoubtedly realized that *Tuberose and Meadowsweet*, a volume that explores love through a series of poems featuring different flowers, is a collection of homoerotic verse. The language of his review specifically evokes a decadent register:

> This is really a remarkable little volume, and contains many strange and beautiful poems. To say of these poems that they are unhealthy, and bring with them the heavy odours of the hothouse, is to point out neither their defect, nor their merit, but their quality merely. And, though Mr. Raffalovich is not a wonderful poet, still he is a subtle artist in poetry. Indeed, in his way he is a boyish master of curious music, and of fantastic rhyme.[23]

The word 'odours' suggests Pater's 'Conclusion', while words like 'strange', 'curious', and 'subtle' have strong associations with his essay 'Leonardo da Vinci' (1869) that hints at the painter's homosexuality.[24] (As Wilde probably knew, Raffalovich and Pater were friends.)[25] Wilde's review also echoes Swinburne's 1862 review of Baudelaire's *Les Fleurs du mal*, a volume described as possessing 'a heavy heated temperature with dangerous hothouse scents in it'.[26] Raffalovich had prefaced his volume with an unattributed epigraph taken from Swinburne's poem 'Relics' (1873) and the collection has in places a marked Swinburnian register.[27]

Wilde apparently outs Raffalovich as a decadent poet but almost immediately undercuts the gesture by questioning his basic credentials. *Tuberose and Meadowsweet* is named after one of the principal poems in the collection in which the word 'tuberose' is continually repeated: 'Of tuberose, O love, of tuberose, | I sing of tuberose, of tuberose!'[28] Referring to the title and doubtless aware of its author's foreign origins, Wilde teasingly charged Raffalovich with failing to pronounce the word 'tuberose' correctly, claiming (falsely as it happens), it should be stressed as a disyllable not a trisyllable, and adding 'though he cannot pronounce "tuberose" aright, at least he can sing of it exquisitely.'[29] This claim sparked a sparring match in the *Pall Mall Gazette* with both parties citing Shelley in their defence.[30] Regardless of the rights of the matter, Wilde sets himself up as a gatekeeper, making the exotic word 'tuberose' a decadent poetic shibboleth. Mispronunciation suggests one's ineligibility as a true English poet, inheritor of Shelley, and rightful claimant to the contemporary poetic scene. In spite of this tussle, Wilde and Raffalovich remained on more or less cordial terms until the 1890s when their relations rapidly degenerated.[31]

Ed Madden, one of few critics to discuss Raffalovich's verse, suggests that he 'turned to the Victorian "language of flowers" — a language of romance and courtship codified in the floral dictionaries and gilt-bound gift-books of the period — and he used this sentimental, heterosexual, and usually feminized language to portray homosexual love.'[32] Madden's legitimate claim that Raffalovich '*queers* the language of flowers — both making it strange and (homo) sexualizing it' nonetheless ignores the fact that prior to 1885 a number of Victorian women poets — such as Michael Field and Agnes Mary Frances Robinson — had used floral poetry as a device to convey love between women and that there are classical traditions of figuring both lesbian and male homosexual love via floral emblems that reach back to 'violet-crowned' Sappho and the homoerotic verse of the Greek Anthology.[33] Indeed the word 'anthology' means a collection or garland of flowers — a poet's poems being traditionally his 'flowers' — *anthoi* in Greek — an association punningly made by Swinburne in the poetic quotation Raffalovich uses for the epigraph to his book: 'Such words of message have dead flowers to say [...] | Before I throw them and these words away.'

Lest we should think his floral imagery merely a convenient veil, it should be pointed out that Raffalovich adored flowers, and one commentator observes that 'ladies envied his exquisite disposition of [them]'.[34] In later life he was apparently 'a stickler for correct botanical names', and cherished his Edinburgh garden 'which was always kept in meticulous order, and gay with flowers according to the season.'[35] Commenting on the soirées and dinner parties he held at this time, Margaret Sackville, one of his visitors, wrote: 'Every week small exquisite blossoms were grouped together in impermanent masterpieces. He possessed the genius the flower painter so often lacks: that is to say, he really *did* make flower *pictures*!'[36] However, by this date, his moral outlook had changed, and another visitor, Janet Grierson, noted his efforts to redefine his tastes as befitting those of an older respectable man of the church. She recalls his displeasure when a guest picked one of his roses to present to her sister,

> for his roses were sacred; of a certain *parti pris* he had for the simple and the healthy, though it was obviously an attitude and part of his revolt against what had once been his tastes. I remember he once advised me with great seriousness what scent to use, and stipulated that it must never be an artificial scent, but a flower perfume.[37]

Of course all manufactured perfume, however apparently natural, is always an artificial affair; moreover, as we have seen, some flowers and flower scents have a complex, decidedly 'unwholesome' aura, as indeed Grierson suggests when she observes the efforts of the older Raffalovich to champion the rose over less 'simple', stranger flowers.

Tuberose and Meadowsweet does include some of those simpler flowers — cranesbill, nettle, love-in-a-mist, ivy, anemone, meadowsweet itself — but the volume's title suggests a union or marriage between the exotic and the simple, and perhaps also between urban sophistication and pastoral innocence. Moreover the perfume of flowers is all-important, as borne out by the title poem in which the speaker celebrates his love for his beloved by evoking two contrasting flowers and their scents, the narcotic tuberose 'Whose scent in living pulses seems to beat: | Magnetic ardour, drowsy scent of love' and the meadowsweet 'most mystical and fresh, | Whose breath can thrill us with a breath most sweet'.[38] In her book on plant aromatics, Jennifer Peace Rhind lists meadowsweet, a wild flower, among those plants that produce the typical agrestic odours of the meadow or hayfield, noting that its 'clusters of creamy flowers' have a 'sweet, honey-floral odour'.[39] In common with other agrestic plants, meadowsweet also contains coumarin, an organic chemical compound with the scent of hay and cut grass — a fresh out-of-doors fragrance. The speaker associates the scent of meadowsweet with 'my passion's purity, | O distant echo, faintness rapt and fresh, | That means my soul to thee, and thine to me' (p. 37). However, lest this look like a straightforward contrast between sexual and spiritual passion, the speaker complicates matters by telling us that meadowsweet is also reminiscent of the touch of 'warm seraphic flesh' (p. 39), an image that somewhat curiously blends the physical and the spiritual. Meadowsweet thus represents the idealized grace and delicacy of the beloved's body: 'Slender and sweet, like honey, like thy hair, | O like my words to thee, like meadowsweet, | Stainless and tender, tall and fair' (p. 39). However, it is the exotic sensuality of tuberose that proves the dominant perfume, taking over from and overwhelming the lighter, more innocent fragrance of meadowsweet. Asking archly 'It may be summer in the woods to-day, | Or winter with the trees, or spring, who knows?' (p. 39), the speaker shifts from the external world of natural beauty to the enclosed realm of the bedroom where seasons or even the time of day are no longer important: 'Behind the soft green curtains half undone, | The fluttering paleness, is it morn or eve, | To-day that ends, to-morrow that's begun?' (p. 40).

In the next stanza we enter the darkened space of that room which is suffused by the erotic perfume of tuberose. Without recourse to more explicit language, the strong carnal presence of the scent seems to signify 'voluptuousness', a sexual pleasure that erases thoughts of anything beyond the moment:

> Here in the vague and close confined room
> All senses are as one acutely blent,
> When speechless, touching not, in silent gloom
> We yearn and languish with a single scent,
> Relentlessly and subtly odorous.
> Here in the vague and close confined room
> And of Lethean pleasures redolent,
> The strong inevitable tuberose
> Surrounds irradiating to a tomb,
> Where half-unconsciousness is well content.
> Here in the vague and close confined room
> All senses are as one acutely blent. (pp. 40–41)

This interlude, a typical Swinburnian interspace between life and death, has both an overcharged awareness and an enervated lassitude. Indeed the oppressive scented atmosphere and synaesthetic merging of the senses — 'All senses are as one acutely blent' — recall Swinburne's Christian knight, Tannhäuser, in 'Laus Veneris' languishing in the enclosure of the Horsel, Venus's subterranean pleasure-palace. Tannhäuser tells us: 'Inside the Horsel here the air is hot; | [...] The scented dusty daylight burns the air', and later says:

> The scent and shadow shed about me make
> The very soul in all my senses ache;
>   The hot hard night is fed upon my breath,
> And sleep beholds me from afar awake.[40]

Raffalovich's speaker describes the tuberose as of 'Lethean pleasures redolent'. Lethe is the river of forgetfulness in the Underworld that the dead must drink from in order to forget their earthly lives. Are Lethean pleasures 'forgotten', or even 'deadly' or 'dangerous pleasures' that, revived by this tuberose-perfumed idyll, can be once more enjoyed, or are they pleasures that require a narcotized obliviousness of the quotidian world? Such shortlived oblivion — the dying to one's everyday life, the temporary dissolve of consciousness and identity along with ecstatic release — is a symbolic form of death. But the fleshly tuberose, manifesting its funereal character, decomposing in sheer beauty and irradiating its scent and its faint phosphorescent light in the dim tomb-like confines of the chamber, also rouses thoughts of death proper which continue into the next stanza:

> If this be death, then we are dead indeed!
> O do not stir lest we find life again:
> What should we have of life? There is no need
> For us to fill the hollow hours in vain
> Or lengthen out the sobbing of our breath.
> If this be death, then we are dead indeed,
> Or waiting for the whole of life to wane,
> After the last sigh, love, the first kiss, death!
> I think that on some battlefield we bleed,
> And I would live once more to be so slain.
> If this be death, then we are dead indeed.
> O do not stir lest we find life again! (p. 41)

Life outside the chamber, where the lovers are compelled to disguise their passionate feelings for each other, might well seem like 'hollow hours' and a prolonged torture, to which sexual consummation, figured as a kind of *Liebestod*, seems entirely preferable. The date of Raffalovich's collection, published in the spring of 1885, reminds us that the August of that year would see the passing of the infamous Labouchère Amendment that criminalized sexual activity between consenting men in private, making it a dangerous pleasure indeed.

In the ensuing final stanzas of the poem, the speaker, now apparently at a distance from his lover and recalling their mutual passion, impresses on us the need for secrecy, addressing his lover as the

> [...] flower, whose name I may not tell
> Save unto one alone who is not here,
> But who perhaps like me remembers well
> One flower, one scent, one hour and one called dear. (pp. 41–42)

To this unnamed absent lover, he announces how the fragrance of the tuberose has become the essence of their secret love.

> For this perfume since then a grave profound,
> Wherein is laid of life the perfect whole,
> Has undivided from desire been wound
> About the inmost longings of my soul.
> And when I sicken of my living now
> This wizard flower brings back again thy breath,
> Touches my mouth and hands: how far art thou?

> For I do feel thee like delight or death,
> Thy shoulders and thy arms, thy shadowed hair,
> Thy speechless lips and thy unaltered stare.
> Of tuberose, desirous tuberose,
> Of tuberose I sing, of tuberose,
> Of tuberose I sing and meadowsweet. (p. 42)

The scent in its carnal-charnel nature is a grave that buries but also commemorates and protects the precious perfect life of the speaker's concealed desire. However, it also has the power to resurrect it, with an intense evocation of the beloved's fleshly presence. That evocation is infused with the reminiscence of another same-sex love as Raffalovich echoes the accents of Swinburne's Sappho hymning Anactoria:

> Ah sweeter than all sleep or summer air
> The fallen fillets fragrant from thine hair!
> Yea, though their alien kisses do me wrong,
> Sweeter thy lips than mine with all their song;
> Thy shoulders whiter than a fleece of white.[41]

That Swinburnian echo helps press home the message that Raffalovich's poem is not a song of heterosexual love.

Yet lesbianism, unlike male homosexuality, was ignored by the Labouchère Amendment, in which 'dangerous pleasures' became specifically criminal pleasures. Raffalovich would go on to become a writer on sexual inversion, the author of a substantial book on the topic, *Uranisme et unisexualité* (1896), and numerous articles contributed from 1894 onwards to the French review *Archives d'Anthropologie Criminelle*. Influenced by his growing religious feeling — he would become a Catholic in 1896 — these later writings advocated a chaste non-physical love between men. (A later anti-decadent sonnet in praise of simpler wholesome flowers marks his turn away from the exotic blooms of his youth that represented sensual love, now denigrated as 'Voluptuous, tawdry, evil, tuberoses, | Orchids uncouth, foxglove or aconite'.)[42] Nonetheless even though Raffalovich's later writings promoted chaste male homosexuality, they still had to be published in France as they would have been condemned, if not criminally prosecuted, in Britain. At least one bookseller would have criminal charges brought against him for stocking Havelock Ellis's book *Sexual Inversion* when it was published in 1897.

We shall return in due course to the dangerous and even criminal pleasures of the carnal flower. In the meantime we move on three years to the short sonnet sequence 'Tuberoses' by the poet Mary Robinson from her collection *Songs, Ballads, and a Garden Play* of 1888. Robinson, who for seven years had been the lover of Violet Paget (better known as Vernon Lee), shocked her partner and her family by becoming engaged in August 1887 to the orientalist James Darmesteter whom she had met on just three occasions. The union seems to have been by mutual consent a *mariage blanc* but was evidently a happy companionable affair. We don't know exactly what prompted Robinson's sudden decision. She may have craved her independence, away from her protective parents, and there is a hint that she may have intended Vernon Lee to live with her and her new husband in Paris.[43] If this was the case, Lee was having none of it. After a temporary breakdown, she found solace in a new partner, the painter Kit Anstruther-Thomson. Following Robinson's marriage in March 1888, the two women continued to correspond and to see each other occasionally, but relations between them were never the same.

Songs, Ballads, and a Garden Play is dedicated to Robinson's sister, the novelist Mabel Robinson. In her dedicatory preface dated 27 February 1888, written just before her marriage, Robinson recalls a conversation about the 'Garden Play' of the title at the Robinsons' out-of-town house in Surrey, 'one happy afternoon, more than a year ago, when Vernon and you and I walked up and down the sunny Epsom garden and laid a deep plan for the acting of that trifle.'[44] She then concludes: 'The only real things, you know, are the things that never happen; and so it will always seem to me that the Play belongs to you and Vernon and the Epsom garden.' This preface has an important thematic link with Robinson's 'Tuberoses' whose final sonnet announces:

> But fashion'd in the mirage of a dream,
>   Having nor life nor sense, a bubble of nought,
> The enchanted City of the Things that seem
>   Keeps till the end of time the eternal Thought.[45]

There is a distinct sense of melancholy and loss that pervades both the preface and the poem; indeed the volume has as its frontispiece plate a reproduction of Dürer's *Melancholia*. The preface seems addressed as much to Lee as it is to Mabel and it is possible that the thematically linked poem 'Tuberoses' may be a reflection on the end of their relationship, as it is an elegy to 'things that perish, | Memory, roses, love we feel and cherish'.[46] The following reading is not primarily biographical, although, according to the garden historian Roy Genders, during the Victorian period tuberose bulbs were brought into Britain from Italy, Lee's adopted homeland, possibly suggesting her identity with this exotic import.[47]

'Tuberoses' is an extremely conflicted poem. Its final sonnet is an apparent celebration of the enduring imaginative ideal over the transient real, the city of fancy over the man-made city that will crumble and decay, evoking Théophile Gautier's aesthetic manifesto poem 'L'Art' which proclaims that 'the sculpted bust survives the city.'[48] Yet the poem's melancholy is more in line with Keats's 'Ode on a Grecian Urn', whose speaker's deliberately over-fervent praise of art's longevity is undercut by his palpable attraction to 'breathing human passion'.[49] Robinson's conclusion proposes that art, aesthetic meditation, and aesthetic imaginings inevitably arise out of our need to deal with death, change, and decay, but also suggests that art is a deceptive illusion, 'having nor life nor sense, a bubble of nought', holding out the lure of permanence, while depriving us of more immediate joys and sorrows.

The conflicted emotion of the conclusion also affects the flower that gives its name to this poem. The opening of Sonnet 1 tells us the tuberose is the gift of the poem's addressee whom we assume is the speaker's lover: 'The Tuberose you left me yesterday | Leans yellowing in the glass we set it in'. Although the first and most subsequent printings of this poem give us 'glass', the version published in Robinson's *Collected Poems* of 1902 gives 'grass', suggesting that the couple planted a flowering tuberose in the speaker's garden. 'Glass' is the more likely reading, but the second one, 'grass', is interesting because it suggests the lover's intention that the flower continue living and blooming as an enduring symbol of their romance. (Indeed later the speaker will refer to 'the flower we lov'd so long', suggesting that the tuberose is part of the couple's shared romantic history.) Tuberoses are not native to Britain but it is perfectly possible to grow them as garden flowers if they are planted out when the weather is warmer, and they were regularly grown in borders throughout the second half of the nineteenth century. Whether cut or growing, the carnal tuberose and its sensual scent should, as we have seen, represent voluptuousness, something the lover may have wanted to signify in giving this flower to the speaker.

However, if the tuberose formerly represented erotic passion to the speaker, she indicates that such passion is now sadly depleted. A cut tuberose spray should remain powerfully fragrant for several days but the speaker suggests the vitality and perfume of the flower are dependent on the presence of her lover, now 'gone away' but addressed as 'my dear'. This tuberose has become a funereal flower but does it represent the speaker herself or her feelings for the absent lover? Does she feel abandoned or bereft or resentful at her lover's absence? Is she pining or does she find that her feelings ebb and diminish once her lover is out of sight? And what about that extraordinary second quatrain in which the fast-fading fragrance of the flower is compared to the misgivings following a short-lived episode of guilty passion? Why does the speaker choose such an analogy? Is she thinking about an experience with the absent lover or with another? There is also an awkwardness in the wording: the 'faint' fragrance of the dying flower is also 'poisoned at the source', although a 'poisoned' fragrance suggests something stronger than a faint odour. And what is this 'source'? Is it the speaker's heart or feelings? Moreover, the lingering guilty 'passion' of the analogy is mismatched, being not 'faint' at all but finding instead 'its sweetness heavy with remorse.'

In the third quatrain of Sonnet 1 the speaker casually merges the specificity of the fading tuberose into generalized 'dying roses', although the tuberose is botanically unrelated to the rose and bears it no physical resemblance. One could interpret this as an act of aggression as well as repression, reinforced by the speaker's suggestion that she 'shut' the 'dying flowers' 'in weighty tomes where none will look' — as if, ashamed of her feelings, she wishes to hide away and forget the emblem of her former love. This suggested concealment is to be accompanied by an amnesia so profound that she will later 'wonder when the unfrequent page uncloses | Who shut the wither'd blossoms in the book?' Robinson may be partly remembering the image of woman as a 'rose shut in a book', used by D. G. Rossetti in his dramatic monologue, 'Jenny', to describe how the prostitute is cut off from other untainted women. Jenny is compared to a flower pressed in a pornographic book in which 'pure women may not look', and thus forgoes the sympathy they would otherwise surely have for her 'crushed' state.[50] Here the speaker implies she will press the dying flower not in an erotic book but in a 'weighty tome' — surely a dry or boring book that she will rarely want to consult.

Sonnet 2 opens with a remembrance of the couple's shared admiration for the tuberose when it was growing 'Alive and white', a vigorous 'spike of waxy bloom' rather than a 'Poor spike of withering sweetness'. This shared memory of the blooming tuberose — not, it seems, the same blossom as the withered cut flower — recalls an earlier time when the couple's own relationship was 'Alive', and thus helps explain the plural 'tuberoses' of the title. Even so, this memory is bound up with the view that the tuberose 'grows and grows | Until at length it blooms itself to death.' The tuberose, whether cut or cultivated, will eventually die. Again strategically shifting us away from the particularity of the withered tuberose and the fading relationship, this sonnet embraces the larger theme that 'everything passes' and adopts a more generalized perspective as it considers how transient experiences or precious memories of them can be preserved. Here the image of the pressed flower in a book is converted into the idea of a commemorative poem in a book as, in a wittily self-reflexive manoeuvre, the emblematic flower becomes the poetic flower, the speaker's poem or *anthos*. The commemorative poem, unlike the pressed flower, is not hidden away, but the speaker signals that there is nonetheless a violence in transforming lived experience into art, that the poetic image can be created only at the expense of the real, by killing or crushing the living referent:

> Everything dies that lives — everything dies;
> How shall we keep the flower we lov'd so long?
> O press to death the transient thing we prize,
> Crush it, and shut the elixir in a song.

As mentioned earlier, tuberose oil was not extracted from the flower by expression but by enfleurage, a gentle death in which the flower gradually yields up its fragrance. Nor is expression, a technique reserved for citrus oils, used for other flowers, which are instead processed by steam distillation. This may sound rather pedantic but the speaker is evidently employing a reference to perfumery-cum-alchemy — perfumery, of course, having its origins in alchemy, with both processes focused on capturing the definitive essence of a thing rather than the thing itself. Both processes also are analogous with aesthetic transformation; the young Yeats, for example, resolutely anti-material and fascinated by alchemy, in 1898 describes the new decadent arts as 'filling our thoughts with the essences of things, and not with things.'[51] In alchemy the *elixir vitae*, elixir of life, prolongs or revives life rather than taking it away, just as perfume or *extrait* preserves and enhances the fragrance of flowers long dead. Robinson's sonnet is clearly in dialogue with Shakespeare's sonnet no. 5, which uses the image of perfume extending the life of transient summer flowers to encourage the fair youth to eternalize his beauty through having fair children of his own. Shakespeare's sonnet concludes by insisting that 'flow'rs distilled, though they with winter meet | Leese but their show; their substance still lives sweet.'[52] And there is the strong suggestion that the condensed and concentrated space of the sonnet is also the container of 'beauty', its essence, or sweetness. However, Robinson's speaker suggests that the commemorative song is a poor substitute for actual experience or beauty, that art seems sterile and lifeless in comparison, its one superiority over life being its longevity:

> A song is neither live nor sweet nor white.
> It hath no heavenly blossom tall and pure,
> No fragrance can it breathe for our delight,
> It grows not, neither lives; it may endure.

This speaker refuses to acknowledge the reviving powers implied by her own use of the word 'elixir', and her insistence that the poem is but a dry husk of an experience and cannot replace the beauty of the living flower — an act of poetic self-contempt — may be her way of finally acknowledging the true loss of the dying tuberose, a bereavement that cannot be compensated by art.

While we know that memory is powerfully activated by smell, the question of whether a smell can be conjured up by a memory or prompted, say, by a poem or artwork, is more debatable, though many perfumers, wine tasters, and chefs claim the ability of olfactory recall. However, though for most subjects a poem or painting may not be able to conjure up an actual smell, it can certainly evoke vivid feelings and images associated with that smell or with an analogous smell sensation. Poems about smell and other sensory experiences clearly speak to emotions deep-rooted in our corporeal existence. There is, of course, a paradox or irony at work in Robinson's poem, which depends on our awareness of what fragrance is and what it might signify, only then to deny the very evocative power on which it calls. In the final lines of sonnet 2 the tuberose is bidden farewell and banished, its place to be taken by the enduring poetic dream or thought, but for the reader of Robinson's poem the flower has always been such a dream or thought, permanently arrested in its long demise.

From the melancholy funereal tuberose of Robinson's sonnets we pass to our final poem from Theodore Wratislaw's collection *Orchids* (1896).[53] Wratislaw, whose other poems in both this and an earlier collection, *Caprices* (1893), reveal a keen interest in perfumes such as frangipani, opoponax, and white lilies, finds himself unable to resist the blandishments of the tuberose. As in our previous two poems where the flower emblematizes a sexual or romantic relationship, associations with both sex and death are in play. Wratislaw intensifies these associations through the figure of the femme fatale, an alluring *fleur du mal*, to produce an archetypal decadent poem. Like various modern tuberose perfumes that capitalize on the sensational impact or attack of the flower, Wratislaw's poem is a deliberate provocation.

The speaker has been sent a spray of tuberose by his mistress, which he smells and kisses as he fantasizes about the giver and the possible implications of her gift. The flower is also a fetish, a synecdoche for the absent mistress, and redolent of certain characteristics that the speaker ascribes or wants to ascribe to her. Although the exotic flower, like the mistress, requires the luxury of warmth in which to flourish, like her, the flower itself is 'Cool', seemingly calculating in its efforts to make its recipient 'heated'. Its 'whiteness' echoes her 'smooth white hands' that have clearly little more to do than cull flowers and please lovers, the 'languid' blossom hinting at her own cultivated lassitude. The speaker declares that she has plucked the flower spray from a tuberose by her bedside; the word 'alcove' has a Baudelairean provenance, signifying a recess for a bed, the flower bringing with it, like an invitation, this suggestion of the heated, scented boudoir and its erotic pleasures, along with the risqué hint at a bodily recess.[54] Asking 'But ah! what missive comes with thee [...]?' the speaker teases us with an allusion to the sentimental language of flowers as conventionally encoded in the lover's proffered posy or bouquet, but the sensuous aspects of tuberose are so evident in its fragrance that it requires no decryption: the skin notes in the fragrance of the flower evoke his mistress's own body scent, 'The languid fragrance of her breast'. In another poem, 'La Fleur du jardin d'ici bas', Wratislaw hymns the 'Odour of women faintly wrought | In folds of silken bodices' as a 'perfume headier than wine'.[55] In the nineteenth century the phrase 'bouquet de corsage' could refer not merely to the fragrance of flowers worn in a woman's bodice, but to the smell of her perspiring skin as savoured by her partner on the dance floor.[56]

Burying his lips in the 'honeyed whirls' of the florets, the speaker hopes to find the kiss that his mistress bestowed on the spray before she sent it to him, but he also fantasizes that the flowers' curled petals hold the less innocuous gift of 'poison'. Yet this idea of poison seems to arouse rather than dismay him. Apostrophized in the final stanza, 'Dear poison' is a sadomasochistic aphrodisiac imagined as conferring a blissful death. It is the essence of the 'murderous flower by whom I die', the dangerous pleasures of the vampish woman as tuberose, because to succumb to her narcotic and deadly spell is at least to suffer no parting from her.

The notion of a poisonous perfume has a long history that predates Wratislaw. In the Renaissance, when perfume was used to scent leather and fabric rather than directly applied to the body, Catherine de' Medici is supposed to have dispatched her daughter's future mother-in-law, Jeanne de Navarre, with the gift of poisoned gloves.[57] Nathaniel Hawthorne's gothic short story 'Rappaccini's Daughter' (1844), features a nefarious Paduan scientist who has brought up his beautiful daughter to be immune to the poisonous perfumed flowers in his private garden. However, in tending these toxic blooms, she herself becomes poisonous to others.[58] In the nineteenth century there were debates about the possibly dangerous, even fatal effects of flower fragrance. In 1843 the periodical *The Garden and Practical Florist* cited Dr Ingenhousz on poisonous exhalations from plants, who opined that 'a person shut up in a small and close room, containing a large quantity of the most fragrant flowers, might lose his life by this most treacherous of all poisons.'[59] The poet Swinburne was convinced that he had been poisoned by the perfume of some Indian lilies left overnight in his bedroom, an experience that he claimed had left him 'prostrated for many wretched or unprofitable weeks'.[60]

Tuberose absolute diluted as an essence was widely used in bouquet perfumes throughout the nineteenth century, and, more specifically, bottled soliflore tuberose perfume was certainly available. However, it may not have had the impact of the actual flower, or at least not for long, because, as Piesse's perfume manual points out, 'essence of tuberose [...] is exceedingly volatile, and, if sold in its pure state, quickly flies off the handkerchief', and he advises the use of fixatives such as storax or vanilla to delay its volatility.[61] Tuberose perfume would really come into its own in the twentieth century when additional use of synthetics and more complex design gave the fragrance more force and staying power. What is interesting, however, is that the associations with the floral fragrance that I have been exploring through these poems — sexuality, death, criminality, poison — uncannily anticipate the great tuberose perfumes of the twentieth century which exploit the sensational aspects of the flower. The poems, if you like, suggest ways of reading and responding to tuberose scent that are later encapsulated in perfumes starting with the violent disturbance of Germaine Cellier's *Fracas* for Robert Piguet (1948), the mother of all famous tuberose fragrances. *Fracas* gives birth to Edouard Fléchier's *Poison* for Christian Dior (1985), Christopher Sheldrake's *Tubéreuse Criminelle* for Serge Lutens (1998), Dominic Ropion's *Carnal Flower* for Frédéric Malle (2005), and Calice Becker's *Beyond Love* for By Kilian (2007). Tessa Williams comments that *Tubéreuse Criminelle* 'is said to have been inspired by a murder that took place in a room full of tuberose', a decadent detail worthy of Wratislaw, while in her perfume guide Susan Irvine cites an article in French *Vogue* for 1997 with regard to *Fracas*: 'This white flower is a torrid poison which acts seductively on men. It is an agony, an olfactory rape'.[62] *Beyond Love*, or *Beyond Love, Prohibited*, to give it its full name, features in Kilian's 'L'Oeuvre Noire' range, the perfumes in their iconic black packaging pitched to suggest an edgy S&M vibe. Apropos of Dior's *Poison*, Irvine comments that 'Scent has always been sold as bottled sex, but it has to be forbidden sex to be truly alluring', a sentiment that in different ways pervades and enhances the appeal of the poems by Raffalovich and Wratislaw.[63] The concept or 'story' that lies behind most modern fragrance is for tuberose perfume already there in the poetry of Victorian decadence, adding piquancy to the saying of the contemporary perfumer Jean-Claude Ellena: 'Smell is a word, perfume is literature'.[64]

Notes to Chapter 2

1. H. G. Wells, 'The Flowering of the Strange Orchid', in *The Stolen Bacillus and Other Incidents* (London: Macmillan, 1904), pp. 17–35 (pp. 30, 35).
2. Walter Pater, 'Conclusion', *Studies in the History of the Renaissance*, ed. by Matthew Beaumont (Oxford: Oxford University Press, 2010), p. 120.
3. Oscar Wilde, *The Picture of Dorian Gray*, ed. by Joseph Bristow (Oxford: Oxford University Press, 2006), pp. 163, 167.
4. Roja Dove, *The Essence of Perfume* (London: Black Dog Publishing, 2008), p. 59.
5. Alec Lawless, *Artisan Perfumery or Being Led by the Nose* (Stroud: Baronia Souk, 2009), p. 75.
6. G. W. Septimus Piesse, *Art of Perfumery and the Methods of obtaining the Odours of Plants, the Growth and General Flower Farm System of Raising Fragrant Herbs*, ed. by Charles H. Piesse, 5th edn (London: Piesse and Lubin, 1891), p. 223.
7. Luca Turin, cited in Chandler Burr, *The Emperor of Scent: A Story of Perfume, Obsession, and the Last Mystery of the Senses* (London: Arrow Books, 2004), p. 18.
8. Denyse Beaulieu, *The Perfume Lover: A Personal History of Scent* (London: Collins, 2012), pp. 128, 125–26.
9. Thomas Moore, *Lalla Rookh: An Oriental Romance*, 3rd edn (London: Longman, Hurst, Rees, Orme and Brown, 1817), pp. 311–12.
10. William A. Poucher, *Perfumes, Cosmetics & Soaps with especial reference to Synthetics*, 2 vols (London: Chapman and Hall, 1925–26), II (1926), 161.
11. John Ingram, *Flora Symbolica or the Language and Sentiment of Flowers* (London and New York: Frederick Warne & Co., 1870), p. 134.
12. Ed Madden, 'Say it with Flowers: The Poetry of Mark-André Raffalovich', *College Literature*, 24 (1997), 11–27 (p. 15). See also Madden's source — Beverly Seaton, *The Language of Flowers: A History* (Charlottesville: University Press of Virginia, 1995), pp. 167–97 (pp. 196–97).
13. *Piesse's Art of Perfumery*, p. 223.
14. Beaulieu, *The Perfume Lover*, p. 129.
15. Emily W. Emmart Trueblood, '"Omixochitl" — the Tuberose (*Polianthes tuberosa*)', *Economic Botany*, 27 (1973), 157–73.

16. Beaulieu, *The Perfume Lover*, p. 130.
17. Percy Bysshe Shelley, *Shelley's Poetry and Prose*, ed. by Donald H. Reiman and Sharon B. Powers (New York and London: W. W. Norton & Co., 1977), p. 211; *Shelley: Poetical Works*, ed. by Thomas Hutchinson, rev. by G. M. Matthews (London, Oxford, and New York: Oxford University Press, 1970), pp. 562–64 (p. 562).
18. Shelley, *Shelley's Poetry and Prose*, p. 492.
19. John Addington Symonds, *Studies of the Greek Poets* (London: Smith, Elder, 1873), p. 33.
20. *Ibid*.
21. See my article 'Paterian Flair: Walter Pater and Scent', *The Pater Newsletter*, 61/62 (Spring/Fall 2012), 21–42. Freely accessible online at http://paternewsletter.org/issues/
22. Walter Pater, 'An English Poet: Imaginary Portraits 2', *Fortnightly Review* (1931), reprinted as 'An English Poet', in Walter Pater, *Imaginary Portraits*, ed. by Lene Østermark-Johansen, MHRA Jewelled Tortoise Series, Volume 1 (London: Modern Humanities Research Association, 2014), pp. 101–13 (pp. 107, 110).
23. Oscar Wilde, 'A Bevy of Poets', *The Complete Works of Oscar Wilde*, ed. by Ian Small and others, 7 vols to date (Oxford: Oxford University Press, 2000-), VI: *Journalism Part 1*, ed. by John Stokes and Mark Turner (2013), pp. 44–47 (p. 46).
24. The word 'strange' occurs 22 times in Pater's essay, 'curious' and 'curiosity' 16 times, and 'subtle' and its variants 7 times.
25. Their relationship dates from when Pater interviewed the young Raffalovich for entry to Brasenose, Oxford, although poor health prevented him from attending university. See Brocard Sewell, *Footnote to the Nineties: A Memoir of John Gray and André Raffalovich* (London: Cecil and Amelia Woolf, 1968), p. 25.
26. Algernon Charles Swinburne, 'Charles Baudelaire', in *Swinburne as Critic*, ed. by Clyde K. Hyder (London: Routledge & Kegan Paul, 1972), p. 29.
27. 'Relics' was originally published as 'North and South' in the *Fortnightly Review* for May 1873. See *The Collected Poetical Works of Algernon Charles Swinburne*, 6 vols (London: Chatto & Windus, 1904), III, 26–28, (p. 28). Raffalovich sent Swinburne a presentation copy of *Tuberose and Meadowsweet* that was sold at Christie's in New York in 1992 for $2,420.
28. Mark André Raffalovich, *Tuberose and Meadowsweet* (London: David Brogue, 1885), pp. 37–43 (p. 39). Full text given in the Appendix.
29. Oscar Wilde, 'A Bevy of Poets', *The Complete Works of Oscar Wilde*, VI, 46.
30. For Raffalovich's reply and Wilde's subsequent response, see the Commentary in *The Complete Works of Oscar Wilde*, VI, 249–51.
31. Although Raffalovich was already disenchanted with Wilde, the final break came in 1892 when he 'rescued' the young poet John Gray from Wilde's affections and started a life-long, devoted, chaste attachment to him. See Jerusha Hull McCormack, *John Gray: Poet, Dandy, Priest* (Hanover and London: Brandeis University Press, 1991), pp. 46–48, 148–49.
32. Madden, 'Say it with Flowers', p. 11.
33. Madden, 'Say it with Flowers', p. 13.
34. Walter Shewring, 'Two Friends', in *Two Friends: John Gray and André Raffalovich: Essays Biographical and Critical*, ed. by Brocard Sewell (Aylesford: St Albert's Press, 1963), pp. 148–51 (p. 149).
35. Peter F. Anson, 'Random Reminiscences of John Gray and André Raffalovich', in *Two Friends*, pp. 134–41 (p. 137).
36. Margaret Sackville, 'At Whitehouse Terrace', in *Two Friends*, pp. 142–47 (p. 143).
37. Cited in Brocard Sewell, 'John Gray and André Sebastian Raffalovich: A Biographical Outline', in *Two Friends*, pp. 7–49 (pp. 35–36).
38. Mark André Raffalovich, *Tuberose and Meadowsweet*, pp. 37, 39. Subsequent references given in the text.
39. Jennifer Peace Rhind, *Fragrance and Wellbeing: Plant Aromatics and their Influence on the Psyche* (London and Philadelphia: Singing Dragon, 2014), p. 282. Peace Rhind, a chartered biologist and aromatherapist, also remarks 'some say it is reminiscent of almonds, but this smell comes from its leaves' (p. 282). The almond smell may come from heliotropin, another chemical constituent.

40. Algernon Charles Swinburne, 'Laus Veneris', *Poems and Ballads & Atalanta in Calydon,* ed. by Kenneth Haynes (London: Penguin Books, 2000), pp. 9–22 (pp. 10, 12).
41. Swinburne, 'Anactoria', *Poems and Ballads & Atalanta in Calydon,* pp. 47–55 (p. 50).
42. Mark André Raffalovich, 'The Green Carnation', *The Thread and the Path* (London: David Nutt, 1895), p. 67.
43. See Sally Newman, 'The Archival Traces of Desire: Vernon Lee's Failed Sexuality and the Interpretation of Letters in Lesbian History', *The Journal of History of Sexuality,* 14 (2005), 51–75 (p. 71).
44. A. Mary F. Robinson, *Songs, Ballads, and a Garden Play* (London: T. Fisher Unwin, 1888), p. 6.
45. Robinson, 'Tuberoses', *Songs, Ballads, and a Garden Play,* pp. 22–24 (p. 24). Full text given in the Appendix.
46. Robinson did send Lee a presentation copy inscribed 'Vernon, with Molly's love. June 29th 88. Epsom Common', now in The Norman Colbeck Collection, University of British Columbia Library. See *A Bookman's Catalogue: The Norman Colbeck Collection of Nineteenth-Century and Edwardian Poetry and Belles Lettres,* ed. by T. Bose and Paul Tiessen, 2 vols (Vancouver: UBC Press, 1987), I, 235.
47. Roy Genders, *Bulbs: A Complete Handbook of Bulbs, Corms and Tubers* (London: Robert Hale & Co., 1973), p. 472.
48. Théophile Gautier, 'L'Art', 'Tout passe. — L'art robuste | Seul a l'éternité. | Le buste | Survit à la cité.' For a dual-language text, see Théophile Gautier, *Selected Lyrics,* trans. by Norman A. Shapiro (New Haven and London: Yale University Press, 2011), pp. 262–67 (pp. 264–65).
49. *Keats: The Major Works,* ed. by Elizabeth Cook (Oxford: Oxford University Press), pp. 288–89 (p. 289).
50. D. G. Rossetti, 'Jenny', *The Collected Works of Dante Gabriel Rossetti* (London: Ellis, 1911), pp. 36–43 (p. 40).
51. W. B. Yeats, 'The Autumn of the Body' (1898), *Essays & Introductions* (London: Macmillan, 1989), p. 193.
52. Sonnet 5 in *Shakespeare's Sonnets,* ed. by Stephen Booth (New Haven and London, 2000), pp. 7–8.
53. Theodore Wratislaw, 'Tuberose', *Orchids: Poems by Theodore Wratislaw* (London: Leonard Smithers, 1896), p. 30. Full text given in the Appendix.
54. See, for instance, 'Le Revenant', in the dual-language text *Baudelaire: The Complete Verse,* trans. by Francis Scarfe (London: Anvil Press Poetry, 1986), p. 143.
55. Theodore Wratislaw, 'La Fleur du jardin d'ici bas', *Orchids: Poems by Theodore Wratislaw,* p. 8.
56. See the comment of an elderly lady surprised by the advent of modern deodorants: 'when I went to balls, the gentlemen used to *like* what we called a "bouquet de corsage".' Cited in Alison Adburgham, *Shops and Shopping 1800–1914: Where, and in What Manner the Well-dressed Englishwoman Bought her Clothes,* 2nd edn (London: George Allen & Unwin, 1981), p. 262.
57. For an informed commentary on the apocryphal poisoning of Jeanne de Navarre (dramatized by Christopher Marlowe in his play *The Massacre at Paris* (1594)), see Evelyn Welch, 'Scented Buttons and Perfumed Gloves: Smelling Things in Renaissance Italy', in *Ornamentalism,* ed. by Bella Mirabella (Ann Arbor: University of Michigan Press, 2011), pp. 13–39 (p. 27).
58. 'Rappaccini's Daughter' (1844), collected in Nathaniel Hawthorne, *Tales and Sketches* (New York and Cambridge: The Library of America, 1982), pp. 975–1005.
59. Cited in Tom Carter, *The Victorian Gardener* (London: Bell & Hyman, 1984), p. 106. 'Dr Ingenhousz' is the Dutch physiologist, biologist, and chemist Jan Ingenhousz (1730–1799) who discovered photosynthesis and the cellular respiration of plants.
60. Letter of 20 March 1877 in *The Swinburne Letters,* ed. by Cecil Y. Lang, 6 vols (New Haven and London: Yale and Oxford University Presses, 1959–62), III, 302. A more cynical interpretation of this incident occurring in the late summer of 1876 is that Swinburne suffered a severe bilious reaction as a result of one of the alcoholic episodes he was prone to at this time. Swinburne mentions his illness to a number of different correspondents. See his letters of 17, 25, 28 October 1876, in *Letters* III, 207, 210, 211.
61. *Piesse's Art of Perfumery,* p. 223.
62. Tessa Williams, *Cult Perfumes: The World's Most Exclusive Perfumes* (London and New York: Merrell, 2013), p. 173; Susan Irvine, *The Perfume Guide* (London: Haldane Mason, 2000), p. 59.

63. Susan Irvine, *The Perfume Guide*, p. 124.
64. Jean-Claude Ellena, *The Diary of a Nose: A Year in the Life of a Parfumeur*, trans. by Adriana Hunter (London: Particular Books, 2012), p. iii (epigraph).

CHAPTER 3

Decadent Sensuality in Rachilde and Wilde

Petra Dierkes-Thrun

There are many connections between Oscar Wilde's work, Paris, and French literature, but one that is surprisingly little known is Wilde's personal and professional relationship with the female French Decadent writer, Rachilde (née Marguerite Eymery, 1860–1953). This essay offers a comparative reading of the hidden intellectual cross-currents and potential influences between Oscar Wilde's and Rachilde's major Decadent and Symbolist works. While Wilde and Rachilde shared a broader Decadent approach to sensuality and pleasure as a conglomerate of aesthetic and erotic transgression with other writers, Rachilde was a major influence for Wilde's interest in sadomasochistic, violent, and gender-bending elements of Decadent sensuality. Both writers also connected Decadent sensuality with triumphant individualism and aesthetic connoisseurship through sensual perversity, and they celebrated violence as an unusually pleasurable, fulfilling experience that approached the level of art.

Although not a household name today except to scholars and enthusiasts of French *fin-de-siècle* literature, Rachilde was a central player on the Parisian writing and publishing scene in the 1890s. She was the author of several scandalous Decadent novels with a reputation for outrageous gender play and sadomasochistic imagery, especially *Monsieur Vénus* (1884), *La Marquise de Sade* (1887), *La Jongleuse* (1900), and some interesting Symbolist plays from the 1890s, including *La Voix du sang* (1890), *Madame la Mort* (1891), and *L'Araignée de cristal* (1894). Rachilde accumulated a list of over sixty literary works in her name by the end of her life. In the 1890s she also hosted vibrant weekly literary salons, held on Tuesdays (just like Mallarmé's *mardis*) that brought together the most cutting-edge writers and journalists and functioned as social networking places for young writers. Wilde attended at least one, if not more, of Rachilde's salons and befriended many of her professional connections in Paris, including Marcel Schwob, Paul Fort, and Henry Davray, who would become his main French translator and trusted friend. Rachilde also co-published, with her husband Alfred Vallette, the influential journal *Mercure de France*, which became the premier publishing outlet for French Decadent, Symbolist, and anarchist writers. Wilde had a special intellectual relationship with French literature and the city of Paris, which he visited often and regularly (especially in the years around 1890–91, in which some of his most important works were written), and many members of the *Mercure*'s inner circle became touchstones for him.[1] Under Rachilde's stewardship as both literary editor and one of its contributing writers from 1890 to 1924, the *Mercure* actively featured and translated Wilde's work in France, and it continued to do so even after the scandal of Wilde's 1895 trials for 'acts of gross indecency', his prison sentence and untimely death in 1900. Although Wilde scholars have not yet explored these biographical and publishing connections fully through archival work, the textual evidence speaks for itself: Wilde most likely learned some lessons about sadomasochistic sensuality from Rachilde and employed them in *The Picture of Dorian Gray* and *Salomé*; conversely, Rachilde admired *Salomé* and honoured Wilde by echoing some of its central themes in her own works.

A Little-Known Decadent Urtext: Rachilde's *Monsieur Vénus*

Rachilde's major claim to fame was her novel *Monsieur Vénus*, first published in Belgium in 1884. Wilde read *Monsieur Vénus* during his 1884 honeymoon with Constance in Paris. And no wonder he did: the sexually explicit and transgressive novel was the talk of the town; in fact, it had just earned Rachilde an obscenity trial and prison sentence (*in absentia*) in Belgium, its first place of publication.[2] In Rachilde's time, *Monsieur Vénus* was at least as well known as Joris-Karl Huysmans's *À rebours* (published in the same year), which now, perhaps unjustly, holds the status of the only 'breviary of the Decadence', as Arthur Symons called it. *Monsieur Vénus* is a Decadent shocker, teeming with sadomasochistic fantasies and role-play that question heteronormative and sexist assumptions about femininity and art, putting forward an openly sexualized, violent version of Decadent desire for sensual pleasure. In a reverse version of the Pygmalion myth, Rachilde tells the story of Raoule de Vénérande, a female aristocrat who fashions her own aesthetic and erotic ideal by turning an effeminate lower-class male lover, Jacques Silvert, into her passive and submissive 'mistress', whom she sexually abuses and later kills, using his most fetishized body parts to graft onto a wax model to immortalize him as a Decadent sex puppet.

The novel's salacious depiction of their relationship abounds with sadomasochistic imagery. Raoule abuses Jacques both emotionally — forbidding him to go out or smoke, calling him 'stupid' — and physically, by slapping him or throwing him down on the floor, digging 'her nails into his flesh' (p. 83), enjoying his humiliation and emasculation:

> Raoule came and went, commanded and acted like a man well past his first affair, although this was his first love. She forced Jacques to bask in his passive happiness like a pearl in its shell. The more he forgot his sex, the more she created around him multiple opportunities to feminize himself and, so as not to frighten too much the male inside him that she wanted to smother, she treated each degrading idea first as a joke, content to make him accept it seriously only later. (p. 94)

Raoule's increasing dominance and Jacques's instinctive submissiveness are intensely pleasurable for both. As they kiss, for instance, Raoule 'bit him full on the nape of his neck. Jacques twisted with a cry of amorous pain. "Oh! That feels good!" he sighed, stiffening in the arms of his wild dominatrix. "I don't want anything else! Raoule, you can love me as you please, provided you always caress me like that!"' (p. 85) Raoule's dominance mingles with her female masculinity and what we would now call transgender performance. When Jacques tries to assert himself in bed, she shows 'complete [physical] indifference' (p. 88), but whenever Raoule manages to 'top' him, she 'covered him with her flanks swollen by savage ardor' (p. 90). In tandem with Raoule's masculine prowess in bed, the novel is tinged with homoerotic and gender-bending desires throughout: 'I'm a man in love with a man, not with a woman!' Raoule exclaims to the Baron de Raittolbe, Raoule's best friend and suitor, who is continually puzzled by Raoule's unusual gender behaviour and wonders if she might be an invert.

The sadomasochistic sex and gender play between Raoule and Jacques extends into a queer love triangle between Raoule, Jacques, and Raittolbe. Raittolbe is attracted to Raoule's masculinity as well as to the effeminate Jacques, whom he wants to seduce, and both Raoule and Raittolbe indulge in voyeurism as they secretly gaze at the naked, often sleeping and drugged, Jacques. When Jacques finally actively resists his more and more brazen physical advances, Raittolbe beats him up, 'seized by a blind rage whose violence he could probably not understand' (p. 120), revealing Raittolbe's own homosexual panic. Jacques challenges Raittolbe to a duel in which he is killed immediately, a helpless doll pierced by Raittolbe's phallic sword.

In the novel's wonderful shocker of a finale, Raoule (who has always preferred Jacques passive, languid, drugged or sleeping) takes possession of Jacques's corpse after the duel and dissects it surgically, cutting it apart in order to then reassemble it to her own taste. She selectively grafts those parts she has always fetishized — Jacques's milk-white skin, his perfect teeth and red hair — onto a medically correct wax model, probably a so-called 'anatomical Venus'. Raoule places her artificially transsexual, Frankensteinian creation into her temple of a private bedroom, where it is ever ready to please her:

> At night, a woman dressed in mourning, sometimes a young man in evening clothes, opens th[e] door. They come to kneel beside the bed, and, after contemplating at length the marvelous lines of the wax statue, they embrace it, kiss it on the lips. A spring hidden inside the flanks connects with the mouth and animates it at the same time that it spreads apart the thighs. This wax figure, an anatomical masterpiece, was made by a German.[3] (pp. 209–10)

Resurrecting the dead, fragmented Jacques as a mechanically modified sex puppet is both shocking and logical, given the strong sadomasochistic and gender-bending sensual trajectory. Katherine Gantz comments, 'In a fittingly depraved Rachildean ending, the novel allows the reader a voyeuristic glimpse of the lovers' final parody of heterosexuality, twisted to the end, in which we may gaze upon the spectacle of two sexual dissidents morbidly simulating the genders of convention.'[4]

Whereas *À rebours* focuses on an effeminate male Decadent anti-hero, Des Esseintes, with hereditary physical degeneracy and an overly sensitive, nervous and borderline hysterical constitution, Rachilde's *Monsieur Vénus* presents a masculinized, dominant heroine and thus openly celebrates a more eroticized, masculinized version of Decadent sensuality. Sadomasochistic imagery, physical violence, aestheticized crime and Decadent religious imagery dominate the novel. As Melanie Hawthorne and Liz Constable have noted, Raoule's last name (de Vénérande) invokes both religious veneration and venereal disease (a dominant medical-sexological obsession at the time), but it also carries the French noun *vénerie*, hunting, which is further expressed in the novel's ekphrastic depiction of a portrait of Raoule with hunting dogs and a riding crop. The riding crop, also a prominent prop in Sadean pornography, symbolizes the novel's prominent sadomasochistic relationship of pleasure between Raoule and Jacques. Raoule is initially attracted to Jacques because of his feminine and childish looks and demeanour (in the first scene of the novel, we see him arranging flowers and positioned like a water nymph, with a garland of roses about his neck that 'slipped between his legs' (p. 8)), but she is also attracted to his lower-class status which she, as an aristocrat, can take advantage of:

> What did the low birth of this man matter for what she wanted to do with him? The envelope, the epidermis, the palpable being, the male sufficed for her dream. [...] The woman who vibrated within her saw nothing in Silvert but *a beautiful instrument of pleasure* that she coveted and, in a latent state, that she already held steadfast in her imagination. (p. 19, my emphasis)

Raoule's dehumanizing, impersonal approach to Jacques as her personal property, her 'beautiful instrument of pleasure', effectively turns Jacques into her prized collector's item. She installs him in a decadent boudoir with an exotic collection of sumptuous, curious, orientalist decadent objects — beautiful furniture, art, and decorative objects (including homoerotically evocative ones such as her tapestry panels depicting Henri III and Antinous, to whom she repeatedly compares Jacques) as well as scandalous erotic books ('the books no one would admit to having' (p. 68)). For both Rachilde and Wilde, bedrooms, boudoirs, and libraries are aesthetic places filed with beautiful, sensual objects and tantalizing books, physical pleasure, sensuous exploration, and transgression.[5] In *Monsieur Vénus*, Jacques takes his place as an *objet* to be manipulated, as Raoule first refashions him with clothes and later operates on his dead body. The collection of objects is a familiar Decadent literary trope, of course, as embodied most famously in Des Esseintes's eclectic and bizarre collection in *À rebours*.

Rachilde's iconic elevation of Jacques as an artistic object for Raoule's sensual consumption is also linked to religious imagery. During their wedding night, Raoule worships the naked, drugged Jacques as her idol, stretched out on the bed, with religious veneration: 'With avid eyes and passionate mouth, Raoule approached the altar of her god and in her ecstasy sighed: "You alone exist, Beauty. I believe in you alone"' (p. 178). Ironically contrasting Raoule's lush decadent taste with the austere, sensually deprived Catholicism of her pious, nun-like aunt Ermengarde, Rachilde describes Raoule's bedroom (and Jacques's final resting place) as a lushly decorated, temple-like room which houses erotic statues, incense burners, and a striking 'nuptial bed' in the middle (a trope she would later take up in *La Jongleuse*). Raoule's behaviour celebrates a transgressive, gender-flexible, *artistic* identity that provides a measure of freedom from the typical restrictions of *fin-de-siècle* femininity.[6] Rachilde's *La Marquise de Sade* (1887) also contains striking depictions of violent, erotic, aggressively assertive femininity, and gender. It further solidified Rachilde's status as the primary female French literary Decadent, whom Maurice Barrès lovingly christened 'Mademoiselle Baudelaire' and whose *cartes de visite* provocatively read '*Rachilde — homme de lettres*'. Rachilde's sadomasochistic, shocking, gender-bending work, as well as the circle of like-minded writers she soon assembled around her at the *Mercure de France* offices (with whom Wilde became intimately acquainted as well), was an important literary influence on Wilde in Paris that shaped his approach to decadent sensuality in *The Picture of Dorian Gray* and *Salomé* (and possibly other works).

Under the Influence: Wilde's *The Picture of Dorian Gray*

Against the background of Wilde's reported enthusiasm for *Monsieur Vénus* and his extensive connections with Rachilde's circle, it is intriguing to investigate some major affinities between Wilde's work and Rachilde's. Wilde's biographer Richard Ellmann notes that Mark André Raffalovich reported (in a 1927 *Blackfriars* article) that Wilde had been so excited about *Monsieur Vénus* that he once held forth about the topic with friends for several hours. Raffalovich recalls that Wilde was especially enthusiastic because in it 'a lesbian dresses her lover as a man', suggesting that Wilde somehow thought the novel was about lesbianism.[7] Melanie Hawthorne comments:

> While it may seem difficult to defend this particular reading (of all the possible permutations, the lesbian seems the least likely, and, in fact, in a conversation with Raittolbe, Raoule specifically denies that her interests are Sapphic), the novel is sufficiently imprecise and vague as to allow many interpretations [...][8]

Whatever the case may have been in the conversation noted by Raffalovich, Wilde was still so enthralled with the novel in the late 1880s (years after first reading it) that he alluded to it in the first manuscript and the typescript version of *The Picture of Dorian Gray* (the text for *Lippincott's Monthly Magazine*) housed respectively at the Morgan Library and the Clark Memorial Library at UCLA. The original manuscript shows that Wilde gave the mysterious 'little yellow book' that so fatally influences Dorian (now most commonly identified as Huysmans's *À rebours*, despite obvious discrepancies in Wilde's chapter descriptions) the fictitious title 'Le Secret de Raoul' by the (fictional) author 'Catulle Sarazzin'. This was a direct allusion to Raoule de Vénérande and perhaps to Rachilde's intimate friend and almost-lover, fellow Decadent Catulle Mendès, Ellmann asserts.[9] But Wilde evidently changed his mind and erased this title for the published version. This is a tactic he seems to have followed with another possible allusion: Dorian's French valet — who often addresses Dorian as 'monsieur' — was originally called Jacques. In the typescript and all subsequent published versions, he is suddenly 'Victor'.[10] As Joseph Bristow and others observe, it is unclear whether Wilde himself or his editor, J. M. Stoddart, at *Lippincott's Monthly Magazine* (which published the serialized original shorter version of the novel), was responsible for the changes.[11] It seems plausible that either Wilde or Stoddart decided to avoid any possible identification with Rachilde's literary scandals. The homoerotic overtones of the novel were generally being toned down through a process of editorial censorship, apparently in response to negative press reviews that openly hinted at the novel's homoeroticism as well as its connections to pathologically unclean, morally suspect French Décadence.[12] In 1890, Wilde was still trying to make a living as a serious literary writer. It may have just seemed too risky to associate *The Picture of Dorian Gray* with Rachilde's scandalous obscenity trial and conviction. A third possibility is that Stoddart, the American editor of the first version, feared that the allusions to *Monsieur Vénus* would create a scandal in more puritanical America.

Dorian's poisonous yellow book, while closest in fictional description to *À rebours* and its hero Des Esseintes, is a blend of at least two influences — Huysmans's novel and Pater's *Studies in the History of the Renaissance* (and perhaps Pater's *Marius the Epicurean*). And yet, Wilde's ostensible summaries of specific chapters of the mysterious yellow book (supposedly an illicit French work, since those were widely known to be bound in yellow covers) seem deliberately vague — actually, Ellmann is quick to point out, 'Huysmans's book has none of these'.[13] Why such evocative deviations from Huysmans's chapters? What if Wilde had intended the following passage from the original, uncensored version not *merely* as an allusion to Des Esseintes's Decadent material-collecting, but *also* to another Parisian, Raoule de Vénérande, with her proclivity for sadomasochism and idiosyncratic sexual pleasure? What if the following sentences, ostensibly summarizing Des Esseintes, were actually an interpretation of *Raoule's* transgendered, masculine-identified sexual adventures, not Des Esseintes's? Let us reread that famous passage with fresh eyes:

> [Dorian's] eye fell on the yellow book that Lord Henry had sent him. What was it, he wondered. He [...] took the volume up. *'Le Secret de Raoul par Catulle Sarrazin'. What a curious title!* He flung himself into an arm-chair, and began to turn over the leaves. After a few minutes, he became absorbed. It was the strangest book he had ever read. It seemed to him that in exquisite raiment, and to the delicate sounds of flutes, the sins of the world were passing in dumb show before him. Things that he had dimly dreamed of were suddenly made real to him. Things of which he had never dreamed were gradually revealed. It was a novel without a plot, and with only one character, being, indeed, simply a psychological study of a certain young Parisian, who spent his life trying to realize in the nineteenth century all the passions and modes of thought that belonged to every century except his own, and to sum up, as it were, in himself the various moods through which the world-spirit had ever passed, loving, for their mere artificiality, those renunciations that men have unwisely called virtue, as much as those natural rebellions that wise men still call sin. The style in which it was written was that curious jewelled style, vivid and obscure at once, *that characterizes some of the French school of Decadents*.[14]

It is easy to see that the narrator's emphasis on the hero's attempt to 'sum up' and 'realize [...] passions and modes of thought' that belonged to other times and places, and the emphasis placed on a purely aesthetic, morally neutral, relativist approach to what has been called 'virtue' and 'sin', speaks just as vividly to Rachilde's presentation of Raoule's daring sexual and violent experimentation and Decadent aesthetic quest in *Monsieur Vénus* as it does to Des Esseintes's preference for the provocative imagery of artists such as Odilon Redon or Gustave Moreau. Even the fact that the little yellow book poisons Dorian has its precedent in *Monsieur Vénus* (and in other Decadent fiction focusing on the transformative nature of a 'fatal book', as Linda Dowling and Matthew Potolsky point out). Potolsky writes about Raoule's 'awakening' by such a book:

> Left alone by her guardian, the adolescent Raoule is transformed by a chance discovery of an erotic book in the garrets of her ancestral mansion [...]. The theme of the fatal book reflects the predominant form of sociality among decadent writers, demonstrating the extent to which decadent 'identity' is an effect of reception.[15]

Wilde's explicit allusions to Rachilde in the original, uncensored passage thus open up a space for reconsidering *Monsieur Vénus*'s broader influence on Wilde's novel. The open sexual perversity and sadistic tendencies of Rachilde's Raoule, read in tandem with the refined decadent tastes of Huysmans's Des Esseintes as literary models for Dorian Gray's character, shed new subtle light on Dorian's dark sexual adventures in the brothels, back alleys, and opium dens of Whitechapel. Dorian's 'wonder at the shallow psychology of those who conceive the Ego in man as a thing simple, permanent, reliable, and of one essence' and his view of man as 'a complex multiform creature that bore within itself strange legacies of thought and passion' in Chapter 11 now also remind us of Raoule's oscillating gender and her rational-irrational mixture of affectionate love and sadistic impulse.[16]

There are other striking parallels between the two novels. Both feature dangerous queer love triangles at the heart of their plots: Basil, Lord Henry, and Dorian in Wilde; and Raoule, Jacques, and Raittolbe in Rachilde. Dorian and Jacques also become the objects of others' fascination with fashioning the perfect body as a new prototype of art. Raoule's adoration of the feminized Jacques finds its expression in her creative moulding of his physical appearance, first only with clothes and later physically, in her Decadent, Frankensteinian, sexualized refashioning of his fetishized dead body. In both novels, the ideal Decadent sensual body appears to be the result of an intentional creative act, which fashions this body according to a superior mental ideal in the mind of the artist: Basil paints Dorian; Raoule cuts up and reassembles Jacques. Both novels also show Wilde's and Rachilde's keen interest in the topics of art and crime and artificiality and criminality, and their tendency to represent criminals as supreme, admirable individuals. In Wilde, these obviously include Dorian Gray and Salomé, but also Thomas Wainewright in 'Pen, Pencil, and Poison' and Lord Arthur in 'Lord Arthur Savile's Crime'. In Rachilde, they definitely include Raoule but also the Marquise de Sade and many other of her strong female heroines. A related interesting detail is that Rachilde was probably also responsible for introducing Wilde to Jean Lorrain, writer of Decadent crime literature extraordinaire and one of Rachilde's protégés. Lorrain became part of Wilde's inner circle in Paris and prompted or intensified Wilde's interest in crime as an aesthetic topic. Jean Lorrain also explicitly recalled discussing Wilde's next important work with him — *Salomé*, a Symbolist play written in French — thus creating even closer Decadent collaborations between Rachilde, Wilde, and others who knew and appreciated them both.[17]

Wilde's *Salomé* and Rachilde's *L'Araignée de cristal* and *La Jongleuse*

Wilde wrote *Salomé* during one of his extended stays in Paris in 1890 and 1891, a season in which he actively networked with the most important French writers and intellectuals of the day and sought their artistic respect. Writing *Salomé* was part of 'Wilde's seduction of Paris', to use one of Ellmann's chapter titles in *Oscar Wilde*. (Many of the individuals with whom Wilde associated at the time of *Salomé*'s conception and writing were intimate friends of both Rachilde's and Wilde's, including Marcel Schwob, who helped Wilde with the French text.)

When scholars discuss the French and Belgian influences on Wilde's *Salomé*, they usually mention Flaubert, Mallarmé, Huysmans, and sometimes Laforgue and Baudelaire, but never Rachilde. Yet, as Diana Holmes and Melanie Hawthorne have pointed out, Rachilde was a very important figure in the Symbolist and Decadent theatre scene in Paris at the same time Wilde was composing *Salomé*. This connection has been completely overlooked in Wilde scholarship, which has focused more on Maeterlinck's theatrical and Mallarmé's poetic influences. Rachilde's role may have been just as crucial for Wilde, however, since she was acting as an adviser, reviewer, and drama writer for the vibrant Symbolist theatrical avant-garde both before and after Wilde wrote *Salomé*. Together with Paul Fort's foundational Théâtre d'Art, Rachilde sought to transform the French theatrical scene and free it from its naturalist focus.[18] Holmes writes:

> Rachilde supported the enterprise practically and artistically. [...] Alfred Vallette supported the venture, and Rachilde actively helped. Fort commissioned and chose plays, mainly from the network of writers associated with the *Mercure* and with Symbolism. She provided favourable reviews of Théâtre d'Art productions and she contributed two plays, one of these, *La Voix du sang* [*The Voice of Blood*], for the opening night in November 1890.[19]

Starting in 1891, Rachilde and her husband were actively serving on the theatre's play selection committee and thus assumed a strong position of artistic influence.[20] When the Théâtre de l'Art was renamed Théâtre de l'Œuvre and Aurélien Lugné-Poë became the director (from 1892 to 1897), Rachilde again lent her support and offered advice. We do not know for certain what moved Lugné-Poë to honour Wilde's *Salomé* with a world première in 1896 (with Wilde still in prison). However, given her central position of literary advisor, Rachilde may have had an active role in convincing him to put on Wilde's play, which remained banned in London in 1892, where the London Examiner of Plays for the Lord Chamberlain, Edward F. Smyth Pigott, had pulled it from the stage during ongoing rehearsals, the French star actress Sarah Bernhardt (who was to play Salomé) notwithstanding.[21]

Just two years later, in 1894, Rachilde also wrote her own play for the Théâtre de l'Œuvre, entitled *L'Araignée de cristal* [*The Crystal Spider*], which included subtle allusions to Wilde's *Salomé*.[22] Rachilde picked up a few things from Wilde, specifically moons, mirrors, and decapitated men. *L'Araignée de cristal* was a single-act play first produced at the Théâtre de l'Œuvre on 13 February 1894 (and subsequently taken on tour to Belgium and Scandinavia), with Lugné-Poë himself taking the lead. In the play, the main protagonist literally loses his head when a broken mirror slashes his throat at the end. The mirror and fatal women are prominent leitmotifs in the play, and the two protagonists, 'the Terror-Stricken Man', Sylvius, and his 'Mother', are reminiscent of Wilde's fearful, superstitious Herod and the wry realist Herodias. The stage setting is a drawing room whose windows open on to a terrace 'full of honeysuckle' and a nightly scene that features the moon and a large 'psyche mirror' (two prominent Symbolist motifs that Wilde combined in *Salomé*):

> The moon illuminates the space where the characters sit. The back remains dark. [...] At the centre of this half-darkness, a tall psyche mirror in empire style [...]. A hazy reflection of light on the mirror, but seen from the lit terrace, this reflection does not seem to come from the moon; it rather appears to emanate from the mirror itself like a light which might be its own.[23]

The Mother comments on the honeysuckle's strong aroma, which pervades the atmosphere like a sweet, intoxicating 'lady's liqueur' (p. 273), introducing the theme of fatal, sensual femininity. The Mother herself has a 'sensual voice' (p. 273), and she exhibits an almost incestuous love for her son (a Herod-like character, incestuously married to Herodias in the synoptic Biblical story underlying Wilde's *Salomé*) who has corresponding incestuous visions of voluptuous women that look like his mother:

> I saw, one evening, while leaving a ball, as I put a fur coat over your shoulders, I saw a lady smiling voluptuously in the mirror, a lady who resembled you, Mother! ... And one morning, [...] I saw through that half-open door, in an immense mirror, the reflection of a beautiful naked girl in a provocative pose! ... Mirrors, Mother, are abysses where the virtue of women and the serenity of men founder together. (p. 276)

The son has a terrible fear of mirrors and women, both of which are connected with death in his mind: 'Women, young girls, creatures with reflections of mirrors at the back of their eyes ... Mother! You want to kill me ...' (p. 274). Specifically, he is afraid of decapitation. He recalls a horrifying vision, as a ten-year-old boy, of a white spider (the crystal spider of the title) advancing towards him from a mirror: 'its head starred with dazzling ridges, its legs along my reflected head, it invaded my forehead, cracked my temples, devoured my pupils, slowly effaced my image, *decapitated me*' (p. 275, my emphasis).

Throughout the play, the Mother negates the man's irrational fears. She does not understand why he imagines phantoms or believes in something he cannot see — as in Wilde's play, the hyper-realist Herodias could not understand Herod's fear of the Angel of Death, see anything unusual in the moon, or believe in Iokanaan's prophecies: 'Ho! Ho! Miracles! I do not believe in miracles. I have seen too many.'[24] In Rachilde, the Terror-Stricken Man, in turn, cannot understand his mother's sober realism:

> So, for you, an intelligent woman, nothing exists inside a mirror except for simple things? In that atmosphere of the unknown, have you not seen an army of phantoms suddenly rising? On the threshold of these doors to dream, have you not unravelled the magic of the infinite lying in wait for you? But it is so very frightening, a mirror is [...]! (p. 275)

For him, 'there is a mirror to catch men, a mirror that lurks at the dangerous turn of their dark existence, a mirror that will watch them die with their faces crushed against the icy crystal of their own enigma ...' (p. 276). In *Salomé*, Wilde's glacial princess of the moon, refracted in mirrors of men's gazes, is fatal to Iokanaan, whose throat she orders to be cut, and indirectly to Herod, whose head she has invaded, similar to Rachilde's idea of the dangerous crystal spider that eats the son's brain. In *L'Araignée de cristal*, the Terror-Stricken Man eventually becomes the victim of his own worst fears as he mistakenly walks into the mirror in the dark and meets his gruesome end as the glass breaks and slashes his throat. The chilling stage direction reads:

> *He launches himself with rage in the direction of the psyche mirror and of the drawing-room door behind it. For a moment, he runs into the deep night ... All at once the terrible jolt of an enormous piece of furniture, the resonant sound of shattering crystal, and the dismal howl of a man whose throat is cut ...* (p. 176)

While we cannot say with certainty that Rachilde's combination of mirror, moon, and throat-slashing decapitation stems from her reading of Wilde's play, the similarities are striking.[25]

The evocative echoes of *Salomé* in Rachilde's work become even stronger when we consider her novel *La Jongleuse*, first published in the *Mercure* in 1900, which Hawthorne calls 'at once one of Rachilde's most carefully constructed novels, a simultaneous expression and parody of Decadence, and a meditation on female power, desire, and sexuality.'[26] Scholars have rightly noted the novel's misogynist and sometimes racist orientalism (its female protagonist Eliante is a French Creole widow in her mid-thirties with a dead, disfigured seafarer husband who fetishized exotic erotica and collected orientalist knick-knacks on his journeys), which intermingles with its more progressive, gender-bending elements. The novel's strategic indirect allusions to Wilde's presentation of Salomé are part of this complex mixture. Salomé desires the aestheticized, eroticized body of a chaste and essentially unavailable love object (Iokanaan), and her own sensual, childish and unavailable body is fetishized by others — and yet she fully, triumphantly inhabits and exhibits it herself.

The novel's dramatic visual opening immediately invokes the opening scene of Wilde's *Salomé*. Eliante is described walking like a queen and exits a lit hall — similar to Salomé, who leaves Herod's banquet hall and steps onto a moonlit terrace. There is an air of 'mystery' around her, and her body is immediately associated with darkness and death. The opening draws attention to her black dress (whose tail spreads around her in circles, as if to evoke Beardsley's drawings for *Salomé*) and her neck (foreshadowing her suicide). The colours red, black, and white are associated with Eliante just as they are a hallmark of *Salomé*'s symbolic colour scheme. The end of the passage even quotes Wilde's central twin leitmotifs, the mirror and the gaze:

> [H]e stopped in front of a mirror [...] The mirror reflected only the marble statue of a nymph holding a candelabrum over there, and here, the dark silhouette of the motionless woman, equally a statue, two twins turning their back on each other, the one very naked, spreading cold in the transparent electric globes, the other magnificently dressed, even less real, and these mute phantoms aroused the idea of an imminent catastrophe. (p. 2)

This first description of Eliante mixes the decadent overtones of *Salomé* with the cold light of modern electricity to create a simultaneously sensual yet cold, virginal, and untouchable impression of the heroine. When Eliante meets the much younger medical student Léon and invites him to come home with her, we learn of the extent of her unusual sensual taste. Eliante is not asexual, but she has a strong aversion to human touch and instead an idiosyncratic erotic preference for an inanimate object, a beautiful tall Greek vase. Just as Raoule keeps the waxen Jacques in her chapel-like bedroom of pleasure, Eliante has installed the torso-like vase in a temple-like boudoir, into which she invites Léon as a fellow worshipper and voyeur:

> [T]here was one admirable objet d'art placed in the middle of the room on a pedestal of old rose velvet, like an altar; an alabaster vase the height of a man, so slim, so slender, so deliciously troubling with its ephebe's hips, with such a human appearance, even though it retained the traditional shape of amphora, that the viewer remained somewhat speechless. The foot, very narrow, like a spear of hyacinth, surged up from a flat and oval base, narrowed as it rose, swelled, at mid-height, to the size of two beautiful young thighs hermetically joined and tapered off towards the neck where, in the hollow of the throat, an alabaster collar shone like a fold of plump flesh, and, higher up, it opened out, spreading into a corolla of white, pure, pale convolvulus, almost aromatic since the white, smooth material with its milky transparence had such lifelike sincerity. This neck spreading into a corolla made one think of an absent head cut off and carried on shoulders other than those of the amphora. 'What a marvel!' cried Léon, completely seduced by this apparition of the adorable chastity of line. (p. 18)

Like Iokanaan for the adoring Salomé, Eliante's urn embodies her ideal of absolute Beauty and a perverse object of desire — something that, like the Biblical prophet's body, should be out of bounds yet is maddeningly irresistible to the heroine. Rachilde's anthropomorphic, oddly sexy description of the vase as a human 'torso' with slender hips and 'two beautiful young thighs', which makes the onlooker think of 'an absent head cut off', as well as the emphasis on the vase's chastity and androgyny, all point in the direction of Wilde's *Salomé* as an important intertext for *La Jongleuse*. In this passage, the sensual and seductive allure of the vase mixes with sexual desire with hints at violence (a head cut off) and voyeurism — the narrative gaze, in this description, is moving up from the foot of the vase over its whole body to linger on the convolvulus-like neck.[27] The vase's androgyny (supported by the alternating male and female grammatical genders of *un vase* and *une urne*, as Melanie Hawthorne points out) is part of its appeal.[28] Eliante says, 'my Tunisian urn is by turns a "he" or "she", for that's the way it likes it. She isn't forced to give an opinion, to prolong her satisfaction at feeling me caress her or to split with joy when I contemplate her. She is chaste, and I leave her chaste' (p. 58).

Eliante is convinced that her intimate relationship with the vase — in its typical Decadent pairing of enthusiastic aesthetic appetite, non-reproductive sex, and autoeroticism — is far superior to human-to-human sensuality. She tries to kindle the same passion in Léon, prodding him to touch the urn's 'virgin's flanks' and make him appreciate the vase's chaste, vaguely dangerous sexiness with his own fingers:

> 'You were telling me about pleasure? This is another thing entirely! This is the power of love in an unknown material, the madness of silent delight. [...] Come and touch. I give you permission. [...] (She seized the young man's hand and moved it carefully over the innocent whiteness of the vase, its virgin's flanks.) [...] It will neither grow nor diminish, it is beauty immutable. Ah, I really want you to know, for at least five minutes, how to be in ecstasy, the right way and over something immortal. [...] This charming body in which life has been replaced by perfume, by wine ... or by blood!' (pp. 20–21)

Eliante's speech moves seamlessly back and forth between invocations of abstract beauty, immortality, and spirituality, to 'ecstasy, the right way'. What Eliante does next though is unique and shocking, even by the standards of Decadent literature: she takes this oscillating physical and metaphysical desire all the way to orgasm. She announces to Léon that she has brought him into the boudoir

> to show you that I don't need a human caress to reach orgasm. [...] I'm disgusted by union, which destroys my strength, I find no delightful plenitude in it. For my flesh to be roused and to conceive the infinity of pleasure, I don't need to look for a sex organ in the object of my love! I am humiliated because an intelligent man immediately thinks of ... sleeping with me ... (p. 22)

What follows is 'probably the most explicit description of female orgasm to be found in the decadent text':[29]

> Eliante, at present standing over the neck of the white amphora, became taut as a bow from head to foot. She was not offering herself to the man; she was giving herself to the alabaster vase, the one insentient person on the scene. Without a single indecent gesture, arms chastely crossed on the slender form, neither girl nor boy, she clinched her fingers little, remaining silent, then, the man saw her closed eyelids flutter, her lips half open, and it seemed that starlight fell from the whites of her eyes, from the enamel of the teeth; a slight shudder traversed her body — or rather a squall lifted the mysterious wave of her dress — and she gave a small groan of imperceptible joy, the very breath of orgasm.[30] [...] He was dazzled, delighted, indignant. 'It's scandalous! Right there ... In front of me ... Without me? No, it's horrible!' (p. 23)

Léon's spontaneous revulsion and hurt at his sensual exclusion and delegation to eye witness faintly echoes Herod's disgusted violent outburst as he sees Salomé caressing and kissing his rival's severed head (inducing him to order the soldiers to 'Kill that woman!')[31] Rachilde's explicit textual display of Eliante's female orgasm in the cited passage is daring and provocative: Eliante's Decadent sensuality, performed for her own pleasure, is autonomous and self-fulfilling, similar to Salomé's auto-erotic play with Iokanaan's head. Eliante's striking suicide — by a knife she deliberately lets fall during a juggling act, slashing her own throat — similarly invokes the decapitation trope, which Rachilde had also already employed in *L'Araignée de cristal*. These three Decadent sensual heroines — Raoule, Salomé, Eliante — are loners in their moment of artistic and erotic apotheosis, be it in death or in orgasm (called *la petite mort* in French).

Any future investigation of these briefly sketched intertextual affinities between Rachilde's and Wilde's shared taste for sadomasochistic, solipsistic, autoerotic Decadent sensuality can not only enlarge and solidify our knowledge of Rachilde's and Wilde's mutual influences on each other's work, but also further illuminate the conceptual range of Decadent sensuality itself. Raoule, Salomé, Eliante are all impressive, ruthless, perverse, and triumphant heroines, regarding not only their unusual tastes in 'men' but their shared aesthetic commitment to a Decadent ideal of Beauty at all costs, including their own life. Salomé is killed by Herod's soldiers after she has fully satisfied herself by kissing Iokanaan's mouth, sighing,

> Ah! I have kissed thy mouth, Iokanaan, I have kissed thy mouth. There was a bitter taste on thy lips. Was it the taste of blood? ... Nay; but perchance it was the taste of love. ... They say that love hath a bitter taste. ... But what matter? what matter? I have kissed thy mouth, Iokanaan, I have kissed thy mouth.[32]

Eliante performs her final dance half-naked and uncaring yet full of joy, 'the living and suffering poem of a body tormented by strange passions [...] no longer concerned with earth. She was dancing for herself' (p. 196). Raoule is the only heroine who is still alive by the end of the novel. Ultimately, in these three Decadent heroines — Raoule, Eliante, and Salomé — we see a transitional Decadent-Modernist type of sexually transgressive, gender-non-conformist, self-reliant, and assertive femininity that finds its highest satisfaction not in full physical union with a lover but in the solo *performance* of passion as self-affirming aesthetic and autoerotic act, passion for passion's sake, for the woman's own pleasure only.[33]

Notes to Chapter 3

1. Wilde was deeply immersed in the Parisian literary scene and at the time of his forced bankruptcy sale, 'the volumes of French fiction comprised around a quarter of Wilde's library — easily the best-represented genre in his collection', Thomas Wright estimates in *Built of Books: How Reading Defined the Life of Oscar Wilde* (New York: Henry Holt, 2009), p. 125.
2. When Wilde read the novel in 1884, it must have been in its first uncensored Belgian edition. The first genuinely French edition was not published until 1889, and even then the French excised certain passages deemed too offensive or shocking. Melanie Hawthorne discusses *Monsieur Vénus*'s publication and censorship history in detail in *Rachilde and French Women's Authorship: From Decadence to Modernism* (Lincoln and London: University of Nebraska Press, 2001), pp. 88–100. All references to Rachilde's novel in this chapter are to Hawthorne's 2004 translation: Rachilde, *Monsieur Vénus: A Materialist Novel*, trans. by Melanie Hawthorne (New York: Modern Language Association, 2004). References to this translation are given parenthetically.
3. The comment on the wax figure's manufacturing by a German may be an allusion to a common view that the best-made anatomical Venuses (popular since the eighteenth century) came from Germany and Switzerland. Anatomical Venuses were often strangely eroticized by being arranged in relaxed poses amidst drapery, with languid or closed eyes and beautifully made up with long human hair, jewellery, and red lips, despite the fact that they were meant for medical study and had an open inner front that made organs, including female sex organs, visible. The Josephinum Museum of the Medical University of Vienna, Austria, and the Museo di Storia Naturale in Florence, Italy, hold many such examples.
4. Katherine Gantz, 'French Theory Makes Room for Rachilde', *South Central Review*, 22 (2005), 113–32.
5. In addition to Raoule's salacious erotic library, one might think of Thomas Wainewright's dangerous library in Wilde's 'Pen, Pencil, and Poison', or Lord Henry's library as a scene of Dorian's seduction in *The Picture of Dorian Gray*.
6. See also Rachel Mesch, *The Hysteric's Revenge: French Women Writers at the Fin de Siècle* (Nashville: Vanderbilt University Press, 2006), pp. 128–29. Many scholars have noted the paradoxical, still puzzling relationship between Rachilde's declared anti-feminism in *Pourquoi je ne suis pas*

féministe (1928) and other works, and her depiction of extremely strong, dominant and often gender-bending heroines, which defy many conventions of femininity and are reminiscent of the New Woman type (in addition to being highly sexualized figures). It is certainly important to acknowledge Rachilde's own wish to distance herself from the suffrage and early feminism movements, as well as from what she perceived as the weak character of her sex. But I agree with Rachel Mesch that 'this resistance to the feminist label should not prevent us from recognizing the ways in which Rachilde's writing may have interrogated relationships among sexuality, language and power that much later feminist theorists would explore explicitly' (Mesch, *The Hysteric's Revenge*, p. 124).

7. Richard Ellmann, *Oscar Wilde* (New York: Knopf, 1987), p. 282; Mark André Raffalovich, 'Oscar Wilde', *Blackfriars*, 92 (1927), 694–702, reprinted in Brocard Sewell, *Footnote to the Nineties: A Memoir of John Gray and André Raffalovich* (London: Cecil and Amelia Wolf, 1968), pp. 108–12 (p. 110).
8. Hawthorne, *Rachilde*, p. 99.
9. Ellmann, *Oscar Wilde*, p. 316.
10. I am very grateful to Emily Eells for drawing my attention to this fact.
11. See Joseph Bristow's very useful summary in his annotated edition of *The Picture of Dorian Gray*, in *The Complete Works of Oscar Wilde*, ed. by Ian Small and others, 7 vols to date (Oxford: Oxford University Press, 2000-), III, *The Picture of Dorian Gray: The 1890 and 1891 Texts*, ed. by Joseph Bristow (2005), p. 392, n.102.16.
12. See the collection of contemporary reviews of *The Picture of Dorian Gray* in *Oscar Wilde: The Critical Heritage*, ed. by Karl Beckson (London and New York: Routledge, 1997).
13. Ellmann, *Oscar Wilde*, p. 316.
14. Typescript of Chapter 8 (1890 version for *Lippincott's Monthly Magazine*), in *The Picture of Dorian Gray*, ed. by Bristow, emphasis mine. The passage continues as follows:

> There were in it metaphors as monstrous as orchids, and as evil in colour. The life of the senses was described in the terms of mystical philosophy. One hardly knew at times whether one was reading the spiritual ecstasies of some mediaeval saint, or the morbid confessions of a modern sinner. It was a poisonous book. The heavy odour of incense seemed to cling about its pages, and to trouble the brain. The mere cadence of the sentences, the subtle monotony of their music, so full as it was of complex refrains and movement elaborately repeated, produced in the mind of the lad, as he passed from chapter to chapter, a form of revery, a malady of dreaming, that made him unconscious of the falling day and creeping shadows. (pp. 142–43)

15. Matthew Potolsky, *The Decadent Republic of Letters: Taste, Politics, and Cosmopolitan Community from Baudelaire to Beardsley* (Philadelphia: University of Pennsylvania Press, 2013), p. 94.
16. Oscar Wilde, *The Picture of Dorian Gray*, in *The Complete Works of Oscar Wilde*, III, ed. by Bristow, p. 288.
17. Jean Lorrain, in 'Salomé et ses poètes', *Le Journal* (11 February 1896), 1–2, recalls a visit in 1891 by Oscar Wilde. Everyone wanted to meet the famous author of *The Picture of Dorian Gray*, which had just been published. Lorrain hosted a lunch for him in his apartment, attended by Marcel Schwob, Anatole France, and Henri Bauer. Wilde admired a severed head of a saint made of plaster in Lorrain's writing studio.
18. The Théâtre d'Art project was formed by a group of Decadent and Symbolist writers in opposition to 'the extreme naturalism' of André Antoine's Théâtre Libre (1887–96), Diana Holmes explains in *Rachilde: Decadence, Gender and the Woman Writer* (Oxford: Berg, 2001), p. 204. In her long 'Préface: De la Fondation d'un Théâtre d'Art', in *Théâtre* (Paris: Nouvelle Librairie Parisienne, 1891), Rachilde praises the Théâtre d'Art's effort as 'une des plus courageuses entreprises artistiques de notre époque' [one of the most courageous artistic enterprises of our era] (p. 1).
19. Holmes, *Rachilde*, p. 205. We do not know whether Wilde attended a performance of *La Voix du sang* (he was actually in Paris in November 1890), or whether he saw or discussed with others the subsequent *Madame la Mort*, performed shortly thereafter (March 1891). Given his involvement with the group of writers around Rachilde, and his own attempts at writing a Symbolist drama with *Salomé*, it would be rather surprising if he didn't.

20. Hawthorne, *Rachilde*, p. 162.
21. Rachilde also used the Théâtre de l'Œuvre to promote her protégé Alfred Jarry. Jarry's sensational *Ubu Roi* had its world première at this theatre in December 1896.
22. According to Hawthorne, Rachilde adapted the play 'from a short story in dialogue that had been published in the *Mercure de France* in June 1892' (Hawthorne, *Rachilde*, p. 166). Wilde's *Salomé* was not officially published in Paris before 1893, but we know that Wilde talked about *Salomé* and circulated the drafts among friends (including Marcel Schwob and Jean Lorrain; see n.17 above). So it is likely that Rachilde either read the play or heard Wilde and others talk about it.
23. Rachilde, *The Crystal Spider*, in *Modern Drama by Women 1880s-1930s: An International Anthology*, ed. by Katherine E. Kelly (London: Routledge, 1998), p. 273. Subsequent references to this translation are given parenthetically.
24. Oscar Wilde, *Salomé*, in *The Complete Works of Oscar Wilde*, ed. by Ian Small and others, 7 vols to date (Oxford: Oxford University Press, 2000-), V, *Plays I: The Duchess of Padua, Salome: Drame en un Acte, Salome: Tragedy in One Act*, ed. by Joseph Donohue (2013), p. 719.
25. Hawthorne and others have pointed out that the use of the mirror is a prominent Decadent theme. It appears as a thematic or structural device in many Decadent works to indicate 'a double, an evil twin through whom the darker, irrational side of the self that Freud was just beginning to expose could be explored' (Hawthorne, *Rachilde*, p. 166). Famously, Wilde himself used the deceptive mirror image for his conception of the portrait, in *The Picture of Dorian Gray*, and to some extent in 'The Portrait of Mr. W. H.'.
26. Melanie Hawthorne, 'Introduction' to Rachilde's *La Jongleuse*, trans. by Melanie Hawthorne (New Brunswick: Rutgers University Press, 1990), p. xvii. Subsequent references to this translation are given parenthetically.
27. For a prominent homoerotic association of the convolvulus, see the famous passage of the bee and the flower in Chapter 2 of *The Picture of Dorian Gray*. As Dorian listens to Lord Henry's seductive words in the garden, he watches 'a bee creeping into the stained trumpet of a Tyrian convolvulus' which 'seemed to quiver'; just as Dorian is 'stirred by some new emotion', the flower 'swayed gently to and fro', signalling that Dorian, like the bee, has been penetrated and inseminated by Lord Henry's influence. (Wilde, *The Picture of Dorian Gray*, in *The Complete Works of Oscar Wilde*, III, ed. by Bristow, p. 187.)
28. Hawthorne, 'Introduction' to *La Jongleuse*, p. xxii.
29. Mesch, *The Hysteric's Revenge*, p. 143.
30. Eliante's auto-erotic orgasm scene is reminiscent of Raoule's in Chapter 2 of *Monsieur Vénus*, where Rachilde hints that Raoule reaches orgasm by merely thinking of Jacques:

> Her entire, delicately nervous being tensed in an extraordinary spasm, a terrible vibration; then, with the immediacy of a cerebral shock, the reaction came and she felt better. She felt a certain undefined intensity in her being, a bizarre effect quite well rendered by the idea of a spring broken in full deployment, a state in which brain activity seems to increase as the muscles relax. [...] With half-closed eyes and a half-open mouth, her head falling on a shoulder raised intermittently by a long calming sigh, she resembled a creature deliciously fatigued by ardent caresses. (Rachilde, *Monsieur Vénus*, pp. 18–19)

31. Wilde, *Salomé*, p. 731.
32. *Ibid.*, pp. 730–31.
33. In my *Salome's Modernity: Oscar Wilde and the Aesthetics of Transgression* (Ann Arbor: University of Michigan Press, 2011), I have called this phenomenon the aesthetics of transgression, a bridge between Decadence and Modernism.

CHAPTER 4

❖

'Things worldly and things spiritual': Huysmans's *À rebours* and the House at Fontenay

Jessica Gossling

The private home of Joris-Karl Huysmans (1848–1907), on the fifth floor of 11 Rue de Sèvres, was a reflection of his singular taste and style.[1] Elevated from the noise of the street, his apartment was described by 'One Who Knows Him' in the *Academy* (1898) as a space where 'things worldly and things spiritual lie side by side, marking the two extremes of his life.'[2] Huysmans's study was a modern hermitage, in which old bibles and religious artefacts were mingled with contemporary literature and works of art (Fig. 4.1). Rather like the anti-hero of his Decadent novel *À rebours* [*Against Nature*] (1884), Huysmans appears to be a contrarian monk embedded in an aesthetic retreat full of *objets d'art* and artefacts.

In his preface to the 1903 publication of *À rebours* Huysmans confesses that at the time of writing the novel he had no religious inclination (his religious awakening and Catholic conversion occurred eight years later, after the publication of *Là-bas* [*Down There*] (1891)). Instead, he comments on his organization of the novel around the sensual and physical worlds, and layered descriptions of 'pierreries, de parfums, de fleurs, de littérature religieuse et laïque, de musique profane et de plain-chant' [jewellery, perfumes, flowers, religious and secular literature, of profane music and plain-chant] (p. ix).[3] Huysmans's focus on sensory pleasures rather than on the actions of the protagonist underpins the structure of the novel.

À rebours can be read as an inventory of decadent pleasures and experiences, each carefully selected and contained within the individual rooms of the villa. As Huysmans comments, 'chaque chapitre devenait le coulis d'une spécialité, le sublimé d'un art différent' [each chapter became the sublimate of a specialism, the refinement of a different art] (p. ix). Like the rooms of the house, the chapters of the novel emphasize a different obsession or collection. David Weir, in his analysis of Huysmans as an innovator of the novel form, notes that Des Esseintes 'disappears from the text for pages at a time, while this or that aspect of decadent taste is explored — the Latin of Petronius, the philosophy of Schopenhauer, the artificiality of exotic plants, the nuances of strange combinations of colours and odours, and so on.'[4] Huysmans describes a collector's paradise and positions Des Esseintes as both the curator of the space and its principal artefact.

Fig. 4.1. Joris-Karl Huysmans in his study.
Dornac, *Nos contemporains chez eux*, fol. 1, photograph. Bibliothèque nationale de France, Département des Estampes et de la photographie.

Fontenay: Suburban Sensorium

In *À rebours*, Des Esseintes retreats to Fontenay-aux-Roses, a suburb of Paris, to escape from his tedious life in the city and to stimulate his flagging senses. The villa is located outside the urban centre, where

> il éprouvait une allégresse d'autant plus vive qu'il se voyait retiré assez loin déjà, sur la berge, pour que le flot de Paris ne l'atteignît plus et assez près cependant pour que cette proximité de la capitale le confirmât dans sa solitude (p. 10).[5]
>
> [he felt a glow of pleasure at the idea that here he would be too far out for the tidal wave of Parisian life to reach him, and yet near enough for the proximity of the capital to strengthen him in his solitude]

The villa is a meticulously designed haven of peace and tranquillity in which he can indulge his extravagant tastes without distraction. However, the house at Fontenay does not offer him an escape from the world. In the threshold space of the villa, his collections become an inescapable reminder of his past and of the limitations of his body. Rather than providing a refuge from the overstimulating effects of the city, the interior of the house reflects Des Esseintes's mind. It is a 'chambre mentale'.[6]

In preparation for writing the novel, Huysmans undertook research into the subject of hysteria and other nervous illnesses, consulting textbooks such as Alexandre Axenfeld's *Traité des Névroses* [*Nervous Traits*] (1883). This interest in the newly emerging body of knowledge — *psychologie nouvelle* — is reflected in his depictions of Des Esseintes's hypersensitivity and obsessive-compulsive tendencies.

These neuroses are taken to a decadent extreme and lead to disorders of sense and motion that manifest themselves as physical symptoms. Before he enters the house, Huysmans describes how Des Esseintes already suffers from certain symptoms of neurasthenia — pains in the back of the neck and shaking hands.[7] For this reason, Fontenay is designed as a restorative space and the architecture of the house replicates the division Des Esseintes wishes to create between his ailing body and overstimulated mind. The house is divided into two, with Des Esseintes's four rooms on one side of the house (a dressing-room, bedroom, library, and dining-room), corresponding to four more practical rooms on the other side (his closets, boudoir, entrance hall, and kitchen). Huysmans makes a distinction between private and public space in the two halves of the building, but the structure of the house also recalls the relationship between the mind and the body as described by René Descartes in his philosophy of dualism. The mental processes on one side of the house run parallel to the material functionalism on the other. For instance, he fills his boudoir with ebony-framed prints by Jan Luyken, images that depict human suffering at the hands of religious fanatics by which Des Esseintes is both repelled and fascinated. The boudoir and adjoining vestibule, hung with works by the contemporary artists Rodolphe Bresdin and Odilon Redon, are the counterpoint to his bedroom — a facsimile of a monastic cell that is separate from but adjacent to his boudoir. Within his calming and almost minimalist bedroom, he attempts to recover from the over-stimulation of his environment. However, as the interconnections and correspondences of his physical living space suggest, there is no clear division; the mind and body are inseparable.

In *À rebours*, Huysmans focuses on sensory experiences, and these are compartmentalised in the rooms of the house. As Joseph Halpern suggests, 'the heart of the book is the house as museum' and we are encouraged to see the chapters as like a series of display cases.[8] The interior of Des Esseintes's villa consists of interconnected rooms, each representative of an aspect of his mind or body. The individual rooms are 'capitonné, hermétiquement fermé' [padded, hermetically sealed] (p. 29) so that smells or sounds are unable to filter from one room to the next. This creates the impression that the different parts — or rooms — of the house are more significant than the house in its entirety. The emphasis is on the part rather than the whole. We can trace historical connections between this compartmentalized interior design and the location of the villa. In the seventeenth century, Fontenay-aux-Roses was the centre for the cultivation of rose varieties, and it specialized in growing the intensely perfumed Bengal rose for the perfumers at the court of Versailles. This process is suggested in Des Esseintes's architectural design. In the extraction of a fragrance from a flower, one sense (smell) becomes disconnected from the other senses (touch and sight). In a similar way to the distillation of a perfume from a flower, Des Esseintes also tries to separate and manipulate the senses. In order to amplify their intensity and to try to gain some control over their suggestive potential, he groups objects by their sensory properties. Similarly, each chapter focuses on a different obsession or collection. For example, Chapter One describes the colour of his rooms, in particular his library and bedroom, Chapter Four focuses on his aesthetic and physical tastes, particularly in relation to jewels and liquor,

Chapter Eight concentrates on the visual and textural properties of his hothouse-flower collection, and Chapter Ten describes his assortment of perfumes.

Huysmans's writing invokes all the senses, but he was particularly interested in olfaction and the evocative power of scent. In Chapter Ten, Huysmans describes Des Esseintes's attempt, prior to entering the villa, to master 'la grammaire, comprendre la syntaxe des odeurs' [the grammar, to understand the syntax of smells] (p. 171). Scents are described as like music and poetry, and he analyses the construction of a scent like the structure of a text. Des Esseintes argues that the language of scents had 'avancée parallèlement avec les autres arts' [advanced side-by-side with the other arts] (p. 173) and he creates perfumes that stimulate correspondent thoughts, directly drawing on the poems of Baudelaire. For instance, he describes how he used to base some of his 'accords en parfumerie' [scented harmonies] (p. 177) on the pantoum form used by Baudelaire in 'Le Balcon' [The Balcony] and 'L'Irréparable' [The Irreparable] from *Les Fleurs du mal* [*The Flowers of Evil*] (1857). This carefully controlled structure, in envelope form, was replicated in the structure of Des Esseintes's recollections when he experimented with scent in Paris. 'Il s'égarait dans les songes qu'évoquaient pour lui ces stances aromatiques, ramené soudain à son point de départ' [He used to roam haphazardly through the dreams conjured up by these aromatic stanzas, until he was suddenly brought back to his starting point] (p. 177).

However, in the house at Fontenay, Des Esseintes's intention is different. Within the controlled space of the villa he uses perfumes to open up a vast and 'sonore' [sonorous] (p. 177) countryside scene. His perception of strong perfumes as deep sounds, or olfactory notes, enables him to compose an imaginary landscape. The objects in Des Esseintes's interiors are the vehicles for his fantasies and synaesthesiac experiences. Through attempting to contain and control the senses, Des Esseintes makes their synaesthetic effects stronger — when one sense is separated from another its associations become clearer. Rather than being carefully controlled, however, the villa becomes a space of mixed sensations. Scents evoke music and memories and, similarly, in Chapter Four, his collection of liquors, the 'mouth organ', create imaginary musical compositions. Traditionally, synaesthesia is viewed as a random association between separate senses. However, through Des Esseintes's explorations in space and sensation, Huysmans anticipates contemporary research suggesting that synaesthesia can be shaped by environmental associations.[9] The objects, when positioned in the rooms of the villa, become the catalyst for Des Esseintes's hypersensitivity and developing nervous disorders.

Des Esseintes's confinement within his suburban sensorium leads to wild thoughts. Within the intense space of the house at Fontenay, correspondences between sensations and memories are cultivated. Alfred Carter asserts that Des Esseintes's 'neurosis develops in the hothouse atmosphere of his retreat at Fontenay like a melon under a bell-glass'.[10] He is both protected and imprisoned in his house and this is perfectly suggested by the metaphor of the glass enclosure. In this heated space, the growth of delicate rare breeds is artificially accelerated. Unlike conservatories in which plants are placed in moveable pots, in a hothouse the plants are permanently planted inside and forced to acclimatize to the artificially created conditions. Similarly, the villa space is not a static display case with collections arranged neatly and gathering dust. It is crammed with objects that suggest shifting moods and the growth of unconscious desires and fears. As Michael Riffaterre proposes, in a hothouse, 'despite their separateness, the inner and outside worlds are mutually visible'.[11] For Des Esseintes, this is manifested in the villa through a frustrating relationship between present sensations and past memories. He is able to recall a time of virility and sexual adventure, but he is unable to take an active part in these recollections or even control when or how they occur.

Previous studies of the novel have tended to consider Des Esseintes's villa as an example of an aesthetic museum house, or a cabinet of curiosities. George Cevasco, for example, describes the structure of *À rebours* as 'essentially a log book of a young aristocrat's response to, and sensations about, the world'.[12] This notion of the novel as a 'log book' is emphasized by Des Esseintes's meticulous attention to aesthetic details when collecting for and organizing the villa space. However, it does not accurately reflect the kind of space represented by the text as museum house and neglects the fact that the collections are not as contained, and the rooms are not as sealed, as Des Esseintes intends. Although Des Esseintes's rooms are connected to each other, 'Ainsi que ces boîtes du Japon qui entrent, les unes dans les autres' [Like those Japanese boxes that fit one inside the other] (p. 29), they are unlike neatly nested Japanese boxes. Huysmans imagines the interior of the villa as a set or series of complex and contrasting spaces, which sometimes contain smaller hidden chambers and secret recesses. The rooms of the villa, and the chapters of the novel, are not separate but interconnected and embedded spaces.

House/Room and Dynamic Compartmentalization

Contrary to the views of some critics, the space in the house is not discrete and contained; it is dynamic. The villa is a liminal space and the collections in the villa, like the rooms in the villa that open onto other rooms, spark imaginative correspondences. Rather than being a hermetically sealed laboratory for sensory experimentation, the rooms in the house, and the chapters of the novel, are connected by Des Esseintes's neurotic associations and memories. In the prologue, Huysmans describes these mental desires as like a physical craving for 'les joies déviées' [perverse pleasures] (p. 10). Des Esseintes designs the villa in order to escape this hunger, but his tastes for the perverse are amplified by his surroundings. For instance, the only full meal that Des Esseintes eats is in Chapter Eleven, when he visits an English tavern in the rue d'Amsterdam. On his return to Fontenay, Des Esseintes is still obsessed with his stomach. In the following chapter, he describes his taste in books using gustatory adjectives. For example, he refers to Baudelaire as 'charnue' [fleshy], and compares reading Pierre Nicole and Blaise Pascal to 'ces moelles condensées en de sévères et fortes phrases' [the pith and marrow of stern, strong phrases] (p. 134). He chooses his favourite writers like dishes on a menu, foregrounding the connection between his refined literary and culinary tastes. This refinement continues in the following chapter, when he awakes with nausea and has a longing for everyday peasant food. In the final chapters, his eating habits become increasingly *à rebours*. He begins consuming food passed through a digester and eventually his diet consists of enemas created by his physician. Initially, Des Esseintes is excited by this gastronomical reversal. He describes it as an insult 'jetée à la face de cette vieille nature' [thrown in the face of old Mother Nature] (p. 194). However, this final amplification of his neurotic impulses is one of the factors that cause his return to Paris.

Des Esseintes's aim when creating the villa space was to escape from the ravages of time and sickness. He creates a fake death, symbolic of his attempt to remove himself from his old life, only to be constantly reminded of it. However, Des Esseintes's uneasy relationship with his body and desires is intensified within the rooms of the villa. The house is not an extension of the outside world but, as Walter Benjamin describes in *Passagen-Werk* [*The Arcades Project*] (1927–40), the occupant's *étui* — a small protective cover or case designed to shield its contents.[13] This image of a tight-fitting shelter suggests proximity and evokes a feeling of claustrophobia. The house is both containing and safe, and yet imprisoning. Des Esseintes's villa is designed to restrict sensory stimulations from the outside world, but he cannot control the visual, aural and olfactory connections that come from within the house. Thus, enclosure in the novel is a paradox. Des Esseintes voluntarily imprisons himself within a space of involuntary memory.

Huysmans demonstrates how Des Esseintes creates and constructs his decadent universe at Fontenay and yet is both within the limits of his house and the limitations of his mind. As Gail Finney describes, the house is an 'aesthetic hermitage', an image that suggests a simple monastic retreat devoted to sensory experiences and beauty.[14] This almost contradictory description is reflected in Des Esseintes's decoration of his bedroom in the manner of 'une loge de chartreux qui eût l'air d'être vraie et qui ne le fût, bien entendu, pas' [a Carthusian monk's cell which would have the air of being real, without, of course, actually being so] (p. 100). He combines ecclesiastical objects with opulent materials to create a luxurious bedroom in which he can imagine that he is in the depths of a cloister. The irony of this is that this monk's cell, while it has all the trappings of the monastic life, is only superficially a renunciation of worldly pleasure in that it is also 'une chambre confortable et tiède' [a pleasant and comfortable bedroom] (p. 102). This small room exemplifies his increasing obsession with 'worldly' sensual extremes and belies his search for religious fulfilment. The interior in which Des Esseintes places himself is not a soothing or regenerative escape from the chaos of the modern world. Instead, the house becomes a virtual replica of his past life in the city. Des Esseintes brings his desire for overstimulation and exhausting contradictions with him to his retreat. He is unable to create a hermetically sealed environment in the villa space as the external world is still evoked through the objects that he has collected.

The connection between the objects and rooms in which they are located is of great decorative importance to the spatial organization in Des Esseintes's house. As Robert de Montesquiou-Fezensac, the real-life dandy and model for Husymans's protagonist, stated of his own apartment, it is 'le groupement des objets, dans une association, presque dans une conversation ingénieuse, et parfois saisissante, qui réveille l'appétit des yeux, et se communique à l'âme' [the grouping of objects, in association, almost in ingenious and sometimes striking conversation, which awakens the appetite of the eyes, and communicates with the soul] (p. 94).[15] In his villa, Des Esseintes attempts to augment the effects of his collections on his senses. This is apparent in his bedroom, but it becomes most obvious in his adjacent library-study, the walls of which he bound 'comme des livres, avec du maroquin, à gros grains écrasés, avec de la peau du Cap' [like books, in large-grained crushed morocco: skins from the Cape] (p. 24). The leather-lined library is a feature adopted from Montesquiou's Quai d'Orsay library. Willa Z. Silverman gives a detailed description of this room and proposes that 'with its glistening, lacquered leather walls and peacock-eye motif, this library was meant to stimulate the intellectual work and inspiration associated with writing and reading.'[16] The library in Montesquiou's apartment not only fostered intellectual activities but also served, Silverman claims, 'as their emblem'.[17] The decoration of the room is more than just an aesthetic choice. It echoes the function of the room and multiplies its intensity.

Des Esseintes manipulates the correspondences between an object and its location. On the one hand, the room intensifies sensory or material objects and, on the other, the interior design appears to be at odds with the functionality of the space. For instance, his dining room resembles a ship's cabin, with one window rendered useless by an aquarium that 'occupait tout l'espace compris entre ce hublot et cette réelle fenêtre ouverte dans le vrai mur' [occupied the entire space between the porthole and the real window in the real house-wall] (p. 30). Instead of being designed around social conviviality and gustatory desires — as we might expect from a dining room — Des Esseintes creates a room that is a feast for the eyes, not the stomach. The aquarium, filled with mechanical fish and artificial seaweed, is an experiment in colour. By dissolving pigments in the water, he manipulates the refracted light from the outside window. These visual effects are enhanced by the other senses, such as the infusion of the room with the smell of tar and the nautical apparatus piled by the door. Des Esseintes designs the space to permanently capture a sense of movement. The dining room is a journey for the senses as it gives the destabilizing, even nauseating, impression of being both on top of and under the water. This potential of creating a *mal de mer* is the opposite of what is usually desired from a dining room, and corresponds to Des Esseintes's eating habits, the limited time he spends on his meals, and their sometimes sickening effects. The deliberate disorder and impermanent appearance of the dining room is purposefully in contrast to the permanent and orderly study that is connected to it. This gives the effect of travel, of moving from one place to a different one, but without the annoyance or fatigue of a long voyage.

Baudelaire's Correspondences

Huysmans's decadent novel-space is a retreat, a space of escape, but it is also a work full of reference to recollections, memory and dreams. These correspondences recall Baudelaire's poem 'Correspondances' from *Les Fleurs du mal*, which describes the relationship between different realms of experience, physical and metaphysical. Through his depiction of sensory correspondences, Baudelaire expands on the writings of the philosopher Emanuel Swedenborg and his suggestion that everything in nature has its spiritual counterpart. In the poem, the space between the worldly and the spiritual is imagined as a 'forê[t] de symboles' [forest of symbols], where 'Les parfums, les couleurs et les sons se répondent' [Perfumes, colours, and sounds correspond] (p. 18).[18] The relationship between the physical and metaphysical realms becomes a preoccupation of Huysmans in À rebours and his admiration for Baudelaire is apparent throughout the novel.

In Chapter Twelve, Des Esseintes praises Baudelaire's poetic style. He describes writers who depict typical human behaviour as like botanists who watch closely 'le développement prévu de floraisons normales plantées dans de la naturelle terre' [the expected development of normal flora planted in natural soil] (p. 215). In comparison, Baudelaire explores the more morbid psychology of the mind. As Des Esseintes comments, it was Baudelaire who found 'couvant sous la morne cloche de l'Ennui, l'effrayant retour d'âge des sentiments et des idées' [hatching in the dismal forcing-house of ennui, the frightening climacteric of thoughts and emotions] (p. 216) and on closer study we can see this Baudelairean idea played out in fictional form. The house at Fontenay is also an inter-sensory and claustrophobic environment that is a breeding-ground for diseases of the mind. Like Baudelaire, Huysmans explores the 'végétations monstrueuses' of human nature grown within a hothouse environment.[19]

In the final pages of the opening chapter, the central room is described. The library-study is a distillation of the purpose of the villa and Baudelaire's poems are a central component. As Huysmans states, 'le seul luxe de cette pièce devant consister en des livres et des fleurs rares' [the only luxuries he intended to have in this room were rare books and flowers] (p. 25), but he also fills it with furs, furniture and curtains made of ecclesiastical material. Above the fireplace in Des Esseintes's study, in the same position as Huysmans's crucifix in his rue de Sèvres apartment, he hangs 'un merveilleux canon d'église' [a magnificent triptych] (p. 26). On these panels are three poems by Baudelaire that exemplify the essential components of the villa space:

> à droite et à gauche, les sonnets portant ces titres 'La Mort des Amants' — 'l'Ennemi'; — au milieu, le poème en prose intitulé: *'Anywhere Out of the World'*

> [right and left, the sonnets called 'The Death of the Lover' and 'The Enemy', in the middle, the prose poem that goes by the English title of *'Anywhere out of the World'*] (p. 26)

'Anywhere Out of the World', from Baudelaire's *Le Spleen de Paris, Petits poèmes en Prose* [*Paris Spleen, Small Prose Poems*] (1869), describes the poet in conversation with his reticent soul, and reflects the initial purpose of the villa as an escape from the monotony of everyday life into a man-made world of art and artifice. However, in 'L'Ennemi', from *Les Fleurs du mal*, the poet expresses his fear that he has reached 'l'automne des idées' [the autumn of ideas] (p. 101). Huysmans includes the poem in the triptych to illustrate the similar fears and desires of Des Esseintes but, unlike Baudelaire, he does not have a desire to regain the lost time of his misspent youth. Instead, the poet is confronted with the 'autumn' of his ideas in a devastated garden, and this is evoked by Des Esseintes's attempt to create a perfect environment in which to grow these new 'flowers'. Des Esseintes hopes that within his villa he will be able to cultivate the new sensations and experiences that will cure his ennui.[20] In the context of *À rebours*, this poem articulates the connection created in the house at Fontenay between the sensual physical world and spiritual transcendence.

The house at Fontenay is not a refuge. It is a hothouse for his mental aberrations and the novel is a multisensory experiment with Des Esseintes at the centre. Everything, from the collections in the villa to the colour of the walls, is centred around the effect they will have on his mind. For instance, in his choice of red, yellow and orange for his villa, Huysmans replicates contemporary ideas about colour stimulation that were first commented on by Grant Allen in *The Colour-Sense: Its Origin and Development* (1879). Allen argues that the 'red and orange end of the spectrum is decidedly the most pleasurable: while the central colours, green and blue, are decidedly the least so.'[21] Huysmans's observation that there is a correspondence between 'la nature sensuelle d'un individu vraiment artiste et la couleur que ses yeux voient d'une façon plus spéciale et plus vive' [the sensual make up of that person with a truly artistic temperament and whatever colour that person reacts to most strongly and sympathetically] (p. 24) also suggests Baudelaire's comments in his essay, *Le Salon de 1845*. Ultimately, Des Esseintes settles on a colour palette consisting of mostly orange, a colour that Huysmans describes as attractive to characters of feeble constitution because of its 'irritante et maladive' [irritating and morbid] (p. 24) effect on the eye.

Fontenay is, in effect, a house of correspondences. There are correspondences between the physical and mental realms, and the more we study the novel, the more we see that the narrative is powered by a modern preoccupation with memory and recollections stimulated by sensory experience. The senses are portals to the complex and shifting realms of the mind. This is particularly evident in Chapter Eight, when the villa becomes a more literal hothouse for Des Esseintes's neuroses. Before the plants even arrive Huysmans hints at the effects that these 'folies de végétation' [floral follies] (p. 134) are having on the unconscious mind of Des Esseintes. After arriving home, he is 'hanté sans trêve par des souvenirs de corbeilles magnifiques et bizarres' [haunted all the while by the memories of bizarre and magnificent blooms] (p. 134). The visual and textural qualities of these plants remind him of the physical symptoms of venereal disease. The chapter is mostly set in Des Esseintes's mind and narrates his sexual adventures of the past. However, he is unable to control these exhausting memories and his neurosis begins to take on new forms.

Judith Ryan observes that Huysmans was one of the first writers to depict an 'impressionistic view of space' not limited by linear time and with an emphasis on subjective reactions to visual stimuli.[22] In Chapter Eight, Huysmans suggests the process of walking along the avenues of a hothouse, where specimens are positioned to attract the eye. As the plants are unloaded by the gardeners into the entrance hall Des Esseintes surveys and groups the plants in terms of their physical similarities. This is exemplified in relation to the *Alocasia metalica*, which he describes as 'd'un modèle similaire à celui des Caladiums' [of a type similar to the Caladiums] (p. 136). While both plants share the characteristic of flat foliage, the tropical Alocasia requires hothouse conditions for survival whereas other species of Caladiums can be grown outdoors. In a hothouse, plants are traditionally grouped into topographical zones both so that their origins can be understood and their requirements easily catered for (so they can in effect receive the correct amount of sunlight, heat and water). In À rebours, the typical hothouse arrangement of plants into topographical zones is undercut by Des Esseintes's predominantly aesthetic considerations. This turns out to have disastrous consequences. Like the death of his bejewelled tortoise, crushed by the weight of its shell, Des Esseintes's hothouse plants die from a lack of proper care.

Sensory Perception and Memory

As I have suggested, the dominating influence of sensory perception is apparent from the beginning of À rebours; however, it culminates in Chapter Eight with the descriptions of the hothouse flowers that enter the villa, which are no stranger than Des Esseintes himself. In his description of the *Albane* and *Aurora borealis*, which 'présentait les deux notes extrêmes du tempérament, l'apoplexie et la chlorose de cette plante' [represented two temperamental extremes, apoplexy and chlorosis, in this particular family of plants] (p. 135), the contrast between the red blood and the green tinge of anaemia sets the focus in the rest of the chapter on the physical and temperamental extremes recognizable in both people and plants.[23] Des Esseintes's sexual peculiarities become particularly discernible in the description of the *Anthurium*, which, Huysmans comments, 'faisait partie d'un lot de cette famille à laquelle appartenait aussi un Amorphophallus' [belonged to a section of the same family as a certain Amorphophallus] (p. 137). Huysmans combines the description of the *Anthurium*, which has 'une queue charnue, cotonneuse' [a fleshy, downy tail] (p. 137), with the name of the *Amorphophallus*, translated as 'misshapen phallus', in order to create a sense that the aroid is the epitome of both strange eroticism and diseased sexuality. Des Esseintes is exultant before this abnormal beauty and is delighted when a fresh batch of monstrosities is unloaded from the carts.

Considering the dominance of scent throughout the novel, Chapter Eight is notably lacking in olfactory sensations. The carrion plants, of which the Amorphophallus is a notable example, are mentioned for their visual, rather than their scented, properties. However, the final plant that is almost omitted from Des Esseintes's list, is the fragrant Cattleya orchid of New Granada, which completes the sensory experience of the hothouse. The pale lilac orchid described by Huysmans is the *Cattleya trianae*, native to Columbia. This winter flowering species, also known as the 'Christmas orchid', has a fetid perfume that is reminiscent of mothballs or damp wood. Huysmans describes it as smelling like cheap varnished wood — a 'boîte à jouets' [toy-box] aroma that is evocative of Des Esseintes's childhood and 'les horreurs d'un jour de l'an' [the horrors of a New Year's Day] (p. 140). It is the only time a flower's scent is described in the chapter and, for Des Esseintes, the smell of the orchid evokes 'les plus désagréables des souvenirs' [the most unpleasant memories] (p. 140). The troublesome associations of this smell are revisited in the dream as the nostrils of the horse ridden by Syphilis personified are described as 'soufflant deux jets de vapeur qui puaient le phenol' [breathing twin jets of vapour that stank of phenol] (p. 146). The smell of phenol has connections to perfumery, in which it is used as a substitute for the musty odour of orchids and ferns. Thus this scent is also an amplification of the mothball smell of the Cattleya orchid, mentioned earlier in the chapter. Angela Nuccitelli makes the connection between the smell of phenol exhaled by the horse and Des Esseintes's memory of a visit to the dentist for a tooth extraction. Having teeth pulled, she argues, is a common symbol of castration and phenol would also have been used as an antiseptic in the nineteenth century.[24] The scent has a manifest association (his childhood) and a latent meaning (his fear of women). This is significant as it demonstrates an engagement with contemporary debates about the unconscious and dreaming, in particular Freud's theory of dream interpretation. The fragrance of a particular flower could conjure a visual memory or resurrect a dead moment.

In the first volume of *A la recherche du temps perdu* [*In Search of Lost Time*] (1913), Proust borrows the lascivious properties of the Cattleya orchid found in Huysmans's novel for the private code between Charles Swann and the courtesan Odette de Crécy. The Cattleyas that Odette wears during a carriage journey are dislodged when her horse suddenly shies at an obstacle. Swann restores the Cattleyas to Odette's bodice and subsequently uses the coded phrase 'faire cattleya' for making love. Proust believed that the past is concealed in sensations that a material object can give us — the taste of 'petites madeleines' is the famous example. Similarly, Bettina Knapp argues that Des Esseintes's 'exaggerated sense of smell (*hyperosmia*) has the power of bringing on hallucinations and dreams. Perfumes and other aromas are able to lead him into ever-profounder levels of introspection'.[25] However, these introspections are an amalgamation of moods and anxieties, rather than an actual manifestation of Des Esseintes's memories.

The two-part structure of Chapter Eight enables Huysmans to depict the correspondences between the thoughts of the day and their distorted expression in the unconscious. In the prologue, Des Esseintes is described as dreaming of 'une thébaïde raffinée' [a refined Thebaid] (p. 10) and the villa is an attempt to make his dreams a reality. The French verb 'rêver' [to dream] is used forty-five times in *À rebours*. However, the only actual dream described in the novel is the one stimulated by the hothouse flowers. As Ruth Antosh explains, even though Des Esseintes purposefully fills his house with nightmarish art in order to flee from reality, 'the only truly personal nightmare he undergoes offers him anything but an escape.'[26] Instead, the associations that are created while he is awake become actualized in the visual narrative of the dream.

The diseased characteristics attributed to the hothouse flowers provide an insight into Des Esseintes's fears and desires. As they enter the villa the ways in which these sickly growths appear to parallel human perversions, especially those associated with prostitution and sexual diseases, is made explicit. For example, when the gardeners bring in more varieties of *Caladium*, Des Esseintes describes them as looking as if they have been 'rongées par des syphilis et des lèpres' [ravaged by syphilis or leprosy] (p. 135). He then attributes the visual and textural elements of these diseases, such as chancres, ulcers, scabs, and scars, to the hothouse plants, describing the usually smooth leaves of the perennials as 'épidermes poilus, creusés par des ulcères et repoussés par des chancres' [hairy surfaces pitted with ulcers and embossed with chancres] (p. 135). Des Esseintes admires the hothouse plants for their unhealthy appearance and selects them for their fleshly properties. He remarks how the leaves of his exotic blooms have 'une apparence de peau factice sillonnée de fausses veines' [the appearance of a factitious skin covered with a network of counterfeit veins] (p. 135).

In his descriptions, Huysmans brings together the medical and aesthetic realms.[27] Like patients in a hospital, the plants are placed side by side, and encompass a range of pre- and post-operative disfigurements. Many of the plants appear as if they have been mutilated by syphilis or leprosy, while others seem to have just had their wounds 'plaquées d'axonge noire mercurielle, d'onguents verts de belladone, piquées de grains de poussière, par les micas jaunes de la poudre d'iodoforme' [coated with black mercurial lard, plastered with green belladonna ointment, dusted over with the yellow flakes of iodoform powder] (p. 136). The description of the skin diseases and medical cures correspond to the preliminary stages of syphilis — characterized by, firstly, small chancres on the skin and, secondly, rashes and wart-like skin growths.[28] However, the markings on the plants are described in an aesthetic way. They are 'marbrées de roséoles, damassées de dartres' [marbled with roseola, damasked with dartre] (p. 135). This description connects skin with paper through its evocation of the rose-coloured rash and the eczema-like skin condition, as well as suggesting techniques used in papermaking in the nineteenth century.[29] Like the scent of the Cattleya, the texture of the flowers is emphasized and distorted in the dream and, as he imagines during the day, the leaves become the skin of the flower woman. He notices 'l'effrayante irritation des seins et de la bouche, découvrit sur la peau du corps des macules de bistre et de cuivre' [the frightening irritation of the mouth and breasts, discovered on the skin of the body spots of bistre and copper] (p. 147). In the dream space the descriptions of first-stage syphilis are developed, and the plant woman has the syphilitic rash of the second stage of the disease.

Women are a source of attraction and repulsion for Huysmans, and the dominant image of the diseased flower-woman is stirred by Des Esseintes's overarching fear of syphilis. In his thesis on the representation of women in Huysmans, Brendan King foregrounds the connection in the dream between the fear of syphilis and the image of woman as the carrier of disease, and he comments that in the final stages of his dream Des Esseintes begins to come to the same conclusion. His 'manie raisonnante persista dans le cauchemar, dériva de même que pendant la journée de la végétation sur le Virus' [reasoning mania persisted even in his nightmare; and as in the daytime, it switched from vegetation to the Virus] (p. 148). Des Esseintes's dominant fear is of the tertiary stage of syphilis, which can occur years after initial infection and can lead to madness and death. However, he is more concerned with the potential of the virus to cause sexual dysfunction, all the more significant given that he is the last of his hereditary line. In the dream, this is imagined through castration imagery. He is drawn towards the figure of Syphilis, and is almost touching her when 'noirs Amorphophallus jaillirent de toutes parts, s'élancèrent vers ce ventre qui se soulevait et s'abaissait comme une mer' [black Amorphalli sprang up on every side and stabbed at her belly, which was rising and falling like a sea] (p. 148). The 'farouche' [savage] Nidularium begins blossoming from under her thighs and has, as described previously in the chapter and repeated at this point in the dream, leaves like 'des lames de sabre' [sword blades] (p. 149). Camilla Paglia proposes that the women in the dream have the power of destruction and creation. She comments that 'Des Esseintes builds a palace of art against nature but in his dreams nature comes to reclaim and devour him.'[30] As a result, the dream is as an example of the virus increasing its hold over him, and the true beginning of his physical decline. The villa intensifies, rather than cures, his illness.

Huysmans suggests that the unnatural villa creates an unhealthy atmosphere for Des Esseintes. Rather than enabling him to escape from the anxieties created by the outside world, the villa increases and enhances his neurotic impulses. He attempts to impose a linear order on the dream but the structure is more akin to a series of associations, in which an element of the previous image triggers the next one. Elements appear and disappear like 'un changement à vue, par un truc de décor' [some transformation scene, some theatrical illusion] (p. 147), and the images in the dream, like the flowers that initiated it, have been imported from strange places. For example, the image of 'immenses et blancs pierrots faisaient des sauts de lapins, dans des rayons de lune' [enormous white pierrots jumping about like rabbits in the moonlight] (p. 146) seemingly draws on the nightmarish images of the Symbolist artist Odilon Redon, who is greatly admired by Des Esseintes in Chapter Five. In À rebours, Huysmans creates a space that is real and imagined, intimate and performative. The villa space encourages impressionistic thoughts that relate to the house as a site of correspondences, as previously mentioned by Judith Ryan and developed by Ruth Weinreb, who states that a symbiotic relationship is developed between the spiritual and the material world in the text: 'Huysmans materializes the spiritual world through Des Esseintes. Des Esseintes spiritualizes the material world through art and his artificial life.'[31] He is the catalyst for the correspondences in the text, resulting in a novel that focuses on the threshold between experiences in the real world and their manifestation in the realm of the unconscious.

Conclusion

In Huysmans's 1903 preface to À rebours, he comments that all the novels he had written since 'sont contenus en germe dans ce livre' [are contained in embryo in that book] (p. xi). This is particularly true of Huysmans's use of the senses to evoke liminal spaces, depictions of which evolve alongside his developing Catholicism. In *En rade* [Stranded] (1887), the use of dreams as an echo of the unconscious mind can be seen as an extension of the structure of Chapter Eight of À rebours, which is divided into the events of the day and the subsequent nightmare.[32] The dilapidated chateau is a repository of dreams and an external depiction of the crumbling mind of Jacques Marles who, like Des Esseintes, is on the verge of lunacy. In *En rade*, Marles retreats into a fantasy world, typified by the dream of fevered exoticism that occurs in Chapter Two. The vegetative dream of the biblical character Esther is infused with floral imagery, scent and precious jewels to create a dream-like version of Des Esseintes's villa. The hothouse is evoked inside the dream palace, where 'partout grimpaient des pampres découpés dans d'uniques pierres; partout flambait un brasier d'incombustibles ceps' [everywhere climbing vine branches were carved into unique stones; around blazed a fire of combustible vines] (p. 30; my translation).[33] In the dream the strange growth is again the figure of the dangerously exotic female and while Huysmans does not make a direct reference to Gustave Moreau, the exoticized description of Esther is reminiscent of Salome in Chapter Five of À rebours.

In Là-bas, both the character of Hyacinthe Chantelouve and the spaces she occupies suggest the connection between the hothouse, scent, and gendered female space. Durtal visits her apartment in Chapter Twelve and comments on her surroundings which 'sentait l'eau des tombes, mais elle exhalait aussi une odeur cléricale' [smelt of damp tombs, but also exhaled a clerical odour] (p. 24).[34] As with the flower-women of the previous novels, Durtal finds Hyacinthe more desirable on account of her environment, with its green iron railings and strange smells. Hyacinthe is a physical embodiment of the threat of female sexuality that is imagined in À rebours. She is the hothouse flower removed from the dream space of the hothouse. In a possible continuation of this allusion, the Black Mass takes place on the rue Olivier de Serres, a street named after the inventor of the first French greenhouse. The debased church, in which the Black Mass is held, embodies Durtal's desire to escape from the mundane nature of everyday existence. However, like Huysmans's other spaces of retreat, this space is also a disappointment. 'Excédé de dégoût, à moitié asphyxié' [Overcome by disgust, almost suffocating] (p. 168), Durtal is affronted by the reality of satanic infection and debasement. In Là-bas, the imagined horrors of À rebours become manifested in real people and experiences. For instance, the 'odeur du sabbat' [smell of the sabbath] (p. 168), a scent of incense and coupling bodies, is reminiscent of Des Esseintes's remembered perversities. However, in Là-bas, the smell is overwhelming as it is no longer a part of a controlled, imaginative space. As Durtal runs outside for a breath of air, the reader is reminded of Des Esseintes when he opens the window at the end of Chapter Ten. In both Là-bas and À rebours, this craving for fresh air marks the beginning of their return to the outside world.

The notion of olfactory sensations circulating within decadent spaces and corrupting those who experience them is not limited to Huysmans's own work. The unique qualities of À rebours were particularly attractive to Francophile English Decadent writers, such as Oscar Wilde. In The Picture of Dorian Gray (1891), Wilde borrows from À rebours in a sensory way. For instance, in the opening paragraphs, time is compressed and this stillness is permeated by 'the rich odour of roses, the heavy scent of lilac, or the more delicate perfume of the pink flowering-thorn.'[35] The artificial studio space is infused with seductive scents in order to create the impression of a carefully curated space. However, it is Wilde's construction of Chapter Eleven that provides an insight into the lasting influences of Huysmans's novel. This chapter describes the liminal period of Dorian's self-corruption and it is like a miniature version of À rebours, with sections on senses that blend into one another. Like Des Esseintes, Dorian studies perfumes and their effects on the psyche, 'seeking often to elaborate a real psychology of perfumes', then devotes himself to music, studies jewels and tapestries, and collects ecclesiastical garments in an array of colours.[36] Wilde describes the detrimental effects that these sensory pleasures have on Dorian's psyche and, at the end of Chapter Ten, the narrator gives an impression of the 'yellow book' (thought to be À rebours) as 'a poisonous book. The heavy odour of incense seemed to cling about its pages and to trouble the brain.'[37] À rebours, 'the breviary of the Decadence' as Arthur Symons termed it, leaves a corrupting legacy, and this corruption is described evocatively in terms of scent.[38]

Des Esseintes fails in his experiment to isolate the senses; they cannot be experienced as discrete. Rather, the senses permeate one another, creating correspondences that he cannot control. In this way, his retreat does not cure him, but makes him worse. In the breeding-ground of his villa that resembles a hothouse, sensations exacerbate Des Esseintes's nervous illness. He is forced, at the novel's conclusion, to return to Paris. Similarly, Dorian Gray is unable to release himself from the 'poisonous' influence of À rebours, remaining trapped in a circle in which the worldly and the spiritual permeate one another interchangeably. In Chapter Sixteen, Dorian recites Lord Henry's credo, 'to cure the soul by means of the senses or the senses by means of the soul', as he makes his way to an opium den.[39] However, it is impossible to manipulate the sensory into a 'cure'. As Huysmans demonstrates in À rebours, reactions to sensory stimulations are involuntary, causing uncontrollable mental associations. The rooms of the villa are not sealed and separate, but are permeated by the sense-impressions Des Esseintes carries with him from room to room. In Des Esseintes's retreat, the worldly and the spiritual are united in the realm of the senses. However, in his Durtal tetralogy, Huysmans moves away from a depiction of sensory experimentation and aesthetic excess, towards an exploration of religious salvation and the realities of a monastic lifestyle.[40] Huysmans's search for spiritual transcendence finally replaces his obsession with 'worldly' sensual extremes.

Notes to Chapter 4

1. Photographs of Huysmans in his apartment form part of the pioneering series of famous figures by Dornac (pseudonym of Paul Cardon), *Nos contemporains chez eux* [*Our Contemporaries at Home*], c. 1887 to 1917. Three albums of these photographs are held by the Bibliothèque nationale de France, and illustrate the fashion for photographing writers and artists in their homes.
2. The 'Academy Portrait', written by 'One Who Knows Him', was published in the 22 October 1898 issue of the *Academy*, 131–32 (p. 132).
3. All parenthetical page references in this chapter to Huysmans's works are to Lucien Descaves's 18-volume edition of the *Œuvres complètes* (Paris: Crès, 1928–34), and, unless otherwise stated, to vol. VII: *À rebours*. Translations into English are taken, and sometimes adapted, from Robert Baldick's *Against Nature* (London: Penguin, 1959).
4. David Weir, *Decadence and the Making of Modernism* (Amherst: University of Massachusetts Press, 1995), p. 96.
5. Des Esseintes's retreat echoes Huysmans's relocation to Fontenay in 1881 in order to convalesce. For three months, Huysmans commuted from the pseudo-countryside of Fontenay-aux-Roses to Paris and during this period he worked on *À Vau-l'eau* [*With the Flow*] (1882).
6. Jules Bois first used this phrase in 'Les Guérisons par la pensée', *La Revue*, 35 (1900), 16–33 (p. 29).
7. In a letter to Zola (dated 25 May 1884), Huysmans explained how he had used medical textbooks throughout *À rebours* in order to be exact in his descriptions of Des Esseintes's symptoms — 'J'ai pas à pas suivi les livres de Bouchut et d'Axenfeld sur la névrose' [I followed step by step the books of Bouchet and Axenfeld on neurosis]. *Lettres inédites à Émile Zola*, ed. by Pierre Lambert (Geneva: Droz, 1953), p. 103.

8. Joseph Halpern, 'Decadent Narrative: A rebours', *Stanford French Review*, 2 (Spring 1978), 91–102 (p. 95).
9. See Richard E. Cytowic, David M. Eagleman, and Dmitri Nabokov, *Wednesday is Indigo Blue: Discovering the Brain of Synesthesia* (Cambridge, MA: MIT Press, 2009).
10. Alfred Carter, *The Idea of Decadence in French Literature, 1830–1900* (Toronto: University of Toronto Press, 1958), p. 85.
11. Michael Riffaterre, 'Decadent Features in Maeterlinck's Poetry', *Language and Style*, 7 (Winter, 1974), 3–19 (p. 6).
12. George Cevasco, *The Breviary of the Decadence: J.-K. Huysmans's A rebours and English Literature* (New York: AMS Press, 2001), p. 5.
13. Walter Benjamin, 'Paris, Capital of the Nineteenth Century, Exposé <of 1939>', *The Arcades Project*, trans. by Howard Eiland and Kevin McLaughlin (Cambridge: Harvard University Press, 1999), p. 20.
14. Gail Finney, 'In the Naturalist Grain: Huysmans's "A rebours" Viewed through the Lens of Zola's "Germinal"', *Modern Language Studies*, 16 (Spring 1986), 71–77 (p. 73).
15. Robert de Montesquiou, *Les Pas effacés: Mémoires*, 3 vols (Paris: Émile-Paul Frères, 1923), II, 94.
16. Willa Z. Silverman, 'Unpacking His Library: Robert de Montesquiou and the Esthetics of the Book in *Fin-de-siècle* France', in *The New Bibliopolis: French Book-collectors and the Culture of Print, 1880–1914* (Toronto: University of Toronto Press, 2008), pp. 141–64 (p. 155).
17. Silverman, 'Unpacking His Library', p. 155.
18. Charles Baudelaire,'Correspondances', *Les Fleurs du mal*, 1857, in *Œuvres complètes*, 5 vols (Paris: Michel Lévy frères, 1868–69), I (1868), 92. Translations are adapted from *The Flowers of Evil*, trans. by James McGowan (Oxford: Oxford University Press, 1998).
19. In his novella *La Fanfarlo* (1847), Baudelaire was the first to use the hothouse in a literary context to describe the bedroom of the dancer Fanfarlo. His interest in this motif is continued in his later prose poetry, with 'La Chambre double' [The Double Room] (first published 1862) explicitly drawing upon 'des sensations de serre chaude' [hothouse sensations]. See 'La Chambre double' in *Le Spleen de Paris: Petits Poèmes en Prose*, *Œuvres complètes* (1869), IV, 12–16.
20. 'La Mort des amants' [The Death of Lovers], from *Les Fleurs du mal*, also contains in the first stanza the description of 'd'étranges fleurs' [strange flowers] that blossom under the 'cieux plus beaux' [most beautiful heavens]. In this harmonious and redolent environment there is a correspondence between colour and scent that enables the lovers to be united in the moment of death. 'La Mort des amants', in *Les Fleurs du mal*, p. 339.
21. Grant Allen, *The Colour-Sense: Its Origin and Development* (London: Trübner and Company, 1879), p. 226.
22. Judith Ryan, *The Vanishing Subject — Early Psychology and Literary Modernism* (London: University of Chicago Press, 1991), p. 43.
23. In this instance Huysmans's sentence structure, which leads the reader to connect *Albane* with apoplexy and *Aurora borealis* with chlorosis, is incorrect. It is the *Albane* that appears bloodless and the *Aurora borealis* that is deep red in colour.
24. Angela Nuccitelli, '*A rebours* — Symbol of the Femme-Fleur: A Key to Des Esseintes's Obsession', *Symposium*, 23 (1975), 336–44.
25. Bettina L. Knapp, 'Huysmans's *Against the Grain*: The Willed Exile of the Introverted Decadent', *Nineteenth-Century French Studies*, 20 (Fall-Winter, 1991–92), 203–21 (p. 217).
26. Ruth Antosh, *Reality and Illusion in the Novels of J.-K. Huysmans* (Amsterdam: Rodopi, 1986), p. 89.
27. This is a technique learned from Émile Zola. In *La Curée* [The Kill] (1871), the hothouse is a setting for clandestine and heated romances. His descriptions of the hothouse flowers foreshadow Huysmans's *À rebours*, and Zola describes the Caladiums as evoking 'la brutalité de caresses sanglantes' [the brutality of bloody caresses]. *La Curée* (Paris: A. Lacroix, Verboeckhoven et Cie, 1871), p. 128.
28. In 1838, the French dermatologist Phillippe Ricord (1800–89) defined the different stages of the disease — primary, secondary and tertiary.
29. Marbled endpapers were common in book binding at the end of the nineteenth century. Damask

is a rich decoration of elaborate patterns on silk or paper, originating from Damascus. By the 1700s, weavers in Lyon, France, made the design and process popular with French aristocrats. See Dard Hunter, *Papermaking: History and Technique of an Ancient Craft,* 2nd edn (New York: Alfred A. Knopf, 1947).

30. Camille Paglia, *Sexual Personae: Art and Decadence from Nefertiti to Emily Dickinson* (London; New York: Penguin Books, 1990), p. 434.
31. Ruth Weinreb, 'Structural Techniques in *À rebours*', *The French Review,* 49 (December 1975), 222–33 (p. 223).
32. The title, *En rade,* evokes a temporary home, a refuge rather than just a retreat. This ambiguity is suggested in the translations of the title as *Becalmed* (1993), *A Haven* (1999) and *Stranded* (2010) by Terry Hale, Rachel Ashton, and Brendan King, respectively.
33. Huysmans, *En rade,* in *Œuvres complètes,* IX.
34. Huysmans, *Là-bas,* in *Œuvres complètes,* XII.
35. Oscar Wilde, *The Picture of Dorian Gray* (1891; Harmondsworth: Penguin, 1979), p. 149.
36. Wilde, *The Picture of Dorian Gray,* pp. 150–56.
37. However, this 'poisonous book' is not simply an intertextual reference to *À rebours*. As Petra Dierkes-Thrun discusses in Chapter 3 (pp. 51–65), Wilde is also alluding to Rachilde's *Monsieur Vénus* (1884). Wilde, *The Picture of Dorian Gray,* p. 140.
38. Arthur Symons, 'The Later Huysmans', *The Symbolist Movement in Literature* (1899; New York: E. P. Dutton, 1919), p. 265.
39. Wilde, *The Picture of Dorian Gray,* p. 204.
40. This tetralogy describes the spiritual progress of Durtal from Satanism to Catholicism. It begins with *Là-bas* (1891), and is followed by *En route* (1895), *La Cathédrale* (1898) and *L'Oblat* (1903). The final novel is set in the Benedictine monastery of Ligugé, near where Huysmans lived from 1899–1901.

CHAPTER 5

'All the senses would melt into one': Theodore Watts-Dunton's *Aylwin* and the Decadent Pleasures of the *Roman-à-clef*

Angela Dunstan

1882 saw the death of one of the Victorian era's most distinctively decadent figures. Notorious for his chloral drinking, velvet wearing, wombat collecting, and scandalous exhumation of his late wife, Dante Gabriel Rossetti was a favourite of the celebrity-centric Victorian public. Sixteen years after his death, the *Athenæum* reflected on the eccentric poet-painter's charisma, embodied in the very sound of his voice:

> It seemed as if in his very name there was an unaccountable music. The present writer well remembers being at a dinner-party many years ago when the late Lord Leighton was talking in his usual delightful way. His conversation was specially attended to only by his interlocutor, until the name of Rossetti fell from his lips. Then the general murmur of tongues ceased. Everybody wanted to hear what was being said about the mysterious poet-painter. Thus matters stood when Rossetti died. Within forty-eight hours of his death the many-headed beast clamoured for its rights. Within forty-eight hours of his death there was a leading article in an important newspaper on the subject of his suspiciousness as the result of chloral-drinking. And from that moment the romance has been rubbed off the picture as effectually by many of those who have written about him as the bloom is fingered off of a clumsily gathered peach.[1]

If the romance was rubbed off Rossetti, it was not for lack of protective impulse on the part of Theodore Watts-Dunton, who had struggled to defend Rossetti's reputation since penning his friend's eulogy. 'Though written many years ago', explained Watts-Dunton in his introduction to the 1901 edition of *Aylwin*, 'this story was, for certain personal reasons easy to guess, withheld from publication — withheld, as *The Times* pointed out, because 'with the *Dichtung* was mingled a good deal of *Wahrheit*'.[2] This tension between poetry and truth permeates all fiction inspired by real-world personalities, but it was amplified in the case of *Aylwin* by the fact that Watts-Dunton was an intimate of Rossetti, the poet-painter his *roman-à-clef* reimagined. Watts-Dunton's novel tapped into the late nineteenth-century desire to see, hear, smell, and touch the real-world celebrity author, even beyond the grave.

Aylwin has not been considered in the context of Decadence, somewhat surprisingly. The novel's most obvious links to the movement are its author's close friendships with Decadent icons Dante Gabriel Rossetti and Algernon Charles Swinburne. However *Aylwin*'s key concerns are also decidedly decadent in nature; several doomed romances foiled by otherworldly interventions, an exhumation, Romany mysticism, spiritualism, mesmerism, animal magnetism, opium use, degeneration of body and mind, homoerotic tension, a preoccupation with aesthetics and even self-flagellation with a cursed Gnostic cross. In addition to subject matter and style, this essay will argue, *Aylwin* may be productively read as a Decadent text in its form: the *roman-à-clef*.

Aylwin is a unique, pleasurable, and decadent intervention in this genre. Through its transparency as a *roman-à-clef*, and its extra-textual materials which proliferated with each new edition, *Aylwin* experiments with and transforms the genre from a guilty pleasure into a decadent one; a pleasurable immersion in its celebrity subject. *Aylwin* was renowned for capturing the essence of Rossetti through the character D'Arcy where other contemporary attempts failed or indeed parodied their subject. By ventriloquizing Rossetti from beyond the grave, *Aylwin* invited a particularly pleasurable confusion between truth and poetry, reality and fiction, and between the very senses themselves.

This essay takes the form of a textual experiment. How might considering *Aylwin* in the context of Decadence enrich and consolidate our understanding of a perplexing Victorian bestseller? Might this experiment be a useful way to reconceptualize and contextualize this surprising literary sensation? I will suggest that the novel's decadence is threefold: *Aylwin* fictionalizes Decadent real-world figures, in a Decadent prose narrative, and provides a Decadent reading experience in which the reader's participation in the decoding of the *roman-à-clef* becomes a sensual aestheticized pleasure in itself.

Guilty Pleasures: *Aylwin*, Decadence and the *Roman-à-clef*

First published in October 1898, *Aylwin* was an instant success. 'We can recall no study of the love-passion that can compare with "Aylwin"', wrote the *Star* reviewer, 'It declines to be classed. It is of no school. It owns no lineage, acknowledges no tradition'.[3] Such hyperbolic reviews typified the novel's critical reception, which was paralleled by its popular success. Nine editions were published within two months,[4] and by 1914 *Aylwin* was in its twenty-sixth edition, having sold over one hundred thousand copies.[5]

Despite its remarkable contemporary critical and popular acclaim, the novel has received only limited attention since the early twentieth century. Like the very genre of the *roman-à-clef*, scholars have hesitated to confidently classify *Aylwin*.[6] Indeed, the novel's success may seem perplexing to the modern reader who unearths only glimpses of what contemporary critics praised as the 'vivid, enthralling, absorbing love story, full of movement and life and vigour'.[7] Scholarship on *Aylwin* has largely centred on its Romany and Celtic themes and, most recently in Catherine Maxwell's illuminating work, its Romantic inheritance.[8] Part of *Aylwin*'s challenge is its generic instability; the almost ethnographic documentation of Romany and Celtic traditions jars with the sentimental portraits of its Romany heroines, whilst the supernatural and spiritual concerns sit uncomfortably with the novel's preoccupation with a recently deceased real-world celebrity poet-painter. The *Star* reviewer was indeed correct: the novel declines to be classed.

The novel can, however, be classified generically as a *roman-à-clef* and this is an underestimated source of its popular success. Watts-Dunton undeniably exploited the contemporary fascination with the late Rossetti, and his representations of the Rossetti-inspired character D'Arcy revel in a strikingly decadent sensuousness that has thus far gone unrecognized in criticism. A much-maligned and critically-neglected genre, the *roman-à-clef* also requires reconsideration — largely on account of its popularity, which has seen it overlooked as a genre. Barthes reminds us that a popular text is often a productive text:

> There are those who want a text [...] without a shadow, without the 'dominant ideology'; but this is to want a text without fecundity, without productivity, a sterile text [...]. The text needs its shadow: this shadow IS *a bit* of ideology, *a bit* of representation, *a bit* of subject: ghosts, pockets, traces, necessary clouds: subversion must produce its own chiaroscuro.[9]

Aylwin encourages its reader to revel in the chiaroscuro of this subversive genre; to touch the past and consume the Decadent celebrity poet-painter through the *roman-à-clef*. Part of the reader's loss in consuming *Aylwin* is the realization that their decoding of the novel doubles others' readings. 'A certain pleasure is derived from a way of imagining oneself as *individual*, of inventing a final, rarest fiction: the fictive identity', writes Barthes. 'This fiction is no longer the illusion of a unity; on the contrary, it is the theatre of society in which we stage our plural: our pleasure is *individual* — but not personal.'[10] Similarly, the reader's relationship with the novel's tragic figure D'Arcy is predicated on their individual conceptions of the character's real-world counterpart, Rossetti. Each reader's realization that D'Arcy is a fictionalized Rossetti therefore hinges on Barthes's notion of the individual in the theatre of society; each individual reader relates to the celebrity figure as 'other', and experiences the revelation as an individual — though not a personal — member of society's audience. The pleasurable process of reading as decoding occurs on a similarly individual basis, with each reader revelling in the illusion that they are individually unlocking a secret identity that allows them to touch that figure.

Despite its popularity the late Victorian *roman-à-clef* is surprisingly under-theorized as a genre, and particularly in terms of the affective pleasures of reading: the cumulative pleasure of decoding textual clues to unmask a recognizable real-world individual camouflaged in the otherwise fictive text. Where earlier *romans-à-clef* depicting the Pre-Raphaelite and aesthetic circles, such as Averil Beaumont's *Thornicroft's Model* (1873) and Vernon Lee's *Miss Brown* (1884), had ostracized the very circles that had inspired them, *Aylwin* was celebrated for capturing the essence of Rossetti through the character D'Arcy. In *Aylwin*, the *roman-à-clef* becomes a genre of Decadent pleasure. Sean Latham, in his book *Modernism, Libel Law and the Roman-à-clef*, argues that despite scholarly neglect of the *roman-à-clef* 'this mode of writing nonetheless played a generative albeit unexamined role in the twentieth-century renovation of the novel, providing a passage beyond Victorian realism and into a far murkier field where fact and fiction pleasurably — and sometimes dangerously — intertwine'.[11] Central to Decadent reading is 'the idea of the dialogic relationship between the writer and the ideal reader [which] was ubiquitous at the time; in England, Vernon Lee, Walter Pater and Oscar Wilde all addressed this issue repeatedly in both fiction and criticism'.[12] This dialogic relationship is equally integral to the *roman-à-clef*; the complete appreciation of the form is dependent on the initiated reader's decoding the fictional character's real-world identity. This becomes explicit in *Aylwin*, where the novel's many editions regularly contained extra-textual material reflecting on the novel's real-world inspiration, as will be explored later. Such prefaces and appendices effectively divert the reader's attention away from the overtly fictional body of the novel itself: a constituent characteristic of Decadent texts. Shafquat Towheed argues that, in Decadent novels, 'part of the text dominates the volume, or even the author's entire oeuvre, invariably results in renewed disappointment, and often precludes, rather than facilitates, an actual reading, or re-reading, of the book at hand.'[13] Quite separately from the climax of the narrative itself, the reader experiences an affective climax in untangling the interplay between the fictional and the real worlds during the process of decoding the *roman-à-clef*'s characters; first, elation at successful unveiling of a real world identity, followed by a sense of loss in the knowledge that the first reading can never be recuperated. The real-world identity, once discovered, cannot be unlearned. Yet this volatility is pivotal to the pleasure of the *roman-à-clef*. Barthes alerts us to the precariousness of textual pleasure: 'everyone can testify that the pleasure of the text is not certain: nothing says that this same text will please us a second time'.[14] This is even more the case in the reading of the *roman-à-clef*, particularly one which exhumes the recently deceased.

As the largely negative reception of other Victorian *romans-à-clef* demonstrated, there were implicit standards for the acceptable appropriation of public personae, as well as expectations as to the suitability of the author to recreate or replicate the renowned subject. Like Vernon Lee's *Miss Brown*, *Aylwin* generated much musing surrounding the real-world 'identity', or 'originals' as the contemporary press referred to them, of the fictional characters.[15] Whilst periodical reviewers were confident in their identification of real-world counterparts to the characters featured in parodies of the Pre-Raphaelites such as *Miss Brown*, they approached the Rossetti-inspired elements of *Aylwin* only obliquely. 'It is not necessary to hint at the persons whose influence on the story may be felt, if not seen.'[16] One of the first reviews of *Aylwin* even suggested that Watts-Dunton had written about Rossetti unconsciously, because of his close association with the late poet-painter. 'For a long time Mr. Watts-Dunton's circle of friends has comprised all that was and is most interesting in the literary and artistic worlds', wrote the *Athenæum* critic, 'For him to write intimately about himself seemed almost like writing intimately about great poets and painters with whom he has lived on terms of more than brotherly closeness and confidence. And it was an axiom of Sir Walter Scott's that it is not easy for a novelist to delineate characters in entire independence of the people by whom he has been impressed.'[17] The review further suggested that Watts-Dunton's fictionalization of celebrity figures 'although easily recognized by the initiated, will be unfamiliar to the general reader', extending the concept of *Aylwin* as a coded work inaccessible to the uninitiated by refusing to name Rossetti. Instead, he is elusively portrayed as 'an eccentric man of genius, respected and admired and beloved by the men of genius among whom he moved, the nature of which is brought out in Mr. Watts-Dunton's description of the painter's designs.'[18]

Many such reviews, which positioned *Aylwin* as a form of cryptically coded secret history, would have been written by friends and associates not just of aesthetic circles but of Watts-Dunton, a respected critic himself. Unlike Lee's *Miss Brown*, Watts-Dunton's more subtle representation left even the closest of Pre-Raphaelite associates guessing as to certain characters' real-world counterparts. Despite attempts to identify an 'original' for each dominant character, such as Thomas Hake's 1902 'Key To Aylwin', the work was carefully constructed by Watts-Dunton to resist such interpretation. Writing to Watts-Dunton with a critique of the early manuscript of *Aylwin* in 1883, Ford Madox Brown commented that 'certainly Wilderspin is a quite original character', questioning 'Is he not intentionally compounded out of Rossetti and Shields? The pictures are Rossetti's and the clothes Shields.'[19] It was precisely this indistinct yet permeating influence of Rossetti, identifiable throughout *Aylwin*, which prevented a definitive identification of anyone but D'Arcy as Rossetti, leaving much to his readership's interpretation and thus allowing Watts-Dunton to reimagine Rossetti 'without peril to the peace of those among whom he moved'.[20] In any case, the publication of a novel sure to generate excessive publicity merely on account of the inspiration for its characters resonates with Hake and Compton-Rickett's belief that 'Watts-Dunton certainly cultivated the mystery surrounding *Aylwin*'.[21]

The Coming of *Aylwin*

Decadent writing and decadent living do not necessarily go hand in hand, as Dennis Denisoff reminds us, and this was certainly true in Watts-Dunton's case. A central though sensible figure in Aesthetic and Decadent circles, Watts-Dunton is perhaps best remembered for his caretaking of Swinburne. Watts-Dunton similarly protected Rossetti both in life and death. Watts-Dunton met Rossetti in his capacity as solicitor, shortly after Rossetti's mental breakdown in 1872, and quickly became a close friend and confidante of the increasingly paranoid poet-painter. Watts-Dunton himself has been remembered not for his literary achievements but for his famous friendships with Rossetti and Swinburne,[22] or as one critic expressed it, his 'dead friend' and his 'living friend'.[23] Watts-Dunton's biographers have defined his life by his capacity for friendship and self-sacrifice. 'Watts-Dunton's life work was not literature nor poetry, but friendship', wrote Coulson Kernahan:

> His best books stand upon our shelves in every part of the English-speaking world, but the name that appears upon the cover is not that of Theodore Watts-Dunton, but of Dante Gabriel Rossetti and Algernon Charles Swinburne. He wrote no Life of either, but how much of their life and of their life's best work we owe to Watts-Dunton, we shall never know [...]. Cheerfully and uncomplainingly Watts-Dunton gave his own life and his own life's work for them, and his own best book is the volume of his devotion to his friends.[24]

Kernahan's account typifies the biographical treatment of Watts-Dunton: Hall Caine and William Michael Rossetti reporting that Rossetti himself had, in his dying breath, called him 'a hero of friendship'.[25] Watts-Dunton's influence over the notoriously difficult personalities of Rossetti and Swinburne was substantial and it was remarkable, as Kernahan observed, 'That any one man should so completely control, and even dominate, two such intellects as Swinburne and Rossetti'.[26] W. Robertson Nicoll concurred, writing 'Very few have been brought into such close relations with dominating minds, but the citadel of his thought has remained inviolate'.[27] Watts-Dunton's guardianship of Rossetti's posthumous reputation proved an extension of the loyal friendship he exhibited throughout Rossetti's later years.

Watts-Dunton was, however, more than merely a devoted friend; indeed, his is a key and neglected Victorian critical voice. He had become the *Examiner's* pre-eminent poetry critic in 1874, and he wrote consistently for the *Athenæum* throughout the final quarter of the century. Swinburne called him 'the first critic of our time, perhaps the largest-minded and surest-sighted of any age', and Richard le Gallienne was rumoured to have bought the *Encyclopaedia Britannica* purely for Watts-Dunton's entry on poetry.[28]

Yet, it was not until his 1897 collection of poetry, *The Coming of Love*, that Watts-Dunton published a substantial literary work in his own name. He had, however, held off publishing *Aylwin* for almost twenty years. Watts-Dunton dismissed this delay as being due 'simply [to] diffidence', yet an examination of his writings about biography indicates that his reasoning related to his protectiveness of Rossetti's memory. Watts-Dunton had been instrumental in defending Rossetti in the periodical press, publishing anonymous articles and rallying his literary contacts to debate the ethics of biography; particularly the biography of a deceased subject.

Sensing the Dead: *Aylwin* as Celebrity Sensorium

Like his Decadent peers Swinburne and Wilde, Watts-Dunton expressed multiple, frequently conflicting viewpoints on the question of the author as a public figure for the public's consumption. Watts-Dunton clearly resented the public for creating a market for scandal-mongering biographies, and frequently invoked Rossetti to sanction his own views. 'That mysterious entity "the public", would no doubt, like to get [a Rossetti biography]', he wrote,

> but we have always shared Rossetti's own opinion that a man of genius is no more the property of the 'public' than is any private gentleman; and we have always felt with him that the prevalence in our time of the opposite opinion has fashioned so intolerable a yoke for the neck of any one who has had the misfortune to pass from the sweet paradise of obscurity into the vulgar purgatory of Fame, that it almost behoves a man of genius to avoid, if he can, passing into the purgatory at all.[29]

The public's guilty consumption of the dead celebrity figure became a preoccupation for Watts-Dunton. This guilty consumption also characterizes the genre of the *roman-à-clef*: what Latham calls a 'reviled and disruptive literary form, thriving as it does on duplicity and an appetite for scandal'.[30]

Watts-Dunton's representations of Rossetti as D'Arcy in *Aylwin* revelled in a striking decadent sensuousness that has gone unrecognized in criticism. In its representation the novel reimagines the decline of the great poet-painter, aligning the novel with the very definition of decadence: 'the process of falling away or declining (from a prior state of excellence, vitality, prosperity)'.[31] For contemporary critics and readers of *Aylwin*, the strength of Watts-Dunton's portrayal of his Rossetti-inspired character D'Arcy outweighed the extremely minor role he plays in the novel. In fact, Rossetti even haunts the work from *without*, from its poetic dedicatory sonnet, titled 'D.G.R.',[32] to the Rossetti-themed appendices which multiply with the publication of new editions of *Aylwin*, evidencing the predominance of a very minor part of the text. Accordingly, reviews of *Aylwin* reflect a preoccupation with Rossetti as the character D'Arcy's real-world counterpart. The *Daily News*, for example, praised the representation of D'Arcy as 'a glittering picture of [...] the mighty dead who but yesterday [was] the mighty living, and who [is] still of the freshest mintage of memory, great painters who were also great thinkers with the great thoughts which were the medium in which their spirits moved.'[33] Such reviews certainly demonstrate the centrality of Rossetti's spectral presence to the novel's persistent contemporary popularity. This continuum of spiritual influence which is so idiosyncratically presented throughout the novel is epitomized by the revivification of Rossetti as the character D'Arcy in *Aylwin*.

Watts-Dunton took great care in preparing new editions of *Aylwin*, writing frequently to his publishers regarding changes he wished to incorporate and taking great pride in *Aylwin*'s new incarnations. In 1914, he wrote to William Michael Rossetti of his changes to the new edition. 'I will seize this opportunity of sending you a copy of the *Illustrated Aylwin*, just out', he wrote,

> because I want you to read the 2 appendices which distinguish this edition from all others. Appendix I. contains something about Swinburne which I should like you to read. Appendix II. contains a reprint of certain articles, which appeared in 1902 in *Notes & Queries*, discussing some of the characters in the novel.[34]

Perhaps with the dismal reception of Lee's *Miss Brown* in mind, Watts-Dunton was concerned to present D'Arcy as a three-dimensional tribute to Rossetti, as is suggested by the content and unequivocal title of Appendix I: 'In Defence of a Great and Beloved Poet whose Character is Delineated in this Story' (p. 491). In this appendix, Watts-Dunton's comparison of Rossetti to Napoleon typifies the honorific tone of all his writing about Rossetti. 'To describe the magnetism of such a man is, of course, impossible', explained Watts-Dunton,

> It would seem, however, that there is another kind of demonic power — the power of shedding quite unconsciously one's personality upon all brought into contact with it. The demonic power of Rossetti, like that of D'Arcy in this story, was quite unconscious. In Rossetti's presence, as in D'Arcy's, it was impossible not to yield to this strange, mysterious power. (p. 496)

Watts-Dunton's belief in the catalysing force of D'Arcy's/Rossetti's 'demonic power' becomes obsessive and he repeats the phrase like a mantra: 'Without D'Arcy, indeed, and the demonic power possessed by him, the story would have no existence' (p. 497). This implicitly reflects Watts-Dunton's recognition that his story would not exist but for Rossetti, also demonstrating his awareness of the primary source of his own fame. The majority of periodical reviews refer, albeit obliquely, to the shadow that the memory of Rossetti cast across the novel. W. L. Courtney's 'Books of the Day' column in the *Daily Telegraph* praised 'the value of its contemporary portraits', whilst *Lloyd's Weekly Newspaper* even invoked the authority of the long-dead Rossetti to praise 'the magic music of [Watts-Dunton's] verse [that] so charmed Dante Gabriel Rossetti that he pronounced one sonnet, "Stars in the River", the most beautiful of the Doppelgänger legend, and intended to make it the subject of a picture.'[35]

In addition to the influence of Rossetti, contemporary reviews certainly suggest the centrality of the Welsh and Romany elements for which the work has been remembered as a source of its popularity, with the senses again playing a primary part. *Lloyd's Weekly Newspaper* praised the novel's 'Welsh scenery [...] seen and pictured as only a poet can see and picture it',[36] and the *Athenæum* marvelled at 'the exposition [...] of the influence of Romany blood on its possessors and their surroundings'.[37] The fact that *Aylwin*'s sequel *The Coming of Love* continued the gypsy storyline rather than resurrecting that of Rossetti's fictional counterpart suggests either that *Aylwin*'s popularity stemmed primarily from its Romany characters and Welsh setting, or that Watts-Dunton felt that his original portrayal of D'Arcy/Rossetti could not be replicated. Catherine Maxwell identifies *Aylwin*'s spiritual message as central to its success, considering it 'likely that the non-sectarian, generalized and positive religious message of the book, attesting the spiritual power of nature, life beyond the grave, and a love that defies death, appealed to a large number of readers who may no longer have felt able to believe in orthodox Christianity.'[38] Certainly, recurring themes of supernaturalism, mysticism, animal magnetism and mesmerism appealed to late nineteenth-century audiences engaged with the sensory and extra-sensory.

Critics concurred that in *Aylwin* Watts-Dunton had produced what 'the Welsh nation has accepted [...] as the representative Welsh novel'.[39] Watts-Dunton was soon considered an authority on the Celtic and the Romany, writing such pieces as the Introduction to the Everyman edition of George Borrow's *Wild Wales* (1906). Whilst the small body of scholarship on *Aylwin* has considered such themes in detail, any consideration of the Celtic and the Romany is augmented by acknowledging the centrality of these themes to the representation of Rossetti in *Aylwin*, with Watts-Dunton's fictional representation of Rossetti as exotic ethnic outsider. In the English imagination, the Welsh, like the gypsies, 'hovered on the outskirts of the English world, unassimilable, a domestic and visible but socially peripheral character.'[40] By virtue of his Italian heritage, Rossetti occupied this same liminal space between Englishman and foreigner, insider and outsider. Deborah Epstein Nord has written of gypsy kidnapping in literature as a 'trope for representing — and indeed accounting for — anomalous types within a homogenous and insular middle-class English world.'[41] Throughout *Aylwin*, the Romany is constructed as representative of this liberating alternative of recognizing the untamed other even within oneself: even in the quintessentially English character of Henry Aylwin. 'In

Aylwin the temperament of the gipsy is at war with the intellect of the cultivated Englishman', wrote an *Athenæum* reviewer, 'and, in the end, the Romany in him prevails.'[42] Ian Duncan has similarly written of the late nineteenth-century preoccupation with the Celtic. 'It is relatively easy to decode many of the later works in the tradition', he explains, 'as they play out the fantasy of a libertarian disengagement from modern life [...]. The nomad clearly represents a sentimental alternative — fulfilling the decorum of pastoral — to those regimented identities proposed by a civil society and an industrial economy.'[43] Throughout *Aylwin*, Watts-Dunton identifies Wales as a type of spiritual home for the disillusioned Englishman or an exotic alternative to those who reject the way of mainstream materialism. Continuing this theme in his Introduction to Borrow's *Wild Wales*, Watts-Dunton wrote that 'It is the blood in a man's veins, it is not the spot in which he is born, that decides the question of his race', later rhetorically questioning 'Does one call the Rossettis Londoners, because it was in London, and not in Italy, that they were born?'[44] In drawing this explicit and unlikely parallel between the Romany-Welsh and Rossetti, Watts-Dunton figured his fictional incarnation of Rossetti within the insider/outsider paradigm that was well-established within English literature.

Sights and Sounds: Writing D'Arcy, Righting Rossetti

The most graphic vignettes in *Aylwin* are filtered through the senses — the smell of D'Arcy's tobacco, the sound of his mesmeric voice, dreadful sights 'unutterable and intolerable', the taste of food cooked by the 'tanned fingers' of Aylwin's love Winifred, the touch — real and imagined — of the longed-for lover. The narrative strives to extend beyond the senses, grasping for experience beyond the sensory to that which would defy description itself. Aylwin himself is frequently struck by the inadequacy of words to capture 'sensation such as I cannot describe' (p. 89). Indeed, his spiritual bond to the long-dead Romany beauty Fenella Stanley is first experienced as great relief at her having articulated what he cannot: the 'Nature-ecstasy' he has experienced but has been unable to express. Her written reflections in family papers 'came upon me like a revelation, for it was the first time I had ever seen embodied in words the sensations which used to come to me in Graylingham Wood or on the river that ran through it' (p. 32). Aylwin then describes his own synaesthetic experience of 'Nature-ecstasy', which he experiences as a unification of the senses:

> The wheels of thought would stop; all the senses would melt into one, and I would float on a tide of unspeakable joy, a tide whose waves were waves neither of colour, nor perfume, nor melody, but new waters born of the mixing of these; and through a language deeper than words and deeper than thoughts, I would seem carried at last close to an actual consciousness — a consciousness which, to my childish dreams, seemed drawing me close to the bosom of a mother whose face would brighten into that of Fenella. (p. 32)

This particular representation of *Aylwin's* Decadent sensorium — in this case, an overwhelming and then an amalgamation of the senses which swells beyond the capacity of expression before returning Aylwin to childhood and to the literal and figurative mother figure — demonstrates the novel's preoccupation with the impossibility of accurately representing sensory experiences.

Sight and touch play particularly significant roles in the novel, both literally and conceptually. *Aylwin* traces the romance between Henry Aylwin, the son of a wealthy English landowner, and Winifred Wynne, who was raised by her aunt in Wales and visits her drunkard church custodian father once a year in England. Through a sequence of dramatic events, the lovers are separated and Winifred disappears in Wales. Aylwin embarks on an extended search for his love, assisted by a young headstrong gypsy woman Sinfi Lovell who secretly loves him, meeting various unusual characters along the way. One such personality is the charismatic artist D'Arcy, whose tragic loss of his beautiful wife has plunged him into depression. Yet the loss of his wife enables D'Arcy's empathetic counsel of the distraught Aylwin as he pursues his search for his own lost love. Despite a series of obstacles, false hopes and temporary despair, the lovers are eventually reunited and Sinfi sacrifices her love for Aylwin to secure his happiness with his beloved Winifred.

As the protagonist, Aylwin's sensitive descriptions prevail throughout. To read the character of D'Arcy through Aylwin's eyes is to engage in a homoerotic decadent sensorium. Aylwin himself provides, and indeed later demands, extremely precise physical descriptions of D'Arcy, as can be seen in one particular exemplary vignette. D'Arcy is depicted in painstaking detail in a manner that is paralleled only by Aylwin's portrayal of Winifred. This congruence with Aylwin's descriptions of his love interest suggests his homoerotic attraction to D'Arcy, with this decadent dynamic of attraction/revulsion seen in his invocation of contradictory analogies to describe his new friend. It is the sound of D'Arcy's voice that first attracts Aylwin:

> This voice, however, was not the one that had uttered the name of Wilderspin. It was from his companion, who sat opposite to him, with his great broad back, covered with a smart velvet coat, towards me, that the talk was now coming. This man was smoking cigarettes in that kind of furious sucking way which is characteristic of great smokers. Much smoking, however, had not dried up his skin to the consistence of blotting paper and the colour of tobacco ash as it does in some cases, but tobacco juice, which seemed to ooze from his face like perspiration, or rather like oil, had made his complexion of a yellow green colour, something like a vegetable marrow. Although his face was as hairless as a woman's, there was not a feature in it that was not masculine. Although his cheek-bones were high and his jaw was of the mould which we so often associate with the prizefighter, he looked as if he might somehow be a gentleman. And when I got for a moment a full view of his face as he turned round, I thought it showed power and intelligence, although his forehead receded a good deal, a recession which was owing mainly to the bone above the eyes. Power and intelligence too were seen in every glance of his dark bright eyes. (p. 222)

Watts-Dunton creates a remarkably unsettling characterization of D'Arcy which, in its combination of attractive and repulsive descriptions, paints an ambiguous and androgynous portrait. The negative suggestion — 'his face was as hairless as a woman's, there was not a feature in it that was not masculine' — powerfully suggests androgyny, and we are offered a catalogue of physical features, what William Greenslade has called elsewhere a 'decadence of detail'.[45] Arthur Symons, in his 1893 article 'The Decadent Movement in Literature', identifies the key notes of Decadence, and these are certainly present here: 'intense self-consciousness, a restless curiosity in research, an over-subtilizing refinement upon refinement, a spiritual and moral perversity'.[46] Winifred then offers Aylwin and the reader a more conventional portrayal of D'Arcy, which unequivocally invokes Rossetti:

> I suppose I must begin with his forehead then. It was almost of the tone of marble, and contrasted, but not too violently, with the thin crop of dark hair slightly curling round the temples, which were partly bald. The forehead in its form was so perfect that it seemed to shed its own beauty over all the other features; it prevented me from noticing, as I afterwards did, that these other features — the features below the eyes, were not themselves beautiful. The eyes, which looked at me through spectacles, were of a colour between hazel and blue-grey, but there were lights shining within them which were neither grey, nor hazel, nor blue — wonderful lights. And it was to these indescribable lights, moving and alive in the deeps of the pupils, that his face owed its extraordinary attractiveness. (pp. 420–21)

Winifred becomes increasingly aware of Aylwin's extraordinary interest in her description of her protector, whom Aylwin has clearly by this time identified as D'Arcy, and she playfully teases him by asking 'Have I sufficiently described him? Or am I to go on taking his face to pieces for you?' (p. 421), coyly questioning whether she should continue her anatomized description of D'Arcy. Aylwin is preoccupied with D'Arcy's mouth and laugh, which Winifred describes as unattractive:

> 'Well, then, between the eyes, across the top of the nose, where the bridge of the spectacles rested, there was a strongly marked indented line which had the appearance of having been made by long-continued pressure of the spectacle frame. Am I still to go on? [...] The beauty of the face, as I said before, was entirely confined to the upper portion. It did not extend lower than the cheekbones, which were well-shaped.'
> 'The mouth, Winnie? Describe that, and then I need not ask you his name, though perhaps you don't know it yourself.'
> 'A dark brown moustache covered the mouth. I have always thought that a mouth is unattractive if the lips are so close to the teeth that they seem to stick to them; and yet what a kind woman Mrs. Shales is, and her mouth is of this kind. But, on the other hand, where the space between the teeth and the lips is too great no mouth can be called beautiful, I think. Now though the mouth of the gentleman was not ill-cut, the lips were too far from the teeth, I thought; they were too loose, a little baggy, in short. And when he laughed—'
> 'What about that, Winnie? I specially want to know about his laugh.'
> 'Then I will tell you. When he laughed his teeth were a little too much seen; and this gave the mouth a somewhat satirical expression.' (p. 421)

Winifred's purposefully pedestrian description of D'Arcy is clearly eroticized and acts as a decadent strip-tease for an increasingly agitated Aylwin. Though focalized through the playful Winifred ostensibly for Aylwin's benefit, the unexpected — even grotesque — homoeroticism of the depiction seems to reflect Watts-Dunton's voice. Given the identification of Watts-Dunton with the character of Aylwin elsewhere, his excitement at the depiction of D'Arcy and, in particular, his oral fixation, suggest a parallel with Watts-Dunton and Rossetti which Watts-Dunton himself may not have intended.

Aylwin's sensorium is further heightened by opium and grief. In a plot twist reminiscent of Rossetti's exhumation of his late wife Elizabeth Siddal's body to retrieve a manuscript of his poems, Phillip Aylwin's tomb is robbed by 'some sacrilegious wretch' (p. 101). As it happens, it is violated by Winifred's father and Phillip Aylwin's curse falls upon poor Winifred. Aylwin is overcome with the shock of trying to hide from Winifred the truth of her father's deception and succumbs to a dreadful fever. When he wakes, he is told that Winifred is dead. Believing that he has lost his love, Aylwin descends into drug addiction and, like Rossetti, is warned by his doctor 'That drug of yours is the most dangerous narcotic of all. Increase your doses by a few more grains and you will lose all command over your nervous system — all presence of mind. Give it up, give it up' (p. 221). Though Aylwin shakes his opium addiction, he discovers yet another Rossetti-reminiscent distraction from his grief at the apparent loss of Winifred through developing a preoccupation with the supernatural, embarking on 'that great struggle between reason and the inherited instinct of superstition which afterwards played so important a part in my life' (pp. 83–84).

D'Arcy's conversation, when it leads to his lost love, invariably wavers into expressive silence, as when he begins to discuss 'my own condition on that never-to-be-forgotten night when she whom I lost...' (p. 472). D'Arcy is drawn to Aylwin as a fellow-sufferer and is almost obsessive in his proclamation that they 'must be friends', implicitly because of their mutual understanding of grief.

> Then springing up from the divan and laying his hand upon my shoulder, he said, 'And you have a great trouble at the heart. You have had some great loss the effect of which is sapping the very foundations of your life. We should be friends. We must be friends. I asked you to call upon me because we must be friends.'
> His voice was so tender that I was almost unmanned. (p. 231)

D'Arcy's spiritualism, like that of Rossetti, was spawned by his grief. He admits his mysticism like a guilty secret to Aylwin, 'As it is evident that we are going to be intimate friends, I may as well confess to you at once that I am a mystic' (p. 239). He directly links this spiritualism to his desire to make sense of the world in the wake of his love's death, viewing madness and corruption as the only option other than 'a spiritualistic theory of the universe' (p. 239).

> Any man who has passionately loved a woman and lost her; ask him at what moment mysticism was forced upon him — at what moment he felt that he must either accept a spiritualistic theory of the universe or go mad; ask him this, and he will tell you that it was at that moment when he first looked upon her as she lay dead, with Corruption's foul fingers waiting to soil and stain. (pp. 239–40)

D'Arcy's fascination with mysticism leads him to urge Aylwin to replace the Gnostic cross in his father's grave. He commands Aylwin to 'Put it back in the tomb [...]. There is the promise to the dead man or woman on whose breast it lay [...]. Promises to the dead must be kept to the letter, or no peace can come to the bereaved heart. You are talking to a man who *knows*!', concluding with the imperative 'You *will* replace the cross in that tomb' (p. 240). Similarly, it is D'Arcy's compulsion to present Winifred to the mesmerist Dr Mirvart which ensures her return to health. The novel's vexed depictions of materiality — its advocacy of the immaterial whilst fetishizing the beloved's body and its relics — forms yet another textual tension; one that is echoed in the book's production history, both as a collectable and an *objet d'art*.

Celebrity Sightings: Touching the Author

In the late nineteenth and early twentieth centuries, fame was mediated by the proliferation of material culture and the collecting impulse that accompanies the phenomenon of fandom. As one contemporary biographer expressed it, Rossetti's celebrity was such that '[he could] excite [the] practical kind of admiration' that inspired women to decorate their houses with antimacassars and fire-grates featuring Rossetti's 'singular circular initials'.[47] Accordingly, *Aylwin* became a desirable item of Rossettiana — a way of touching the dead author. Publishers capitalized on the novel's collectability by producing new editions featuring Rossetti-centric appendices and illustrations that were overseen by Watts-Dunton. For the Victorian collector of Rossettiana, owning multiple editions of *Aylwin* was another way of consuming the late celebrity poet-painter, particularly in those editions which encouraged a multi-media reading of the novel which further confused reality and fiction.

It is in the 1904 illustrated edition of *Aylwin* that D'Arcy's parallel with Rossetti becomes particularly manifest and their respective identities indistinguishable. In choosing to illustrate *Aylwin* with paintings of Pre-Raphaelite locations by artists associated with the Pre-Raphaelite circle, the edition escalated the work's mingling of life and art to confusing effect. For example, the illustrated edition displays May Morris's watercolour of Kelmscott Manor, the property her father William Morris had jointly leased with Rossetti in 1871 to conceal Rossetti's affair with her mother Jane. This real-world location finds its fictional parallel in D'Arcy's home 'Hurstcote'. This illustration of Hurstcote in *Aylwin* (Fig. 5.1) is accompanied by a caption that reads 'the country-house jointly occupied by Rossetti and William Morris in which takes place what has been called "the crucial scene in *Aylwin*"' (p. 497). This alignment of Rossetti with D'Arcy, and confusion of real-world locations with those of the novel, reveal the pleasurable slippage between reality and *Aylwin*'s imaginary world that the text encourages.

In the same edition, D'Arcy's London house is illustrated by the inclusion of the famous image of Rossetti's drawing room at 16 Cheyne Walk which had been painted by his pupil, Henry Treffry Dunn (Fig. 5.2). This is a significant visual reference to Rossetti, as it is the residence which had been associated with his more eccentric later years as he accumulated his private menagerie, and it is a painting that had been featured in many of the biographies of Rossetti since his death. In the illustration, Watts-Dunton is also portrayed listening to Rossetti as he reads what the illustration's caption tells us are his *Sonnets and Ballads* — the painting's subject, as its title implies, is the mesmeric sound of Rossetti's voice. The correlation of this illustration with the depiction of D'Arcy's home and menagerie in *Aylwin* creates a

Fig. 5.1. May Morris, *Kelmscott Manor*, n.d., watercolour on paper.

Fig. 5.2. Henry Treffry Dunn, *Dante Gabriel Rossetti; Theodore Watts-Dunton*, 1882, gouache and watercolour on paper, 54.3 × 81.9 cm. © National Portrait Gallery, London.

persuasive visual and literary confusion of art and life into which even the work's author is imaginatively inserted, emphasizing the instability with which Watts-Dunton, and by extension the reader, differentiates the living man from the fictional character. This parallel textual and visual confusion of life and art constitutes a playfully pleasurable confusion and consumption of Rossetti and D'Arcy for readers of the *roman-à-clef*. For collectors of *Aylwin*'s illustrated edition, the novel therefore provided multiple points of sensory access beyond merely reading the written text: the physical luxuriousness of the edition toyed with the readers' tactility, the lavish illustrations melded real and imaginary worlds. In this way *Aylwin*'s illustrated edition functioned as a multi-media publication; an item which, as Colligan and Linley have emphasized, 'permeated domestic space with the touch and smell of the physical artifact, the music of the words on the page, and the dual perspective of reading and gazing at images'.[48] The illustrated *Aylwin* therefore functions as the ultimate decadent sensorium, providing both an allegorical and a literal sensory experience for the reader.

Decadent Double Vision: Sensing the Past

Watts-Dunton questioned the ethics of biography in his 1916 memoir *Old Familiar Faces*, asking 'Can any biography, by whomsoever written, be other than inchoate and illusory — nay, can it fail to be fraught with danger to the memory of the dead, with danger to the peace of the living, until years have fully calmed the air around the dead man's grave?'[49] Perhaps, in resurrecting Rossetti to speak from beyond the grave through the mouth of D'Arcy, in granting Rossetti a Decadent literary afterlife, Watts-Dunton offered an ingenious answer to his own question. The character of D'Arcy is emblematic of the inexplicable magnetism the book itself exudes. The reader's unveiling of D'Arcy's real-world counterpart parallels Winifred's playfully anatomized description of D'Arcy for Wilderspin; the pleasure is derived in matching the description to its real-world correspondent.

In *Aylwin*, the book itself doubles as a fetishistic object just as D'Arcy is a shadow of Rossetti; the reader is a replica of other readers; the pleasures of decoding a mass reading rather than that of an individual. Just as *Aylwin*'s 'Nature-ecstasy' would see 'all the senses [...] melt into one', so the possible interpretations of *Aylwin* converge in the initiated reader's consumption of the novel as a decipherable *roman-à-clef*, inviting its readers to enjoy the pleasures of touching the decadent past.

Notes to Chapter 5

1. Anonymous, review of 'Letters of Dante Gabriel Rossetti to William Allingham, 1854–1870', *Athenæum* (26 March 1898), 395–96.
2. Theodore Watts-Dunton, *Aylwin* (London: Oxford University Press, 1914), p. xvii. I have relied on this World's Classics edition as it is the most complete in terms of supplementary material, and was published within Watts-Dunton's lifetime. Subsequent references are cited parenthetically.
3. Quoted in Hurst and Blackett advertisement for third edition of *Aylwin*, *Athenæum* (22 October 1898), 560.
4. Catherine Maxwell, 'Theodore Watts-Dunton's *Aylwin* (1898) and the Reduplications of Romanticism', *Yearbook of English Studies* 37 (January 2007), 1–22 (p. 4).
5. Ibid., p. 1.
6. Since James Douglas's 1904 publication *Theodore Watts-Dunton: Poet, Novelist, Critic*, the only dedicated scholarly consideration of *Aylwin* has been Catherine Maxwell's 2007 article 'Theodore Watts-Dunton's *Aylwin* (1898) and the Reduplications of Romanticism'.
7. Hurst and Blackett advertisement, p. 560.
8. See Catherine Maxwell, 'Theodore Watts-Dunton's *Aylwin* (1898) and the Reduplications of Romanticism', and her *Second Sight: The Visionary Imagination in Late Victorian Literature* (Manchester: Manchester University Press, 2011), particularly Chapter 4, 'Theodore Watts-Dunton's *Aylwin* and the Reduplications of Romanticism', pp. 166–96.
9. Roland Barthes, *The Pleasure of the Text*, trans. by Richard Miller (New York: Hill and Wang, 1998), p. 32.
10. Ibid., p. 62.
11. Sean Latham, *Modernism, The Art of Scandal: Libel Law and the Roman-à-clef* (Oxford: Oxford University Press), p. 7.
12. Shafquat Towheed, 'Containing the Poisonous Text: Decadent Readers, Reading Decadence', in *Decadences: Morality and Aesthetics in British Literature*, ed. by Paul Fox (Stuttgart: Ibidem, 2006), pp. 1–32 (pp. 4–5).
13. Ibid., p. 4.

14. Roland Barthes, *The Pleasure of the Text*, p. 52.
15. James Douglas, *Theodore Watts-Dunton: Poet, Novelist, Critic* (London: Hodder and Stoughton, 1904), p. 51.
16. Anonymous, '*Aylwin* By Theodore Watts-Dunton', *Athenæum* (22 October 1898), 561.
17. Ibid.
18. Ibid.
19. Letter from Ford Madox Brown to Theodore Watts-Dunton, 13 October 1883, in *Life and Letters of Theodore Watts-Dunton*, ed. by Thomas Hake and Arthur Compton-Rickett (London: T. C. and E. C. Jack, 1916), p. 125.
20. Theodore Watts-Dunton, *Old Familiar Faces* (London: H. Jenkins, 1916), p. 78. Whilst Rossetti was clearly the inspiration for D'Arcy, and Watts-Dunton largely identified as the model for Aylwin, other characters were much less recognizable. The inspiration for the character of Henry Aylwin's father, Phillip Aylwin, generated much debate. Originally thought to be Watts-Dunton's father, Douglas claims that the character was based on Watts-Dunton's beloved uncle, James Orlando Watts, who shaped Watts-Dunton's interest in mysticism. Wilderspin generated the greatest argument, with 'originals' suggested from Whistler to William Morris, however Watts-Dunton's friend Gordon Hake claimed the writer's brother, Alfred Eugene Watts, as the inspiration (James Douglas, *Theodore Watts-Dunton*, p. 88; Thomas Hake, 'Aylwin', *Notes and Queries* (7 June 1902), 451). This may well be the case, as Watts-Dunton had closely supervised Douglas's critical biography from which these 'solutions' to the characterization debate are sourced; either that or he decided to preserve the eclectic nature of the inspiration for his characterization.
21. *Life and Letters of Theodore Watts-Dunton*, ed. by Thomas Hake and Arthur Compton-Rickett, p. 69.
22. For biographical information on Watts-Dunton, see James Douglas, *Theodore Watts-Dunton: Poet, Novelist, Critic*, *Life and Letters of Theodore Watts-Dunton*, ed. by Thomas Hake and Arthur Compton-Rickett, Catherine Maxwell, 'Theodore Watts-Dunton's *Aylwin* (1898) and the Reduplications of Romanticism', and Megan A. Stephan, 'Dunton, (Walter) Theodore Watts-(1832–1914)', *Oxford Dictionary of National Biography*, Oxford University Press, Sept 2004; online edition, Jan. 2012 [http://www.oxforddnb.com/view/article/36785; accessed 30 March 2012].
23. James Douglas, *Theodore Watts-Dunton: Poet, Novelist, Critic*, p. 26. Douglas's work is the most complete critical biography of Watts-Dunton thus far, and provides an excellent overview of critical responses to Watts-Dunton's writing. Douglas, then the literary critic and assistant editor of the *Star*, wrote the biography under the close supervision of Watts-Dunton, who carefully regulated all biographical writing about himself.
24. Coulson Kernahan, 'Theodore Watts-Dunton as "A Hero of Friendship"', in *Life and Letters of Theodore Watts-Dunton*, ed. by Thomas Hake and Arthur Compton-Rickett, pp. 215–32 (pp. 223–24).
25. William Michael Rossetti, *Dante Gabriel Rossetti: His Family Letters with a Memoir by William Michael Rossetti* (London: Ellis and Elvey, 1895), p. 391.
26. Coulson Kernahan, 'Theodore Watts-Dunton as "A Hero of Friendship"', p. 216.
27. W. Robertson Nicholl, 'The Significance of "Aylwin"', *The Contemporary Review*, 74 (December 1898), 798–809 (p. 802).
28. James Douglas, *Theodore Watts-Dunton: Poet, Novelist, Critic*, p. 1.
29. Theodore Watts-Dunton, *Old Familiar Faces*, pp. 77–79.
30. Sean Latham, *Modernism, The Art of Scandal: Libel Law and the Roman à clef*, p. 7.
31. *OED*. For a thorough consideration of literary Decadence, see *Decadence: An Annotated Anthology*, ed. by Jane Desmarais and Chris Baldick (Manchester: Manchester University Press, 2012).
32. This sonnet appears as an epigraph to early editions of *Aylwin* but is contained within the Appendix of the World's Classics editions.
33. Quoted in Hurst and Blackett advertisement, p. 560.
34. Letter from Theodore Watts-Dunton to William Michael Rossetti, 31 January 1914, Angeli-Dennis Papers, University of British Columbia Rare Books and Special Collections.
35. Hurst and Blackett advertisement, p. 560.
36. Ibid.

37. Anonymous, 'Aylwin By Theodore Watts-Dunton', p. 561.
38. Catherine Maxwell, 'Theodore Watts-Dunton's *Aylwin* (1898) and the Reduplications of Romanticism', p. 4.
39. James Douglas, *Theodore Watts-Dunton*, p. 311.
40. Deborah Epstein Nord, '"Marks of Race": Gypsy Figures and Eccentric Femininity in Nineteenth-Century Women's Writing', *Victorian Studies*, 41 (Winter 1998), 189–210 (p. 189).
41. *Ibid.*, p. 190.
42. Anonymous, 'Aylwin By Theodore Watts-Dunton', p. 561.
43. Ian Duncan, 'Wild England: George Borrow's Nomadology', *Victorian Studies*, 41 (Spring 1998), 381–403 (p. 382).
44. Theodore Watts-Dunton, 'Introduction', in George Borrow, *Wild Wales: The People, Language and Scenery* (London: J. M. Dent, 1906), pp. vii-xxiii (p. xii).
45. William Greenslade, 'Naturalism and Decadence: the Case of Hubert Crackanthorpe', in *Decadent Poetics: Literature and Form at the British Fin de Siècle*, ed. by Jason David Hall and Alex Murray (Basingstoke: Palgrave Macmillan, 2013), pp. 163–80 (pp. 163–64).
46. Arthur Symons, 'The Decadent Movement in Literature', *Harper's New Monthly Magazine*, 87 (1893), 858–59.
47. William Tirebuck, *Dante Gabriel Rossetti: His Work and Influence* (London: Elliot Stock, 1882), p. 33.
48. Collette Colligan and Margaret Linley, 'The Nineteenth-Century Invention of Media', in *Media, Technology, and Literature in the Nineteenth Century: Image, Sound, Touch*, ed. by Collette Colligan and Margaret Linley (Farnham: Ashgate, 2011), pp. 1–22 (p. 6).
49. Theodore Watts-Dunton, *Old Familiar Faces*, p. 78.

CHAPTER 6

'Use my body like the pages of a book': Decadence and the Eroticized Text

Kostas Boyiopoulos

[One of the] five common methods by which sex gains an entrance into literature [is ...] not the language of love, but the love of language [...] not what the tongue touches, but what it forms, not lips and nipples, but nouns and verbs.

WILLIAM H. GASS, *On Being Blue* (1976)[1]

A recognizable feature of late nineteenth-century Decadence is the irresistible magnetism of books, texts, and indeed language itself. Famously, in Chapter 11 of *The Picture of Dorian Gray* (1891), Dorian is 'poisoned by a book'.[2] Oscar Wilde toys with the idea of the lurid and dangerous 'fatal book' not only as a means of exploring the paradoxes of morality, but crucially as an agent of sexual ravishment. Walter Pater was one of the early scholars who was interested in the erotic possibilities *in* and *of* language, expressed as 'soul in style': Pater writes that by 'mind' the literary artist reaches us through design; but by 'soul' he reaches us through a 'kind of immediate contact'.[3] For Pater language is most inebriating when imbued with religious sentiment, which when it 'enkindle[s] words', 'through no mere phrase-worship, an unconscious literary tact has, for the sensitive, laid open a privileged pathway'.[4] 'Soul in style' is suggestive of a spectral excess emanating from the text that spellbinds the reader like a subtle yet overpowering perfume. The Decadent text eventually goes a step further. By appealing to the senses, it acquires the properties of flesh — 'nouns and verbs' replace 'lips and nipples' as the author William Gass vividly submits. It is erotic on a meta-level — to use terms that are both fleshly and textual — in its *body* of words, its sinuous *lines*, its *tissue* of phrases and quotations, its *corpus*.

This text does not only seduce us but is a personified lover, a *texte fatal*, that we perversely seek to possess. It is, to various degrees, a pulsing landscape that is sensual, gendered, dangerous, contaminating, and contaminated by the self through immersion and embodiment. In this chapter I discern ways in which the Decadent text behaves as a resplendent bodily surface that appeals seductively to and interacts erotically with the reader and the author. I consider the text as erotic body and, inversely, the body as erotic text. I pay special attention to Arthur Machen's *The Hill of Dreams* (1907), written in 1895–97, and Peter Greenaway's film *The Pillow Book* (1996), two works that exemplarily celebrate the interplay between textuality and bodily eros in the last two *fins de siècle* respectively.

In *Le Plaisir du texte* [*The Pleasure of the Text*] (1973), Roland Barthes fetishizes language as an erotic space that electrifies the reader with its splintering structures: '*I love you all* (words, phrases, sentences, adjectives, discontinuities [...])'.[5] These linguistic parts make up a 'marble, iridescent text',[6] not dissimilar from Paul Verlaine's love letter to the word 'décadence': 'I love [...] this word decadence, all shimmering in purple and gold.'[7] *The Pleasure of the Text* is a poststructuralist quasi-literary work that celebrates the tangibility of style just as Pater's sensuous prose suggested a hundred years earlier in *The Renaissance: Studies in Art and Poetry* (1873). Susan Sontag, that maverick of literary theory, insightfully classes Barthes with the Wildean aesthetes.[8] Sontag closes her essay 'Against Interpretation' (1964) with the famed dictum: 'In place of a hermeneutics we need an erotics of art.'[9] Barthes fulsomely unfurls the idea of erotics as a replacement of hermeneutics in his writing which itself is an erotic performance diffused in a style of sprezzatura, staccato rhythms, elliptical, and disconnected clauses. He asserts that the 'text' is an 'anagram' 'of our erotic body' yet its 'pleasure is irreducible to physiological need'.[10] Barthes distinguishes between 'text of pleasure' and 'text of bliss' (*jouissance*); the first refers to comfortable, conventional reading in line with cultural mores; the second one breaks with culture, imposing a 'state of loss' as in inebriating disorientation.[11] Textual *jouissance* operates as a *petite mort*: 'like that untenable, impossible, purely *novelistic* instant so relished by Sade's libertine when he manages to be hanged and then to cut the rope at the very moment of his orgasm, his bliss.'[12] That 'instant' indicates a hiatus between the suspension of pleasure in textuality and its potential fulfilment. Like Verlaine's 'décadence' which itself hangs on, poised and postponed at the phantasmagorical cusp of its demise, the text of bliss has the propensity to precipitate yet closure never comes, agreeing with what Ben Hutchinson calls 'deferral' and Linda Dowling terms 'aesthetics of delay'.[13]

Dowling's 'seductiveness of style' and Hutchinson's 'erotics of style' consider the rhetorical implications of Decadent 'style' as having partly an erotic effect on the reader. By discussing a selection of late-Victorian aesthetes in light of Romantic philology, Dowling recognizes Pater's 'profane "soul in style"' which inhabits 'the fatal book' with its 'sensual presence'.[14] She advances the idea of 'linguistic autonomy' which 'becomes in a precise sense Decadent, however, only when portrayed as a poisonous or seducing power'.[15] More recently, by examining work by Édouard Dujardin, Thomas Mann, Paul Valéry, and Rainer Maria Rilke, Hutchinson scrutinizes the continuities between literary style and eros. He argues that the 'erotic tension' of much Modernist literature is owing to the Bourgetian 'decomposing signifier, deriving in the first instance from the decadent style of the 1880s.'[16] On discussing the deferral of satisfaction in *Death in Venice* (1912), Hutchinson claims that 'erotic tension is sublimated into stylistic pleasure: the aesthetic becomes the erotic.'[17] In this erotics of language the text falls apart through decomposition from the page to the phrase to the word as Paul Bourget contends in his familiar definition of 'Decadent style'.[18] This ongoing dissection implies an erotic fixation on the ever-specialized linguistic unit through a synecdochic, protean fetishism. In what reads as a paraphrase of Bourget's definition, Gass writes: 'What a page before was a woman is suddenly a breast, and then a nipple, then a little ring of risen flesh, a pacifier, water bottle, rubber cushion'.[19] The text, therefore, also falls *away* by transcending and transgressing its own textual condition, overreaching into the contiguity of sensual matter. To use a befitting pun, rupture in the unity of the text induces rapture.

Decadent Bibliomania

The erotic nature of literary style is a central thematic preoccupation in Decadent fiction of the 1880s and 1890s that features aesthete bibliomaniacs: Jean des Esseintes in J.-K. Huysmans's *À rebours* (1884), Edward Dayne in George Moore's *Confessions of a Young Man* (1886/1888), Pater's eponymous protagonist of *Gaston de Latour* (1888) and his delighting in Pierre de Ronsard, Wilde's Dorian Gray and Thomas Griffiths Wainewright in 'Pen, Pencil and Poison' (1891), and Machen's Lucian Taylor in *The Hill of Dreams*. These characters are learned and sophisticated *connoisseurs* of literature. They interact sensuously and sensually with fatal books which are often personified. Pater's Winckelmann, for instance, treats lyrical language lustfully, with sculptural tactility: he 'had handled the words only of Greek poetry, stirred indeed and roused by them, yet divining beyond the words an unexpressed pulsation of sensuous life.'[20]

Holbrook Jackson, a man of letters who championed the generation of the 1890s, develops the subject of 'burning book-love' fully in his enormous study *The Anatomy of Bibliomania* (1930).[21] An encyclopaedic book about books, *The Anatomy of Bibliomania* itself is a pastiche of copious references and quotations on literature and print culture. It is a more specialized version, we might argue, of the inventories that parade in *À rebours*. With chapters that treat the literary artefact and the physical book in terms of anatomy, personification, 'bibliophagy', book-drinking, medicine and disease, hunting and collecting, courting, and many more, Jackson's idiosyncratic study turns into a morbid fixation on the book as the locus reflecting the entire spectrum of emotion and human experience. One of the chapters is even dedicated to the five senses of textuality and 'bookhood' as 'The Five Ports of Book-Love'. For Jackson the personified book is richly sensuous, alluring, and flirtatious. He feminizes 'bookhood' and savours its private spaces like *'the lover in the arms of his mistress'*.[22] The ultimate goal of the bibliophile is comparable to the Decadent tenet about impossible desire: 'women and books are symbols of some exquisitely imagined bliss which remains exquisite, Heaven itself, because it cannot be captured or reached.'[23] One of the earliest, most famous cases of eroticized 'bookhood' documented by Jackson is expressed in *Philobiblon* by Richard de Bury (1287–1345), a wealthy Bishop of Durham and compulsive book collector. De Bury fetishized books, cherished their virginal condition, and considered libraries sanctified places. Jackson quotes from *Philobiblon*: 'Nulla tuum nobis subducet femina lectum' [no woman shall filch thy place of love with me].[24] In medieval monasticism, possessing a woman was replaced by possessing a library, a seraglio of books. The late nineteenth-century aesthetes' morbid penchant for monastic retreat into mausoleums of scholarship, as documented by Jackson, seems to descend from privileged clerics' private rituals of physically adoring books.

In the *fin de siècle* the epitome of the private and dangerous, sensual seduction of literature is captured in Octave Uzanne's short story 'Le Cabinet d'un éroto-bibliomane' [The Cabinet of an Eroto-Bibliomaniac] (1878). Uzanne (1851–1931) was a notable bibliophile, eclectic publisher, and author. He was associated with the Symbolists and Decadents of the day, including Stéphane Mallarmé and Aubrey Beardsley. The narrator of his tale approaches the dandified book-lover Chevalier Kerhany, in the hope of accessing his eclectic library. Kerhany is modelled on Frederick Hankey (1828–82), a notorious British bibliophile who lived in Paris and specialized in pornographic and subversive literature. He supplied erotica to A. C. Swinburne and Sir Richard Burton.[25] For the eponymous Kerhany in Uzanne's tale, both literature and women merge in the eternal feminine. The tale reads like a condensed *À rebours*, heaped with curios, luxurious materials, and décor. The aesthete's hoarding of beautiful editions mirrors the Decadent text's obsession with the literary trope of catalogue: asyndetic lists of bric-à-brac, luxury objects, and obscure words. The narrator, drawn first to Kerhany's private art gallery, is intoxicated and eventually nauseated after viewing a torrent of gleaming paintings of carnal women. The next day he enters the inner sanctum of his host's personal library. The host is a 'selfish Pluto' who treats the encounter with the rare and obscure erotica of his bookshelves as first-time opium intoxication in a bibliographic hell.[26] The luxury of sultry and voluptuous clandestine literature overwhelms the narrator to the extent that his hands begin to tremble — the manifested stigmata of textual/sexual excess.[27]

The process of seduction reaches out in *mise en abyme* from the fictionalized book to its fictional reader (protagonist) to us. In Chapter 9 of *À rebours*, Des Esseintes hires a beautiful female ventriloquist, orders miniature statues of a Sphinx and a Chimera, and has them magnified by light manipulation in a makeshift shadow theatre. He becomes enraptured as the ventriloquist animates a scene from Gustave Flaubert's novel *La Tentation de Saint Antoine* (1874): 'Spellbound by Flaubert's wonderful prose, he listened in breathless awe to the terrifying duet, shuddering from head to foot when the Chimera pronounced the solemn and magical sentence: "I seek new perfumes, larger blossoms, pleasures still untasted."'[28] The Chimera's desire to leap beyond the dimension of its own existence, to transcend and reach out to the mirage of unattainable art, mirrors that of Des Esseintes. He confronts his own 'feverish desire for the unknown, the unsatisfied longing for an ideal'; he longs to 'cross the frontiers of thought, to grope after a certainty, albeit without finding one, in the misty upper regions of art!'[29] Des Esseintes yearns to merge sexually with the very textures of words; his orgasmic 'shuddering' stems precisely from the impossibility to realize the senses within the novelistic space of ever new stylistic configurations. The moment he apprehends the impossibility of vanishing entirely into the province of the textual, he resorts to carnal entanglement with the mediator of the text, the ventriloquist. Flaubert's book is assimilated into the eroticized body of the ventriloquist: by making love to her, Des Esseintes makes love to Flaubert's book.

Taking its cue from *À rebours*, Moore's *Confessions* is an ostentatious and flamboyant autobiographical memoir that treats books of fiction and verse capriciously as lovers. Here we have the clearest articulation of the idea that language can be a sexual seducer.[30] The protagonist, Edward Dayne, is a compulsive reader and aspiring writer. Immersed in the bohemian, avant-garde art world of 1880s Paris, he finds more sensual pleasure in literature than in human sexual relations. He proclaims that books are 'individuals' that can 'create a sense within the sense' and can 'madden you in blood and brain'.[31] His formulation contains a playful semantic ambiguity: 'sense' as in *meaning*, for Dayne, transfigures into physical 'sense'. The realm of words is governed by the laws of carnal tactility. He suggests that literature is

> ruled by the same caprices — those of the flesh? [...] No doubt that there is the brain-judgment and the sense-judgment of a work of art. And it will be noticed that these two forces of discrimination exist sometimes almost independently of each other, in rare and radiant instances confounded and blended in one immense and unique love. Who has not been, unless perhaps some dusty old pedant, thrilled and driven to pleasure by the action of a book that penetrates to and speaks to you of your most present and most intimate emotions. This is of course pure sensualism[.][32]

By associating the delights of literature with those of the 'flesh', Dayne collapses the thin line between hermeneutics and erotics. In his articulation of sexual intimacy with books, Dayne as reader is penetrated by the 'action of a book' that mirrors his mood of the moment. His description confounds gender roles. As he writes, 'I only love woman or book, when it is as a voice of conscience, never heard before', confessing that he is 'feminine, morbid, perverse.'[33] With such preferential, exclusionary taste, he implies that the fusion of intellect with sensuousness in the eroticized text is selective; and certainly this text is not of the Dickensian variety but that which can be found on the bookshelves of Des Esseintes and Chevalier Kerhany. Dayne's syllogisms and analogies, we might add, anticipate those by Barthes and William Gass. The *fatal book* is an efficacious novelistic entity only if the language it is made of is conceived in its power to seduce, in its infectious capacity on its reader. Hence the physical volume that contains the text must necessarily be defined against the reader's presence. Its typographical boundaries that enclose it into an object must also be part of its fiction. Consequently, for those aesthetes, the bibliomaniacal worship of the book as an *objet d'art* always mirrors the worship of the Barthian signifier blazing within its covers.

Erotic Bodies Textualized

Not only is the text an eroticized, gendered body, but, in reverse, the human body of desire can also be a text to be deciphered or *read*. The body-as-text is not a clear metaphor; in its Decadent version it collapses the figurative and the literal, straddling the curious line between the fictional body, in the Aristotelian sense, and that which is written. The depiction of woman as text was a well-trodden conceit, elaborately explored by Renaissance and Metaphysical poets. Woman was frequently likened to a 'two-leued booke'.[34] Thomas Carew's *The Masque: Coelum Britannicum* (1634) provides a striking example: 'religiously kissing the two-leav'd

Book, never to stretch his limbs more betwixt adulterous sheets'.[35] Women 'are mystique bookes, which only wee | Whom their imputed grace will dignify | Must see reveal'd', writes John Donne in 'Elegy 19: To his Mistris Going to Bed'.[36] Thomas Moore in 'The Devil among the Scholars: A Fragment' and James Shirley in *The Cardinal* (1640) explore this metaphor further by indulging in the delicious 'errata' of the woman-book.[37] Sir John Mennes writes in an epigram that making love to woman is synonymous with studying her.

In late Victorian poetry this conceit was developed into a trope in which the sophisticated male readership was fascinated with the mystery of what was clothed, what lay hidden beneath the figurative covers. D. G. Rossetti's scandalous poem 'Jenny' (1870) is a pivotal work in which woman is an object of male pleasure that has textual dimensions as 'a volume seldom read' (l. 158),[38] a descriptor of rarity. Rossetti's speaker compares the 'room' of the static, slumbering prostitute Jenny with his own which is 'so full of books' (l. 23). He is an eroto-bibliomaniac who luxuriates in the private sphere of sexual indulgence in the same manner he does in the private refuge of scholarship. He aestheticizes Jenny, contemplating the textual properties of her sensuality and beauty. Instead of penetrating her body, the speaker — as Richard Cronin states — attempts 'to penetrate her mind':[39]

> For all your wealth of loosened hair,
> Your silk ungirdled and unlac'd
> And warm sweets open to the waist,
> All golden in the lamplight's gleam, —
> You know not what a book you seem,
> Half-read by lightning in a dream! (ll. 48–53)

The body of Jenny tantalizes with its mannered, enthralling posture fashioned teasingly by partial clothing and illumined by artificial light as if it was an exhibition object. It is her commoditized sensuality that fixes her into a half-read book which is resistant to yet rouses interpretation. The half-naked languorous Jenny anticipates Symons's 'White Heliotrope' where a 'half dressed' mistress is frozen in the disorderly *mise-en-scène* of her private bedroom. In Symons's poem the room that is littered with a 'novel flung half-open' along with 'tumbled skirts' and spread-out 'Hat, hair-pins, puffs, and paints'[40] represents an instant of intimacy fixed like a Pre-Raphaelite painting fraught with enigmatic clues that calls for a reading:

> The feverish room and that white bed,
> The tumbled skirts upon a chair,
> The novel flung half-open, where
> Hat, hair-pins, puffs, and paints are spread;

In Rossetti's poem, Jenny's heart is compared to a dead 'rose shut' inside a forbidden, salacious book 'which pure women may not look | For its base pages claim control' (ll. 253–55). Jenny is 'a vile text' in which 'a lady's cheek' can be 'read' more than a 'living rose' (ll. 259–61). Later on, the speaker attempts to have the 'volume' (Jenny) 'opened halfway' (l. 159), so that, in an image suggestive of sexual violation, 'the pages of her brain | Be parted' (ll. 160–61); but the book is impervious as it closes back upon the 'dusty sense' (l. 162). Jenny is a reverse Paterian-Wildean *fatal book*.

These variants of Jenny as a text show that her commoditized flesh does not only harbour and even eclipse her obscene, venereal narrative, but it remains dangerous. Paradoxically, the explicitness of pornographic literature to which Jenny is compared is closed off and mystified in the ghostly meaning of flesh as it is stylized and textualized by the cerebral male gaze.

Likewise the music-hall dancers, actresses, and prostitutes that populate Symons's poems are themselves living poems, full of ambiguity, double meanings, enigmatic *maquillage*, and body language that plays with invitation and resistance. Symons wrote in order to re-enact and relive his sexual adventures, either real or imagined. Yet, even in this context, he pronounces that woman is 'the masterpiece of flesh',[41] a brilliant work of art. The bodies of Symons's lovers and objects of adoration call for an interpretive approach. His speakers are perceptive readers, or rather critics, who decipher and analyse women's appearances as if they were texts, from gazing as part of music-hall etiquette to direct sexual interaction. 'At the Foresters', a poem in a cycle titled 'Décor de Théâtre' from *London Nights* (1895), reinforces unequivocally the idea of woman as textual enigma, analogous to Rossetti's 'Jenny'. Symons's speaker is submerged in the space of artistic performance; positioned in the wings, he regards Flo, a female performer who is on the gas-lit stage, dodging the 'Prying and indiscreet' lights as she is outfitted with 'prince's dress' and 'yellow tights'.[42] Flo's made-up 'quaint grimace' is that of indeterminacy and ambiguity. Her allure oscillates between the spontaneous exuberance of her body and the artifice of cosmetics: 'The charm and pathos of your youth | Mock the mock roses of your face.'[43] In the penultimate stanza the speaker scrutinizes her with an erotic yet intellectualizing curiosity:

> And there is something in your look
> (Ambiguous, independent Flo!)
> As teasing as a half-shut book;
> It lures me till I long to know
> The many meanings of your look[44]

As with Rossetti's Jenny who is a 'half-read book', halfness and teasing and partial disclosure, are also recurrent techniques in Symons's work. Flo's look is a 'half-shut' book in the same way she is half-concealed in her male costume and semi-natural in her affectations. Her ambiguity, however, is what constitutes her complex artificiality. The speaker is in thrall to the erotic undertones of the living fatal book which is polysemous ('many meanings' — and many senses). The plethora of meanings that the speaker/reader elicits from Flo/text agrees with Barthes's notion of the 'writerly' text in which the reader actively participates in the orgasmic production of meaning.[45] Like language in its semantic slipperiness, artistic performance fuels and sustains eroticism through indefinability ('something'). He longs to 'know', a phrase that suggests bibliomaniac desire for scholarship. The speaker, we might say, is a subtler version of Des Esseintes who in the act of reading engages the ventriloquist performer of Flaubert's novel sexually. George Moore's idea of 'sense within a sense' is also here relevant. The word 'look', referring to the changing disposition imprinted in her 'eyes' in the last stanza, has a lexical ambiguity denoting bidirectionality: gaze at and from; it can also signify Flo's appearance. The woman's eroticized presence is itself *written*, presented and enshrined in her body language and by extension in the poem's textual artifice, glimpsed at through the seams and interstices of words.

Another way in which the object of desire is textualized is through Ernest Dowson's metonymic fetishism. Dowson sublimates the object of his desire. In 'Preface: For Adelaide' to *Verses* (1896) he notably begins his dedication: 'To you, who are my verses',[46] transforming his muse into the poetic corpus itself. Dowson uses the romantic etiquette of the dedicatory epistle as a subterfuge to spin erotic desire in textual performance. He gives a quotation from Flaubert's *L'Éducation sentimentale* (1869) where he eroticizes Adelaide's synecdochic 'nom' [name], conflating the act of speech with that of carnality: 'je me répétais en tachant de le baiser sur mes lèvres' [I keep repeating to myself while kissing it with my lips] (my translation).[47] Dowson emulates John Keats who writes to Fanny Brawne: 'I shall kiss your name and mine where your Lips have been'.[48] But where the textual trace in Keats seems to be a substitute of the object of desire, Dowson's delirium is an authentic engagement with the fetish itself, the erotic essence of femininity incarnated in language.

Eroticism is most effective when the object of desire is entirely unreachable and yet regulated. In 'Villanelle of His Lady's Treasures' Dowson's speaker recreates, while fragmenting, the female body in the environment of the mannered villanelle form: 'I took her dainty eyes, as well | As silken tendrils of her hair: | And so I made a Villanelle!'[49] The eyes and hair are highly charged Victorian fetishes. In this fragmented bundle of fetishes the speaker adds her 'whiteness virginal' and 'from her cheek two roses rare'.[50] Like a Frankensteinian scientist, the speaker takes apart the female body and makes a beautiful poem out of it. He is also a dexterous watchmaker who affixes to the ensemble her 'voice, a silver bell, | As clear as song, as soft as prayer', stealing 'her laugh, most musical' which he 'wrought [...] in with artful care'.[51] This image of the human voice is linked to the preface to *Verses* (1896): 'Quelquefois vos paroles me reviennent comme un écho lointain, comme le son d'une cloche apporté par le vent' [Sometimes your words return to me like a distant echo, like the sound of a bell transported by the wind] (my translation).[52] The voice of the written body instigates a double artifice, or a double textuality. The speaker does not create a perfectly personified and gendered villanelle in order to preserve the memory of the girl. On the contrary, as he muses, 'It may be possible | Her image from my heart to tear!'[53] — As with the 'cold eyes' of 'Flos Lunae' that the poet would not change, the object of desire is transformed, effaced, and replaced by the steely surface of the textual.

Enraptured by the Text: *The Hill of Dreams*

Machen's *The Hill of Dreams* (1907) figures the realm of the textual and presents the intricate ways it interacts with the senses, physically and cerebrally, on multiple levels. Described 'without the shadow of a doubt [as] the most decadent book in the whole of English literature' (my translation),[54] it is a semi-autobiographical *Künstlerroman* that follows a writer's creative tussle in the art of literature. Through the perspicacious, daydreaming writer Lucian Taylor, it goes as far as to enact George Moore's cogitations on the text's sexual possibilities. In the opening of the narrative, Lucian's 'eyes had looked on glamour'.[55] The word 'glamour' is cryptic: it is of medieval origin and etymologically hails from *grammar*.[56] Hence, Lucian's existence is that of language and learning. What he inhabits is the realm of configured text.

The narrative amalgamates language, the rural and urban landscape with its patterns and sensations, and imagination. In this derangement of ontological categories 'the hills and hanging woods, the brooks and lonely waterpools; books, the thoughts of books, the stirrings of the imagination, all fused into one phantasy' (p. 31). Moreover, hills, woods, vales, matted thickets, ruins, brooks, lanes, and other topographical features have a punctuating and periodical presence throughout the narrative that suggests an arcane textual system. Lucian's visible world is made out of text-like 'symbols' (p. 33) that operate much like Baudelaire's conceit of metalanguage as landscape in 'Le Soleil'. On the other hand, the book is written in symbols manifested as 'wonderful foliage' that 'creep[s] about the text' (p. 80). Where does nature end and textuality begin? Botanical imagery and calligraphic flourishes fuse into one. The novel's physical spaces in which Lucian drifts and meditates, the rural landscapes of Caermaen, and the urban vistas of London, make up a grammatical structure. The natural terrain is a text in which Lucian can *read*, for instance, 'the simulacra of the wood' (p. 15). He is ensconced in a bizarre, intoxicating setting that behaves as if it is a language.

Machen writes in *Hieroglyphics: A Note upon Ecstasy in Literature* (1902) that 'style' yields 'a peculiar kind of aesthetic delight.'[57] This peculiarity is a slippery notion that, nonetheless, endows words and text-making in the novel with a sensual ambience. In the capacity of literary theorist, Lucian reveres language in sybaritic terms, calling it 'ravishing' and prizing its enkindling materiality: 'the secret of the sensuous art of literature' is that of 'causing delicious sensation by the use of words' (p. 110). His own literary productions are conveyed in phrases of inebriating allure and febrility: they seem 'of amorous fire' (p. 39) and his writing is 'glowing; and action and all the heat of existence quickened and beat on the wet page' (p. 60); he is moreover 'rapt by the cadence of a phrase' (p. 176). Lucian's writings are Pygmalionic, amounting to an indefinable Galatea made out of words.

Lucian is infatuated with the lithe, stately country girl Annie Morgan. He builds around her a series of elaborate fairy-tale fantasies. But as we soon realize, Annie serves for him a sensory complement to his textual world. She is not a real lover but a novelistic one, 'the symbol of all mystic womanhood' (p. 193), the *princesse lointaine* of medieval romance, kept at bay in order for Lucian to facilitate and maintain his quixotic, enclosed fantasy. Lucian is preconditioned to see women as 'literary conventions borrowed from the minor poets and pseudo-medievalists' (p. 64). Yet he does not clearly draw from the reservoir of legend; he is chiefly interested in the sealed-off style, the web of artificiality delivered by the formal structures of texts which he mediates in the form of religious ritualism. Although he is an adherent of the Paterian 'soul in style', in his case religious ecstasy does not come from Roman Catholicism but from literature itself. In this vein, Ellis Hanson writes that 'in their cult of artifice, the decadents often eschewed sex for the more refined pleasure of writing about it — for the highly erotic pleasures of writing itself.'[58] Lucian declares that 'woman's body had become his religion' (p. 72), apotheosising it as an idol. He comes into erotic, tactile contact with its proxy, the textual space that preserves her:

> He slept with [manuscripts] next to his heart, and he would kiss them when he was quite alone, and pay them such devotion as he would have paid to her whom they symbolized. He wrote on these leaves a wonderful ritual of praise and devotion; it was the liturgy of his religion. Again and again he copied and recopied this madness of a lover; dallying all days over the choice of a word, searching for more exquisite phrases. No common words, no such phrases as he might use in a tale would suffice; the sentences of worship must stir and be quickened, they must glow and burn, and be decked out as with rare work of jewellery. Every part of that holy and beautiful body must be adored; he sought for terms of extravagant praise [...] (p. 74)

The object of desire is displaced and transposed onto the textual corpus. Machen clearly frames the act of writing as an act of lovemaking. Lucian is sexually obsessed with his own artistic efforts. His compulsive re-copying of the erotic, encomiastic manuscript suggests a crucial antithesis: Lucian imbues with sensuality the creative process in which every choice of word is agonized over and yet he is locked in a circle of repetition which is indicative of sterility and stagnancy. In this species of sophisticated eroticism, Lucian favours the linguistic obscurity advocated by such Decadent stylists as Théophile Gautier, Huysmans, Wilde, and M. P. Shiel with whom Machen was well acquainted. As Barthes avers, 'the word can be erotic on two opposing conditions, both excessive: if it is extravagantly repeated, or on the contrary, if it is unexpected, succulent in its newness'; in agreement with Lucian's behest that words 'must glow and burn', Barthes adds that 'in certain texts, words *glisten,* they are distracting, incongruous apparitions'.[59] The pulsing and shimmering language of Machen's eroticized text-body is entirely fetishistic: because of its fragmentation its words and clauses are titillating, synecdochic fetishes that stand out and become ends in themselves. It is never entirely clear whether that 'holy and beautiful body' is that of Annie or, by default, of the manuscript.

Both the craft of writing and its process, or in other words, the cultivation of style and the ceremony of luxuriating in handwriting, copying, and revelling in dazzling calligraphy respectively, equally induce intolerable orgasmic symptoms in Lucian — the eroticized text is so intense that in its caress it is 'a knife | Too sharp to hurt' as Olive Custance writes in 'The Song Spinner'.[60] Lucian is inebriated by his own creative productions:

> [H]e copied and recopied the manuscript nine times before he wrote it out fairly in a little book which he made himself of a skin of creamy vellum. In his mania for acquirements that should be entirely useless he had gained some skill in illumination, or limning as he preferred to call it, always choosing the obscurer word as the obscurer arts. [...] There were stranger things written in the manuscript pages that Lucian cherished, sentences that burnt and glowed like 'coals of fire which hath a most vehement flame.' There were phrases that stung and tingled as he wrote them, and sonorous words poured out in ecstasy and rapture, as in some of the old litanies. (pp. 74, 76)

In his indulgence in style Lucian is both wounded and seduced, agreeing with Barthes who writes: 'I am interested in language because it wounds or seduces me'.[61] The sustained motif of glowing words is suggestive of a philological sublime, the distraction of the signifier, and a blinding passion that consumes the senses with its excessive heat. These 'sentences that burned and glowed' lend conflagrating effulgence to the entire narrative of *The Hill of Dreams*. Indeed, Machen's novel opens and closes with the 'glow in the sky as if great furnace doors were opened' (pp. 1 and 219). The difference is that in the opening the furnace is in the sky and at the close of the novel it is in Lucian's brain. Even Lucian's name etymologically points to this burning ecstasy. These rapturous stinging and tingling phrases in their botanical and pontifical splendour are the very testament of Barthian *jouissance*, assaulting Lucian's senses more in a bodily and less in a hermeneutic manner. Lucian hoards lexical obscurities and pretty words; these consist of a decadent 'mania for acquirements': like a zealous bibliomaniac, Lucian is both a collector of rare words and a fastidious stylist. Essentially, his pursuit becomes *thesaurical* (*thesaurus* in Greek means 'treasure'). Moreover, Lucian highlights the obscure jewel-like word through the painstaking art of calligraphy in all its rituals of preparing the instruments of writing, making script-ocular 'experiments in inks' in the same way Des Esseintes experiments synaesthetically with liquors (Chapter 5) and perfumes (Chapter 10).

Eventually, Lucian's obsessive encounters with literature drive him to intolerable, orgasmic ecstasy which culminates in a masochistic, elaborate rite:

> taking off his nightgown, [he] gently lay himself down on the bed of thorns and spines. Lying on his face, with the candle and the book before him, he would softly and tenderly repeat the praises of his dear, dear Annie, and as he turned over page after page, and saw the raised gold of the majuscules glow and flame in the candle-light, he pressed the thorns into his flesh. At such moments he tasted in all its acute savour the joy of physical pain; and after two or three experiences of such delights he altered his book, making a curious sign in vermilion on the margin of the passages where he was to inflict on himself this sweet torture. [...] his body would be all freckled with drops of blood; he used to view the marks with pride. Here and there a spine would be left deep in the flesh, and he would pull these out roughly, tearing through the skin. On some nights when he had pressed with more fervour on the thorns his thighs would stream with blood, red beads standing out on the flesh, and trickling down to his feet. (p. 81)

This key passage is packed with Decadent motifs: violence, eros, obsession, fetishism, and Roman Catholic overtones, particularly of the Crucifixion. The 'graceful form' of the imbrued, ensanguined Lucian appears as the body of a 'tortured martyr' (p. 82). From the sensuous stripping of his body to the self-infliction of erotic wounds, Lucian is a feminized icon coalescing St Sebastian with Christ. And as Linda Dowling observes, it is not Annie Morgan that Lucian worships 'but the fetishistic book itself.'[62] This juncture, and indeed confusion, between bodily responsiveness and the textual condition here is quite nuanced. The text of the book, both in its aural incantation and its visual shimmering, is a charged fetish that thrills Lucian to orgasm in a series of *petites morts*. At the same time, Lucian's body is a living book, a palimpsest, on which the thorns, like lancinating quills, write, producing a mystical text in blood. This kind of writing on Lucian's own body signifies a coital act that is sustained by his subjective sensibility. In a voodoo fashion, he creatively 'alter[s]' the book by inflicting wounds on its pages in vermillion ink, mirroring his own wounds in anticipation. Here, two *books* blend erotically: the inanimate, actual one, and the figurative book of flesh. The intermingling or inter-writing of book and flesh is conducted with calculated ritualism that symbolizes the formal aspect of Decadent style.

Intermedial Eros: *The Pillow Book*

> There are two things in life which are dependable: the delights of the flesh and the delights of literature. I have had the good fortune to enjoy them both equally. (Section 172) (Peter Greenaway, *The Pillow Book*)[63]

The text aspiring to be a tactile body and vice versa is staged sumptuously by Peter Greenaway in his film *The Pillow Book* (1996) which is loosely based on and inspired by the book of the same name (枕草; *Makura no sōshi*) by Sei Shōnagon, an imperial courtesan in tenth-century Japan. Shōnagon's work exemplifies the genre of *zuihitsu* (随筆) which consists of reflections, essays, fragments, and adages loosely strung together. Susan Sontag called Shōnagon's *The Pillow Book* 'that breviary of consummate dandy attitudes'.[64] Greenaway said in an interview that Shōnagon's 'continual fragmentation of ideas' in her use of the 'diary form' ties her 'to Baudelaire', while Murasaki Shikibu's *The Tale of Genji* is more associated with Tolstoy or Zola.[65] Japanophilia, of course, was a late-Victorian phenomenon, championed by the aesthetes. Also Shōnagon's fragmentary observations resonate with postmodernist attitudes that characterize Greenaway's film. Her book is a diary fixated with trifle rules of aesthetic taste and etiquette, making up a literary universe backdropped by the elegances of the imperial court. In a way, the theme of her book is style.

Greenaway's film is marked by the director's signature recurring luxurious, hypnotic visuals, expanding from *Prospero's Books* (1991). It extracts from Sei Shōnagon's literary distillation of sensuous morsels a meta-cinematic vision in which eroticism is propagated through the tension and collapse of antithetical media: flesh and script, image and text, skin and film, lovemaking and writing. We watch the conflation of texts with bodies in a visual feast of free-floating signs and textures (Fig. 6.1). The film features textuality and flesh as the ingredients of a new cinematic language in the way smells and scents serve as the inherent narrative idiom in Patrick Süskind's novel *Das Parfum* (1986) for instance. In the film's idiosyncratic idiom, calligraphic flourishes and textual landscapes feature not only on skin but are also superimposed on screens and props within the streaming *mise-en-scène*. Text appears in a variety of fonts, shapes, colours, luminosity, and languages, and interacts with screens and split-screens, or screens-within-screens, and static visuals; these are in colour, black and white, sepia, blue, and negative print. In short, following Gautier's definition of 'decadent style' as one that pushes 'the boundaries of language, borrowing specialist vocabularies from everywhere',[66] Greenaway pushes the film's cinematic vocabulary to its limits in intermedial interactions.

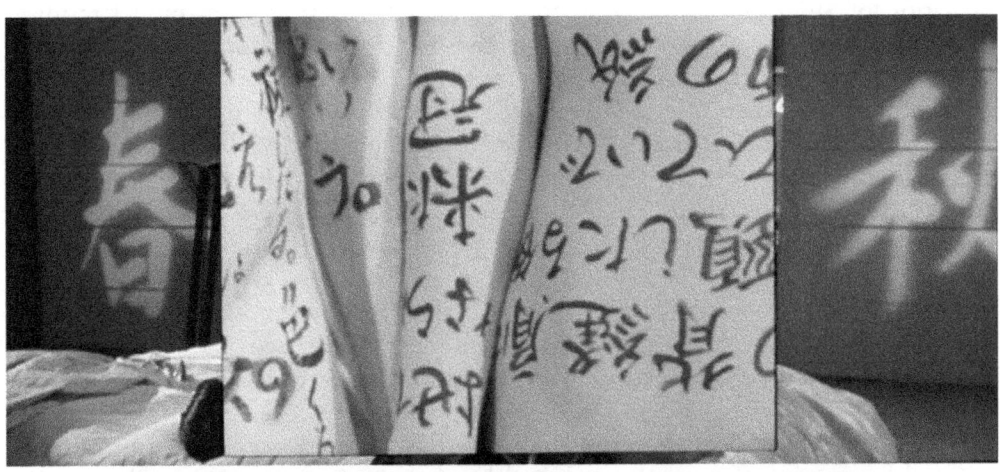

Fig. 6.1 (above). Still from *The Pillow Book* (dir. Peter Greenaway, 1996), at 00:47:06. In this frame-within-a-frame, Nagiko is photographed alongside the body of an unconscious random Englishman (whose services she has commissioned) after creating a calligraphic text on his and her own body.

Fig. 6.2 (below). Still from *The Pillow Book* (dir. Peter Greenaway, 1996), at 00:56:44. This is a composition from the highly stylized sequence of Nagiko's seducing the 'publisher's lover', Jerome, who is foregrounded by stacks of books like a library item. On Jerome's back, one can discern the well-known program used in printing presses, 'The quick brown fox jumps over the lazy dog.'

The story centres on Nagiko Kiyohara (Vivian Wu) who is a symbolic reincarnation of Shōnagon. She grows to become a Japanese fashion model residing in Hong Kong and pursues fastidiously sensual pleasure through fine literature and the act of calligraphic writing on her body. The film opens with a ritual in which Nagiko's father inscribes her face with bloodlike calligraphic characters, accompanied with the mantra: 'When God made the first model of a human being, He painted in the eyes, the lips, and the sex. Then He painted in each person's name Lest the owner should ever forget it.' The ritual is performed annually on Nagiko's birthday. This recurring scene suggests that the human entity is a living parchment, a divinely authored text. Nagiko gradually perceives herself as a body written on and as body writing. She is in search of 'lovers who would remind me of the pleasures of calligraphy', adding that in an ideal lover the art of lovemaking and calligraphy should be balanced. Nagiko is a connoisseur of letters and an aspiring writer just like Machen's Lucian Taylor; her penchant for calligraphy also matches Lucian's. She seeks to exact revenge on the homosexual publisher Yaji-san who rejected her work and sexually exploited her father as payment for publishing the latter's own work. Nagiko plots and seduces the publisher's new lover, the British translator Jerome (Ewan McGregor) (Fig. 6.2). She uses Jerome's inscribed naked body as the text which she sends to the publisher. Yet in a fit of jealousy Nagiko rejects Jerome who, in order to win back her favours, overdoses on pills. As a result he accidentally dies and Nagiko realizes only too late that she is in love with him. The plot is entirely mediated through an intricate and dynamic web of textual and sensual imagery.

Amidst flashing images of fashion clothing and quirky catwalk women's apparel, near the beginning of the film, Greenaway references Section 150 presumably of the original *Pillow Book*, which talks about the beauty of the many layers of silk clothing worn by the Empress. Considering Nagiko's body as a book, this image suggests that her splendidly covered body is an unopened, exquisite book that teases with its secret content, or a palimpsest that intrigues with its possibilities. The film is punctuated with interpositions of Shōnagon's text throughout: it achieves a rich intermedial effect by overlaying voiceover with a fluid typeface — featuring antique bowls and serifs (in typographic terms) — and is accompanied by hypnotic illustrations. At a key moment, Nagiko confesses 'I enjoy the smell of paper of all kinds. It reminded me of the scent of skin.' By organic associations, eroticism merges the human epidermis with stationery, the space of writing. A little later, Greenaway gives us Section 167:

> The smell of white paper is like the scent of skin of a new lover who has just paid a surprise visit out of a rainy garden. And the black ink is like lacquered hair. And the quill? Well, the quill is like that instrument of pleasure whose purpose is never in doubt but whose surprising efficiency one always, always forgets.

In this titillating succession of similes, the body of a lover, including his private parts, is transmogrified into writing materials. The opposites of whiteness and blackness, paper and quill, generate erotic energy and contrast. The transience indicated by the elaborate *petrichor* image (the smell of earth after rain) is consonant with Greenaway's assertion in an interview that the perishability of paper is akin to the ephemerality of the body.[67] The 'efficiency' of the double-dealing 'instrument of pleasure' points to both sexual as well as stylistic economy. Furthermore, Greenaway evokes the preciousness of body and book imagery in Shōnagon's taxonomies; in the 'lists of anatomical comparisons' Nagiko recounts:

> Nipples like bone buttons
> An instep like a half open book
> A navel like the inside of a shell
> A belly like an upturned saucer
> A penis like a sea slug or a pickled cucumber

Nagiko adds to that last line: 'not a special writing instrument at all.' There are other instances of taxonomy in the film via Shōnagon's *The Pillow Book*, such as the 'list of elegant things' (Sections 29 and 16) and the 'List of Splendid Things' (Section 57). These lists are delivered with ceremonial daintiness. Shōnagon, like a genuine dandy as Susan Sontag deduces, resembles Des Esseintes and Dorian Gray in their penchant for collecting and cataloguing books, fabrics and vestments, precious gems, perfumes and oils, and beautiful objects. In a way, Shōnagon's and by extension Nagiko's lists are twice-over artificial. These authors do not just collect objects, but brilliant epigrammatic lines and titbits that describe these objects. In their textual manifestation, these enchanting diary entries become the sensuous objects they refer to.

When Nagiko turns into 'the pen, not just the paper' after Jerome's encouragement to use his 'body like the pages of a book', she first experiments by hiring a random Englishman; she writes on his inert, corpse-like body as well as on hers, and has the result photographed. The book that grows out of this process is rejected by the publisher because the material 'is not worth the paper it's written on'. The production of the rejected book is clinical and devoid of eroticism. By contrast, eroticized textuality is fully fledged in the centrepiece of the film, the dreamy sequence of Nagiko's entanglement with Jerome. Sex and text or rather the act of writing, intermingle multifariously. Nagiko and Jerome handle exquisite stationery, have sex in a bed full of manuscripts, and write intimately on each other's naked bodies. The capriciousness of the lovers-writers in possessing each other in changing variations is the same as that of Des Esseintes who, with a fond lover's touch, binds Baudelaire's *Les Fleurs du mal* lavishly, as if it was made of flesh with Japanese paper of 'milky whiteness faintly tinged with pink' and dressed in 'flesh-coloured pigskin', indulging in its contents whilst tucked away in his private world of artifice.[68] Nagiko's and Jerome's spontaneity as they experiment on each other also evokes the changeable mood of Dorian Gray who 'procured from Paris no less than nine large-paper copies of the first edition' of the fatal book from Lord Henry 'and had them bound in different colours'.[69]

Jerome projects Latin calligraphy on Nagiko's body in the same manner subtitles are superimposed on the surface of the film itself. He kisses her while in voiceover Nagiko says: 'His writing in so many languages made me a signpost pointing east, west, north and south. I had shoes in German, stockings in French, gloves in Hebrew, a hat with a veil in Italian. He only kept me naked where I was most accustomed to wear clothes'. Nagiko turns into a postmodern, chimerical artefact that transcends cultural constraints whilst her body like a vast atlas encompasses the polyglossia of humanity, fracturing the body. Their lovemaking ritual then changes into staged and stylised, painterly vignettes in which they make love in various traditional Japanese clothes, imitating erotic prints of the school of shunga (春画), by such art masters as Katsushika Hokusai, overlaid on screen. In the last part of the sequence the camera in scopophilic close-up pans along Nagiko's body as it is inscribed with Biblical text in English and Latin while she is pinned on bookshelves with hands outstretched in the posture of the Crucified. Then the camera halts languorously on Nagiko's *mons pubis* covered by her palm in the manner of a Botticellian Venus (Fig. 6.3). The Decadent trappings of affected artificiality are present in the merging of Roman Catholicism and Classical aesthetics. This dreamy sequence is complemented by French pop singer Guesch Patti's entrancing aria-like French song 'Blonde' both as sound and as drifting subtitles. This song, about 'Un ange blonde', a potential reference to Jerome, could be a counterpart to Lionel Johnson's lyric 'The Dark Angel' (1893). It is characterized by sexual ecstasy, gender confusion, suggestions of the Fall, and semantic ambiguity: 'S'échange-t-il d'aile en elle | Un homme sombre change en elle' [Is he trading his wings for her | a sombre man changing into her] (my translation). It is a lyrical presentation of lovemaking in which disturbance and harmony alternate; 'Déloge' [unsettle] and 'Dérange' [disturb] fluidly overlap with the 'Parfait mélange' [perfect blend]. The gender oscillation and neutrality of the angel suggests that the sexual interaction between Nagiko and Jerome is symmetrical. Their bodies are quills and parchments, writing and being written on in a circuit of pleasure and ecstasy.

The image of sexuality as a site of artistic creativity taps into the theme of the artist-lover, which was prevalent amongst the Pre-Raphaelites and in the 1890s. One such instance is John Gray's poem 'The Barber' from *Silverpoints* (1893). Symptomatically, the title of *Silverpoints* is a reference to stylish engraving technique and the volume itself stands testament to a lavish edition. The Barber-artist of the poem paints women's faces and bodies. He transforms them into wonders of artificial beauty; and yet his action is highly sensual. Eroticism and creativity become perfect synonyms *in situ*:

> I moulded with my hands
> The mobile breasts, the valley; and the waist
> I touched; and pigments reverently placed
> Upon their thighs in sapient spots and stains,
> Beryls and crysolites and diaphanes,
> And gems whose hot harsh names are never said.
> I was a masseur; and my fingers bled
> With wonder as I touched their awful limbs.[70]

The imagery of touch, palpation and tactility has various nuances, from scriptorial and authorial involvement to sculptural Pygmalionism. The barber who uses 'pigments' to adorn bodies with 'spots and stains' is a calligrapher who writes on flesh like Nagiko and Jerome. The bleeding fingers are like instruments of penmanship emitting ink (this image is the reverse of Lucian Taylor's creative

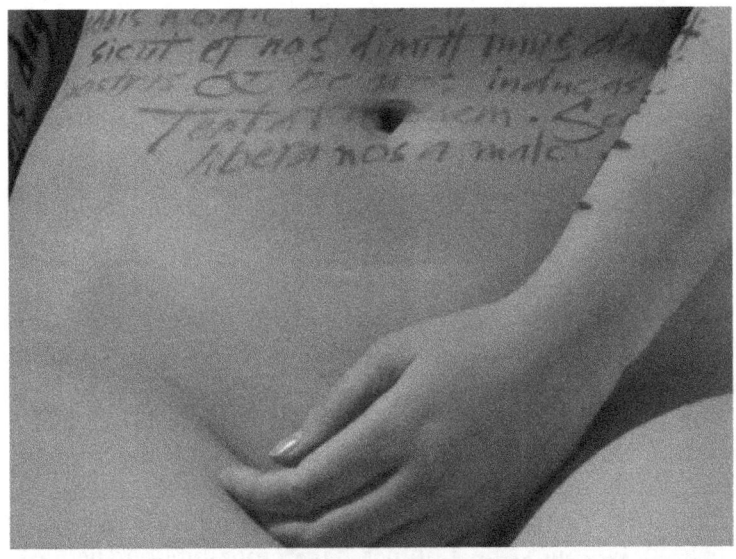

Fig. 6.3 (above). Still from *The Pillow Book* (dir. Peter Greenaway, 1996), at 01:00:06. The sensual immediacy of Nagiko's epidermis is most prominent here. Revisiting a familiar Decadent conceit, the Pater Noster prayer in English, including doxology, with parallel text from the Vulgate becomes sacrilegiously the meeting point between eroticism and text-making.

Fig. 6.4 (below). Still from *The Pillow Book* (dir. Peter Greenaway, 1996), at 01:33:12. The publisher Yaji-san is carving the blanched, written-on skin of Jerome's exhumed body in order to master and bind *The Sixth Book: The Book of the Lover*.

scrawling in the masochistic ritual of puncturing his own body). Aptly in *A Lover's Discourse* Barthes conjures the analogy of 'words instead of fingers, or fingers at the tips of my words.'[71] The precious gems 'whose hot harsh names are never said' are lexical obscurities, pure components of style. As they are applied on flesh, these closed-off signifiers literally transform the body into a brilliant surface of Decadent style that exists for its own sake.

Greenaway's film explores the flesh/text convergence further as a political tool between the author Nagiko and the publisher Yaji-san. Nagiko creates '*The First Book of Thirteen*' on Jerome's skin and sends him to Yaji-san who is aroused by the naked, inscribed, feminized body of this 'ange blonde'. In having sex with Jerome, he has sex with the book. Later, Yaji-san in a macabre twist manufactures and binds '*The Book of the Lover*' out of Jerome's written dead body (Fig. 6.4) and, naked, comes into lecherous contact with it in an ostensible act of necrophilia. It is worth noting that book necrophilia is a variety that Holbrook Jackson discusses in a section titled 'Books Bound in Human Skin', in which 'bibliopegic dandies' indulge in the 'fetishism' of books bound in human skin.[72] Accordingly, in an odious anecdote, the flagrant, eccentric book collector Frederick Hankey, the inspiration behind Uzanne's 'Le Cabinet d'un éroto-bibliomane', asked Richard Burton to bring him the '*peau de femme*' of a living negress's backside to bind his *Justine*.[73] Despite how close book necrophilia comes to eroticizing and even defiling the text, it is supremely ironic: it epitomises perverse pleasure and yet a double inaccessibility as it implies an unresponsive, dead body, or *volume*, that is also made from inert language.

To recap, the works I have discussed in this chapter reflect what really makes Decadence distinctive: the reader participates in creating the fantasy through style and texture and the typographic medium itself, thus becoming an accomplice, privately exploring the Decadent text's open, transcending possibilities of pleasure. He or she succumbs bewitched by the *texte fatal*, resembling Dorian Gray who is in thrall, with 'parted lips', 'vibrating and throbbing to curious pulses': 'Words! Mere words! How terrible they were! How clear, and vivid, and cruel!'[74]

Notes to Chapter 6

1. William Gass, *On Being Blue: A Philosophical Inquiry* (Boston: David R. Godine, 1976), pp. 10, 11.
2. Oscar Wilde, *The Complete Works of Oscar Wilde: Stories, Plays, Poems, Essays* (1966; London: Collins, 1986), p. 115.
3. Walter Pater, *Appreciations, with an Essay on Style* (London and New York: Macmillan, 1889), p. 22.
4. Ibid., pp. 22–23.
5. Roland Barthes, *The Pleasure of the Text*, trans. by Richard Miller (New York: Hill and Wang, 1975), p. 8.
6. Ibid.
7. William Gaunt, *The Aesthetic Adventure* (1945; [London]: Pelican, 1957), p. 119.
8. Susan Sontag, 'Writing Itself: On Roland Barthes', in *A Susan Sontag Reader*, introd. by Elizabeth Hardwick (1963; Harmondsworth: Penguin, 1983), p. 446.
9. In *A Susan Sontag Reader*, pp. 95–104 (p. 104).
10. Barthes, *The Pleasure of the Text*, p. 17. Elsewhere Barthes confounds the 'sexiness of a body' with '*sexy sentences*', and 'erotic practice with linguistic practice'. Roland Barthes, *Roland Barthes by*

Roland Barthes, trans. by Richard Howard (Berkeley: University of California Press, 1977), p. 164.
11. Barthes, *The Pleasure of the Text*, p. 14.
12. *Ibid.*, p. 7.
13. Ben Hutchinson, 'Modernism and the Erotics of Style', in *Modernist Eroticisms: European Literature after Sexology* (Basingstoke: Palgrave Macmillan, 2012), pp. 213–31 (p. 220); Linda Dowling, *Language and Decadence in the Victorian Fin de Siècle* (Princeton: Princeton University Press, 1986), p. 130.
14. Dowling, *Language and Decadence*, p. 20. For the 'fatal book' see pp. 104–74.
15. *Ibid.*, p. 165.
16. Hutchinson, 'Modernism and the Erotics of Style', p. 215.
17. *Ibid.*, p. 220.
18. Paul Bourget, *Essais de psychologie contemporaine* (Paris: Gallimard, 1993), p. 14.
19. Gass, *On Being Blue*, pp. 16–17.
20. Walter Pater, *The Renaissance: Studies in Art and Poetry*, ed. by Adam Phillips (Oxford: Oxford University Press, 1998), p. 118.
21. Holbrook Jackson, *The Anatomy of Bibliomania* (1930; London: Faber and Faber, 1950), p. 627.
22. *Ibid.* Emphasis in original.
23. *Ibid.*, p. 629.
24. *Ibid.*, p. 604.
25. See Ian Gibson, *The English Vice: Beating, Sex and Shame in Victorian England and After* (London: Duckworth, 1978), pp. 244–45.
26. In Octave Uzanne, *Les Caprices d'un bibliophile* (Paris: Édouard Rouveyre, 1878), p. 142.
27. *Ibid.*, p. 144.
28. J.-K. Huysmans, *Against Nature*, trans. by Robert Baldick (London: Penguin, 1959), p. 114.
29. *Ibid.*, pp. 114–15.
30. See Dowling, *Language and Decadence*, pp.164–65 on 'the power of language to seduce its readers in a specifically sexual sense' (p. 165) by considering Moore's *Confessions*.
31. George Moore, *Confessions of a Young Man*, ed. by Susan Dick (1888; Montreal and London: McGill-Queen's University Press, 1972), p. 76.
32. *Ibid.*, p. 99.
33. *Ibid.*, p. 76.
34. Gordon Williams, *A Dictionary of Sexual Language and Imagery in Shakespearean and Stuart Literature* (London: Athlone Press, 1994), p. 131.
35. *Ibid.*
36. *The Metaphysical Poets*, ed. by Helen Gardner (1957; London: Penguin, 1985), p. 54.
37. For example, see Williams, *A Dictionary of Sexual Language*, p. 132.
38. Dante Gabriel Rossetti, *Collected Poetry and Prose*, ed. by Jerome McGann (Yale: Yale University Press, 2003), pp. 60–69 (p. 64). All quotations of the poem are from this edition, line references cited parenthetically.
39. Richard Cronin, *Reading Victorian Poetry* (Chichester: Wiley-Blackwell, 2012), p. 41.
40. Arthur Symons, 'White Heliotrope', in *London Nights* (London: Smithers, 1895), p. 49.
41. Symons, 'Idealism', in *London Nights*, p. 43.
42. Symons, 'At the Foresters', in *London Nights*, p. 23.
43. *Ibid.*
44. *Ibid.*
45. Roland Barthes, *S/Z*, trans. by Richard Miller (1974; New York: Hill and Wang, 2000), p. 5.
46. Ernest Dowson, *The Poetical Works of Ernest Christopher Dowson*, ed. and intro. by Desmond Flower (London: Cassell; Lane, 1934), p. 3. All Dowson's poetry quotations are from this edition.
47. *Ibid.*
48. John Keats, *The Letters of John Keats*, ed. by Maurice Buxton Forman, rev. edn (London: Oxford University Press, 1960), p. 473.
49. Dowson, *The Poetical Works*, p. 40.
50. *Ibid.*

51. *Ibid.*
52. *Ibid.*, p. 3.
53. *Ibid.*, p. 40.
54. 'The Hill of Dreams est sans doute le livre le plus décadent de toute la littérature anglaise.' Madeleine L. Cazamian, *Le roman et les idées en Angleterre: II. L'Anti-intellectualisme et l'esthétisme (1880–1900)* (1923; Paris: Les Belles Lettres, 1935), p. 260.
55. Machen, *The Hill of Dreams*, p. 1. Subsequent references given parenthetically.
56. See Machen, *The Hill of Dreams*, p. 221, n.1.
57. Arthur Machen, *Hieroglyphics*, The Caerleon Edition of the Works of Arthur Machen, 9 vols (London: Secker, 1923), V, 88.
58. Ellis Hanson, *Decadence and Catholicism* (Cambridge, MA: Harvard University Press, 1997). p. 23.
59. Barthes, *The Pleasure of the Text*, p. 42.
60. Olive Custance, *Opals* (London: John Lane, 1897), p. 4.
61. Barthes, *The Pleasure of the Text*, p. 38.
62. Dowling, *Language and Decadence*, p. 155.
63. *The Pillow Book*, dir. by Peter Greenaway, Kasander & Wigman Productions, *et al.* 1996. [On DVD].
64. Susan Sontag, 'Writing Itself: On Roland Barthes', p. 439.
65. *Peter Greenaway: Interviews,* ed. by Vernon Gras and Marguerite Gras (Jackson: University Press of Mississippi, 2000) pp. 180–81.
66. *European Literature from Romanticism to Postmodernism: A Reader in Aesthetic Practice,* ed. by Martin Travers (London: Continuum, 2001), p. 140.
67. Alan Woods, *Being Naked Playing Dead: The Art of Peter Greenaway* (Manchester: Manchester University Press, 1996), p. 268.
68. Huysmans, *Against Nature*, p. 146.
69. Wilde, *The Complete Works*, p. 102.
70. John Gray, *Silverpoints* (London: Matthews and Lane, 1893), p. xii.
71. Roland Barthes, *A Lover's Discourse*, trans. by Richard Howard (London: Penguin, 1990), p. 73.
72. Jackson, *The Anatomy of Bibliomania*, p. 402.
73. See Gibson, *The English Vice*, pp. 242–44.
74. Wilde, *The Complete Works*, p. 30.

CHAPTER 7

Bittersweet:
Michael Field's Sapphic Palate

Sarah Parker

This chapter explores the 'flavours' of female homoeroticism in the poetic works of Michael Field. 'Michael Field' was the collaborative pseudonym of Katharine Bradley and Edith Cooper, an aunt and niece who enjoyed an intimate romantic and creative partnership spanning a thirty-year period, beginning in 1884 with the verse-drama *Callirrhoë* and culminating in two volumes of Catholic poetry published in 1912 and 1913, the year of Cooper's death (Bradley died a year later in 1914). Bradley and Cooper were prolific; they published poetry, verse dramas and also documented their lives in an extensive joint diary *Works and Days* (1888–1914). Despite being neglected for the majority of the twentieth century, in the last ten years critical work on Michael Field has increased dramatically, prompting a renewed recognition of Bradley and Cooper's varied literary productions.

Bradley and Cooper moved in a circle comprised mainly of male aesthetes and Decadents, including Lionel Johnson, Arthur Symons, Charles Ricketts, Charles Shannon, Walter Pater and Oscar Wilde. They shared their fellow aesthetes' interests in the refinement and appreciation of the senses. This manifests itself in their diaries in detailed descriptions of the colours of flowers, the scents of perfumes, the texture of fabrics, the rhythms of classical music (they were admirers of Wagner), among other sensory experiences. In this chapter, I intend to focus specifically on taste in Michael Field's lyric poetry, examining the juxtaposition of 'bitter' and 'sweet' flavours across Bradley and Cooper's oeuvre, with a particular emphasis on *Long Ago* (1889), their debut volume as 'Michael Field'. I will consider these flavours as reflecting their engagement with the Ancient Greek poetess Sappho, their direct poetic precursors and their own homoerotic desires. Before commencing this discussion, however, some clarification of the connection between homoeroticism and the senses is required.

Synaesthesia and Homosexuality

Synaesthesia has long been associated with sexual inversion — the late nineteenth-century term for homosexuality.[1] Sexologists such as Richard Freiherr von Krafft-Ebing and Karl Heinrich Ulrichs believed that the invert was a hypersensitive, often creative individual, and linked both hypersensitivity and sexual 'perversity' to the theories of congenital degeneration popularized by Max Nordau. In *Degeneration*, Nordau examines literary texts such as Joris-Karl Huysmans's *À rebours* (1884) as case studies, linking synaesthesia (epitomized by Des Esseintes's 'sniffing of the colour of perfumes') to sexual perversity (his prurient interest in 'sexual aberrations' and corruption of a young boy').² However, whilst Nordau argues that synaesthesia can be linked to degeneracy and criminality, the British sexologist Havelock Ellis does not view either synaesthesia or sexual inversion as a dangerous disease, just as an abnormality:

> we may compare inversion to such phenomenon as colour-hearing, in which there is not so much defect, as an abnormality of nervous tracks producing new and involuntary combinations. Just as the colour-hearer instinctively associates colours with sounds [...] so the invert has his sexual sensations brought into relationship with objects that are normally without sexual appeal.³

A typically 'degenerate' writer to whom Nordau refers in his study is the poet Algernon Charles Swinburne. Synaesthesia manifests in his work in the form of 'intricate rhyme schemes and other sound patterns' combined with 'fusions and overlaps of visual imagery' which make 'excess demands on the reader's consciousness'.⁴ Swinburne's use of synaesthetic imagery can be linked to his blurring of other boundaries, such as those of gender and sexuality. As Alison Pease argues, the 'repetitive sexuality' of Swinburne's poems results in 'a bestial, sensual chaos that tends to collapse constructed taxonomies'.⁵ We find this tendency expressed through the figure of the androgyne — featured in Swinburne's poem 'Hermaphroditus' (1863) — who combines male and female genitalia, resulting in a 'double blossom of two fruitless flowers'.⁶ We also find this blurring of the genders in Swinburne's desire to 'become one' with Sappho, who was for him, 'beyond all question the greatest poet that ever lived'.⁷ In poems such as 'Anactoria' (inspired by Sappho's Fragment 16) and elsewhere ('Faustina', 'A Match'), Swinburne flaunts his fascination with the powerful *femme fatale*, until this fascination blurs into a kind of female identification: the effeminate man becomes one with the dominant woman.

Swinburne's poetry therefore seems to bear out Ellis's suggestion that synaesthesia and inverted sexuality can be connected — both conditions dissolve the boundaries between categories, whether sensory, or in terms of the body, gender roles, and sexual desire. However, in this chapter, I want to address two neglected aspects of this discussion. Firstly, whilst connections have been drawn between theories of synaesthesia and *male* homoeroticism in *fin-de-siècle* literature, links between female homoeroticism and the senses have been less frequently forged by critics.⁸ Secondly, whilst scent, visual stimuli and sound have featured in this dialogue, taste and flavour have figured less prominently. I propose that for Bradley and Cooper, writing together as Michael Field, the contrasting flavours of bitterness and sweetness came to embody their experience of female homoerotic desire *and* their identification with Sappho as an important poetic precursor. These flavours are detected on the tongue — which is, significantly, the organ of taste, the shaper of lyric speech, and a potential instrument of sexual pleasure.

'Heart-trainèd to the tongue': Singing Sapphic Desire

In 1885, Bradley and Cooper obtained a copy of new English translations from Sappho, Henry Thornton Wharton's *Sappho: Memoir, Text, Selected Renderings and A Literal Translation* (1885). They were instantly inspired by these translations, which were the first to reproduce Sappho's love lyrics with the female pronouns intact (previous translations had changed the addressee to male, or suggested that the love poems were spoken by male personae). In the Preface to *Long Ago*, Michael Field states their 'audacious' intention to extend 'Sappho's fragments into lyrics' — an idea that was eagerly welcomed by their mentor Robert Browning.[9] The result was a volume of sixty-eight lyric poems, each taking lines from Sappho (in Ancient Greek) as an epigraph and expanding them into an original poem.

Bradley and Cooper appeal to Sappho in order to signal their inheritance as women poets. As the most famous and celebrated woman poet, Sappho offered an unparalleled model for female creativity that inspired many women poets during the nineteenth century (and male poets too, as we have seen in relation to Swinburne). Yet, as Margaret Reynolds observes, Sappho offered a far from unproblematic model of female poetic identity:

> At a time when women were becoming increasingly radical in their demands for political and social freedoms at the expense of domestic claims, this fated nineteenth-century Sappho sang a song where art and love were mutually exclusive [...] the results for women poets were ambivalent. To be identified as a 'modern Sappho' was both an inspiring blessing and an inhibiting curse.[10]

Sappho's story seems to epitomize the suffering of the woman poet who must choose between art and love. The impossibility of this choice, and her rejection by Phaon (the boatman she loved, according to Ovid and later classical writers) results in her suicidal leap from the Leucadian cliffs. This narrative continues in Madame de Staël's influential novel *Corinne* (1807), which imagines the woman poet as a captivating performer who enjoys public adulation before her tragic death. The nineteenth-century poetesses L. E. L. (Letitia Elizabeth Landon) and Felicia Hemans continued this theme in 'The Improvisatrice' (1824) and 'Corinne at the Capitol' (1830).

But for Bradley and Cooper, writing later in the nineteenth century, Sappho represents an empowering example of a woman who made desire the very subject of her song. Rather than being the passive object of love poetry — the silent muse with which women had long been associated — Sappho's lyrics instead address men and women as *her* muses, placing her firmly in the position of poet. This was a model of creativity that Bradley and Cooper wished to emulate. This aspiration is expressed in an early poem by Bradley (published under her first pseudonym 'Arran Leigh') entitled 'The New Minnesinger' which articulates her belief that women must add their own voices to the tradition of love poetry, hitherto dominated by men:

> O Woman, all too long by thee
>   Love's praises have been heard;
> But thou to swell the minstrelsy
>   Hath brought no wealth'ning word.

> Thou, who its sweetest sweet canst tell
> Heart-trainèd to the tongue,
> Hast listened to its music well
> But never led the song![11]

The image of the 'tongue' is significant here, recalling Ovid's myth of Philomela, another important origin story for female creativity. As in the case of Sappho's unrequited love, the myth of the nightingale associates poetic creativity with both femininity and pain.[12] Drawing on this myth, Bradley asserts that rather than being silenced, woman must learn to use her tongue — trained to detect 'sweetest sweet' music — in order to 'lead the song'. Elsewhere, she and Cooper declare that it is 'Sweeter to sigh than be sighed over, | Sweeter to deal the blow than bear the grieving, | That girl will learn who dares become a lover'.[13] Sappho's poetry, full of love lyrics expressed to various named addressees, offers an inspiring example of a woman who 'dared become a lover' *and* a poet.

Sappho was also a particularly inspiring model for Bradley and Cooper because of her ambiguous sexuality. Whilst increasingly associated with lesbian desire by the end of the nineteenth century (thanks to the work of poets with strong classical abilities, such as Swinburne, who envisioned Sappho as a homoerotic figure), 'Victorian Sappho' continued to represent heterosexual desire. Thus, for the late Victorian 'educated reader, up-to-date with the developments in Greek scholarship, Sappho represented a sexual ambivalence: still the lover of Phaon, but now also clearly linked with a homoerotic female community'.[14] Sappho appealed to Bradley and Cooper as a model for their poetics precisely because 'she represents a category-defying mixture of sexual imagery which usefully tropes the identity configured within the space that is "Michael Field"'.[15]

Finally, in addition to her enabling sexual ambiguity, Sappho's lyric fragments offered Bradley and Cooper a treasure-trove of sensual imagery to incorporate into their own verse. Her poetry is replete with descriptions of luxurious objects, intoxicating scents, scintillating colours, and delicious flavours. The modernist poet H.D. alludes to this in her essay 'The Wise Sappho' (1918), associating Sappho with tints 'of rich colour [...] violets, purple woof of cloth, scarlet garments, dyed fastening of a sandal, the lurid, crushed and perished hyacinth'.[16] Jane McIntosh Snyder notes that: 'Such details of appearance, clothing, and adornment are essential aspects of the Sapphic texture of desire', connecting this to a female tradition of writing about clothes, fabrics and dyes.[17] In their diaries, Bradley and Cooper also participate in this tradition, focusing intently on details of clothing which they often incorporate into poems.[18] However, they also draw upon a language of taste and flavour derived from Sappho's lyrics, to which I now turn.

'Of love, the bitter-sweet, I sang': Flavour in Michael Field's *Long Ago* (1889)

Our modern understanding of flavour is itself a late nineteenth-century phenomenon. Research during the *fin-de-siècle* period focused on the idea that different areas of the tongue detected different tastes. In 1880, the Austrian physiologist Maximilian von Vintschgau concluded that there were four basic tastes: sweet, sour, bitter, and salty.[19] It is interesting to note that Bradley and Cooper's lyric poetry is written at precisely the moment that science is defining the location of tastes on the tongue, and these flavours — particularly bitterness, saltiness, and sweetness — pervade Michael Field's *Long Ago*.[20] For example, the word 'sweet' occurs thirty-one times in the volume. In 'Poem III', addressed to Phaon, Michael Field's Sappho hungers for sweet honey; a metaphor for her unrequited desire:

> Oh, not the honey nor the bee!
> Yet who can drain the flowers
> As I? Less mad, Persephone
> Spoiled the Sicilian bowers
> Than I for scent and splendour rove
> The rosy oleander grove,
> Or lost in myrtle nook unveil
> Thoughts that make Aphrodite pale.
>
> [...]
>
> Honey! clear, soothing, nectarous, sweet,
> On which my heart would feed,
> Give me, O Love, the golden meat
> And stay my life's long greed —
> The food in which the gods delight
> That glistens tempting in my sight!
> Phaon, thy lips withhold from me
> The bliss of honey and of bee.[21]

This poem is based on Sappho's fragment 'Neither honey nor bee for me', which, according to Wharton, was composed as an epithalamion poem. The phrase is spoken by a bride who wishes for 'good unmixed with evil'.[22] Field's poem, however, seems to express a different wish — their Sappho is hungry to experience pleasure (the sweetness of honey) even if it comes with a potential sting in its tail. The language of temptation and danger implies that consuming this honey will result in bitterness — like Persephone, this desirous woman will pay an awful price for revelling in the sensual delights of nature. This grim fate is hinted at by the presence of 'rosy oleander' which, despite its pleasing appearance, is a highly poisonous plant.

In 'Poem XVII' of *Long Ago*, presumably having consorted with Phaon, Sappho reaps the consequences of her rash actions, crying to Artemis for her lost 'maidenhood':

> And Sappho touched the lyre alone,
> Until she made the bright strings moan.
> She called to Artemis aloud —
> Alas, the moon was wrapped in cloud! —
>   'Oh, whither art thou gone from me?
>   Come back again virginity!'[23]

When Artemis rejects her, Sappho's suffering is figured as bitterness: 'O Sappho, bitter was thy pain!'[24] The golden honey in 'Poem III' is contrasted with the cold silver moon in 'Poem XVII', just as the sweetness of pleasure is juxtaposed with the bitterness of rejection. *Long Ago* ends with an unnumbered poem which imagines

Sappho's leap off the cliffs — a stark coastal setting that contrasts with the floral fecundity of earlier lyrics in the volume:

> O free me, for I take the leap,
> Apollo, from thy snowy steep!
> [...] let me be
> A dumb seabird with a breast love free,
> And feel the waves fall over me.[25]

Reading across *Long Ago* as a whole, I suggest therefore that two opposing flavours can be identified — honey, nectar, sweetness, and bee imagery, on the one hand, which is addictive and (eventually) cloying, and bitter, salt, sweat, tears, and sea-spray flavours, which represent the bitterness of unrequited or impossible love. These two flavours are drawn from a distinctly Sapphic palate derived from Sappho's fragments. As the poet Anne Carson observes: 'It was Sappho who first called eros "bittersweet"'.[26] In Fragment 130, Sappho describes love as: 'Sweetbitter, impossible to fight off, creature stealing up'.[27] Two poems from *Long Ago* make direct reference to this famous fragment: in 'Poem XXVIII', Michael Field's Sappho describes love as a 'fatal creature, bitter sweet'. In 'Poem LXII', she states: 'Of love, the bitter-sweet, I sang | Because I owned a glory in its curse'.[28]

The Greek word 'glukupikron' translates literally as 'sweetbitter', implying, as Diana Collecott notes, 'that Eros brings sweetness and then bitterness, in that order: the usual English translation inverts these elements'.[29] Catherine Maxwell argues that Sappho's 'characterization of the oxymoronic bittersweetness of love has pervaded lyric poetry ever since' and during the Renaissance was 'used extensively without realization of its original source'.[30] Edgar Wind confirms that Sappho was the originator of the term 'bittersweet', which was later incorrectly attributed to Orpheus by the Italian Renaissance philosopher Ficino: 'there can be no doubt that the cult of ambivalent love as defined by Sappho, and now proclaimed by Ficino as an Orphic tradition, had an influence on the "bitter-sweet" style of the Petrarchists who regarded themselves as Platonic poets'.[31]

As avid readers of Ancient Greek literature, it is likely that Bradley and Cooper used 'bittersweet' with an awareness of the Sapphic origins of the term. Bradley attended summer courses in classical languages at Newnham College, Cambridge, in 1874. She and Cooper also studied Latin and Ancient Greek at University College, Bristol, on moving to the city in 1879. Hence, the two women were well-versed in Ancient Greek *before* encountering Wharton's volume in 1885. As a result of this classical education, we can observe Sappho's influence on their poetry before *Long Ago*. In an early poem, entitled 'Bitter-Sweet' (in *The New Minnesinger*, 1875) Bradley uses the term in connection with memory, loss, and homoerotic love, suggesting her consciousness of the Sapphic roots of this word.[32] 'Bitter-Sweet' laments the loss of a female beloved, contrasting this with a natural setting of late summer in full bloom:

> O roses that for her are sweet!
>   O scent of new-mown hay!
> O grand old chestnuts, at whose feet
>   The happy children play!

> What bitter memories ye may be,
>   What memories bitter-sweet;
> Again beneath the chestnut tree
>   The little ones may meet;
>
> The roses bloom in pinken spray
>   'Mid briary thickets fair;
> But she who made the summer-day
>   May be no longer there.
>
> O what, an' if the roses red,
>   The hay about our feet,
> Should mind us of the darling dead
>   For whom they once were sweet![33]

This poem demonstrates Bradley's early awareness of Sappho, whose fragments use the imagery of bitterness and sweetness to lament the absence of past lovers or bemoan their unattainability — as in Fragment 31 when Sappho listens to her lover's 'sweet speaking' to another man:

> He seems fortunate as the gods to me, the man who sits opposite you and listens to your sweet voice and lovely laughter. Truly it sets my heart trembling in my breast. For when I look at you for a moment, then it is no longer possible for me to speak; my tongue is snapped, at once a subtle fire has stolen beneath my flesh, I see nothing with my eyes, my ears hum, sweat pours from me, a trembling seizes me all over, I am greener than grass, and it seems to me that I am little short of dying.[34]

It is possible to detect faint echoes of Sappho's fragment in Bradley's 'Bitter-Sweet': the 'new-mown hay' and 'briary thickets' evoke 'greener than grass', the blooming of the roses parallels the blush of Sappho's cheeks, and, of course, the preoccupation of both poems is imminent death and loss (in Bradley's case, this is perhaps a reference to the death of her mother in 1868; *The New Minnesinger* is dedicated to 'My Mother's Memory'). Matthew Mitton detects an echo of Sappho's fragments in another of Bradley's early poems, 'From the Ballads of Göthe': 'Alas that gentle feet should tread | Upon a violet's lowly head! | And must I die? O still 'tis sweet | To perish at the lov'd one's feet!'[35] Mitton notes that these 'four lines recall Sappho's fragment — "As on the hills the shepherds trample the hyacinth under foot and the purple flower [is pressed] to earth" — which Bradley and Cooper [...] turn into "V" from *Long Ago*'.[36]

'Bittersweet', along with other poems from *The New Minnesinger*, therefore supports the suggestion that Bradley was aware of Sappho's work *before* reading Wharton's edition of the fragments. Bradley and Cooper would also have been aware of Sappho through their reading of Swinburne. According to Elizabeth Prettejohn, Swinburne's 'Sapphic poems of the 1860s were an avowed inspiration' for Wharton in making his translations.[37] Swinburne links 'bittersweetness' to explicitly erotic scenarios in poems such as 'Fragoletta' and 'Anactoria'. For example, in 'Fragoletta' — again inspired by a hermaphroditic figure — the speaker is overcome with the 'bitterness of things too sweet!' Another poem, 'Anactoria', spoken by Sappho, opens with the statement: 'My life is bitter with thy love'.[38] Later in the poem,

Sappho sadistically fantasizes about consuming Anactoria's body:

> Ah that my mouth for Muses' milk were fed
> On the sweet blood thy sweet small wounds had bled!
> That with my tongue I felt them, and could taste
> The faint flakes from thy bosom to the waist!
> That I could drink thy veins as wine, and eat
> Thy breasts like honey! that from face to feet
> Thy body were abolished and consumed,
> And in my flesh thy very flesh entombed![39]

The lover's body, described here through the language of tastes found in such sensual Biblical passages as the 'Song of Songs' (in which the Bride's lips drip 'honey and milk' and her navel is 'a round goblet') and from the symbolism of the Eucharist itself, is almost cloying in its sweetness.[40] Sappho's unrequited love may be 'bitter', but her lover's body is sickly sweet (the words 'sweet' or 'sweeter' occur twenty-four times in the poem).

The entire poem plays on parallels between bodily eroticism and lyric composition; for example, Swinburne uses the word 'feet' to refer to the metrical units of the poem: 'seven times sweet, | The paces and the pauses of thy feet'.[41] In the same way, Sappho wishes to taste Anactoria's blood with her tongue, in order to compose her orally into a poem: 'thy body is the song, | Thy mouth the music'.[42] In a similar way, in her own Fragment 31, Sappho's 'broken tongue' signifies her bittersweet suffering — and uncannily anticipates her shattered poetic corpus (and her violent death): 'What is spoken [...] is the violence of Sappho's fragmentation'.[43] Thus, Swinburne's poem employs Sappho's own imagery of the tongue to simultaneously signal acts of lesbian oral eroticism *and* lyric (de)composition.

Pater also references Sappho's fragment in his *Greek Studies* (1895), describing Bacchus as: 'the god of the bitterness of wine, "of things too sweet"; the sea-water of the Lesbian grape become somewhat brackish in the cup' (brackish means 'slightly salty').[44] This description refers to the painting of *Bacchus* (1867) by the Pre-Raphaelite artist Simeon Solomon which depicts the god as a dark-haired youth with strikingly feminine features. While the quotation is taken from Swinburne's 'Fragoletta', Pater also indirectly references his 'Anactoria', in which Sappho refers to 'all the broken kisses salt as brine | That shuddering lips make moist with waterish wine' and 'stinging lips wherein the hot sweet brine | That Love was born of burns and foams like wine'.[45] Pater thus implicitly connects male and female homoeroticism by subtly layering references to Sappho's original fragment and to Swinburne's 'Anactoria', couched within his suggestive description of this homoerotic painting, thus uniting both homoerotic traditions within the same sensual Hellenistic world. This description may also signify Pater's awareness that Solomon himself was in fact as fond of portraying Sapphic subjects as he was male homoerotic figures — he completed a *Study of Sappho* in 1862, a watercolour *Sappho and Erinna in a Garden at Mytilene* (1864) and *Erinna Taken from Sappho* (1865), a sketch which dramatises Fragment 31.

'A little cave that cleaves': Landscape, Sensuality and the Female Body

Michael Field therefore inherit their Sapphic palate from their admired Decadent contemporaries, Swinburne and Pater, and use it in a similar way to represent the pleasures and pains of homoerotic love. However, theirs is also a specifically *female* homoerotic aesthetic. Bradley and Cooper use natural imagery of sweet flowers, honey, dew, and salty moisture to implicitly draw parallels to the flavours of the female body. This approach is derived from Sappho herself: as Snyder observes, Sappho's fragments blur descriptions of nature with a specifically female geography. For example, in Fragment 96, Sappho writes of a woman who surpasses all others just as:

> the rosy-fingered moon
>
> surpasses all the stars; the light
> spreads over the salty sea
> equally as over the many-flowered fields.
>
> And the dew grows beautifully liquid
> and roses and tender chervil
> flourish, and flowery honey-lotus.[46]

Snyder notes that in Sappho's fragments (and in Homer's writings) 'the dew is described as "female" [...] because women were associated with fluids and moisture (blood, amniotic fluid, vaginal secretions)'. In Fragment 96, Sappho therefore 'seems to be capitalizing on an already established pattern of symbolism whereby dew-covered flowers represent the female body'.[47]

In several poems from *Long Ago*, Bradley and Cooper forge a similar connection; for example, in 'Poem I', where amorous maidens twine dewy garlands and recline on mossy beds together, or other lyrics where moist flowers offer veiled imagery of female genitalia. For example, in 'Poem LII', Michael Field's masterful rewriting of the Tiresias myth, female sexual pleasure is described using the metaphor of a budding tree and a blooming rose:

> the thrill of
> springtide when the saplings fill.
> Though fragrant breath the sun receives
> From the young rose's softening leaves,
> Her plaited petals once undone
> The rose herself receives the sun.[48]

This gives the tastes described elsewhere a remarkably erotic charge — the licking of honey or the sweetness of the dew-soaked flower petal become symbols of female homoerotic desire. This sensuality is vividly evoked in 'Fragment XLIII' which describes the home of the nymphs:

> Cool water gurgles through
> The apple-boughs, and sleep
> Falls from the flickering leaves,
> Where hoary shadows keep
> Secluded from man's view

> A little cave that cleaves
> The rock with fissure deep.

Here, the imagery of the hidden grotto recalls the secreted spaces of the female body. This poem drips with moisture and fecundity, from the gurgling stream to the cave where the nymphs dwell, secluded 'from man's view':

> Worshipped with milk and oil,
> There dwell the nymphs, and there
> They listen to the breeze,
> About their dewy hair
> The clustered garlands coil,
> Or, moving round the trees,
> Cherish the roots with care.[49]

Like their fertile surroundings, the nymphs are fed 'milk and oil', their hair 'dewy' with fresh garlands. This is an idyllic world of mutual nourishment. This poem is based on Sappho's Fragment 2, which ends with an entreaty to Cypris (an alternative name for Aphrodite) to 'pour gracefully into golden cups nectar that is mingled with our festivities'.[50] Yopie Prins observes that the synaesthetic 'commingling of sensations in the first three stanzas [...] anticipates the commingling of the nectar in the fourth'. Once again, it is flavour — in this case, nectar — that provides a metaphor for erotic commingling, since the Ancient Greek word '*ommemeichmenon* [mingle] also has sexual connotations, as in the intermingling of bodies'.[51]

The poem epitomizes Bradley and Cooper's 'homoerotic topography' in which the 'language of place shades into the language of the body'.[52] The cleft — concealed by coils of dewy foliage, leading to hidden, fertile roots — evokes a suggestively vulvic landscape. This landscape draws its inspiration from Wharton's Preface, in which he cites a passage from John Addington Symonds's *Studies of the Greek Poets* (1873) where Symonds describes the sensual delights of Lesbos:

> All the luxuries and elegance of life which that climate and the rich valleys of Lesbos could afford, were at their disposal: exquisite gardens, in which the rose and hyacinth spread perfume; river-beds ablaze with the oleander and wild pomegranate; olive groves and fountains [...] fruits such as only the southern sea and sea-wind can mature [...] In scenes such as these the Lesbian poets lived, and thought of Love. When we read their poems, we seem to have the perfumes, colours, sounds and lights of that luxurious land distilled in verse.[53]

As Prins observes, in this passage: 'the landscape of Lesbos, with its valleys and rivers, spreading perfumes and feathery maidenhair, assumes the contours of a female body'.[54] Bradley and Cooper, in turn, build on this approach in order to create the decadent, sensual world of *Long Ago*.

Flavour is key here, as the sea-ripened fruits, olives and fresh herbs that Symonds mentions populate Bradley and Cooper's verse, signifying the flavours of the female body. This sensuality is evoked through the act of garland-weaving. Dewy flowers are joined together; an apt metaphor for lesbian love-making, echoing Swinburne's Sappho's demand in 'Anactoria': 'Let fruit be crushed on fruit, let flower on flower | Breast kindle breast'.[55] Skilful garland-weaving also requires dexterous finger-work — reminding us of Virginia Blain's entreaty 'not to overlook the importance of hands as signifiers of erotic power' in Michael Field's poetry.[56] In 'Poem XIII', Dica is praised for her garland-wreathing: 'Dica, the Graces oft incline | To watch thy fingers' skill | As with light foliage they entwine | The aromatic dill'.[57] This weaving can be read as an erotic, possibly masturbatory act, as Dica's deft fingers 'seek the fount where feathery, | Young shoots and tendrils creep'.[58] If this seems far-fetched, consider that Bradley and Cooper wrote openly of Giorgione's painting 'The Sleeping Venus': 'Her hand the thigh's tense surface leaves, | Falling inward. Not even sleep | Dare invalidate the deep, | Universal pleasure sex | Must unto itself annex'.[59]

Bradley and Cooper's garlands are tactile, scented and flavoured. They are composed of herbs that are aromatic, succulent and visually appealing: of 'piercing, languorous, spicy scent, | And thousand hues in lustre blent'.[60] This lends them a distinctive oral eroticism — the flavour and scent of the garland is suggestive of the salt, spice, and sweet aromas of female genitalia. This sensuous connection between landscape and the female body can be discerned in a later poem 'Circe at Circaeum', written by Cooper around 1900 and published in the posthumous 1914 collection *Dedicated*. The poem re-imagines the myth of Circe, Glaucus and Scylla from Circe's point of view. In the original tale, Circe's jealous love for the sea-god Glaucus led her to transform Scylla into a monster, by poisoning the water where she bathed. Cooper's poem envisages Circe brewing her potion at her island home: 'the shaggy rims | Of the shore's last rock-pool'.[61] Circe's potion 'bleeds' a 'drooping poppy leaf' into 'the vast glitter of the brine', but it is her sweet breath itself that gives the spell its potency:

> She breathes as if the rustling ferns set free
> The evening dew; she looses from her bosom
> A trail of jasmine-flower; her breathing stirs
> All that bees ravish from auriculas
> Of drugged, delicious, smothering meal; she closes
> With tremor to the shadowy breeze her lids,
> And lets her sweetness overlap the salt.[62]

Here, Circe's body and nature merge deliciously — it is her sweetness that infuses the salt of the sea. In this sense, Circe's body becomes one with that of her coastal surroundings — the salty rock pool — just as Scylla becomes yoked to dogs and other monstrous parts in Ovid's original myth: 'In vain she offers from herself to run | And drags about her what she strives to shun'.[63] As Marianne Govers Hopman observes, we can read Scylla's corrupted nether regions as embodying horror at female genitalia (anticipated in Scylla's rejection of Glaucus's tail).[64] Cooper's poem offers a counter-point to that myth; the imagery in 'Circe at Circaeum' describes a cave dripping with brine, but transforms disgust at female genitalia and fluids into a celebration of women's power and autonomy. The poem manages to revise a story of female rivalry and body-horror into a portrait of Circe's self-sufficient sensuality. The flavours of saltiness and sweetness are key to this — far from experiencing the 'bittersweetness' of love, Circe instead blends the sweetness from her bosom and her breath with the brackish 'ocean-ooze' that swirls around her lower half, resulting in orgasmic 'spasm-waves in coiling current spread'.[65]

'Lay upon our tongues Thy holy Bread': Later Poetry

Bradley and Cooper continue to develop their symbolic language of taste in their later poems. The title of their 1908 volume *Wild Honey from Various Thyme*, written during the period in which Bradley and Cooper converted to Catholicism, refers to John the Baptist's sustenance in the desert:

> Wild was the honey thou did'st eat;
> The rocks and the free bees,
> Entombed thy honeycomb.
> [...] no more we roam
> Or taste of desert food
> We have beheld thy Vision on the road.[66]

Here, Bradley and Cooper compare the experience of conversion to the ingestion of honey. This trope is derived from the Bible in which 'the gift of prophecy is figured [...] as an eating of the book which tastes like honey in the mouth'.[67] But elsewhere in the volume, Bradley and Cooper continue to utilize the Pagan imagery we find in their earlier lyrics (including *Long Ago*); for instance, in the pair poems 'The Feeding of Apollo' and 'The Feeding of Bacchus'. Bradley and Cooper's creative conversion is aided by their use of bee imagery that has both Pagan and Christian connotations. Thain points out that the bee was revered in Ancient Greece, where poets were often named after bees 'because of their noise and their ability to produce sweetness'.[68] Bradley and Cooper were clearly aware of this when writing *Long Ago*; in 'Poem XXVI', Sappho describes a young woman she is training to become a poet 'whose soft lips are dumb; | The golden bees about them hum'.[69] The use of bee symbolism therefore connects the sweet honey Sappho yearns for with John the Baptist's wild honey in the desert.

Another poem from *Wild Honey* entitled 'Festa' celebrates Bradley and Cooper's life together as delicious banquet of the senses. The speaker of the poem sits with her beloved in a 'white river room' (which may represent the poets' Richmond home by the Thames, The Paragon, where they moved in 1899). Here, the 'festa' (an Italian word for a religious festival) marks the celebration of their relationship:

> A feast that has no wine! O joy intense,
> Clear ecstasy in one white river-room!
> To-night my Love is with me in the bloom
> Of roses — laughing at their redolence:
> 'A cedar-coffer, a miasma dense
> With suck of honey' ... Dote on their perfume,
> Find tropes! I, shuddering at thy rescued doom,
> Sigh for some wider token to my sense
> Of the wonder that I have of thee, my bride,
> My feast ... The candles burn: they are too few.
> But, hist! the river-night hath heard my sigh:
> The candles reappear and multiply.
> Procession-wise in filmy lights outside;
> And the oar plashes as from singing dew.[70]

Fragrance plays a central role in this poem, as the beloved challenges the speaker to 'find tropes' for the evocative perfume of the roses. But flavour is also present via the speaker's synaesthetic response: the feast needs 'no wine', for the banquet is 'the suck of honey' exuded by the roses. The companion is also hailed as 'my bride, my feast', recalling verses from the Song of Songs: 'I am come into my garden, my sister, my spouse: I have gathered my myrrh with my spice; I have eaten my honeycomb with my honey; I have drunk my wine with my milk: eat [...] drink abundantly, O beloved' (5:1). These lines are also reminiscent of Swinburne's Anactoria, who desires to consume the beloved, describing her fingers as 'good to bruise or bite | As honeycomb of the inmost honey-cells, | With almond-shaped and roseleaf-coloured shells'.[71] The image of 'singing dew' at the close of the poem evokes the dew-wet foliage of *Long Ago* with all its connotations of feminine sexuality. The beloved reawakens the speaker's senses (giving 'wider token of my sense') culminating in 'clear ecstasy' — and in poetic creation: the dew is 'singing' like the poet.

Another poem from *Wild Honey* that employs flavour symbolism is 'Cherry Song'. The speaker dreams of 'Where I ate cherries with thee in a valley, | And the fruit was red' and 'the juice was sweet'.[72] The location of this poem in a dream-like space, combined with its regular nursery rhyme-like quatrains, works to play down the erotic connotations of the juicy cherries. The poem calls to mind Christina Rossetti's 'Goblin Market' (1862). In Rossetti's much-analyzed poem, sisterly love shades into erotic desire as Lizzie begs her sister:

> Come and kiss me.
> Never mind my bruises,
> Hug me, kiss me, suck my juices
> Squeez'd from goblin fruits for you,
> Goblin pulp and goblin dew.
> Eat me, drink me, love me;
> Laura, make much of me[73]

Critics such as Mary Wilson Carpenter describe the poem as 'undeniably homoerotic': 'The result of Laura's totally unrestrained, orgiastic consumption of the "juices" on her sister's body is her restoration to life and health and [...] to desire'.[74] Rossetti was the only contemporary woman poet openly revered by Bradley and Cooper — in their poem 'Why are Women Silent?' they place her alongside Sappho as an example of female poetic mastery resulting from unrequited passion:

> O Christina, by thy cry of pain,
> Sappho by thy deadly sweat, I answer women can attain
> The great measures of the masters only if they love in vain.[75]

This 'deadly sweat' recalls Fragment 31, in which Sappho's body is shaken by a cold sweat. We can also detect 'bittersweetness' in this image: the word 'sweat' bears a visual resemblance to sweet, yet it is salty to taste. Given their admiration of Rossetti and the incestuous nature of their own relationship, it is likely that Bradley and Cooper found inspiration in Rossetti's 'Goblin Market', a poem that combines religious symbolism, mouth-watering fruits and female homoeroticism.

Thus, these poems from *Wild Honey* demonstrate that despite their conversion to Catholicism, Bradley and Cooper continued to employ the language of flavour to represent desire. In keeping with this, their later religious poetry, published in *Poems of Adoration* (1912) and *Mystic Trees* (1913), features erotic imagery of Eucharistic consumption and of Christ's wounds. Consider, for example, the poem 'A Crucifix' that describes Jesus as 'a welcoming open fruit' and the poem 'Imple Superna Gratia' (meaning 'Fill up with divine grace') which expresses a vampiric desire to feed on the wounds:

> We may enter far into a rose,
> Parting it, but the bee deeper still:
> With our eyes we may even penetrate
> To a ruby and our vision fill;
> [...]
> Give me finer potency of gift!
> For Thy Holy Wounds I would attain,
> As a bee the feeding loveliness
> Of the sanguine roses. I would lift
> Flashes of such faith that I may drain
> From each Gem the wells of Blood that press![76]

In this poem, the speaker desires to penetrate and feed on Christ's wounds just as a bee pollinates a rose. This is strikingly reminiscent of *Long Ago*'s 'Poem III', in which Sappho longs to drain the flowers of their honey and nectar. The disturbingly vampiric imagery of this poem transforms transubstantiation — the transformation of Christ's body and blood into the bread and wine taken at communion — into 'a sexualized feeding on Christ'.[77] This feeding also encodes a specifically *female* homoeroticism, as the speaker imagines 'parting' the leaves of the rose to reach its deepest centre. As Paula Bennett notes, flowers, jewels, and bees — all of which are found in this poem — function as clitoral symbols in nineteenth-century women's poetry.[78] Oral eroticism permeates the poem; the speaker wishes to drink and 'drain' the flower of its 'ruby' nectar, evoking menstrual imagery.

Another poem, 'That He Should Taste Death For Every Man' also meditates on the process of transubstantiation, focusing on the wafer received on the tongue in the Sacrament. The speaker expresses gratitude that Christ himself 'ate' death, so that his followers could receive salvation:

> No grinding of the cornfield had sufficed
> To lay upon our tongues Thy holy Bread,
> Unless Thou hadst Thyself so harshly fed
> With grindings of the bone of death[79]

Finally, a poem entitled 'After Anointing' revels in the sensuality of Catholic ritual. As Ellis Hanson observes, the Church appealed to many Decadent writers because of its sensory extravagance: 'The sheer sensuality of its ritual, whether Anglo or Roman Catholic, exposed the Church to accusations of Paganism, even hedonism, rendering it the ideal stage for the subversive gestures of the Catholic dandy'.[80] Bradley and Cooper were not immune to this; 'After Anointing' revels in the 'joy of the senses' they discovered in the Catholic Church: 'joy of all | And each of them, as fall | The Holy Oils!'[81] In the second stanza, the five points upon which the holy oils are applied (representing Christ's five wounds) are compared to the 'fivefold garland' of the senses:

> Joy ripples through each covered lid;
>   Nor are the ears forbid
> Sounds as of honeycomb, so sweet is Heaven
> Afar, such sweet, such haunting sound!
> O nostrils, myrtle ye shall love!
> The lips taste fully, as if God were found.
>   Swift, under peace, toward Heaven
> The hands, the feet, so still, like still lakes move.
> Delighted Powers of Sense, ye dance,
>   Woven in such a lovely chance![82]

This poem attests to the fact that Bradley and Cooper were still weaving garlands of sensory delight twenty-three years after the publication of *Long Ago*. Whether through Sappho's honey, sea-ripened fruits, or the touch of the communion wafer on the tongue, flavour played a key part in catalysing the significant poetic transformations which led their work from Ancient Greece to the Catholic Church. Despite their conversion from Paganism to Christianity, Michael Field's use of flavour to represent desire remains constant across their oeuvre. Their Sapphic palate, trained on bittersweetness, remains sensitive to the end.

'Like a mermaid': Tasting Sappho in the Twentieth Century

Michael Field's use of bittersweet flavours forms part of an ongoing tradition in women's writing. We can, for example, trace links between *Long Ago* and the modernist poet H.D.'s debut collection *Sea Garden* (1916):

> H.D.'s 'Sea Garden' is indeed a garden of flowers [...] but it is always a garden whose sweetness and comfort is tempered by sea-salt and rock, by sand and wind. There is always the undertow of bitterness to counter the honeyed delight of the flowers — the glukupikron ('sweet-bitter') element of eros with which Sappho is constantly preoccupied.[83]

Equally, in *Long Ago*, as we have seen, although some poems are brimming with lush woodland and sweet-smelling flowers, other poems are set in the 'bitter' world of the cliffs, waves, and salt-spray, where Sappho meets her death. H.D.'s life-long companion Bryher also published a volume, *Region of Lutany* (1914), which draws on Sapphic landscapes and synaesthetic imagery, forging a 'homoerotic topography' that has parallels with *Long Ago*. For example in 'Corfu', the island is depicted as a lover with a sensual 'wave-curved mouth', 'quivering' and 'breathing' with a 'cypress-breast'.[84]

In a posthumously published poem by Amy Lowell, entitled 'To Two Unknown Ladies' (1927), flavour provides a covert means for writing about lesbian relationships. The 'ladies' in question are Somerville and Ross (Edith Somerville and Violet Florence Martin) whose personal and creative partnership bears a striking resemblance to that of Michael Field. On reading their work, Lowell's speaker is strangely 'haunted' by these two dead spinsters: 'I go back to you again, | Evening and evening, in a kind of thirst, | Surprising my tongue upon an almond taste'.[85] The significance of the almond flavour is never explained, though it is reaffirmed later on: 'Almonds, I said, | Smooth, white, and bitter, wonderfully almonds'.[86]

The significance of the almond flavour is clarified, however, if we consider that Lowell describes her beloved as an almond in the 'Two Speak Together' section of *Pictures of the Floating World* (1919). These love poems have been read as addressed to Lowell's long-term partner Ada Dwyer Russell. 'Aubade' compares undressing the beloved to shelling an almond: 'As I would free the white almond from the green husk | So would I strip your trappings off, | Beloved'.[87] 'White and Green' depicts the naked beloved as 'an almond flower unsheathed | Leaping and flickering between the budded branches'.[88] In her last volume before her death, *What's O'Clock* (1925), Lowell included a poem entitled 'In Excelsis'. This poem employs Eucharistic imagery, as the beloved is consumed by the speaker, filling her as water (or milk) fills an empty vessel:

> I drink your lips,
> I eat the whiteness of your hands and feet.
> My mouth is open,
> As a new jar I am empty and open.
> Like white water are you who fill the cup of my mouth [...][89]

Drawing on these and other examples, Collecott identifies a language of fluidity in modernist women's writing which she links directly to a Sapphic aesthetic. This emphasis on '*licking, tasting, eating*' confounds 'the boundary between inside and out', between self and other, in addition to situating these poems within an ongoing tradition of writing about female desire.[90] Contemporary poets writing during the era of second-wave feminism continue to experiment with such imagery, linking taste even more explicitly to lesbian eroticism. For example, Olga Broumas's 'Sleeping Beauty' describes love-making as an exchange of bitter and salty fluids:

> Blood. Tears. The vital
> salt of our body. Each
> other's mouth.
> Dreamlike
>
> the taste of you
> sharpens my tongue like a thousand shells,
> bitter, metallic. I know
>
> as I sleep
> that my blood runs clear
> as salt
> in your mouth, my eyes.[91]

Adrienne Rich's early poem 'Holiday' is set in a Sapphic idyll of 'dripping leaves' where 'The senses flourished like a laden tree'. The speaker and her beloved dine together:

> From wicker baskets by a green canal,
> Staining our lips with peach and nectarine,
> Slapping at golden wasps. And when we kissed,
> Tasting that sunlit juice, the landscape folded
> Into our clasp, and not a breath recalled
> The long walk back to winter, leagues away.[92]

With its ripe fruits and golden wasps, this poem is strikingly similar to Bradley and

Cooper's lyric productions; indeed, it would not be out of place in *Wild Honey*. Rich continues to develop this Sapphic imagery in her later work. 'The Floating Poem, unnumbered' from *Twenty-One Love Poems* (1976) describes lesbian lovemaking as 'like the half-curled frond | of the fiddlehead fern in forests | just washed by sun' and the lover's fingers 'reaching where I had been waiting years for you | in my rose-wet cave'.[93]

Finally, we can identify a cluster of later twentieth-century novels and films that draw on a Sapphic palate — if obliquely. Consider, for example, Patricia Highsmith's *The Price of Salt* (1952), May Sarton's *Mrs Stevens Hears the Mermaids Singing* (1975) — its solitary coastal setting reminiscent of Sappho's island — and Rainer Werner Fassbinder's strange portrait of lesbian sadomasochism, *The Bitter Tears of Petra von Kant* (1972). Most recently, Sarah Waters's neo-Victorian novel *Tipping the Velvet* (1998) opens with the line 'Have you ever tasted a Whitstable oyster?' before the heroine, Nan, informs us that Whitstable oysters are 'the juiciest, the savouriest yet the subtlest, oysters in the whole of England.'[94] Waters knowingly employs the oyster here as a symbol for female genitalia (just as the title of the novel plays on Victorian slang for cunnilingus). The young Nan's appreciation and intimate knowledge of the oyster foreshadows her lesbian destiny. Later, Nan worries that she tastes 'like a herring' when Kitty kisses her hand, to which Kitty replies: '"perhaps, maybe, like a mermaid..." And she kissed my fingers.'[95] Kitty's reaction suggests that she too revels in the salt flavours of the female body. Drawing on the same Sapphic palate as Bradley and Cooper, these texts, whether consciously or unconsciously, figure Sapphic desire as a flavour — one that can be, by turns, both bitter and sweet.

Notes to Chapter 7

1. 'Sexual inversion' refers to the theory that the homosexual had a female soul in a male body (or vice versa). For more on Victorian sexology, see *Sexology in Culture: Labelling Bodies and Desires*, ed. by Lucy Bland and Laura Doan (Chicago: University of Chicago Press, 1998).
2. Max Nordau, *Degeneration* (London: William Heinemann, 1898), pp. 304–05, p. 309.
3. Havelock Ellis and J. Addington Symonds, *Studies in the Psychology of Sex, Vol. 1 Sexual Inversion* (London: Wilson and Macmillan, 1897), pp. 186–87.
4. Catherine Maxwell, *The Female Sublime from Milton to Swinburne: Bearing Blindness* (Manchester: Manchester University Press, 2001), p. 196.
5. Alison Pease, 'Questionable Figures: Swinburne's *Poems and Ballads*', *Victorian Poetry*, 35 (1997), 43–56 (p. 45).
6. Algernon Charles Swinburne, 'Hermaphroditus' (1863), in *Algernon Charles Swinburne: Selected Poems*, ed. by Catherine Maxwell (London: J. M. Dent, 1997), pp. 33–35 (p. 34). All subsequent references are from this volume.
7. Swinburne, 'Sappho', *Saturday Review*, 117 (1914), 228.
8. See discussions in Maxwell (cited above), Dominic Janes, 'Seeing and tasting the divine: Simeon Solomon's homoerotic sacrament', in *Art, History and the Senses: 1830 to the Present*, ed. by Patrizia di Bello and Gabriel Koureas (Farnham: Ashgate, 2010), pp. 35–50, and Charlotte Ribeyrol, *Étrangeté, passion, couleur, L'hellénisme de Swinburne, Pater et Symonds* (Grenoble: ELLUG, 2013).
9. Michael Field, 'Preface', *Long Ago* (London: George Bell & Sons, 1889), no pagination.
10. Margaret Reynolds, '"I lived for art, I lived for love": The Woman Poet Sings Sappho's Last Song', in *Victorian Women Poets: An Anthology*, ed. by Angela Leighton and Margaret Reynolds (Oxford: Blackwell, 1995), pp. 277–306 (p. 278).

11. Arran Leigh (Katharine Bradley), *The New Minnesinger and Other Poems* (London: Longmans, Green and Co, 1875), pp. 1–8. A 'minnesinger' is the name for a medieval German troubadour.
12. In Ancient Greek mythology, Philomela is raped by her brother-in-law Tereus. He cuts out her tongue so that she cannot relate her experience. She is eventually transformed into a nightingale — a symbol of the poet's song used by male poets such as Milton, Keats, Shelley, and Tennyson (see Maxwell). For women poets' use of this myth, see Cheryl Walker, *The Nightingale's Burden: Women Poets and American Culture Before 1900* (Indiana: Indiana University Press, 1982).
13. Michael Field, 'I would not be a fugitive', *Underneath the Bough* (London: George Bell & Sons, 1893), pp. 131–32.
14. Marion Thain, *Michael Field: Poetry, Aestheticism and the Fin de Siècle* (Cambridge: Cambridge University Press, 2007), p. 53.
15. *Ibid.*, p. 50.
16. H.D. 'The Wise Sappho', in *The Penguin Book of Lesbian Short Stories*, ed. by Margaret Reynolds (London: Penguin, 1993), pp. 26–34 (p. 26).
17. Jane McIntosh Snyder, *Lesbian Desire in the Lyrics of Sappho* (Columbia: Columbia University Press, 1998), p. 94.
18. See Sarah Parker, 'Fashioning Michael Field: Michael Field and Late-Victorian Dress Culture', *Journal of Victorian Culture*, 18 (2013), 313–34.
19. The 'tongue map' originated in a 1901 paper by German scientist David Hänig. This paper was translated by the Harvard psychologist Edwin G. Boring in 1942. However, the diagram was misinterpreted, leading to the enduring misconception that different parts of the tongue can *only* pick up certain tastes: bitter (back of the tongue), sour and salty (the middle), and sweet (on the tip).
20. Flavour also features in *Works and Days*: for example, on 6 January 1901, Cooper gives a detailed menu for their 'New Century Dinner' with Ricketts and Shannon which includes 'Plum Pudding, Cherry Pudding, Stone Cream, Croûte au Caviar, English Pine, Almonds and Raisins, Newtown Pippins' followed by 'Coffee, Crème de Mocco, Cigarettes', quoted in Marion Thain and Ana Parejo Vadillo, *Michael Field, The Poet* (Plymouth: Broadview, 2009), p. 270.
21. Field, *Long Ago*, pp. 5–6.
22. Henry Thornton Wharton, 'Fragment 113', *Sappho: Memoir, Text, Selected Renderings and A Literal Translation* (London: David Stott, 1885), p. 131.
23. Field, *Long Ago*, p. 27.
24. *Ibid.*
25. *Ibid.*, p. 128.
26. Anne Carson, *Eros the Bittersweet: An Essay* (Princeton: Princeton University Press, 1996), p. 3.
27. Quoted in Carson, *Eros the Bittersweet*, p. 3.
28. Field, *Long Ago*, p. 46; p. 114.
29. Diana Collecott, *H.D. and Sapphic Modernism* (Cambridge: Cambridge University Press, 1999), p. 193.
30. Maxwell, *The Female Sublime from Milton to Swinburne*, p. 32.
31. Edgar Wind, *Pagan Mysteries in the Renaissance* (London: Faber and Faber, 1958), p. 163.
32. In 1891, Bradley writes that she originally came to Newnham with 'the pulpy lyrics of the N. M. [*New Minnesinger*] in my brain'. This suggests that her early poems were written at the same time she was receiving her classical education (quoted in Thain and Vadillo, *Michael Field, The Poet*, p. 245).
33. Arran Leigh (Katharine Bradley), *The New Minnesinger*, pp. 29–30.
34. David A. Campbell, trans., 'Fragment 31', *Greek Lyric I: Sappho & Alcaeus* [Loeb Classical Library] (Cambridge, MA: Harvard University Press, 1994), pp. 79–81.
35. Leigh (Bradley), *New Minnesinger*, pp. 17–20.
36. Matthew Mitton, 'Before Michael Field: Katharine Bradley as "Arran Leigh"', *Philological Quarterly*, 89 (2010), 311–35 (p. 325).
37. Elizabeth Prettejohn, 'Solomon, Swinburne, Sappho', *Victorian Review*, 34 (2008), 103–28 (p. 120).
38. Swinburne, 'Anactoria', in *Algernon Charles Swinburne: Selected Poems*, p. 37; p. 25.
39. *Ibid.*, p. 28.

40. *Song of Solomon, The Holy Bible* (King James Version. Cambridge Edition: 1769), *King James Bible Online*, 2015. 4.11, 7.3. <http://www.kingjamesbibleonline.org>.
41. Swinburne, 'Anactoria', p. 28. See Yopie Prins, *Victorian Sappho* (Princeton: Princeton University Press, 1999), p. 127.
42. Swinburne, 'Anactoria', p. 27.
43. Prins, *Victorian Sappho*, p. 28.
44. Walter Pater, *Greek Studies: A Series of Essays* (London and New York: Macmillan and Co: 1895), p. 37.
45. Swinburne, 'Anactoria', p. 27.
46. Quoted in Snyder, *Lesbian Desire in the Lyrics of Sappho*, p. 46 (Snyder's translation).
47. Snyder, *Lesbian Desire in the Lyrics of Sappho*, p. 51.
48. Field, *Long Ago*, pp. 90–91.
49. *Ibid.*, p. 68.
50. Campbell, 'Fragment 2', p. 57.
51. Prins, *Victorian Sappho*, p. 98.
52. *Ibid.*, p. 99; p. 98.
53. John Addington Symonds quoted in Wharton, *Sappho: Memoir, Text, Selected Renderings and A Literal Translation*, pp. 12–13.
54. Prins, *Victorian Sappho*, p. 100.
55. Swinburne, 'Anactoria', p. 26.
56. Virginia Blain. 'Sexual Politics of the (Victorian) Closet; or, No Sex Please — We're Poets', in *Women's Poetry, Late Romantic to Late Victorian, Gender and Genre, 1830–1900*, ed. by Isobel Armstrong and Virginia Blain (London: Macmillan, 1999), pp. 135–63 (p. 137).
57. Field, *Long Ago*, p. 20.
58. *Ibid.*
59. Field, *Sight and Song* (London: Elkin Matthews and John Lane, 1892), pp. 101–02.
60. Field, *Long Ago*, p. 21.
61. Michael Field, 'Circe at Circaeum', *Dedicated: An Early Work* (London: George Bell & Sons, 1914), pp. 72–74 (p. 72).
62. *Ibid.*, p. 73.
63. Ovid, *Metamorphosis*, trans. by John Dryden (Ware: Wordsworth Editions, 1998), p. 460.
64. Marianne Govers Hopman, *Scylla: Myth, Metaphor, Paradox* (Cambridge: Cambridge University Press, 2012), pp. 138–40.
65. Field, 'Circe at Circaeum', p. 73.
66. Michael Field, *Wild Honey from Various Thyme* (London: T. Fisher Unwin 1908), no pagination.
67. Thain, *Michael Field*, p. 141.
68. *Ibid.* Sappho was named the 'Pierian bee' after the spring of the Muses: see Hilda M. Ransome, *The Sacred Bee in Ancient Times and Folklore* (1937; New York: Dover Publications, 2004).
69. Field, *Long Ago*, p. 42.
70. Field, *Wild Honey*, p. 176.
71. Swinburne, 'Anactoria', pp. 28–29.
72. Field, 'Cherry Song', *Wild Honey*, p. 28.
73. Christina Rossetti, *Goblin Market and Other Poems* (London and Cambridge: Macmillan and Co, 1865), p. 25.
74. Mary Wilson Carpenter, '"Eat Me, Drink Me, Love Me": The Consumable Female Body in Christina Rossetti's "Goblin Market"', *Victorian Poetry*, 29 (1991), 415–34 (p. 416).
75. Michael Field, *Underneath the Bough* (London: George Bell & Sons, 1893), p. 59.
76. Michael Field, *Mystic Trees* (London: Everleigh Nash, 1913), p. 35; Field, *Poems of Adoration* (London: Sands and Co, 1912), p. 92.
77. Thain, *Michael Field*, p. 177.
78. Paula Bennett, 'Critical Clitoridectomy: Female Sexual Imagery and Feminist Psychoanalytic Theory', *Journal of Women in Culture and Society*, 18 (1993), 235–59 (p. 236).
79. Field, *Poems of Adoration*, p. 14.
80. Ellis Hanson, *Decadence and Catholicism* (Cambridge, MA: Harvard University Press, 1998), p. 6.

81. Field, *Poems of Adoration*, p. 105.
82. *Ibid.*
83. Snyder, *Lesbian Desire in the Lyrics of Sappho*, p. 143.
84. Bryher [as A. W. Ellerman], *Region of Lutany* (London: Chapman & Hall, 1914), p. 7.
85. Amy Lowell, *The Complete Poetical Works of Amy Lowell* (Boston: Houghton Mifflin, 1955), p. 563.
86. *Ibid.*, p. 564.
87. *Ibid.*, p. 73.
88. *Ibid.*
89. *Ibid.*, p. 444.
90. Collecott, *H.D. and Sapphic Modernism*, p. 197.
91. Olga Broumas, *Beginning With O* (New Haven: Yale University Press, 1977), pp. 61–62.
92. Adrienne Rich, *Poems: Selected and New: 1950–1974* (New York: W. W. Norton & Company, 1975), p. 20.
93. Rich, *The Dream Of A Common Language: Poems 1974–1977* (New York: W. W. Norton & Company, 1978), p. 32.
94. Sarah Waters, *Tipping the Velvet* (London: Virago, 1999), p. 3.
95. *Ibid.*, p. 33.

CHAPTER 8

Dancing the Image: Sensoriality and Kinesthetics in the Poetry of Stéphane Mallarmé and Arthur Symons

Katharina Herold

> Dance is life [...] more natural than nature, more artificial than art [...].
> ARTHUR SYMONS, 'The World as Ballet' (1907)

Symbolism, as an avant-garde movement of the late nineteenth century, promoted the exploration of dance across the art disciplines. At the *fin de siècle* the French poet and pioneer of Symbolist aesthetics, Stéphane Mallarmé (1842–1898), and his English translator and disciple Arthur Symons (1865–1945), innovated ways in which to recreate the virtuality of dance by the means of language. As Susan Jones and Mark Franko have pointed out, Mallarmé and Symons even anticipated (post)modernist standards in connecting dance and literature that reached an unmatched level of 'mobility, intermediacy, multiplicity, reflexivity'.[1] With these abstract poetic qualities, dance becomes the ideal Symbolist art form, as Frank Kermode outlines in his seminal study *Romantic Image*.[2] Moving away from Kermode's focus on periodization, this essay is concerned with the technicality underlying both dance and Symbolist and Decadent dance poetry.

Dancing, as well as the reading of Symbolist dance poetry, requires kinesthetic awareness, the ability quite literally to 'move (from Greek *kinein*) with the sensation (*aisthēsis*)' and identify the position and movement of the parts of the body by means of sensory organs. By examining Mallarmé's and Symons's dance poetry I argue that through so-called *transpositions d'art*,[3] Symbolist poetics consciously play with kinesthetics to actively engage their readers in a sensory experience. Accordingly, both poets attempted to re-define the limits of linguistic sensoriality in their treatment of dance as an image set in motion, trying to capture its unique characteristics, namely fleetingness, virtuality, and suggestiveness.

Mallarmé establishes the semiotics of dance — the act of signifying instead of telling, the inseparability of form and subject, and a constant oscillation of referential meaning in space — as the central mechanism of two of his most masterful poems, *Hérodiade* [*Herodias*], fully published only in 1926, and *Un coup de Dés jamais n'abolira le Hasard* [*A Dice Throw At Any Time Never Will Abolish Chance*] (1897).

This 'choreographic potential of writing'[4] actively engages the reader, who is to re-create and share in the dance of signs. In contrast, Symons introduces the dancer as metaphorical subject matter and reconsiders poetic language to describe the impressions of momentary transcendence through sensory experience. Unlike Mallarmé's attempts to equate the dancer and the metaphor of dance, Symons's treatment of the metaphor in his early verse collections, *Silhouettes* (1892), *London Nights* (1895), and *Images of Good and Evil* (1899), ranges from dance as an abstract metaphor for the fleetingness of life, the Decadent dancer as eroticized female body, to the dancer as a mysterious Symbolist image of escapism.

In reaction to Mallarmé's celebrated series of lectures on the relationship between music and literature delivered at Oxford and Cambridge in 1894, his work received critical attention primarily for its musicality. The affinity between literature and the performing arts, specifically dance, takes centre stage in Mallarmé's aesthetics.[5] Mallarmé's critical writings render a concise catalogue of the unique qualities of dance. In particular Loïe Fuller represented for him 'la forme théâtrale de poésie par excellence' [the theatrical form of poetry par excellence].[6] Fuller, performing her 'serpentine' dance in front of astounded Parisian audiences in 1892, sought 'a new dance vocabulary independent of ballet'.[7] Her innovative, proto-futurist style of dancing (Fig. 8.1) challenged the traditional ballet, and embodied for Mallarmé the ultimate union of subject and form. The images conveyed by her movements exemplify Mallarmé's ideal of dance and poetry alike:

> comme invention, sans l'emploi, comporte une ivresse d'art [...] Au bain terrible des étoffes se pâme, radieuse, froide la figurante qui illustre maint thème giratoire où tend une trame loin épanouie, pétale et papillon géants, déferlement, tout d'ordre net et élémentaire.
>
> [an invention without utility, includ[ing] an intoxication of art [...] In the fearsome bath of the materials swoons — radiant and cold — the interpreter who illustrates many gyratory themes towards which stretches a thread in full bloom: an unfolding, like giant petals or butterflies, all very clear and straightforward].[8]

Mallarmé imagines the dancer as writing the audience's vision 'à la façon d'un Signe, qu'elle est' [in form of a Sign, the sign that she herself is].[9] Fuller allows the audience to read meaning into abstract shapes created by the animation of her billowing robes, so that the observer watching her dance has to piece together a narrative and interpret it as a 'synthèse mobile' [a synthesis — constantly moving].[10] In this way the dancer becomes the 'révélatrice' [revelation] (my translation) of poetry.[11]

Similarly, Mallarmé investigates ephemerality and vagueness as linguistic assets. In 'Crise de vers' [Crisis in Poetry] (1897) Mallarmé argues for the capacity of language to evoke the concrete through abstracted form, concluding that the subject of poetry is merely a representation of an idea instead of the realization of an object; as practised by other impressionists, words serve an evocation of sensory experience rather than the determination of fathomable facts. Mallarmé had developed this idea in 'Crayonné au théâtre' [Sketched in the Theatre] (1887) going so far as to claim that — when dancing — the performer transforms into a sexless impersonal object,

Fig. 8.1. Samuel Joshua Beckett, *Loie Fuller Dancing*, 1900, gelatin silver print. Metropolitan Museum of Art, New York.

losing all subjectivity. The dancer becomes an abstract, an enigma, which again is '*fictif ou momentané*' [sic] [*fictitious and momentary*].[12]

From 1864 until his death in 1898, Mallarmé troubled himself with the search for the ideal metaphor of pure poetry in his work on *Hérodiade*.[13] In a letter to Henri Cazalis, he explicates his goal to replace imagery by poetic movement:

> [J']invente une langue qui doit nécessairement jaillir d'une poétique très nouvelle, que je pourrais définir en ces deux mots: *Peindre, non la chose, mais l'effet qu'elle produit*. Le vers ne doit donc pas, là, se composer de mots; mais d'intentions, et toutes les paroles s'effacer devant la sensation [...].
>
> [I am inventing a language which must necessarily arise from very new poetics, which I could define in these two words: *To paint not the thing, but the effect it produces*. Therefore the verse must not, in this case, be composed of words, but of intentions, and all language must be erased in the face of feelings [...].][14]

Perhaps because of the disjointed, partly posthumous publication of the three individual parts ('Ouverture' (1926), 'Scène' (1869) and 'Le Cantique de Saint Jean' (1913)), *Hérodiade* has often been considered a 'drama of Mallarmé's own complex evolution toward maturity' as a poet.[15] However, I suggest, considering the poem's formal criteria, it functions rather like an organum of Mallarmé's theoretical work. The poem's structure is intimately linked with Mallarmé's theoretical interpretation of dance. The triptych of 'Ouverture', 'Scène' and 'Cantique' render the dramatic poem in its entirety a metaphor for Symbolist poetry and a prime example of Mallarmé's ingenious skills as an engineer of kinesthetic effect.

Hérodiade conflates the conceptualization of dance and poetry in two essential ways. Firstly, Hérodiade's character as the subject in the 'Ouverture' and 'Scène' is constructed out of contradictory imagery and alternating movements of presence and absence. Secondly, this antagonism, set up in the imagery of the first two parts, structurally unfolds as 'visual movement' when placed in a triptychal arrangement with the concluding and contrastingly dynamic part, the 'Cantique'. The dual nature of Hérodiade as a character is emblematically resumed by the dipolar dynamics of the poem as a whole. The constant ambivalent shift between subject and form in dance is hence mirrored by the poem's oscillation of referential meaning between Hérodiade the character (the ostensible subject) and *Hérodiade* the poem (form), as an allegory for the Symbolist's 'dream of perfect poetry'.[16]

Hérodiade is defined by paradoxes: she is spiritually agile, yet unmoved, she desires ('Par quelle attrait | Menée [...] Le sais-je?' [by what affinity | I am drawn [...] Do I know?] ('Scène', ll. 8–11)), but is physically untouchable. References to her body — except those to her hair — are static and present her as a remote phantom. Hérodiade's non-existence is stressed in the first line of the 'Scène' when the nurse doubtfully addresses her: 'Tu vis! ou vois-je ici l'ombre d'une princesse?' [You are alive! Or do I see the ghost of a princess?] (l. 1). In the ensuing dialogue all attempts of her nurse to substantiate Hérodiade's physicality, for example to kiss her hand, perfume and rearrange her hair are refused by the princess: 'Reculez. [...] réprime | Ce geste, impiété fameuse' [Stand back there! [...] repress that gesture, that notorious blasphemy] (l. 3; l. 55). Hérodiade's insubstantiality makes her a sacred surface, pure beauty, that the slightest human touch destroys: the reader is not to touch the poem's indecipherable sacredness, in order not to ruin its 'mystère' by bestowing straightforward meaning onto it, in the attempt to 'songer [...] | le dieu' [envisage the divinity] (ll. 71–72). The paradoxical oscillation of language then creates an ambiguous surface for the reader's imagination. Even when Hérodiade beholds herself in the mirror, her form is 'une ombre lointaine' [a distant shade] (l. 49). Like the reader she can only find a shadow as a suggestion of her body that seems to be simultaneously shifting between an absent and present mode.

Unlike other literary sources of the time, most famously by Gustave Flaubert ('Hérodias', 1877), Joris-Karl Huysmans (*À rebours*, 1884), and later Oscar Wilde (*Salomé*, 1894), Mallarmé represents Hérodiade as a conflation of the mother and her daughter Salome. She is a cold, rather abstract and ephemeral apparition.[17] Unlike her daughter, often interpreted as the fleshly *femme fatale* par excellence, Mallarmé's *Hérodiade* — despite the text's conception as a performance piece in early stages of its genesis — does not actively seduce her readers.[18] She longs for 'rien d'humain' [nothing human] (l. 82) rendering her a solitary, unsexed Hamlet-like figure torn apart by the conflict between passivity and action. She remains 'sculptée [...] | les yeux perdus aux paradis' [a statue with eyes lost in paradise] (l. 83), forcing the reader likewise to accept an oxymoronic notion of animated *stasis* in the reading process. The conveyed kinesthetics of frozen movement emblematically portrayed in this 'problematic dancer'[19] explicate the mechanics of poetry in Mallarmé's understanding. As Leo Bersani comments, 'Hérodiade's refusal to dance serves to turn the poem away from the idea of show, from visual imagery to abstraction.'[20] 'As a moving image rather than a story',[21] Mallarmé's poem captures sensory motion by *not* letting its protagonist dance. Instead the poet constructs her as an enigma for the whole poem that dances in its overall structure.

Compared to the 'Ouverture' and 'Scène', the short 'Cantique' of John the Baptist shows a succession of expressive, dynamic verbs that oppose the first two rather heavy static and sterile parts. The 'Cantique' addresses in form and imagery a much clearer cut physicality in contrast to Hérodiade's 'indicible pas' [inexpressible steps] (l. 72) in the 'Ouverture'. Even the saint's beheading defines a kinesthetic moment of liberation. A close sequence of agitating images such as 'aux vertèbres | S'éployer des ténèbres | Toutes dans un frisson | A l'unisson' [shadowy wings unfurl [...] which are shuddering one and all in unison] (ll. 6–8), that free the mind from 'Les anciens désaccords | Avec le corps [...] [E]n quelque bond haggard' [an immemorial war so long fought against the torso [...] in some wild flight] (ll. 15–16 and 19–20), support the impression of a liberating 'dancing free'. The original French onomatopoeically re-enacts the motion of a conflicted separation of the mind from the body by doubling 'désa-ccords' in 'corps'. The prominent image of wings as a symbol of transcendence and departure from the purely bodily realm echoes Mallarmé's critical dance agenda: 'La danse est ailes, il s'agit d'oiseaux et des départs en l'à-jamais' [Dance is wings, it concerns birds and departures into the evermore].[22] The act of killing is aligned with the metaphors of dance and wings; all three images suggest a departure into the realm of the unknown. The separation of head and torso figuratively helps the body to 's'opiniâtre à suivre [...] son pur regard' [commit itself to lasting pursuit of its pure sight] (ll. 18–20). The body now liberated from rationality, 'tête surgie | Solitaire vigie' [head now full-blown | a watchman on his own] (ll. 9–10), can finally experience pure feeling — the same liberation gained by dancing, where only the body and the soul speak.[23]

The 'Cantique' relates directly to dance in its kinesthetic imagery. Moreover, and most importantly, the physical element of this section contrasts sharply with the first two parts and adds a spatial tension to the poem's layout as a whole. This formal trajectory between the parts creates the whole poem as an abstract enigma that oscillates between physical presence (as seen in the 'Cantique') and absence ('Ouverture', 'Scène'). Through its threefold structure the parts comment on each other, much like an animated panel painting.

The poem's relation to dance is evident in the line endings of the verse.[24] All stanzas and even partly the dialogue of the 'Scène' have parallel end rhymes. These rhyming, sometimes identical, words at the end of the line (for example in the 'Cantique': 'halte — exalte'; 'redescend — Incandescent') evoke dynamic movement. Like a sequence of steps that evolve one from another in dance, the sounds of words are carefully arranged to create a smoothly flowing choreography of language, a synaesthetic *Gesamtkunstwerk*, in which 'every word is a jewel, scattering and recapturing sudden fire, every image is a symbol, and the whole poem is visible music'.[25] This interweaving of visuals and phonetics, accentuating 'la valeur tonale des mots' [the tonal value of words][26] fulfils Mallarmé's aim of 'spiritualizing [...] the world'[27] through artistic correlations. Thus *Hérodiade* displays both 'the inadequacy of language'[28] as well as the belief in the power of its suggestiveness and dynamic metaphors, in this case 'the symbolic use of dancers as inhuman ciphers for the *Idéal*'.[29] By maintaining its poetic purity by declaring 'c'est pour moi, pour moi, que je fleuris' [for myself alone I bloom] ('Scène', l. 86), *Hérodiade* remains inaccessible if read for the sake of cohesive narration. As a consequence, Hérodiade's untouchable yet temptingly ambiguous purity becomes an abstract symbol for the suggestive quality of dance and Symbolist poetry alike.

Continuing the experimentation with sensoriality as seen in *Hérodiade*, *Un coup de Dés* (1897) plays even more radically with kinesthetic movement visualized in writing. This poem explores poetry's choreographic potential through two key innovations: Mallarmé replaces character-based narrative with the layout and spatial arrangement of individual words and phrases on the blank page. Secondly, the reader becomes a vital instrument in the creation of the poem. As a collaborative artist the reader actively navigates a kinesthetic choreography of isolated words in space. This, as the avant-garde composer John Cage testifies, demands a certain degree of 'polyattentiveness',[30] which turns the reader into a performer. Cage worked closely with the choreographer Merce Cunningham, both of whom based their artistic processes on Mallarmé's 'chance' procedures and mobile structures visualized in *Un coup de Dés*.

The poem's layout is its most striking and alienating feature. In twelve double pages the reader encounters a seemingly loose arrangement of words in different sizes and typefaces. What seems a random assemblage of words is a neatly crafted pattern, which enables a reading of the poem as an image of dance itself. Dee Reynolds explains how the 'disruption of established semiotic codes'[31] in space limits the possibility of extracting definite meanings from the language while simultaneously emphasising its suggestive potential. Mallarmé exposes the materiality of words as 'sensual objects'[32] that react to one another, thus inviting the reader to enter a sensory exchange with the text. The title already implies Mallarmé's experimentation with the unstable dynamics of linguistic structure. Borrowed from dance, the form of the poem imposes a distinction between real and 'imaginary space'[33] as a constitutive dimension. The juxtaposition of textual space and imaginary space creates a visual structure, just as in a dance performance the movement in space corresponds with the figurative kinesthetics of movement. Freed from any traditional ordering principle, such as coherent syntax, verse or punctuation, the space renders each double page a formally abstracted, yet constructed word-image.

Double page eight provides the perfect example of the use of disjointed language in space in which words are distinguished by capitalization, bold print and italicization, making them almost vanish or stand out on the page.[34] This visual emphasis on single phrases gives the page what Reynolds calls 'spatial rhythm'.[35] The word groupings are arranged in a diamond-shaped form (Fig. 8.2), encircling an empty space while de-centring the space of the page.

The shifted centre of attention is 'LE HASARD' [CHANCE]. The italicized '*C'ÉTAIT*' [*IT WAS*] and '*CE SERAIT*' [*IT WOULD BE*] flow from the left side of the page in vertical steps towards the centre. The 'HASARD' seems to bring this

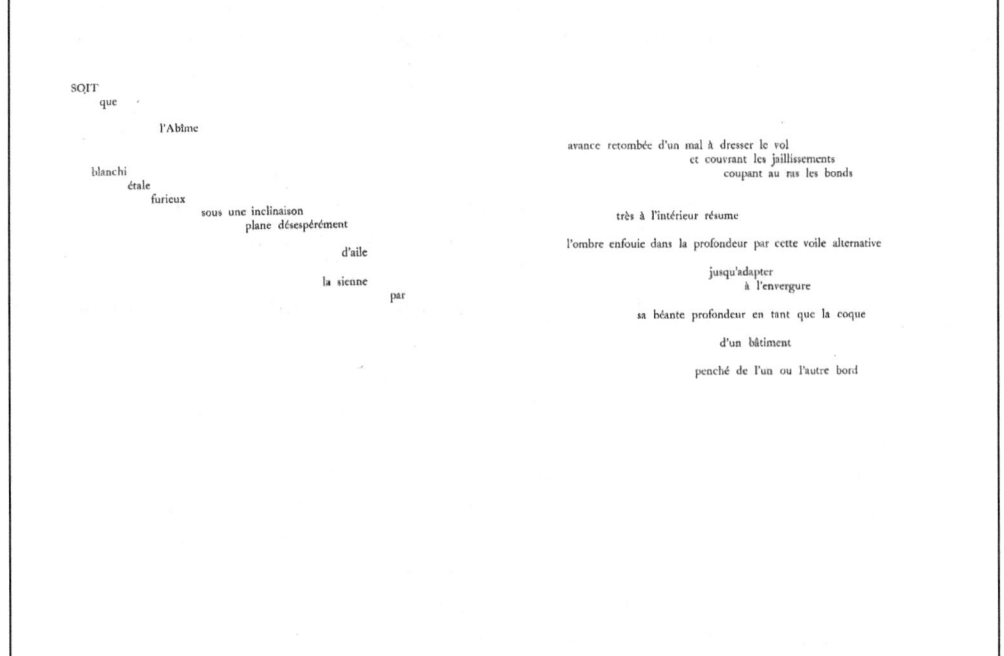

FIGS. 8.2, 8.3. Double pages (p. 9 and p. 3) from Stéphane Mallarmé's *Un coup de Dés*. Bibliothèque nationale de France.

cascading movement (mimicking the movement of a throw of the dice) to a sudden hold, reinforced by the page's margin that serves as an axis of orientation. The italicization enhances this linguistic re-enactment of movement. Pierre Duplan ascribes to the italics an 'obliqueness [that] suggests a sliding motion'[36] which encourages a 'relatively greater speed'[37] of reading. The diversity of typesetting and the directive of the words in space indicate a qualitative differentiation of movement and textual 'gestures'. The significance of words seems to depend firstly on the font size and secondly on their position on the page. The smaller-sized words appear elusive and quick, whilst the grave importance of 'LE HASARD' as a guiding theme of the whole poem cannot be ignored. Ultimately this page renders a pattern of individual units that interact just as a *corps de ballet* would dance around its prima ballerina, so all words dance around 'LE HASARD', each of them at their own speed and rhythm.

Double page two exhibits how the page itself replaces metre as a kinesthetic structuring device. Again Mallarmé juxtaposes elliptic syntactical phrases in a variation of typographical styles. Reynolds points out how the text 'falls' from the top left to the bottom right corner of the page, throwing the reader into its 'gravitational field' (Fig. 8.3).[38] The reader has to follow the text's diagonal axis. At the same time the eyes follow the dice throw's movement, tracing its 'desire for ascent'[39] when leaping over 'l'Abîme' [the Abyss]. Reynolds aligns the diagonal position of the text to the destabilization of a body in movement. The central margin of the double pages becomes for her 'a locus of balance, equivalent to the function of the spine in a body'.[40] As the spine of the text bends so the reader needs to adapt to the movement — intellectually and with the physical movement of their eyes and breath. By following this kinetography, as Paul Valéry suggests, the reader enters the dance of signs.[41]

Reynolds's observation that 'like dance, the art of poetry requires a concrete space, that of the page'[42] accordingly manifests Mallarmé's idea of an 'écriture corporelle' [corporeal writing].[43] Similarly to *Hérodiade*, the poem's subject (chance) merges with its idiosyncratic form. However, the poem's innovative treatment of space relates *Un coup de Dés* in its abstract formal qualities more distinctively to dance. The materialization of words, as Henry Weinfield remarks, makes the typography, layout and spacing an 'integral aspect of the poem itself'.[44] And indeed, Valéry understands the poem, seeing Mallarmé's drafts for it in 1897 for the first time, as 'la figure d'une penseé [...] une tempête spirituelle menée de page en page jusqu'à l'extrême de la pensée' [pattern of thought [...] a whole spiritual tempest carried page by page to the extremes of thought].[45] The visual animation of words thereby relates directly to Mallarmé's concept of dance as the essence of thought, 'l'Ideé' visualized in language as a 'tissu de sens multiples' [multi-sensory network] (my translation).[46] The interconnection of dance and writing in the abstraction of thought is aesthetically most successfully expressed in 'exploiting the visual, musical and performative potential of language'.[47] Judy Kravis even suggests that *Un coup de Dés* 'creates its "language" out of movement and out of the ephemeral capturing of space'[48] derived from the relation between *stasis* and motion in dance.

The second distinct feature of the poem, apart from the extraordinary use of space, lies in its interactive potential. Virginia La Charité points out that its 'space directs the reading process'.[49] The reader needs to reconstruct the abstract choreography of words on the page on an intellectual, imaginative and almost physical level, and becomes a 'revelateur' of the image: they become an intellectual dancer. The poem's 'espacement de la lecture' [spacing of reading],[50] as Mallarmé describes in his preface, aims to create an 'experience of kinesthetic empathy',[51] which provokes spontaneous emotional responses and physical reactions in the reader. For example, bold printed words catch the eye immediately, whilst other more 'silent' phrases appear to be remote. Thus the text is perceived as 'embodying attributes of effort qualities' continuously shaping associations.[52] The reader must adapt to, and evaluate, the spatial complexity of this non-linear layout as a chance to experience new forms and constellations of meaning. In this way the author vanishes completely behind his work; instead the reader takes his place, who actively crafts the text and literally has to take steps towards a purposeful reading. Reading turns into a performative act, an artificially contrived and challenging 'signifying process'.[53] Thus Mallarmé 'maximizes [...] potential meanings by mobilizing language and elevating chance as an aesthetic principle',[54] a practice he further explores in his last work 'Le Livre' which was never completed during his lifetime.

As a poet and reputable dance critic, Arthur Symons clearly owes his theoretical conception of dance in poetry to Mallarmé's poetics. In *The Symbolist Movement in Literature* (1899) Symons admires '[the] breaking up of the large rhythms of literature, and their scattering in articulate, almost instrumental, [...] nervous waves'.[55] Individual words are given 'value only as a notation of the free breath of the spirit'.[56] Yet, Symons's own impressionist poetics are a development of Mallarmé's ideas towards a stronger emphasis on the fleetingness of sensory images and their captivating force. Symons's 'amateur enthusiasm',[57] captured in the erotically charged atmosphere of his early poems, contrasts with the sobriety of his critical reviews and theoretical mediations on dance. Noting this discrepancy, Jan B. Gordon observes that the poems' narrative perspective oscillates between the 'author, participant and watcher'.[58] Drawing on his many visits to and intimate connoisseurship of dance shows performed at the Alhambra and Empire theatres in London, Symons's poetry focuses on the body of the dancer:

> As they dance, under the changing lights, so human, so remote, so desirable, so evasive, coming and going to the sound of a thin, heady music which marks the rhythm of their movements like a kind of drapery, they seem to sum up in themselves the appeal of everything in the world that is passing [...].[59]

First published in *The Dome* in 1898, Symons's essay 'The World as Ballet' re-invents Mallarmé's theoretical Symbolist approach. Petra Dierkes-Thrun argues that Symons's treatment of the dancer instead evolves from a combination of Symbolist ideals and his own sensual experience as a spectator and critic of dance: his language brings the metaphor of dance as a symbol of Symbolist aesthetic theory in dialogue with the self-experienced male projection of desire onto the female dancing body. In comparison to Mallarmé, Symons linguistically stages the 'ecstasy of patterned movement'.[60]

The following selection of dance poems sketches the transition of Symons's fascination with the 'winding motion' of dance.[61] In his early poetry, produced in the 1890s, Symons emphasizes the sensory immersive quality of dance and thus departs from a Mallarméan intellectualism. Instead he immerses the poetic speaker and also the reader in gyratory excesses of language. In his verse Symons sculpts the image of the dancer, shaping the image of her as an eroticized, exposed object of desire. He uses her in various ways; in *Silhouettes* she is a priestess, in *London Nights* a variant of the *femme fatale*, and in *Images of Good and Evil*, the dancer is an abstracted metaphor for Decadent poetry. Arguing against early critical responses to Symons being 'little more than a daring hothouse poet [and] credulous imitator [and] an uninspired disciple of Walter Pater',[62] the virtuality of Symons's dance poems illustrates how vividly Symons establishes a unique, impressionistic style in his literary treatment of dance. Roger Holdsworth remarks that Symons's 'ability to focus sharply on the telling detail' captures 'the flavour of a *scene* with swift, sure strokes'.[63] These linguistic strokes re-create an oscillating mosaic of individual moving 'atoms of ethereal femininity'.[64]

'La Mélinite: Moulin Rouge',[65] a homage to Symons's favourite danseuse Jane Avril, juxtaposes the intersensory exuberance of a 'mysterious night' at the Moulin Rouge with the Symbolist image of the isolated dancer beholding herself in the mirror. In the first stanza the eye is drawn to 'the rouge of petals in a shower', dancers revolving in their rose costumes. At first glance, the poem opens up a panoramic overview of the music-hall stage for the reader. Symons's language evokes geometrical images 'painted' on the performance space by the *corps de ballet*. At the same time the poem plunges the reader into a vortex of movement, music, colour and twirling bodies, 'a rhythmic shower'. Multiplied through the mirror imagery, the music hall is shown as an artificial world, spinning around its own centre, a virtual cinematic pan 'arrested in mid-flight'.[66]

Symons consciously directs and thereby disorients his readers' senses. The image of 'the dance returning | Rounds the full circle, rounds' in the second stanza produces a sense of disorientation placing the reader in the centre of this 'dance of shadows'. This is stressed in the poem by the dizzying density of prepositions such as '*down* the long hall', '*into* the circle', '*apart*', '*before* the mirror', '*between* the robes' and '*back to* a shadow' (my italics), which direct the reader's 'gaze'. The swift change of sensory attention demanded by the text, creates a flip-book of dancing images that rapidly pass before the mind's eye.

The rhyme scheme (*abbab*) imitates the ever-returning rhythm and repeated sound pattern of the maddening and repetitive waltz-music in a kinesthetic way. In contrast to Mallarmé, who pleads for a liberation of language from rhyme, Symons consciously employs metre to evoke a kinesthetic sense of gyration. The waltz-movements implied by the repetitive end-rhymes or reoccurring words ('roses', 'shower — flower', 'rounds — sounds') linguistically recreate the circles and geometrically arranged synaesthetic patterns formed on stage by the *corps de ballet* ('the perfect rose of lights and sounds'). The full-rhyme line endings additionally convey the sense of a tumbling movement. This sensation is enhanced by the onomatopoeic — as much as metaphorical — use of the sound 'o', with the letter representing in itself a never-ending movement in form of a circle. Whereas

Mallarmé uses isolated words in an imaginary space to create the sense of movement, Symons uses rhyme to achieve the same effect. He conjures up the visual arrangements of dancers as, to borrow Alexandra Carter's term, 'convenient units'.[67]

In 'On the Stage', Symons creates synaesthetic movement by a quasi-synecdochic fragmentation of the dancers.[68] Only 'glimpses of profiles' can be made out in the 'whirling mist of multi-coloured lights'. 'Indigo' and 'amethyst', very specific hues of blue and purple, intensify the multi-sensual sensation. The lights in the opening line emphasized by a syntactical inversion, almost 'blind' the reader. The very first sensual impulse in the poem causes the dancers to appear like 'phantoms' moving in 'mist', or, as Bernard Shaw described, 'masses of colour in rhythmic motion'.[69]

The fragmentation of the dancers' bodies, concealed and yet defined through sensory detail, corresponds to the dance hall as a space of liminality. The hazy dance performance becomes a spiritual experience. Seeing only 'faces', 'eyes' and 'mist' and 'rouge', and 'always tights, and wigs, and tights' puts the reader in the midst of the sensually disorienting, and therefore quintessentially modern, chaos of elusive smells, colours and images, that seem to repeat themselves relentlessly over and over again. Enhanced by the endrhymes of the lines, Symons successfully anatomizes not only the dancers' bodies, he also deconstructs a cohesive sense of time. The disjointed, asyndetic syntax ('Then faces, then a glimpse of profiles, then eyes …') offers an excess of sensory stimuli affecting the speaker and the reader. Language here seems insufficient to match the capacity of dance to express 'life's spontaneity'.[70]

The second stanza zooms away from the dance hall as 'distraction factory'[71] and focuses on one isolated dancer 'who smiles', recalling 'memories' and promising secret 'messages' to the onlooker. The dancer as sphinx-like image relates back to *Hérodiade* and the dancer as a mysterious and unpredictable enigma. As an example of a picture captured in 'mid-flight' in Mallarmé's sense, the poem poignantly arrests a moment of kinesthetic movement. Symons thus again successfully 'spatializes time'.[72] Set apart from the busy atmosphere, one image — for a second only — is impressed on the spectator's vision. The isolation and *stasis* of the dancer with her gaze fixed on the spectator, intensify the erotic tension of this poem. Reading the poem equals an elusive erotic encounter with Symons's 'phantom of delight'.[73]

For Symons, dance represents both control over the physical realm of the modern *Zeitgeist* and thereby its transcendence. The attraction of the ephemerality of dance as an image for art lies precisely in its ambivalent position between the physical and the spiritual, in the 'intellectual as well as the sensual appeal of a living symbol'.[74] Paradoxically, however, at its most extreme, the treatment of dance in terms of the Symbolist aesthetic does away with the physical dancer altogether. As early as 1886, Mallarmé had assimilated the dancer completely to language in his essay 'Ballets':

> la danseuse n'est pas une femme qui danse, pour ces motifs juxtaposés qu'elle n'est pas une femme, mais une métaphore résumant un des aspects élémentaires de notre forme, glaive, coupe, fleur, etc., et qu'elle ne danse pas, suggérant, par le prodige de raccourcis ou d'élans, avec une écriture corporelle ce qu'il faudrait des paragraphes en prose dialoguée autant que descriptive, pour exprimer, dans la rédaction: poème dégagé de tout appareil du scribe.

[she is not a girl, but rather a metaphor which symbolizes some elemental aspect of earthly form [...] she does not dance but rather, with miraculous lunges and abbreviations, writing with her body, she suggests things which the written work could express only in several paragraphs of dialogue or descriptive prose. Her poem is written without the writer's tool].[75]

Symons does not go as far as Mallarmé in abstracting the dancer. In fact, his treatments of dancers are divided in a 'highly abstract appreciation of them as art and an equally strong sensuous appreciation of them as female bodies'.[76] This very sensuous, and I argue, sensory appeal of Symons's dance poems draws out the relationship between sensation, action, and reaction involved in the reading process.

'La Mélinite: Moulin Rouge' and 'On the Stage' demonstrate how Symons exposes one dancer in the midst of a literally 'dancing', artificial world of escapism, one oscillating image of moribund delirium. In 'To A Dancer',[77] however, Symons focuses more and more on the female dancer as a kind of *femme fatale* figure. The ballet dancer of the music hall becomes both an elusive performer and object of desire subjected to the male gaze, sparking 'a quickening fire'. Symons works with a paradox here: although the dancer is never seen fully but is instead represented in fragments ('gleaming eyes', 'poising feet') he conjures her up as a fleshly image of an 'intoxicatingly' erotic woman. Dance becomes the 'body's melody', a 'thrill to the sense of all around' that initiates a private communication of erotic desire. However, the dancer remains without voice and full physical appearance. As a consequence she herself (and not the buzzing music hall) becomes, as Kerry Powell puts it, a 'temporary refuge from terrors of life — and death'.[78]

In her cultural-historical research on music-hall dancers, Carter emphasizes how Symons's 'little painted angels [...] winged in gold', remain a pure fantastic vision for the audience. Carter points out how the dance stars of the English Belle Époque were in reality working women, earning their living in a rather unglamorous way to 'maintain their families'.[79] She argues that for Symons 'the ballet girl is constructed as a sexual being' and 'a female body for public consumption'.[80] When the dancer at the end of 'To A Dancer' 'dies into the rapture of repose' the female body, illuminated and elevated by the artificially green gaslight, is transformed into a remote image that 'might be accessible but not attainable'.[81] The dancer is cast as a private vision of escape 'danc[ing] for her own delight',[82] but most of all for that of her solipsistic spectator.

The speaker of 'To a Dancer' imagines the dancer performing for him alone, promising a 'moment of sensuous culmination'.[83] The dancer's sensory impulses are repeatedly rephrased in the refrain ('her eyes that gleam for me', 'her feet that poise to me', 'her body's melody [...] thrills alone for me') and physically reflect the nervous agitation of the speaker. Although the dancer is objectified, the speaker is disempowered and, as Dierkes-Thrun observes, portrayed as a 'victim of the dancer's enchantment'.[84] The dancer becomes an 'amazing mistress of worlds without words'.[85] Surpassing verbal expressions, the dancer's body language initiates an immediate communication with the speaker's as well as the reader's senses. As seen in 'On the Stage', language again fails the speaker; the coherence of sentences is interrupted by an interjection ('And oh') or associative parenthesis ('the wine of

FIG. 8.4. John Singer Sargent, *Heads and Faces of Javanese Dancers* (from *Sketchbook of Javanese Dancers*), 1889, graphite on off-white wove paper. Metropolitan Museum of Art, New York.

Fig. 8.5. John Singer Sargent, *Heads and Faces of Javanese Dancers* (from *Sketchbook of Javanese Dancers*), 1889, graphite on off-white wove paper. Metropolitan Museum of Art, New York.

love, the wine of dream'). The explosive sounds of the adverb and one-word trimeter 'intoxicatingly' in the opening line of the poem emanate a sense of stammering admiration and indicate how the speaker is too overcome by erotic desire to express himself in sophisticated terms and orderly sentences. The desperate euphoria of the speaker is thus mirrored in fleeting, enumerative language that reaches its literal and figurative climax in the 'magic moment's close'. Gordon compares the kinesthetic quality of the poem, which is designed to be read aloud and thereby sensorially processed, to an 'aesthetic copulation' in which the speaker tries to unify himself with the dancer in a desperate attempt 'to achieve a dissolution of the ego'.[86]

Moving away from the adoration of the Decadent dancing bodies of 'footlight immortality',[87] 'Javanese Dancers' explores the Symbolist notion of dance as a holy ritual.[88] In comparison to 'The Armenian Dancer', a later poem from 1906, in which the speaker exhausts himself by a ritualistic feverish dance, 'Javanese Dancers' effuses a sublime, silently tense and mystical atmosphere. The American expatriate painter John Singer Sargent's sketchbooks for his painting *Javanese Dancers* (1889) capture in drawing the kinesthetic quality of Symons's poem (Figs. 8.4 & 8.5). Both artists shared a taste for the 'exotic' and had witnessed a dance performance at the 1889 Exposition Universelle in Paris.[89] 'The little amber-coloured dancers' embody Symons's ideal dancers who inscribe space with their 'interthreading' body movements. They seduce by their mystifying, rather than exciting, performance. Desire is awakened by the 'exotic' presentation of meandering, animalistic movements such as the 'cat-like steps that cling', twining 'fingers into mazy lines', 'lingering feet that undulate' and 'sinuous fingers, spectral hands'. These smooth movements are poetically translated in enjambments, indicating the spectator's breathtaking fascination with the meandering forms. The speaker's tone is now a much more admiring one, more the tone of a worshipper than of a man thrilled by ecstasy. The poem develops its incantatory dramaturgy by a change of rhythmical patterns in each stanza and thus creates a set of qualitatively differing shapes and durations of movements.

The first stanza illustrates the initial majestic entrance of the 'stealthy dancer' in musical terms. '[T]he clang of metal' and 'drums' musically announces the almost frightening appearance of the cat-like performers. The onomatopoeia of hard cutting consonants 't', 'c', 'k', 'cling' (as if to mimic the material of the instruments) and the sibilant 'twitched strings' and 'steps' emphasize the sensual anticipation that 'disquieting[ly]' tantalizes the spectator's expectations.

The second stanza formally resumes the meandering lines 'written' by the hands of the mysterious dancer. Her gestures hypnotize the onlooker as a snake would its prey: the repetition of 'smile' in the first line creates a circular impression; in a serpent-like undulating movement the first line begins and closes with 'smiling'/'smile'. Symons shows the dancer 'motionless' yet animated when he concentrates on the revealing and hiding of the dancer's palms and her minimalistic movements. He breaks the focus on the hands' spiritual signification — the focus on the hands is framed by an embracing rhyme scheme *abba* in the second stanza — by an acceleration of rhythm in the third stanza. The movement seizes space in quick changes of direction ('to and fro'). The anaphora ('now') stresses the elusiveness of fast motion while enhancing the effect of the 'interthreading' of the dancer's gestures and her veils, an image which Symons structurally re-enacts in the syntax. Just as the steps of the dancers continuously flow into one another so does the language. The internal half-rhyme of 'row', 'slow' 'fro' and 'now' interconnects the whole of the stanza and creates the image of a sequence of dance routines. This 'sustained effort' in Rudolf Laban's words,[90] is interrupted in the fourth stanza with the dancer's eyes suddenly fixed 'still', and returns to 'inanimate' holy gesturing ('sinuous fingers, spectral hands'). As if transformed by their transcendental ritual the dancers appear as 'painted figures on a screen', as mere projections and embodied premonitions of an otherworldly 'magic grove'. As powerfully as they appeared they vanish almost invisibly ('haply seen') as shadows in the distance. In comparison to the music-hall poems these 'phantom-dancers' have the air of priestesses. The spectator maintains an awed distance.

Finally, 'The Dance of the Daughters of Herodias'[91] presents the reader with Symons's meta-authorial mediation on his own use of the dance metaphor. The poem encompasses the complete transition of dance as literary trope moving from an inherently Decadent treatment (Salome) to a Symbolist transfiguration (Herodias), and eventual anticipation of its later significance in Modernist writing. It is not without accident that the re-definition of the metaphor of dance in this poem between Decadent, Symbolist, and Modernist elements coincides with Symons's reworking of 'The Decadent Movement in Literature' (1893) as *The Symbolist Movement in Literature* (1899).

The opening question 'Is it the petals falling from the rose?' (p. 42) establishes the reflexive and distanced perspective of the narrator if not the author himself on the usage of dance as a metaphor in Decadent poetry. In challenging the process of a disintegration of the idiosyncratic Decadent image of the rose (often a metaphorical substitute for dance in Symons's poetic idiom), it comments on the deformation and the development of the dance trope in Symons's own work. In it Symons conjures up a canon of stock Decadent tropes associated with the Salome legend ('lips are moist', 'emeralds coloured like the under-sea', 'gold serpent nestling in her hair' (pp. 43–44)), a haunting fresco of a 'pale and windy multitude beaten about the air' (p. 42). These Decadent images, embodying 'The Daughters of Herodias', form the 'eternal enemy' (p. 45) of man. On a second level, as mere descriptive words they represent the poet's opponents in his ambition to capture on paper the intangible sensoriality of beauty ('I behold | Their rosy-petalled feet upon the air | Falling and falling in a cadence soft [...] But they smile innocently, and dance on' (p. 47)).

By exposing the poet's struggle with this 'eternal enemy', namely the attempt to reproduce the relationship between art and life (and in this case a poeticized condensation of life that is dance), Symons comments on his own creative process in which 'Dance is life [...] more natural than nature, more artificial than art [...]'.[92]

The poem's final lines illustrate the centrality of dance as a literary practice in Symons's understanding. Like the teasing promises of a *femme fatale*, the re-creation of movement on the page is simultaneously thrilling and frustrating, 'when they dance, for their delight, | Always a man's head falls because of them' (p. 45). As a result the poem gives the impression of a poet exhausted by the search for imagery:

> Dance in the desolate air,
> Dance always, daughters of Herodias,
> With your eternal, white, unfaltering feet,
> But dance, I pray you, so that I from far
> May hear your dancing fainter than the drift
> Of the last petals falling from the rose. (p. 48)

Written three years before the turn of the century and after the turning point for Decadence marked by Wilde's trials in 1895, Symons captures the sense of the decline of 1890s Decadent culture in the image of the 'petals falling from the rose'. In the juxtaposition of Decadent imagery (Salome 'has forgotten everything, | But that the wind of dancing in her blood | Exults [...]' (p. 44)), Symbolist tropes showing the dancers as '[s]hapes on a mirror, perishable shapes, | Fleeting, and without substance' (p. 47), and proto-Modernist images concerned with the clash of tradition and modernity ('the double-handed sword | Scrape on the pavement' (p. 44)), this poem palimpsestically conflates the dance-hall atmosphere with Mallarmé's enigmatic Hérodiade whilst anticipating the Modernist reinvention of the mystic dancer as seen in W. B. Yeats's *At the Hawk's Well* (1916).[93] The poem's panoptic scope thus draws together the animated image of dance as a 'paradise of physical poetry'[94] that offers the author as well as the reader the possibility of 'letting humanity drift into a rhythm so much of its own'.[95]

The responsive reader of Mallarmé and Symons is rewarded by the engagement in the kinesthetics of dance in poetry. Mallarmé and Symons succeed in incorporating the sensoriality and kinesthetic qualities of dance into their work to different degrees. While both Mallarmé and Symons capture the virtuality of dance in their poetry, Mallarmé is concerned with an 'encounter on the page between the poet and his words, their shared spectacle, and, consequently, reader reaction to that spectacle'.[96] The focus is on a spatial, technical and most of all abstract experimentation with language reminiscent of images of Fuller's dancing. *Hérodiade* as a non-dancing dancer establishes the dancer as a poetic theorem that Mallarmé explores to the extreme in *Un coup de Dés* in which he experiments with formal aspects of abstraction as choreographic movement, adopting the kinesthetic of dance to 'move' the reader to engage with the text. Symons's dance poetry concentrates on the poem and dance as expressions of desire and transgression. Symons's linguistic sophistication in expressing the sensoriality of dance renders his poems a representation of life itself. The poems' physical and erotic presence foster sensory tensions between the reader and the text.

Mallarmé's and Symons's different treatments of the dance trope both provide the groundwork for Modernist poets regarding the re-creation of spatial virtuality and kinesthetics of language. Yeats, Ezra Pound, and T. S. Eliot develop the Symbolist paradox of poetry which Kermode identifies in its potential of being 'both concrete and obscure'.[97] It is through these characteristics that *fin-de-siècle* poets pioneered cutting-edge experimentation; through the innovative integration of visuality and virtuality into their poetry, they prefigured today's self-understood medial mobility within the disciplines of the arts. Symbolist and Decadent dance poetry thus manages to fabricate a volatile encounter in which subject and form merge, enticing the reader to enter a *Sinnenrausch* — a textual as much as kinesthetic dance of the senses.

Notes to Chapter 8

1. Susan Jones, *Literature, Modernism, and Dance* (Oxford: Oxford University Press, 2013). Mark Franko, 'Mimique', in *Bodies of the Text: Dance as Theory, Literature as Dance*, ed. by Ellen W. Goellner and Jacqueline Shea Murphy (New Jersey: Rutgers University Press, 1995), pp. 205–15 (p. 206).
2. Frank Kermode, *Romantic Image* (London: Routledge, 1957). A. J. Bate, 'Yeats and the Symbolist Aesthetic', *Modern Language Notes*, 98 (December 1983), 1214–33 (p. 1217).
3. John M. Munro, 'Arthur Symons as Poet: Theory and Practice', *English Literature in Transition, 1880–1920*, 6 (1963), 212–22 (p. 217).
4. Dee Reynolds, 'The Kinesthetics of Chance — Mallarmé's *Un coup de Dés* and Avant-garde Choreography', in *Symbolism, Decadence and the Fin de Siècle: French and European Perspectives*, ed. by Patrick McGuinness (Exeter: Exeter University Press, 2000), pp. 90–105 (p. 90).
5. For an analysis of the interconnection with theatre and music, see Mary Lewis Shaw, *Performance in the Texts of Mallarmé: The Passage from Art to Ritual* (University Park: Pennsylvania State University Press, 1993), p. 4.
6. Stéphane Mallarmé, 'Autre étude de danse: Les fonds dans le ballet', in *Divagations*, ed. by Eugène Fasquelle (Paris: Charpentier, 1897), pp. 179–86 (p. 180). Translation by Mary Ann Caws and Rosemary Lloyd, 'Another Dance Study', in *Mallarmé in Prose*, ed. by Mary Ann Caws (New York: New Directions Publishing Corporation, 2001), p. 114.
7. Reynolds, 'The Kinesthetics of Chance', p. 91.
8. Mallarmé, 'Autre étude de danse', in *Divagations*, p. 179 / 'Another Dance Study', in *Mallarmé in Prose*, p. 114.
9. Mallarmé, 'Ballets', in *Divagations*, pp. 171–79 (p. 178) / 'Ballets', in *Mallarmé in Prose*, p. 113.
10. *Ibid.*, p. 172 / *Ibid.*, p. 109.
11. *Ibid.*, p. 178.
12. Mallarmé, 'Crayonné au théâtre', in *Divagations*, pp. 153–64 (p. 158) / 'Sketched in the Theatre', in *Mallarmé in Prose*, p. 104.
13. Stéphane Mallarmé, *Hérodiade*, in *Collected Poems and Other Verse with Parallel French Text*, trans. by E. H. and A. M. Blackmore (Oxford: Oxford University Press, 2006), 'Ouverture', pp. 192–99; 'Scène', pp. 28–38; 'Cantique', pp. 212–17. All references are to this edition. Hereafter, line numbers are provided in the main body of the text.
14. Mallarmé, letter to Henri Cazalis (Tournon, October/November 1864), in *Stéphane Mallarmé, Correspondance 1862–1871*, ed. by Henri Mondor (Paris: Gallimard, 1959), pp. 137–38 (p. 137). Translation by David Lenson, 'Introduction to a translation of Herodiade', *The Massachusetts Review*, 30 (Winter 1989), 573–88 (p. 573).
15. Robert Greer Cohn, *Toward the Poems of Mallarmé* (Berkeley: University of California Press, 1965), p. 55.
16. *Ibid.*, p. 52.
17. Gustave Flaubert, *Trois Contes*, ed. by Emilia Ndiaye (Paris: Bertrand-Lacoste, 1922); Joris-Karl Huysmans, *À rebours*, ed. by Françoise Court-Pérez (Paris: Presses universitaires de France, 1978); Oscar Wilde, *Salomé* (Paris: Librairie de l'art indépendant; London: Elkin Mathews and John Lane, the Bodley Head, 1893).
18. Mallarmé's conception of *Hérodiade* as a tragedy reverberates with ideas of passivity/activity which he explores in 'Hamlet', in *Divagations*, pp. 164–70.
19. Felicia McCarren, *Dance Pathologies: Performance, Poetics, Medicine* (Stanford: Stanford University Press, 1998), p. 130.
20. Leo Bersani, in McCarren, *Dance Pathologies*, p. 135.
21. McCarren, *Dance Pathologies*, p. 152.
22. Mallarmé, 'Ballets', in *Divagations*, p. 174 / 'Ballets', in *Mallarmé in Prose*, p. 109.
23. Paul Valéry, *Dance and the Soul: The Original French Text with a Translation by Dorothy Bussy* (London: John Lehmann, 1951).

24. Even if aspects of this relationship are lost in translation from French into English, the scholarly translation by E. H. and A. M. Blackmore preserves the sense of movement. Symons's translations of Mallarmé's poetry, including 'Scène' from *Hérodiade* published as a fragment in the December number of *The Savoy* in 1896 and in 1899 in full were read and appreciated by Aubrey Beardsley, W. B. Yeats and Mallarmé himself. Symons esteemed this 'magnificent and mysterious fragment' of *Hérodiade* Mallarmé's personal 'masterpiece'. However, a detailed consideration of Symons's artistic translation is beyond the scope of this chapter. *Stéphane Mallarmé: Poésies translated by Arthur Symons*, ed. by Bruce Morris (Edinburgh: Tragara Press, 1986).
25. Arthur Symons, *The Symbolist Movement in Literature* (New York: E. P. Dutton, 1958), p. 69.
26. Mallarmé, 'Crise de vers', in *Divagations*, pp. 235–55 (p. 240). Translated as 'Crisis in Poetry', in *Mallarmé: Selected Prose Poems, Essays, & Letters*, ed. by Bradford Cook (Baltimore: Johns Hopkins Press, 1956), p. 37.
27. Symons, *The Symbolist Movement in Literature*, p. 75.
28. Petra Dierkes-Thrun, 'Arthur Symons's Decadent Aesthetics: Stéphane Mallarmé and the Dancer Revisited', in *Decadence: Morality and Aesthetics in British Literature*, ed. by Paul Fox (Stuttgart: Ibidem, 2006), pp. 31–62 (p. 36).
29. *Ibid.*
30. John Cage, cited in Reynolds, 'The Kinesthetics of Chance', p. 92.
31. Dee Reynolds, *Symbolist Aesthetics and Early Abstract Art: Sites of Imaginary Space* (Cambridge: Cambridge University Press, 1995), p. 226.
32. Vincent Leitch, 'Stéphane Mallarmé', in *The Norton Anthology of Theory and Criticism* (New York: Norton, 2010), pp. 730–40 (p. 731).
33. Reynolds, *Symbolist Aesthetics*, p. 225.
34. The poem's publication in *Cosmopolis: An International Review*, 6 (May 1897), 417–28, includes Mallarmé's instructions to the reader, 'Observation relative au poème'. All textual references here are to *Un coup de Dés* from the *Collected Poems and Other Verse with Parallel French Text*, trans. by E. H. and A. M. Blackmore (Oxford: Oxford University Press, 2006). The images are taken from the poem's publication in *Éditions de La Nouvelle Revue Française* (July 1914), [http://gallica.bnf.fr/ark:/12148/bpt6k71351c/f8.image]. Numbers are assigned to each double page in order to help the reader follow the progression of the poem.
35. Reynolds, 'The Kinesthetics of Chance', p. 101.
36. Pierre Duplan, in Reynolds, *Symbolist Aesthetics*, p. 111.
37. Reynolds, 'The Kinesthetics of Chance', p. 103.
38. *Ibid.*, p. 98.
39. Reynolds, *Symbolist Aesthetics*, p. 109.
40. Reynolds, 'The Kinesthetics of Chance', p. 98.
41. Paul Valéry, 'Philosophie de la danse', in *Paul Valéry Œuvres I*, ed. by Jean Hytier (Paris: Gallimard, 1957), pp. 1390–1404 (p. 1400): 'Commencer de dire des vers, c'est entrer dans une danse verbale.' [To begin to recite verse is to enter a dance with words] (my translation).
42. Reynolds, *Symbolist Aesthetics*, p. 88.
43. Mallarmé, 'Ballets', in *Divagations*, p. 173 / Mallarmé, 'Ballets', in *Mallarmé in Prose*, p. 109.
44. Henry Weinfield, *Stéphane Mallarmé: Collected Poems* (London: University of California Press, 1994), p. 265.
45. Valéry, 'Le coup de Dés — Lettre au Directeur des *Marges*', in *Paul Valéry Œuvres I*, pp. 622–30 (p. 624) / Weinfield, p. 265.
46. Valéry, 'Le coup de Dés', p. 626.
47. Reynolds, *Symbolist Aesthetics*, p. 108.
48. Judy Kravis, *The Prose of Mallarmé: The Evolution of a Literary Language* (Cambridge: Cambridge University Press, 1976), p. 161.
49. Virginia La Charité, *The Dynamics of Space: Mallarmé's Un Coup de Dés Jamais n'abolira Le Hasard* (Lexington: French Forum Publishers, 1987), p. 9.
50. Mallarmé, 'Observation rélative au poème', pp. 417–18 (p. 417) / Reynolds, 'The Kinesthetics of Chance', p. 97.
51. Technical dance vocabulary coined by choreographer and dance theorist Rudolf Laban (1879–1958) relates to proto-Modernist poetic explorations of movement by Mallarmé and Symons. Shaw, *Performance in the Texts of Mallarmé*; Reynolds, 'The Kinesthetics of Chance', pp. 97–98.

52. Reynolds, 'The Kinesthetics of Chance', p. 98.
53. Reynolds, *Symbolist Aesthetics*, p. 226.
54. Reynolds, 'The Kinesthetics of Chance', p. 103.
55. Symons, *The Symbolist Movement in Literature*, p. 73.
56. *Ibid.*, p. 70.
57. Barry J. Faulk, *Music Hall and Modernity: The Late-Victorian Discovery of Popular Culture* (Athens, Ohio: Ohio University Press, 2004), p. 51.
58. Jan B. Gordon, 'The Danse Macabre of Arthur Symons's *London Nights*', in *Victorian Poetry*, 9 (Winter 1971), 429–43 (p. 429).
59. Symons, 'The World as Ballet', in *Studies in Seven Arts* (London: Archibald Constable and Company, 1906), pp. 387–91 (p. 369).
60. Gordon, 'Danse Macabre', p. 429.
61. Symons, 'The World as Ballet', p. 388.
62. Karl Beckson and John M. Munro (eds.), *Arthur Symons: Selected Letters, 1880–1935* (London: Macmillan, 1989), p. ix.
63. Roger Holdsworth, *Arthur Symons: Selected Writings* (Manchester: Carcanet Press, 2003), p. 12.
64. Karlien van den Beukel, 'Arthur Symons's Night Life', in *Babylon or New Jerusalem? Perceptions of the City in Literature*, ed. by Valeria Tinkler-Villani (Amsterdam: Rodopi, 2005), pp. 135–53 (p. 142).
65. All quotations are from Arthur Symons, 'La Mélinite: Moulin Rouge', in *London Nights* (London: Leonard Smithers, 1895).
66. Symons, *The Symbolist Movement in Literature*, p. 67.
67. Alexandra Carter, 'Blonde, Bewigged and Winged with Gold: Ballet Girls in the Music Halls of Late Victorian and Edwardian England', *Dance Research: The Journal of the Society for Dance Research*, 13 (Autumn/Winter 1995), 28–46 (p. 36).
68. All quotations are from Arthur Symons, 'On the Stage', in *London Nights* (London: Leonard Smithers, 1895).
69. Bernard Shaw, in Alexandra Carter, 'Over the Footlights and under the Moon: Images of Dancers in the Ballet at the Alhambra and Empire Palaces of Varieties, 1884–1915', *Dance Research Journal*, 28 (Spring 1996), 7–18 (p. 12).
70. Gordon, 'Danse Macabre', p. 429.
71. Beukel, 'Arthur Symons's Night Life', p. 140.
72. Gordon, 'Danse Macabre', p. 432.
73. Beukel, 'Arthur Symons's Night Life', p. 141.
74. Symons, 'The World as Ballet', p. 82.
75. Mallarmé, 'Ballets', in *Divagations*, p. 173 / 'Ballets', in *Mallarmé in Prose*, p. 109.
76. Amy Koritz, *Gendering Bodies/Performing Art: Dance and Literature in Early Twentieth-Century British Culture* (Ann Arbor: University of Michigan Press, 1995), p. 64.
77. All quotes are from Arthur Symons, 'To a Dancer', in *London Nights* (London: Leonard Smithers, 1895).
78. Kerry Powell, 'Arthur Symons, Symbolism and the Aesthetics of Escape', *Renascence*, 29 (Spring 1977), 157–67 (p. 161).
79. Carter, 'Blonde, Bewigged and Winged', p. 33.
80. *Ibid.*, p. 42.
81. Carter, 'Over the Footlights', p. 12.
82. Symons, 'La Mélinite: Moulin Rouge', p. 24.
83. Gordon, 'Danse Macabre', p. 432.
84. Dierkes-Thrun, 'Arthur Symons's Decadent Aesthetics', p. 56.
85. *Ibid.*, p. 47.
86. Gordon, 'Danse Macabre', p. 431.
87. R. K. R. Thornton, 'Introduction' to *Arthur Symons: Images of Good and Evil* (New York: Woodstook Books, 1996), p. v.
88. 'Javanese Dancers', *Silhouettes*, 2nd edn (1896; London: Leonard Smithers, 1897), p. 33.
89. D. Dodge Thompson, 'John Singer Sargent's Javanese Dancers', *Antiques*, 138 (July 1990), 124–33. Symons, letter to James Dykes Campbell, 6 October 1889, in *Selected Letters*, ed. by Beckson, p. 53.

90. Vera Maletic, *Approaches to Semiotics: Body — Space — Expression: The Development of Rudolf Laban's Movement and Dance Concepts* (Munich: Walter de Gruyter, 2011), p. 99.
91. All quotes are from Arthur Symons, 'The Dance of the Daughters of Herodias', in *Images of Good and Evil* (1899; New York: Woodstook Books, 1996), pp. 42–48.
92. Symons, 'The World as Ballet', p. 81.
93. Ian Fletcher explores Yeats's influence on the mysticism of Symons's poem in 'Explorations and Recoveries — II: Symons, Yeats and the Demonic Dance', *The London Magazine* VII, 6 (June 1960), 49–60 (p. 57).
94. Dierkes-Thrun, 'Arthur Symons's Decadent Aesthetics', p. 51.
95. Symons, 'The World as Ballet', p. 82.
96. La Charité, *The Dynamics of Space*, p. 25.
97. Kermode, *Romantic Image*, p. 137.

CHAPTER 9

Decadent Sensations: Art, the Body and Sensuality in the 'Little Magazines' (1885–1897)

Matthew Brinton Tildesley

Within the pages of *The Picture of Dorian Gray*, there is one seminal moment of transition, where Dorian resolves to take up Lord Henry's challenge of living the Paterian life of the senses:

> Yes, there was to be, as Lord Henry had prophesied, a new hedonism that was to re-create life, and to save it from that harsh, uncomely puritanism that is having, in our own day, its curious revival. It was to have its service of the intellect, certainly; yet it was never to accept any theory or system that would involve the sacrifice of any mode of passionate experience. Its aim, indeed, was to be experience itself, and not the fruits of experience, sweet or bitter as they might be. Of the asceticism that deadens the senses, as of the vulgar profligacy that dulls them, it was to know nothing. But it was to teach man to concentrate himself upon the moments of a life that is itself but a moment.[1]

This 'new hedonism' is thus a 're-creation' and a reaction; a necessary measure to combat the 'harsh, uncomely puritanism' that was itself experiencing a fully-fledged revival as Wilde was composing the tale. Puritanical Protestantism is today something of a cliché of Victorian Britain, and even a caricature that has a faintly comic edge. However, at the time of *The Picture of Dorian Gray*'s composition, the puritan movement in Britain was a serious militant force, which was not to be engaged with lightly, as Wilde ultimately discovered in 1895. The watershed moment for the broader purity campaigns was the publication of the infamous 'British Matron' letters in *The Times*, beginning on 20 May 1885, which called for a complete ban on the representation of the nude in British museums and art galleries. The Matron herself was actually the painter and treasurer of the Royal Academy, John Callcott Horsley, who, donning women's weeds, railed against the 'indecent pictures that disgrace our exhibitions'. The 'display of nudity at the [...] Academy' resulted in 'a burning sense of shame' within the poor 'woman', and the gallery, we are told, became a nightmarish vision of debauchery, forcing her 'to turn from them with disgust and cause only timid half glances to be cast at the paintings hanging close by [...] lest it should be supposed the spectator is looking at that which revolts his or her sense of decency.' The Matron therefore announced that a 'noble crusade of purity [...] has been started to check the rank profligacy that abounds in our land'.[2] As Alison Smith illustrates, the campaign of opposition to the nude in Victorian Britain actually started several years earlier, but Horsley's letter was 'the catalyst for igniting a national controversy around the exhibition of the nude'.[3] Letters flooded *The Times* on the subject over the next week. A great many of them took up arms against the Matron, and included letters from women, parents, young girls, and the artist Edward J. Poynter (whose work at the Academy included a nude based on the statue of the Esquiline Venus). One notable opponent of the Matron was Jerome K. Jerome, who wrote in support of her attempted ban, agreeing 'that the human form is a disgrace to decency' but begged her not to castigate the artists 'who merely copy Nature. It is God Almighty who is to blame in this matter for having created such an indecent object.'[4]

However, the strength of language and the zealous fervour in those letters supporting the Matron spoke louder than any reasoned argument or wit. On Thursday 21 May, 'Clericus' lent his voice to the Matron's cause, damning the paintings as 'an outrage on decency and injurious to morality'.[5] The following day 'Senex' expanded on the issue of morality, claiming that artists' models were necessarily exploited, and likened their profession to that of prostitutes.[6] Two days later 'Another British Matron' claimed that her predecessor's letter was 'an expression of the feelings of every right-minded man and woman'. Describing herself as a mother of children 'whom I hope to train up to be an honour to their religion and their country', she launched a singularly vitriolic attack upon contemporary artists, full of religious and nationalistic fury, concerning the influence of nude paintings:

> What has the passion for the nude in art done for our neighbours across the Channel that we should view without fear and alarm its introduction and spread among ourselves? [...] Our honour for ourselves, our love for our daughters, and our regard for the future welfare of our country, whose warriors, statesmen, and citizens are to be born of our daughters, compel us to decry and discountenance, with all our powers, these stealthy, steadfast advances of the cloven foot.[7]

Satan himself was stalking Britain in the guise of sensuous art and reeking of French cologne. Furthermore, this puritanical attack upon art was not confined to the pages of the old 'Thunderer'. Campaign groups caused serious disruption to art schools, insisting on the segregation of sexes within art classes, as well as a total ban on the nude; and this horror of all things bodily and sensuous applied to all artistic endeavours, as the purity movement challenged the realms of literature and the performing arts in its attempt to rid them of sinful sensuousness. Shortly before the British Matron letters, Alfred Sayce Dyer published the pamphlet *Facts for Men on Moral Purity and Health* (1884) in which he stated that

> If you would keep yourself pure, you must set yourself against sensuous Literature and Art as resolutely as against foul tongued companions [...] An artist, or writer, whether in poetry or prose, who knowingly uses his talents to excite the animal passions, whatever the conventionalities of society may term him, is a mental prostitute.[8]

Once again, the enemies are depictions or descriptions of the sensuous, animal (or bodily) passions, and artists are again compared to workers in the sex trade. In 1888, the Local Government Act gave the newly created Local Councils of Britain direct control over issuing licences to music halls.[9] The purity movement therefore lobbied Councils in a partially successful attempt to close down the music halls (distinctly reminiscent of the original puritans' closing of the theatres in the seventeenth century). The mouthpiece for this campaign was Laura Ormiston Chant, who opposed the licence for *The Empire* on the grounds that 'the place at night is the habitual resort of prostitutes in pursuit of their traffic, and that portions of the entertainment are most objectionable, obnoxious, and against the best interests and moral well-being of the community at large.'[10] For this lady and a great many others, there was little distinction to be made between the prostitutes on the promenades, and the performers on the stage. Theatres and music halls were closed, pending investigations into the lyrical content of songs and the physical performances of singers and dancers, along with attempts to separate prostitutes from their clientele within the music halls themselves. (The owners of *The Empire* made structural alterations to the building in an attempt to screen off prostitutes from the theatre's clientele. This was, however, pulled down by the crowds when the theatre reopened.)[11]

Hence, as Wilde was penning his single, singular novel, puritanism was indeed a powerful force to be reckoned with, and its aim was to obliterate all forms of artistic representation, depiction or description of things bodily and sensuous. To the late Victorian puritan, artists, writers, dancers, and singers were synonymous with prostitutes, if their art had any trace of the sensuous or erotic. For the Decadent artist, writer, and poet, such sentiments added new value to the illicit and the sensuous, in terms of both libertarianism and sheer deviance.

As with much of Wilde's novel, Dorian Gray's transition from a socially detached Aestheticism to a morally and socially engaged Decadence is allegorical, and emblematic of the society from within which Wilde was writing. The national furore stirred by the British Matron letters forced artists to take sides with either the nude's detractors or its defenders. Preserved within the pages of the Little Magazines is a detailed and multifaceted rebuttal of Victorian puritanism, akin to Dorian's decision, from the time of the letters in *The Times* to Wilde's conviction a decade later, and beyond.

One early and erudite voice who spoke out against the puritans was Selwyn Image, who, along with the architects Herbert Percy Horne and Arthur Heygate Mackmurdo founded, edited, and shaped *The Century Guild Hobby Horse* from 1884 to 1894. In the mid 1880s, Image was an artist and designer who had recently left the Anglican priesthood. He was a passionate defender of the music halls, and dancers in particular. (After years of escorting the belles of the halls with such Decadent luminaries as Ernest Dowson, Horne and Arthur Symons, Image married the music-hall dancer Janet McHale in 1901.) Writing on 'The New Puritanism' in the *Church Reformer* in 1894, Image saw the attempts to close the music-hall promenades as '*Essentially* [...] the spirit of Puritanism: the spirit which condemns the human body as a vile thing, and regards the free life of the senses as evil.'[12] Image's defence of sensual living is distinctly Paterian, and this is a repeated theme in his rhetorical essays which grace the pages of the *Hobby Horse*.

His playful essay 'On the Representation of the Nude' (1886) recalls his own inner struggle between religion and art, and he clearly identifies the opposing parties of the sensuous world of Art, and a morality based on Protestant teaching; yet his purpose in writing the essay was not to attempt to reconcile these opposed parties with Arnoldian, liberal rhetoric; rather he condemns those who try to do so:

> I cannot help feeling [...] that when artists or critics or amateurs in general grow very contemptuous over such letters, and are indignant in their protests that all fine art tends towards fine morality, — by which they assume to understand *Christian* morality, — and that therefore these presentations of the nude, which may be undoubtedly fine art, tend towards fine morality, I cannot help feeling, I say, in part that they must consciously be posing.[13]

His argument rests upon the fact that the number of those for whom the appreciation of painted nudes is purely a matter of educated aesthetics — a detached appreciation of beauty itself — is remarkably small. For the many, in varying degrees, painted nudes must represent titillation, and he argues that

> when you hear Christ say that even the imagination of fleshly indulgence is adultery, and that no adulterer can enter into his kingdom; when you know how the temptation to such imaginings is everywhere, and that yielding to it is the easiest and the commonest of human yieldings, the victory over it the hardest won of human victories:– with what sort of honour can you say [the 'Lord's Prayer'] while you put yourself at all events within the reach of sensuous allurements, and study the fascinations of nakedness?[14]

Prefiguring the decision made by Dorian Gray (and, indeed, to some extent the semantics of its articulation) in the opening quotation, Image states that the Protestant ideal 'is an ascetic ideal [...] with the exuberant and joyous life of the senses, it is in perpetual and deadly antagonism'.[15] The life led in accordance to Art is necessarily sensuous, and therefore necessarily sinful. To Image, the 'gospel of sensuousness', was 'the very foundation for fine art';[16] and thus, popular Protestant Christianity and Art are fundamentally opposed and should remain so. His conclusion is not, therefore, one of reconciliation, but is simply a matter of choice: 'We *must* make up our minds. It is a radical question in art come just now to the surface for us: and we must make up our minds what we ought to believe.'[17] Rather than directly countering the attack upon Art in the letters to *The Times*, the *Hobby Horse*, represented in Image's essay, clearly sought to further the divisions between the puritans and the defenders of Art.

In his article, 'On the Unity of Art' in Volume 2 (1887; i, 2–8), Image expands on his ostensible title to critique narrowness in thought regarding both art and religion, thereby attacking both the British Matron's rigid definition of what is and what is not art, along with the strict, puritanical Protestantism that underpinned such views. 'On Catholicity of Taste' sees Image taking up the nationalistic themes of 'Another British Matron', but decries the fact that there is nothing 'more feeble, and in the way of our advancement, more obstructive than narrowness of sympathy'.[18] Although never a convert to Catholicism, Image rather enjoyed donning Roman robes metaphorically, if it assisted him in opposing or ridiculing Protestantism's attempted stranglehold on Art.

> In the Catholic Church there are many things that move my admiration and win me; but there is nothing I think more admirable and winning, nothing indeed in which the note of Catholicity is more surely struck, than in the freedom with which she deals with the spiritual life. [...]
> From St. Philip Neri or St. Francis of Sales to the Carthusians and the Trappists:– conceive the pliability, the endless variety of sympathetic methods with which the Great Mother educates her children. Far enough is she from casting them in one mould, setting them to one task, making them walk along one line: but adapting herself with the sure instinct of a genius to their various and divergent and contradictory natures she has for each of them a gracious acceptance, an end which they will heartily desire, a method which they will devotedly use.[19]

As Image's rhetoric unfolds, he clearly contrasts the warmth and humanity of the 'Great Mother' with its cold, empirical 'other', Protestantism: 'Now in Art as in Religion it is a great thing to be of such a spirit as this, to have such freedom from mechanical rigidity.'[20] The contrast could not be sharper. As stated before, Protestantism, in Image's view, works against 'human interests' and in this article, when compared to Catholicism, it is depicted as cold, inhuman and unnatural. Catholicism is praised as having an 'excellent understanding of human nature', with the unstated implication being that any such sympathies are denied within Protestantism.[21] Posing as a Romanist, Selwyn Image further antagonized sensuous Art's detractors, but also sought to defend artistic explorations of the body and the senses, from a solid bastion of sensual art founded upon Classicism, which the *Hobby Horse* posited as a continued influence in the world via the Holy Roman Empire.

Image's essays countering the Matron in 1886 and 1887 were the template for many scholarly essays defending sensuous art against puritanical attackers in the Little Magazines for the next decade. John Gray's 'Les Goncourts' from *The Dial* (1889) is a defence of French literary techniques, and in praising the Goncourt brothers, Gray lambasts the narrowness of thought found in puritanical England. Aping the xenophobic rantings of Another British Matron, Gray asks,

> And what shall we, we English, say? we the chosen? we who understand so well that a book, to be good, must recount a series of good actions? we who like the shadow thrown across the hero's path only for the pleasure of seeing it swept away again? who feel impatient if the wedding is delayed? Germinie Lacerteux stayed out late at night? stole from her mistress? Manette Saloman was not married to Coriolis? Put it away! put it away! Dear me! if Freddy should get hold of it! Shocking blemishes, happily so soon discovered. Let us beware the glittering poison.[22]

Whilst ridiculing the Matron's opinion that the French nation has been corrupted by its acceptance of sensuous art, Gray turns this purportedly French attitude towards art around to attack British nationals: 'For the French can certainly claim a higher intelligence than we, in that at least some appreciable proportion of them understand the phrase "art for art's sake".'[23] Hubert Crackanthorpe's 'Reticence in Literature: Some Roundabout Remarks' in *The Yellow Book* (1894) is a response to another piece of in-house self-criticism in *The Yellow Book*, 'Reticence in Literature', a conservative, and singularly sexist, diatribe from the pen of Arthur Waugh (father of Evelyn). Crackanthorpe's work is a well-structured piece of rhetoric, tackling bourgeois attitudes towards art in general, and literature in particular, which would sit perfectly alongside the writings of Image, and other writers in the *Century Guild Hobby Horse*. He clearly identifies the enemies of Art as being 'the *bourgeois*', and recognizes Arnold's labelling of them as 'Philistines'.[24] Arnold and Pater are brought to mind throughout the essay, as Crackanthorpe makes statements such as 'The business of art is to create for us fine interests, to make of our human nature a more complete thing', as he delineates between morality 'in the wide and truer sense of the word', and the 'moral ogre's' simplistic view of morality as concerning only 'relations between the sexes and [...] between man and man'.[25] Pater's central philosophy in *Studies in the History of the Renaissance* is invoked specifically as we are told that literary works of art

> are inevitably stamped with the hallmark of [the artist's] personality [...] Every piece of imaginative work must be a kind of autobiography of its creator — significant, if not of the actual facts of his existence, at least of the inner working of his soul.[26]

The personality is thus central to the true spirit of Art, in terms of both creation and appreciation, as Crackanthorpe espouses the Paterian philosophy that 'individual interpretation' is the key to all. Image himself is practically paraphrased as Crackanthorpe builds his case for interpretation over replication in matters of art, stating, 'Art is not invested with the futile function of perpetually striving after imitation or reproduction of Nature.'[27] The fact that this essay is firmly rooted in the issues raised by the letters in *The Times* a decade earlier is made plain by an oblique reference to Horsley's British Matron campaign:

> If imitation be the sincerest form of flattery, then our moral ogre must indeed have experienced a proud moment, when a follower came to him from the camp of the lovers of Art, and the artistic objector to realistic fiction started on its timid career.[28]

Havelock Ellis's defence of 'Zola: The Man and His Work' within *The Savoy* (1896) is another example of such scholarly, rhetorical essays, battling against Matron-inspired Purity campaigns of the 1890s. Puritanical values in the circulating libraries business led to a tacit censorship of any literature dealing with the body and senses. Ellis blamed an 'exaggerated purism' for rendering language too 'bloodless and colourless for the artist's purposes' and complained that this 'ever-encroaching process of attenuation and circumlocution [is] extending into literature also, and here it is disastrous.'[29] According to Ellis, late Victorians had 'all but lost the indispensable words "belly" and "bowels" both used so often and with such admirable effect in the Psalms.' Both words had to be replaced with the literarily bland, and anatomically incorrect 'stomach'.[30] Indeed, he quite rightly claimed that were the works of Chaucer, Shakespeare, and even the Bible to be screened by the editorial boards of Mudie's and Smith's, they would not pass muster. Certainly to Ellis's mind, the puritans' abhorrence of any mention of the human body and its functions was virtually killing literary art, a full decade after the Matron began her campaign.

However, the scholarly essay was not the only weapon in the Little Magazines' arsenal. *The Yellow Book* and *The Savoy* revelled in deviant images and prose, as a wanton mark of defiance against puritanism. Aubrey Beardsley's scandalous illustrations, which graced both publications' pages, are well known. (*The Yellow Book* publisher John Lane claimed that, before publication, he had to turn every image of Beardsley's through 360 degrees to ensure that there wasn't a phallus hidden in there somewhere.) As the puritans struck out against the music halls, the Decadents took delight in them, frequenting the halls by night, and then writing up the experience for publication by day. Arthur Symons's 'At the Alhambra: Impressions and Sensations', in *The Savoy*, is one such example. If the puritans sought to damn sensuous art by linking it to prostitution, Decadent writers embraced prostitutes, both figuratively and literally. Henry Harland's 'To Every Man a Damsel or Two', in *The Yellow Book*, is a wry, comic tale of an encounter with a prostitute who gets the better of a naïve young music-hall goer. Arthur Symons's 'Lucy Newcombe' tales in *The Savoy* are a very thinly veiled fictionalization of the real-life prostitute Muriel Broadbent, who used the splendid working name of Amaryllis, and had been mistress to both Symons himself and Herbert Horne of the *Hobby Horse*. Transgression, in the form of brazen declarations of the sensuous life, the erotic, and the illicit, all took on a profound new importance in the defence of artistic freedom in the face of late-Victorian puritanism.

The Little Magazine which has the closest relationship with Wilde's novel and its philosophy is, however, comparatively unknown. The *Dial*'s obscurity, and its status as the apex of Decadent sensibilities are inextricably linked, and are best understood in comparison with its more famous descendant, *The Yellow Book*. John Lane and Henry Harland worked tirelessly to produce an edition of *The Yellow Book* every quarter, and made sure that it represented value for money for its readers. The original contract between literary editor Henry Harland and the owner (and *de facto* editor-in-chief) John Lane, stated that *The Yellow Book* should sell for five shillings and each volume be 'at least 250 pages' long.[31] From the second number onwards, the title page of *The Yellow Book* is prefaced by a note from Harland detailing the conditions for the return of rejected, unsolicited manuscripts. In fact a great many contributions, and notable contributors, such as Ella D'Arcy, were introduced to the editors in this manner. *The Yellow Book* was thus a commercial venture first and foremost, and one that cast its nets very wide indeed, in terms of contributors, their styles and philosophies. Hence, within *The Yellow Book*'s artwork, Sir Frederick Leighton (President of the Royal Academy at the time) may be seen rubbing shoulders with the Decadent *enfant terrible* Aubrey Beardsley.

By contrast, the *Dial* was 'to appear, [...] at such intervals as the sun of inspiration will permit; hence the name', according to its first advertisement in the *Hobby Horse* in 1889.[32] Indeed, this proved to be the case, as only five issues were ever produced, in 1889, 1892, 1893, 1896 and 1897, each more expensive than a year's subscription to *The Yellow Book*. Furthermore, this 'sun of inspiration' was only to shine on a very select band of individuals. Charles Haslewood Shannon and Charles Ricketts were the artistic couple at the centre of the *Dial*, and the only other regular contributors were their close friends John Gray and Thomas Sturge Moore.

From its very inception, the *Dial* put far more importance on the Paterian ideas of momentary inspiration and the individual personality than any base, commercial considerations. Moreover, when one begins to examine the lives of these men, profound connections begin to emerge between the *Dial* and Wilde's text of *The Picture of Dorian Gray*. Ricketts and Shannon represented the quintessence of young, fashionable artists-about-Chelsea in the late 1880s and early 1890s. Sexually ambiguous, but probably homosexual, both men have been cited by Wilde's biographers as the inspiration behind the character of Basil Hallward.[33] In addition, the exquisite décor of Basil's studio in Wilde's book was simply a description of Ricketts and Shannon's actual home studio at the Vale in Chelsea. The third member of the *Dial*'s elite coterie comes with excellent Wildean credentials, being the poet John Gray. Gray was famed for his beauty, particularly in the years leading up to the publication of *The Picture of Dorian Gray*, and he had been Wilde's muse before Alfred Douglas. Although Gray certainly sought to distance himself from Wilde as his notoriety developed more towards infamy, they had been close for a brief period around the time Wilde was writing his novel. Dorian's surname was quite probably chosen in order to flatter the young poet (Richard Ellmann called it 'a form of courtship')[34] and Gray did indeed sign himself 'Dorian' in at least one letter to Wilde at the time. Hence, if one were to picture Ricketts, Shannon, and Gray discussing their artistic endeavours at the Vale, one would only need Wilde to saunter in as Lord Henry, and the room, decor and characters would mirror the opening pages of *The Picture of Dorian Gray*, perfectly.[35] It is therefore unsurprising to find the most daring, flagrant and creative interpretations of Lord Henry's 'new hedonism' within the pages of this lesser known Little Magazine that is so closely tied to the story of Dorian Gray.

The *Dial* did include some rhetorical pieces attacking the purity movement, such as Gray's 'Les Goncourts' mentioned above, Reginald Savage's 'Notes' (*Dial*, 1, 1889), the anonymous 'The Unwritten Book' (most likely penned by Ricketts, *Dial*, 2, 1892), and Gray's 'The Redemption of Durtal', being a review of J.-K. Huysmans's 1895 novel *En route* (*Dial*, 4, 1896). However, their most strident opposition to puritanism was the sheer revelry with which they celebrated bodily sensations within their artwork and letterpress. Gray's poetry in the *Dial* fuses the religious with the homoerotic, as his poem 'Parsifal, after Verlaine' and a supposed translation of St Francis ably demonstrate. Catholic dogma can all too easily lend itself to the misogynist, and in 'Parsifal' woman is depicted as being the essence of temptation and sin, seeking to ensnare the virtuous youth:

> Conquered the flower maidens, and the wide embrace
> Of their round proffered arms that tempt the virgin boy:
> Conquered the trickling of their bubbling tongues; the coy
> Back glances; and the mobile breasts of supple grace.
> Conquered the woman beautiful; the fatal charm
> Of her hot breast; the music of her babbling tongue:
> Conquered the gate of Hell;[36]

For Gray, female sexuality — from her coy glances, trickling tongue and hot, supple breasts, to the very 'gate of Hell' — represents sin itself; that is to say, separation from God. When the youth has conquered the temptation that is woman, the holy ritual that follows is entirely homosocial. This transition, midway in the poem, also marks a significant shift in imagery, from the clear and direct description of female sexuality, to the much more symbolic world of the holy males. The impressionistic imagery of the male ritual is ambiguous but certainly generous enough to allow a homoerotic reading of Gray's all-male ideal. The boy enters into the presence of 'the dying king' and heals him by means of his 'heavy trophy' that is 'The holy javelin that pierced the Heart of God'. Restored, the King becomes also 'high priest of that great gift the living Blood' and by means of this gift of living bodily fluid, 'In robe of gold the youth adores the glorious Sign | Of the green goblet; worships the mysterious Wine. | And oh, the chime of children's voices in the dome!'[37]

The exact nature of this exchange is unclear, although the 'children's voices in the dome' of the last line could represent a more innocent, non-sexual realm, or indeed the idea of Catholic abstinence. However, the notion of a 'youth' who gives a physical gift to the older 'king' and receives enlightenment in return has obvious parallels with the Socratic model of the master-pupil-lover relationship.

This essentially masculine, physical element to Gray's interpretation of Catholic ritual is repeated in the following issue for 1893 in his poetic interpretation of 'A Hymn Translated from the Italian of Saint Francis of Assisi'.[38] The opening stanza begins, and each stanza ends, with the repeated refrain 'Love setteth me a-burning', and the whole is depicted as a marriage between the saint and God. Unquestioningly, God is represented as the male partner in the ritual, as He 'Had set His ring upon me'. The groom is represented as having conquered his bride, and the saint is literally penetrated by his 'new Spouse':

> The Conqueror's prize returning,
> Love's knife had all undone me,
> All my heart broke with yearning.
> Love setteth me a-burning.

Once again, the imagery of the 'holy javelin' is evoked, but in terms much less obscure, and once more piercing the body of the saint:

> I die of very sweetness.
> Yet be thou not astounded.
> That lance of Love's completeness
> So sorrowfully wounded!
> Oh, broad the iron's meetness!
> Not one arm's length, a hundred
> Has pierced me with its fleetness.
> Love setteth me a-burning.

Without the title of the poem suggesting a spiritual interpretation of the tale, this stanza could indeed be read as being flagrantly homoerotic. The very act of salvation is portrayed as being a physical struggle with Christ, in itself reminiscent of the story of Jacob's struggle with the Angel, but given the marriage analogy of the poem as a whole, Gray's depiction of the saint and Christ has powerful homosexual overtones:

> On Christ I warred right knightly.
> Great skill against him urging,
> I grappled with him tightly,
> The dastard in me purging.
> Love setteth me a-burning.

In the final stanza, Christ's love overcomes and conquers the saint entirely, 'Love lavished without measure | To Christ at length united'. Clearly Francis's, and by extension Gray's, relationship with Christ is depicted as a marriage in a very real sense. Although a common metaphor for Christ and the Church within the scriptures themselves, this metaphor of holy, homosexual marriage can be used on any number of levels, from the purely chaste and devotional ideal of a spiritual unity with God, to an essentially physical and sexualized perception of the deity, or perhaps a deification of the sexual act. Gray's poems in the *Dial* certainly interweave religious notions with homosexual desires and fantasies, resulting in works that are dialogic, ambiguous or ambivalent, uniting the spheres of bodily sin and spiritual sanctity. This idea of uniting sin and sanctity has distinctly Catholic overtones. Most unlike puritanical Protestantism, Catholicism embodies the idea of sin within the holy sacrament of Confession (if you must confess every week, you must therefore sin every week). Therefore these elements of Catholic imagery and ideology within Gray's poetry are diametrically opposed to the purity movement's wider sensibilities, as can be found within the more militantly Protestant literature of the time.

The dialogic quality of the poems' messages can certainly be read as an attempt to avoid prosecution for obscenity by cloaking erotic content in religious garb. This was a commonplace practice at the time, along with using classical themes and imagery in order to legitimize or veil sexual content in literature. Pierre Louÿs's novel, *Aphrodite*, is an interesting example of this technique, as are the many collaborations between Sir Richard Burton and the publisher Leonard Smithers.[39] Gray's interpretation of the classical tale of Leda and the Swan, which appeared in the *Dial* in 1897 is a further example of this practice, and is particularly bold in its imagery:

> [...] the swan floats near;
> And bidding Leda not to fear
> Adventure with him by the beck
> Of his keen eyes and writhing neck,
> Enticeth till her breast
> Beyond the parapet doth rest;
> Until a timid hand leans out
> And folds the downy breast about.
>
> Over the margin slips
> The lithe blithe line of Leda's hips;
> And straightway hence the swan doth speed,
> Exultant for his rapturous deed.
>
> The glory of his course:
> Whence his quick gesture and his force
> Excite the like in Leda's limbs,

> Who like a sturdy swimmer swims
> Beside her feathered lord
> And swift assistance doth afford.[40]

Classical veil notwithstanding, the sexual nature of Leda and the Swan is made abundantly clear in Gray's interpretation of the tale. This poem was published by the *Dial* a mere two years after Wilde's conviction, demonstrating the periodical's audacious defence of the Decadent artist, and his most brazen avowal of the sensuous and the erotic. Indeed, the erotic quality of this particular poem retains its potency for modern readers, an uncommon attribute for openly published late-Victorian literature.

The idea of voyeurism is present in much of the artwork, and even in some of the letterpress represented in the *Dial*. In a remarkable number of the works included, nudes and sensual representations of the female form are almost invariably depicted in a room with a mirror.[41] This image of the mirror, encapsulating as it does the notions of both voyeurism and narcissism, is the central conceit in Thomas Sturge Moore's masterful adaptation of the classical tale of 'Danaë'. The opening stanza playfully introduces the idea of voyeurism, or rather the lack of it, in describing the solitude in which Danaë's father has placed her in order to preserve her chastity:

> In her fresh silent mind — in nudity,
> No flush-faced shame dared hinder to enjoy,
> Her beauty — purely with no least alloy
> of vanity, since she had never seen
> Eyes like those to which modest maidens screen
> Themselves from [...].[42]

However, the presence of a mirror violates this temple of chastity, as Danaë views herself for the first time, and through her eyes the poet paints the picture of her maturing body for the voyeuristic reader. Believing her reflection to be her twin, Danaë reflects upon the changes in the perceived other, that is herself:

> Not once had she yet missed her,
> As o'er their earliest chubby limbs had come
> A gradual change, a whimsical, winsome
> Awkwardness peeping out till plumpness went:
> O'er salient points a certain tightness lent
> A peevish pinched appearance; in sight too
> Their shoulder blades moved looselier: a new
> Sly meagreness had crept over them.[43]

Inevitably, this process leads Danaë on to a gradual appreciation of the effects of her dawning sexuality:

> Strange inner effervescence sparkled gaily
> Out through their eyes. The undecided place
> Of budding breasts, dissimulating grace
> As March flakes feign the snowdrops calm, shows forms
> Hazy like mushrooms when the night-time warms,
> That globe and gleam, yet leave the stars in doubt
> If on the dewy slopes they shift about.[44]

In depicting the further maturation of the female form, Moore uses the sensuous metaphor of the potter's wheel in describing God's designing of woman:

> When moulds the potter on his whirling wheel
> Dumb clay, a hint of final curves will steal
> From clever hands in sapience sure; just so
> Quaint querulous suggestions of a flow
> Of contour simpler, more capacious, slips
> From God's thumb when he moulds a woman's hips.
> Her thighs will lengthen faster than they round,
> Till their delightful devious line be found.
> The heels, too narrow, of the little feet
> Will give her steps a wayward wav'ring sweet.
> As when unwrapped, the heavy dahlias lean,
> Her head nods, nods.[45]

Moore's anatomization of Danaë's body guides the reader's imagination, as the poem lingers on each aspect of her maturing figure in turn, shifting the focus, in measured tones, from her eyes, shoulders and breasts to the sensual curves of her hips and legs. Furthermore, the analogy of the potter's wheel adds an almost tangible, tactile quality to the poem, drawing further senses into the interpretation of the story. The same issue of the *Dial* includes another, though slightly more veiled, allusion to the development of the female form, as Shannon quotes from Sappho in his illustrations for the Vale Press edition of *Daphnis and Chloe*.

Entitled *The Topmost Apple*, Shannon's illustration depicts the naked, young Daphnis reaching out towards an apple, far beyond easy reach, as Chloe waits below hiding her head in her hands. The picture is accompanied by the quotation

> DAPHNIS PLUCKS FROM THE TOPMOST BOUGH WHERE THE GATHERERS HAD FORGOTTEN IT THE TOPMOST APPLE LEST PERCHANCE FALLING IT SHOULD BE TRODDEN INTO THE PURPLE GROUND OR BITTEN BY THE VENOUS LIPS OF SOME SERPENT.[46]

These lines are a fusion of fragments 93 and 94 of Wharton's *Sappho* (1885), the first of which reads 'As the sweet-apple blushes on the end of the bough, the very end of the bough, which the gatherers overlooked, nay overlooked not but could not reach.'[47]

Wharton's notes expand upon Sappho's poetry; citing Himerius, he states that 'It was for Sappho to liken the maiden to an apple, allowing to those who would pluck before the time to touch not even with the finger-tip, but to him who was to gather the apple in season to watch its ripe beauty.'[48] Obviously, Shannon's illustration is alluding to Chloe's developing body, and Daphnis's desire to 'reach' her. The erotic content here is therefore doubly veiled in classical allusion when compared to Gray's and Moore's poetry above. However, such playful obfuscation only serves to increase the titillation for the cognizant reader.

The artwork in the *Dial* was consistently of a high and highly sensuous quality, blazoning the Nude in every single issue. One such example is Ricketts's initial illustration to an essay on Maurice de Guérin, which could be described as impressionistic pornography (Fig. 9.1). A brooding centaur watches over a singularly

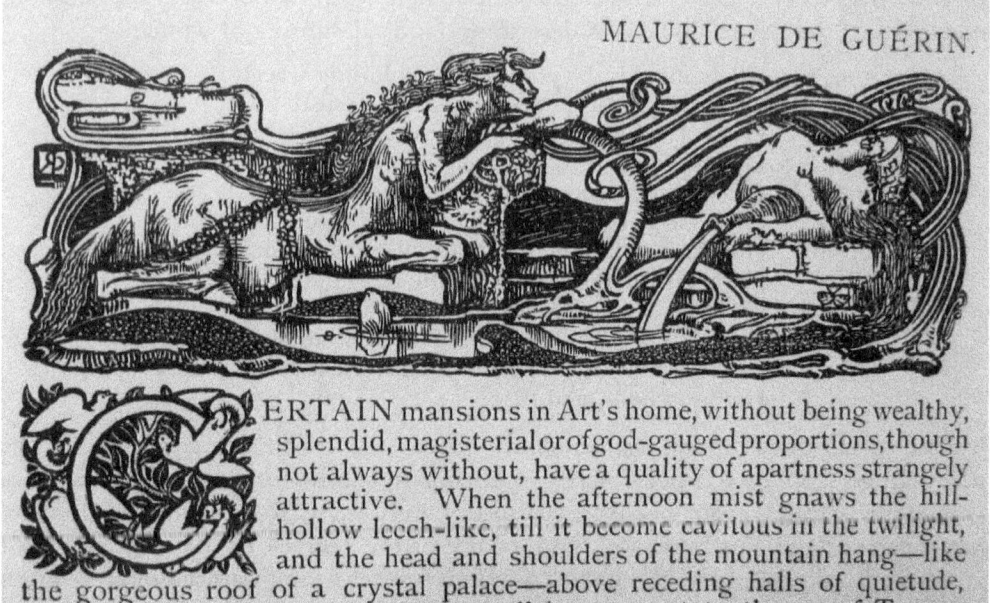

FIG. 9.1. Charles Ricketts, initial piece to 'Maurice de Guérin', c. 1892, *The Dial*, 2, p. 11. Reproduced by permission of Durham University Library.

voluptuous nude who is posing in a way suggestive of recent ravishment. Lacking the energy to keep it aloft, the woman's pitcher spills forth a stream of water or wine which gushes thunderously into a pool (an idea saturated with sexual metaphor), and she lies surrounded by swirling arabesques, which Ricketts used elsewhere to suggest certain masculine bodily emissions (and which was a distinctly probable influence on Aubrey Beardsley, in this latter regard).

However the *Dial*'s interpretation of the importance of the body and the senses was not limited to sexual images, description or metaphor. There are several images and texts that certainly appear to represent a concerted effort to portray, or suggest, as many of the five senses as is possible on the printed page. In Shannon's illustration, *The Queen of Sheba*, the central figure of a nude at toilet is surrounded by images set to excite almost every sense (Fig. 9.2). Hot steam rises from the pool, along with incense from a censer, enveloping the soft white flesh of the Queen. Fresh, crisp lotus flowers float upon the water, and what look like bottles of perfume or oil sit upon a shelf below the mirror, suggesting yet more rich aromas. A very similar image, this time by Ricketts, is used as the initial piece to an early, experimental text in the first issue of the *Dial*, entitled 'Sensations' (*Dial*, 1, 1889, 34–36). In this image, a nude woman, partly submerged in a bathtub, plays her fingers through her long, wet hair. The scene is reflected in a mirror, and the bath is once again surrounded by open bottles of oils and perfumes, and the whole scene is ringed with cut flowers, their heavy heads drooping, as if rich with scent. Although disconnected from the story in terms of narrative content, this image sets the tone for the tale, in terms of suggested sensory stimulation. A highly fragmented tale, 'Sensations' begins with a very tactile, visual and olfactory sense of the protagonist's surroundings:

Fig. 9.2. Charles Shannon, *The Queen of Sheba*, 1889, *The Dial*, 1, AD. Reproduced by permission of Durham University Library.

> Little by little the air grew thick and oily; the sky, colour of oil, was strangely streaked with slowly lengthening shafts of smoke, rising from the whitish houses. The window panes, instead of being cool and soothing, gave a harsh shock, almost painful, suggesting a shudder.[49]

What follows is a depiction of a thunderstorm, experienced though the senses of a frail and sickly dandy, somewhat reminiscent of Huysmans's Des Esseintes. The storm physically assaults the senses of the fragile man, adding a touch of synaesthesia to the imagery:

> The room danced. Each repetition of the vivid light gave almost the impression of a blow; the eye, puzzled, seemed to see from the back of the head — flash! flash! — blue, lilac, rose — flash! flash! Then other sensations rushed upon me, the consciousness of an awful tearing, crackling, and rolling sound; something rolling wantonly in the glory of its strength, falling in key like a phrase of Bach; and still that awful sensation of dancing light — flash! flash! destroying all sense of touch, of space; all, save that of hearing, concentrated into one awful sense of sight.[50]

The story then turns to a memory, which suggests a direct comparison with Thomas de Quincey's *Affliction of Childhood* (1845). For de Quincey, the death of his sister at the height of summer forever linked that season with a sense of morbidity.[51] In Ricketts's tale, the previous thunderstorm's emotional intensity is explained by the presence of another such storm, while the hero was standing over the 'deathbed of a friend', years earlier.[52] The tale progresses to a malodorous Catholic mass, the air 'oppressive from the earlier celebrations', either the night of this storm or of that where the hero becomes morbidly fascinated by the bodily writhings and convulsions of a paralytic.[53] The story ends in a whirl of confused sensations, filled with disjointed and grotesque Catholic imagery, all wreathed in scented tobacco smoke. The end of the story leaves the reader rather unsure as to whether this final scene is present action or dream-like memory.

'Sensations' may be deemed an experimental piece of literature, akin to others in the first issue of the *Dial*, such as Ricketts's 'The Cup of Happiness', which wilfully disrupt or disregard plot, focusing instead on style, image, and effect. It is perhaps a little crude, bringing to mind Michael Field's rather harsh appraisal of the first issue of the *Dial*: 'that mad journal? with some good line work in it, and rubbish for prose.'[54] However, what 'Sensations' demonstrates, in its title, initial illustration, and content, is an exploration of the senses, and a laudable effort to represent as many of them as possible on the printed page. The continued importance of representing sensual experience for the Decadent *Dial*'s central coterie can be seen in a later periodical, *The Pageant*. The two annual editions of the *Pageant* (1896 and 1897) were edited by Shannon and J. W. Gleeson White, and were far more sumptuously bound than the ephemeral *Dial*. Large format, hardback and heavy, the *Pageant* was clearly made with posterity in mind. The *Dial* coterie was again at the heart of the publication, and once more, Decadent themes and preoccupations may be found in relation to the senses.

In the second edition of the *Pageant*, John Gray published a most singular work of fiction, in terms of anti-puritan, Decadent literature. 'Light' fuses bodily ecstasies and excesses with Catholic propaganda and Paterian philosophy, and is quite uncommon in its choice of protagonist. The central character is not a young, dandified and androgynous male, but rather a middle-aged, lower-middle-class housewife, as she undergoes a particularly sense-laden conversion from Protestantism to Catholicism.[55]

The tale begins by stating that the first forty years of the woman's life had been unremarkable, for whom God's very existence was a matter of 'settled fact'. This statement, rooted as it is in empirical *knowledge*, may be seen as typically Protestant, in stark contrast to the story that follows. Any notion of her knowledge of the Divine being fixed was challenged, when, upon hearing her husband (a blacksmith) suggest that she attend 'Winter Street' church one Sunday, 'a voice inside her finished the sentence' with 'Newbury Park' instead. The voice, we are told, emanated 'from her chest rather than from her head'.[56] This movement from the intellectual to the bodily becomes more pronounced when the woman attends the church service at Newbury Park, where, after hearing the gospel, as she had done numerous times before, 'A ray fell from distant heaven. Alighting in her, it exploded her soul into radiant, conscious being. In an instant [...] herself and the visible and invisible world were created anew.'[57]

This new consciousness focuses the woman on the 'now', the present moment, as it is experienced through the senses. In an episode that at once recalls both the Paterian 'gem-like flame' and Buddhist-Hindu transcendence as well as the Catholic ecstatic tradition, it is from within this moment of supreme sensory consciousness, separate from thought, that she touches the divine. The fact that this is a *bodily* rather than intellectual experience is emphasized by Gray, who states that her 'tempestuous, chaotic prayer' came with 'no movement of the lips, no activity of the brain; it throbbed [...] from her chest'.[58] Pater's concept of the 'gem-like flame' that can be maintained in a state of perpetual ecstasy is animated by Gray, as the woman now experiences a new wonder in every act of life however seemingly mundane, bringing her 'ecstasy beyond thought'.[59]

Decadent London is brought to life, firstly in a dream where the woman sees a golden poem amidst a town square that has an 'Oriental aspect'. This later transpires to be the Alhambra Theatre in Leicester Square. However, upon waking from the dream, the woman experiences another moment of sensory transcendence, this time uniting her with the Holy family:

> she offered thanks for her existence, that she was her very self, that she was a *woman*. The Lord had been born of a *woman*. She could understand a little of what it must have been to be the holy mother of God.[60]

It is from this bodily revelation that a sexual element enters into the tale. Meditating upon the physical nature of Christ, 'born of his mortal mother in mortal flesh' she connects herself with the Christ through her female body,[61] and feels an ability 'to light the world from one's own body, to bear the Light within one, to be the genetrix — it surpassed reason.'[62] God therefore becomes her 'Divine Lover' and Gray the narrator compares her husband to St Joseph. Seemingly at a loss to describe the woman's physical and spiritual sensation, Gray compares the woman's experience to poetry that highlights the fleshly, bodily nature of God as Christ:

> Johann Scheffler has shown the nativity in sentences of tenderness which human speech has poor hope to ever excel, so frail that they cannot be stirred from the tongue in which they were first set; Frederich Spe has expressed physical contact with Christ in words which swoon upon his lips; the English language holds the pomp and glory of song in Crashaw's poem on the circumcision. If these three masters could be distilled into one and their concentrated sweetness impinged direct upon a sensitive heart, the victim might present a parallel to the overwhelmed blacksmith's wife, fallen the most pitiable heap of flesh.[63]

'Light' is therefore a singularly subversive text, both in its subject matter of Catholic conversion and in its detailed portrayal of the bodily sensations that accompany such a spiritual journey. Obvious parallels can be drawn between this and other contemporary studies of female hagiography and hysteria, such as Cesare Lombroso's 'A Mad Saint', translated by Havelock Ellis in the first issue of *The Savoy*, or the various tales of religious mania in females in Richard Freiherr von Krafft-Ebing's *Psychopathia Sexualis* (1886). However, the conclusions of these works suggest the women's religious fervour was either the result of delusion or a manifestation of perverted sexuality, if not indeed both, simultaneously. 'Light' draws no such conclusions about the woman herself. Gray does not analyse or diagnose his subject, but recounts her story with sympathy and at least an attempt at understanding (as may be seen in his use of poetic analogy, quoted above). The tale is presented as a reality: a woman attaining the godhead, in religious terms; or an individual who '[succeeds] in life' by maintaining Pater's 'gem-like flame' of total awareness of herself and her surroundings, physically and spiritually.

'Light' is unusual when compared to contemporary interpretations of religious mania, yet it is perfectly aligned with the many Decadent works which all sought to oppose puritanism by embracing the life of the senses as proposed by Pater and Wilde. These works of poetry, criticism, art, and creative prose were not just rebellions for the sake of it, *scandale pour scandale*. They stand as testament to the very real war that was raging between the puritans and the defenders of Art within the last two decades of the Victorian era. One need only dwell upon Wilde's trials in 1895 to see the severity with which judicial puritanism dealt with subversive behaviour and ideas. Indeed, the Wilde trials illustrate precisely how dangerous it was to publish subversive ideas in periodicals. When Wilde's accusers quoted from *The Picture of Dorian Gray*, it was the earlier *Lippincott's Monthly Magazine* edition that they used. Furthermore, the prosecution's use of 'The Priest and the Acolyte' from the single-issue, undergraduate magazine, *The Chameleon*, showed that no periodical, however obscure or small the print run, lay beyond the gaze of the judicial beasts roused by Wilde's arrest. In the wake of Wilde's conviction *The Yellow Book* famously shed its Decadent affiliations, firing Beardsley and a host of others, tainted by their perceived connections with the 'High Priest of the Decadents'.[64] By comparison, the *Dial-Pageant* fraternities were most strident in their defence of Decadence and their continued defiance of the puritan's anti-sensual creed.

Thus these works within Little Magazines remain as evidence of the sustained struggle between puritanism and the defenders and champions of artistic, sexual, and religious freedom at the close of the Victorian age. The human body was their battleground, and bodily sensations and ecstasies their blazon; and as history demonstrates, they were victorious eventually, as defenders of the Decadent faith, and steadfast torchbearers, lighting up the road to Modernism, and ultimately the libertarian victories of the *Lady Chatterley* trial in 1960.

Notes to Chapter 9

1. Oscar Wilde, *The Portrait of Dorian Gray and the Picture of Mr. W. H.* [sic]. Excerpts from *Lippincott's Monthly Magazine* 1890 and *Blackwood's Edinburgh Magazine* 1889 (privately bound by Gleeson White, c. 1890), p. 66.
2. A British Matron [John Callcott Horsley], 'A Woman's Plea: To the Editor of *The Times*', *The Times*, 20 May 1885, p. 10. Along with negative press reactions from the likes of *Punch*, which gave him the sobriquet 'clothes-Horsley', Whistler lampooned Horsley's campaign, exhibiting 'a pastel of a nude at the Society of Artists in December 1885 with a note attached reading "Horsley soit qui mal y pense".' See Helen Valentine, 'Horsley, John Callcott (1817–1903)', *Oxford Dictionary of National Biography*, ed. by Lawrence Goldman (Oxford: Oxford University Press, 2004); <http://www.oxforddnb.com/view/article/33998> [accessed 3 September 2007].
3. Alison Smith, *The Victorian Nude: Sexuality, Morality and Art* (Manchester: Manchester University Press, 1996), p. 227.
4. Jerome K. Jerome, 'Nude Studies: To the Editor of *The Times*', *The Times*, 23 May 1885, p. 10.
5. Clericus, 'To the Editor of *The Times*', *The Times*, 21 May 1885, p. 6.
6. Senex, 'To the Editor of *The Times*', *The Times*, 22 May 1885, p. 5.
7. Another British Matron, 'Nude Studies: To the Editor of *The Times*', *The Times*, 23 May 1885, p. 10.
8. Cited in Alison Smith, *The Victorian Nude*, p. 218.
9. 'Information Leaflet No. 47: Sources for the History of London Theatres and Music Halls at London Metropolitan Archives', *London Metropolitan Archives*, June 2006, p. 2. <https://www.cityoflondon.gov.uk/things-to-do/visiting-the-city/archives-and-city-history/london-metropolitan-archives/Documents/visitor-information/47-theatre-and-music-hall-sources-at-lma.pdf> [accessed 28 November 2014].
10. *Ibid.*
11. *Ibid.*
12. 'The New Puritanism', undated fragment from *The Church Reformer*, 1894. Miscellaneous Papers of S. Image. Oxford, Bodleian Library, Ms. Eng. Misc. c.310, 247–48.
13. Selwyn Image, 'On the Representation of the Nude', *The Century Guild Hobby Horse*, 1 (1886), 8–13 (p. 12).
14. *Ibid.*, p. 10.
15. *Ibid.*, p. 9.
16. Image, 'The New Puritanism'.
17. Image, 'On the Representation of the Nude', p. 9.
18. Selwyn Image, 'On Catholicity of Taste', *The Century Guild Hobby Horse*, 1 (1886), 91–94 (p. 91).
19. *Ibid.*
20. *Ibid.*
21. *Ibid.*, p. 92.
22. John Gray, 'Les Goncourts', *The Dial*, 1 (1889), 9–13 (p. 12).
23. *Ibid.*
24. Hubert Crackanthorpe, 'Reticence in Literature: Some Roundabout Remarks', *The Yellow Book*, 2 (1894), 259–69 (pp. 262–63).
25. *Ibid.*, pp. 264–65.
26. *Ibid.*, p. 261.
27. *Ibid.*, p. 260.
28. *Ibid.*, p. 265.
29. Havelock Ellis, 'Zola: The Man and His Work', *The Savoy*, 1 (1896), 67–80 (pp. 75–76).
30. *Ibid.*, p. 78.
31. Publishing contract between John Lane and Elkin Mathews as publishers and Henry Harland

and Aubrey Beardsley for the production of *The Yellow Book*, signed on 19 April 1894. John Lane Photocopy Archive (UCE, Birmingham), *The Yellow Book* File, 1.
32. Un-numbered page of advertisements, *The Century Guild Hobby Horse*, 4 (1889), verso.
33. See Richard Ellmann, *Oscar Wilde* (New York: Alfred A. Knopf, 1988), p. 313; Horst Schroeder, *Additions and Corrections to Richard Ellmann's Oscar Wilde*, 2nd edn (Braunschweig: Privately printed, 2002), p. 106; Philippe Jullian, *Oscar Wilde*, 2nd edn (London: Paladin-Granada, 1969), p. 183.
34. Ellmann, *Oscar Wilde*, p. 307.
35. Furthermore, Fiona MacCarthy asserts that Wilde first met John Gray in this very studio, just as Lord Henry first met Dorian in the novel. See Fiona MacCarthy, 'Falling out with Oscar', *The Guardian*, 30 August 2008. <http://www.theguardian.com/stage/2008/aug/30/matthewbourne.wilde> [accessed 25 May 2015].
36. John Gray, 'Parsifal', *The Dial*, 2 (1892), 8.
37. Ibid.
38. John Gray, 'A Hymn Translated from the Italian of Saint Francis of Assisi', *The Dial*, 3 (1893), 31. Interestingly, there is no readily available evidence to support Gray's claim that this is a translation from the work of St Francis. This poem may then be included amongst those artistic works that seek to legitimize risqué, erotic content by using a religious framework.
39. Such as their joint work *Priapeia* (1890), and Smithers's and H. S. Nichols's editions of Burton's *The Arabian Nights* (1894–97).
40. John Gray, 'Leda and the Swan', *The Dial*, 5 (1897), 13.
41. These include Ricketts's illustration *My Hair is Filled with the Drops of the Night* (Vol. 2, facing p. 19), Shannon's *With Viol and Flute* (Vol. 2, facing p. 16), Shannon's *The Dressing Room* (Vol. 5, facing p. 8), and Sturge Moore's poem 'Some Shadows of a Thought' (Vol. 3, p. 1) as well as his 'Danaë', Shannon's 'Queen of Sheba' and Ricketts's initial piece to 'Sensations', all discussed in this chapter.
42. Thomas Sturge Moore, 'Danaë', *The Dial*, 3 (1893), 1–9 (p. 2).
43. Ibid.
44. Ibid.
45. Ibid.
46. Charles Haslewood Shannon, 'The Topmost Apple', *The Dial*, 3 (1893), facing p. 26.
47. Henry Thornton Wharton, *Sappho: Memoir, Text, Selected Renderings, and a Literal Translation*, 3rd edn (London: John Lane, 1895), p. 132.
48. Wharton, *Sappho*, p. 133.
49. Charles Ricketts, 'Sensations', in *The Decadent Short Story: An Annotated Anthology*, ed. by Kostas Boyiopoulos, Yoonjoung Choi and Matthew Brinton Tildesley (Edinburgh: Edinburgh University Press, 2014), pp. 65–68 (p. 65).
50. Ricketts, 'Sensations', p. 66.
51. Thomas de Quincey, 'Suspiria de Profundis: The Affliction of Childhood', in *Romanticism: An Anthology*, ed. by Duncan Wu (Oxford: Blackwell, 1996), pp. 688–92.
52. Ricketts, 'Sensations', p. 66.
53. Ibid., p. 67.
54. Cited by Maureen Watry, 'At the Sign of the Dial: Charles Ricketts and the Vale Press 1896–1903,' University of Liverpool Library (2004); <http://sca.lib.liv.ac.uk/collections/exhibs/ValePress.html> [accessed 17 Oct. 2007]. Michael Field did however change their view of the magazine's worth, contributing to both the 1896 and 1897 issues.
55. John Gray, 'Light' in *The Decadent Short Story*, pp. 253–72. It is worth noting that conversion to Catholicism in the late Victorian era was a notably subversive act. Protestantism and Englishness were taken as being almost synonymous in many circles, and therefore 'going over to Rome' was tantamount to treason.
56. Gray, 'Light', p. 257.
57. Ibid., p. 258.
58. Ibid., p. 259.
59. Ibid., p. 262.
60. Ibid., p. 263.

61. *Ibid.*, p. 266.
62. *Ibid.*, p. 267.
63. *Ibid.*, pp. 269–70.
64. *National Observer*, 6 April 1895, p. 547.

CHAPTER 10

'Selecting, transforming, recombining': John Singer Sargent's *Madame X* and the Aesthetics of Sculptural Corporeality

Liz Renes

In 1884, John Singer Sargent submitted his now infamous *Madame X* (Fig. 10.1), a striking portrait of the well-known 'professional beauty' Virginie Gautreau, to the Paris Salon. Exposed, in profile, and in a questionable state of déshabillé, the painting caused such a scandal that Sargent was found 'dodging behind doors' to avoid inevitable accusation, and the work was eventually withdrawn.[1] Though this *succès de scandale* has often been cited as the main cause of Sargent's eventual relocation to London, there has been little discussion about why exactly *Madame X* may have been quite so controversial. One answer may lie in the fact that the painting was viewed outside its intended original context, as Sargent had initially planned to exhibit it alongside a very different painting of a 'woman in white', *Mrs. Henry White* (1883) (Fig. 10.2), a portrait of the wife of an American diplomat.[2] Sargent's intentions, however, were thwarted partly because Mrs White had a lingering illness due to the effects of typhoid, which resulted in a series of rescheduled sittings and constant reworking of the paintings. *Mrs. Henry White* went to the Royal Academy, while *Madame X* remained in Paris for the Salon.

The complex story of these two paintings and their exhibition is nothing short of intriguing. The twinning of two images of women in 'white', or Sargent's 'white girls' as they might be described in homage to Whistler, prompts us to wonder what exactly Sargent wished to communicate by displaying two such seemingly disparate images together. For *Madame X*, in particular, we might wonder about her enigmatic 'whiteness', especially considering the highly sculptural and affected form of her pose. I suggest that a way of understanding this is to consider the discussions of corporeal whiteness and the sculptural body in the Aesthetic texts Sargent was reading and talking about in the years leading up to the exhibition of these portraits. By exploring the visual translation of these texts into Sargent's paintings it may be possible, I argue, to perceive a deeper layer of meaning in his complex compositional choices, specifically in relation to *Madame X*, as well as to comprehend his intentions about a dual exhibition.

For Aesthetes like Baudelaire and Pater, and those working later in the century,

Fig. 10.1. John Singer Sargent, *Madame X*, 1883–84, oil on canvas, 208.6 × 109.9 cm. Metropolitan Museum of Art, New York.

like Vernon Lee and Henry James, the white sculptural body acted as a fertile metaphor for Aestheticism's engagement with such taboo subjects as alternative sexuality, sensual hedonism, and unnatural desire. Statuesque and forcefully posed with crisp white skin set against the dark velvet of her dress, *Madame X* was perhaps not merely an exercise in conveying the eccentricities of the toilette, but (if we consider it alongside Sargent's plan to exhibit it with *Mrs. Henry White*) an exploration through contrasting imagery of Aestheticism's decadent obsession with the white sculptural body.[3] As such, I intend to argue that *Madame X* is a type of Baudelairean *biographie dramatisée,* where 'nothing, if one examines it, is indifferent in a portrait. Gesture, facial expression, clothing [...] everything must be used to represent a character'.[4] As a fashionable Parisienne posed in the diadem of Diana, *Madame X* can be viewed as an embodiment of the intersection between the classical and modern, the eternal and the transient, signifying far more than a mere young painter's desire for success and establishment. This portrait, and its intended dual exhibition, may represent Sargent's desire to proclaim an intellectual alignment with the complex boundaries being explored by Aesthetic and early Decadent figures, who saw whiteness as a highly symbolic motif through which to explore their more provocative concerns.

Relatively little attention has been paid to the fact that Sargent was deeply embedded in the Aesthetic circles in Paris and London in the 1870s and 1880s. Though it could possibly have been much earlier, Sargent was first connected to the movement in 1881, when he was just twenty-five and still studying under the portraitist Carolus-Duran in Paris. He writes to his childhood friend, Vernon Lee, initiating a dialogue with the enquiry: 'Tell me what you think of Pater's essays, I like one or two of them very much.'[5] The next month Lee met Pater in Oxford, beginning a friendship that she extended to Sargent. Her letters note that the three of them, along with Henry James, met at social gatherings at least twice in the summer of 1884.[6] During this period Sargent did not limit his scope to British Aestheticism, however; he also showed a sustained interest in French Aestheticism and 'l'art pour l'art'. In a postcard to her mother in 1884 Lee recounts a day spent sitting on the grass with Sargent at the Pre-Raphaelite model and painter Marie Spartali Stillman's house, discussing 'fantastic, weird, curious, cigarettes, bonbons, Baudelaire'.[7] Sargent also counted among his acquaintances in Paris many key figures in the Aesthetic circle in France: the writer and critic Judith Gautier, daughter of the novelist Théophile Gautier; Count Robert Montesquiou de Fezensac, who was rumoured to be the model for both Huysmans's Des Esseintes and Proust's Baron de Charlus; Paul Helleu, close friend of Proust; as well as Dr. Pozzi, who had significant ties to Sarah Bernhardt and who also most likely fostered Sargent's introduction to Montesquiou and his circle.[8] The majority of these figures were all captured in paint by Sargent in his early career, which suggests that in the most nascent stage of his artistic explorations Sargent actively cultivated Aesthetic and avant-garde contacts on both sides of the Channel.

Between 1881 and 1884 Sargent surrounded himself with writers and fellow artists who had a keen interest in the question of aesthetics in contemporary art and literature. At the end period of this slow Aesthetic simmer, Sargent would exhibit

FIG. 10.2. John Singer Sargent, *Margaret Stuyvesant Rutherfurd White, or Mrs. Henry White*, 1883, oil on canvas, 225.1 × 143.8 cm. Courtesy of the National Gallery of Art, Washington D.C.

Madame X, a work decidedly different in method, colour scheme, and composition than his previous Salon works, such as *Oyster Gatherers at Cancale* (1878) and *Fumée d'Ambre Gris* (1880). If, as evidenced in the letters, he was reading Baudelaire and Pater in the years leading up to painting *Madame X*, it is possible that the development in Sargent's creative practice was influenced by his discussion with friends like Lee and also by the texts he was reading. The notion of the sculptural body appeared with some frequency in the works of Pater, and to a lesser extent Baudelaire, so Sargent's readings of their work may perhaps have been a source of influence for the dramatic way in which he decided to depict Virginie's highly contemporary form of beauty.

The concept of whiteness found in Aesthetic texts embodied a number of dualities, including bodily sensuality versus classical rationalism, purity and naturalism in contrast to the perverse and synthetic, matter versus form, male versus female. In Baudelaire and Pater, this combination of whiteness, sculptural-ness and the body was a useful allegorical vehicle for exploring complex dichotomies, but each writer had a different focus. For Pater, whiteness signified the wider principles of idealization, immortality, and transcendence. While it signalled the fleshliness of the (predominantly) male form, it also functioned to inspire the aesthete to transcend that corporeality in pursuit of a higher aesthetic purpose, one epitomized by the rational intellectualism of the Ancient Greeks. Whiteness simultaneously symbolized aspects of homosexual (i.e. 'perverse') desire and higher forms of creative expression and thought. While Sargent may have adopted aspects of this archetype to some degree, he modified the body and unlike Pater, made it female. This immediately changed the significance that the white sculptural body had for Aestheticism, creating correspondences between Pater's discussions and those of Baudelaire and Vernon Lee. By choosing to depict a white, sculptural *female* body in *Madame X*, Sargent added a rich and complex later of meaning to surrounding feminine beauty and virtue. In its broad range of influences, *Madame X* symbolized the uncanny and unnatural intersections between whiteness, the female body, and sculpture.

In this chapter I shall situate *Madame X* within the context of wider Aesthetic discussions about the white sculptural body — both male and female — principally in relation to issues raised in the work of Baudelaire and Pater, and also in the work of later writers, James and Lee. By studying the composition of *Madame X* and both its alignment to and divergence from Aesthetic discussions on bodily sensuality, femininity, and artificial theatricality, the work can be viewed as an early cypher of the tenuous boundaries between Symbolism and Decadence, as one which, as Andrew Stephenson has remarked in regards to later male Decadent artists, 'saw clothes and cosmetics, alongside striking a pose in public, as linked to modernity and as a sign of the breaking up of old-fashioned Victorian conventions'.[9] *Madame X* became Sargent's modern Diana and reverse Pygmalion's statue, one that advertised Sargent's cosmopolitanism.

The Baudelairean Diana

On first impression, it is difficult to deny *Madame X*'s visual connection to classical sculpture, considering her vast expanse of white skin and affected pose. Such connections were even made by Claude Phillips, a contemporary reviewer, who commented that it 'displays the sculpturesque beauty of her form with a liberality remarkable, and remarked, even in modern Paris.'[10] The posture itself is puzzling for a portrait, the focus of which is usually the facial features of the sitter. In Sargent's painting, the woman's pose explicitly obscures half of the sitter's face. This was not the first time Sargent had focused on compositional choice over mimetic rendering. His 1883 Salon submission, *Portraits d'enfants,* now known as *The Daughters of Edward Darley Boit,* worked on a similar principle by depicting one of the girl's faces in profile obscured by shadowy darkness. This piqued at least one critic, M. B. Wright, who proclaimed that 'One naturally considers the living objects the chief consideration of portraiture, and does not ask for a portrait of fantastic light or for ostentatious proof of the painter's cleverness.'[11] The question that presents itself here is why would Sargent choose to paint portraits that do not show the entirety of the face? Perhaps it is possible that Sargent did not intend the painting to be a portrait at all, but rather a visual exercise in the boundaries between different forms of art, notably the painterly and the sculptural, in an exploration of Pater's concept of *Anders-streben,* by which 'each art may be observed to pass into the condition of some other art'.[12]

The transference between the arts that Pater emphasizes in the concept of *Anders-streben* also contributes to the overall synaesthesia of the portrait, in its evocation of rounded sculptural flesh projected onto a flat two-dimensional surface. It both invites and rejects touch, while simultaneously suggesting cold and warmth by the cool white of her skin and the flushed tint of her ears; she is both 'corpse-like' and a living being: she is both statue and human. This contradictory state of allure and rejection mimicked the unnatural magnetism that sculptural bodies had for many artists in this period. As Michael Hatt notes:

> On the one hand, sculpture is the most abstract of the arts; it is defined, at mid-century at least, as pure form, as the body transformed into an allegory of virtue or morality [...] Unlike the illusory window of painting with its own space, its own world, the statue is here with us, as substantial as if not more so than — those who view it, and while this presence is one of the elements that elevates sculpture, it also threatens its status, for this materiality can threaten sculpture's purity. The moral idea can turn into object; it can be reified, turned to a lump of inert stuff rather than the immaterial ethical ideal it represents.[13]

Aestheticism found particular validity in this idea of the infusion of the 'immaterial ethical ideal' into the inert matter of the sculptural body; as a literal blank space, it became a screen onto which one could project one's own desires, fantasies, and even contemplate the complexities of modern reality. However, it was not solely the white sculptural body itself that proved particularly meaningful, but rather its association with the art of the Ancient and Classical worlds. The rise in archaeological discoveries of ancient Greek and Roman sculpture during this period inspired a renewed interest in and revisitation of classical Antiquity. As Frank Turner notes, these statues and the lost culture they represented quickly became a focal point for wider retrospection, and were a way for many to address 'the spiritual problems and aspirations of modern life and thought'.[14]

As once a powerful empire that spanned in all directions of the globe, ancient Rome had many similarities with the imperialistic culture prevalent in Britain at the end of the nineteenth century. Not only did it inspire new directions in scholarly discussion, but it was also seen to represent 'forms and symbols once alive in the human mind and spirit and still capable of new life.'[15] For Aestheticism in particular, this came in the form of seeing these chiselled ancestors as a symbol of the primitive sensual self before its confinement within the rigid structure of Christian ethics. Paganism, hedonism, and the widespread acceptance of homoeroticism and other forms of alternative sexuality in the ancient world, provided great contrasts to the oppressive social strictures of Victorian Britain. As a movement that espoused the cultivation of the senses — or as Pater put it, the regard of 'all works of art, and the fairer forms of nature and human life, as powers or forces producing pleasurable sensations' — Aestheticism was particularly drawn to these more liberated aspects of Ancient society.[16] The classical naked sculptural body became representative of personal corporeal liberation, and as such Aesthetic writers often used this symbol in their writings to indicate the call to the inner sensual self, as a way to speak of knowledge and dedication to the pursuit of such desires to a like-minded audience.

One such example of this was John Addington Symonds's *Studies of the Greek Poets* (1873–76), in which he encouraged his readers to embrace the fluidity of the ancient identity for self-exploration:

> We must imitate the Greeks, not by trying to reproduce their bygone modes of life and feeling, but by approximating to their free and fearless attitude of mind [...]. We ought still to emulate their spirit by cheerfully accepting the world as we find it, acknowledging the value of each human impulse, and aiming after virtues that depend on self regulation rather than on total abstinence and mortification.[17]

Symonds's view that modern society should embrace the Greeks' ability to harness the 'human impulse' leads directly to Aestheticism, Pater, and his emphasis on the cultivation of sensual experience through aesthetic stimuli, as described in his well-known preface to *The Renaissance: Studies in Art and Poetry* (1873). But for Pater, the white sculptural body was also a site of profound eroticism. As Stefano Evangelista and Linda Dowling have emphasized, studies in classicism during this period, particularly by the Oxford sect of aesthetes which included Pater, Wilde, and Symonds, were often part of a veiled exploration into aspects of perverse or censored sexuality, particularly if one studied Plato's concepts of *eros* in the *Symposium* (375–80 BCE), which 'persistently connects male love to higher forms of culture'.[18] As Dowling notes through David Halperin, these ancient texts allowed the aesthetes to perceive a state of 'sexual deviance' in the classical tradition that was similar to their own. Such 'object choice was viewed as merely one of a number of pathological symptoms exhibited by those who reversed or "inverted" their proper [hetero] sex roles.'[19]

Inversion is apropos here, for not only did several aesthetes transpose their socially defined 'proper' sex roles through their desire for other males, but in their admiration for the classical sculptural bodies as a symbol of Platonic love, they were also 'inverting' their desire for flesh-and-blood bodies onto the symbolic ones represented by the sculptures — an exploration much safer than the illegal physical act itself. Thus when referring to oneself or another as a 'Platonist', as Swinburne does in his oft-quoted letter to Watts after the arrest of Simeon Solomon for indecency in 1873, it was a veiled allusion to contemporary homosexuality. Dowling posits this term, and 'Dorian' too, as part of Aestheticism's homosexual 'code', a set of literary signifiers that enabled dialogue of the unspeakable without concern over censure.[20] To this code, Catherine Maxwell has more recently added the word 'curious' amongst such signifiers, specifically as it relates to Sargent and Lee.[21] Sargent thus appears to be connected to an Aesthetic culture which not only used certain types of veiled language in order to speak of their subversive desires, but which also used the white sculptural body within these symbolic paradigms to allude to such concerns.

It was most likely Pater's *The Renaissance* that Sargent alluded to when he implored Lee in 1881 to 'tell me what you think of Pater's essays'.[22] The publication of *The Renaissance* was key in steering Aestheticism to focus on the primacy of subjective experience. In that book Pater placed Symonds's 'human impulse' above all other sources of inspiration with his repeated attention to the word 'impression'. But Pater also used the essays to discuss his understanding of the symbolic nature of the sculptural body. When it is mentioned, as in the case of Winckelmann and his epiphanic discovery, the ancient form acts as a priming point for a period of intense self-exploration and a stimulation of sensory awakening. Sculpture arouses a corporeal and intellectual response, and thanks to its generalized form, does not intrude on the spectator's internal reveries. Pater emphasized that sculpture does not have those modes of expression — colour, narrative, and context — that lend themselves to the implication of certain feelings. By this limitation it 'unveils man in the pose of his unchanging characteristics', unlocking aesthetic contemplations and drives:

> Its white light, purged from the angry, bloodline stains of action and passion, reveals, not what is accidental in man, but the god in him, as opposed to man's restless movement. [...] The base of artistic genius is the power of conceiving humanity in a new, striking, rejoicing way [...] of generating around itself an atmosphere with a novel power of refraction, selecting, transforming, recombining the images it transmits, according to the choice of the imaginative intellect.[23]

Pater's insistence on the synthesis of sculpture, on its ability to 'recombine' images it transmits, relates directly back to *Madame X* and the image's seeming fluidity between modern and classical forms. As regards the latter, Sargent appears to do this quite literally, by making Virginie Gautreau's body an almost direct composition of classical sculptural poses. Consider, for example, the fact that she is depicted in an unnatural, uncomfortable position, one quite difficult to hold for the long periods of time a portrait required. By choosing this pose, and also by pairing it with the diadem of the crescent moon of Diana placed on top of her head, it seems that Sargent intended to evoke a classical sculptural body. Further compositional elements also lend weight to this interpretation. Gautreau's right hand, which appears to hold the fabric of her gown bunched in order to aid movement, echoes visual depictions of the Venus Pudica or 'modest Venus' type, which frequently used either a hand or the hand holding fabric to shield the goddess's modesty from prying eyes. A well-known classical sculpture of this type, the *Aphrodite of Cnidus* by Praxiteles (4th century), was frequently copied (see, for example, the *Aphrodite of Menophantos* (1st century BCE)). Later replicas of these works would have been widely reproduced for educational purposes in art schools in the Louvre, Rome, and Florence, and it is likely that Sargent would have seen these images in his studies in Paris and abroad.

Another interesting feature of the painting is Sargent's decision to depict the fallen shoulder strap, evidenced in a contemporary photograph of the painting currently housed in the Metropolitan Museum of Art. This decision may again relate to an intentional part of his classical agenda — the fallen strap had historical associations with the Amazonians, and Diana whose strap was frequently shown slipped down on the right side to allow access to the quiver of arrows on the back. A copy of a sarcophagus depicting Artemis and Apollo murdering the children of Niobe from the second century, now in the Glyptothek in Munich and the *Diana de Gabies* in the Louvre (1st century) both show the fallen strap and exposed shoulder.[24] In analyzing the portrait in this way, the work becomes less about Sargent using the fallen strap to court publicity, and more about his use of Gautreau as a representation of a new type of classical beauty, one who artfully blends Baudelaire's and Pater's concepts of the eternal and transitory, the historical and the modern, in pursuit of new, unique forms of personal corporeal aesthetics.

Madame X's classicism, in combination with the stark modernity of its sitter's corseted form and fashionable black gown, seamlessly blends the contemporary and the historical. To echo Pater's words, like classical sculpture she 'conceiv[es] humanity in a new, striking, rejoicing way' and generates 'an atmosphere with a novel power of refraction, selecting, transforming, recombining the images it transmits'.[25] But *Madame X* can also be viewed as a visual embodiment of the intersections between the various types of texts Sargent was reading at this point. If Pater can be seen to have inspired the classical elements of *Madame X* and its white sculptural body, then it can be argued that Baudelaire was the point of animus for Gautreau's contemporary and dramatically painted self-fashioning. Gautreau was often called a 'professional beauty' in the press, a phrase possibly taken from Baudelaire's *The Painter of Modern Life* (1863).[26]

By painting a Baudelairean 'professional beauty', Sargent first establishes a frame of modernity for his figure, as such celebrities were indicative of à la mode standards of feminine allure, fashion, and social status. These aspects of modernity are, by their nature, fleeting and ephemeral, but the true aesthete or *flâneur* is able to 'distil the eternal from the transitory', or to see the 'poetry within history'.[27] Baudelaire also saw this ability as one of the aptitudes of the 'true' artist — one who was able to capture the beauty of a past age without focusing on its ugliness — and as such is able to marry the modern with the eternal, the transitory with that element of beauty that is present in all ages. Baudelaire states at the outset of *The Painter of Modern Life* that 'the past is interesting not only by reason of the beauty which could be distilled from it by those artists for whom it was the present, but also precisely because it is the past, for its historical value'.[28] Modernity will one day become antiquity, and an artist must learn to embrace both the immutable and fugitive elements of his age in order to ease the transition from one to the other in his work. Baudelaire uses historical fashion plates as a prime example of this, for in them 'man ends by looking like his ideal self. These engravings can be translated either into beauty or ugliness; in one direction, they become caricatures, in the other antique statues.'[29]

Baudelaire sees the fluid blending of the historical and the modern as key to the timelessness of the art of the Old Masters. They were able to infuse spirit in the immaterial, to see the small elements of beauty present in their time, and in using this as their focus they did not fall victim to a falseness or 'mistranslation' by blindly copying current trends. In this estimation, it is also possible to transfer such views onto Sargent's choice of colour and composition for *Madame X*. If, as Baudelaire states, beauty can become either 'caricature or antique statue', then it is positioned as one of two opposing extremes — as either a focus on intensive individual detail, which becomes exaggerated, grotesque and 'caricature', or a minimalization of such detail to the point where the person becomes pure form, or 'antique statues'. *Madame X* oscillates between both types, dedicating itself to the capturing of Gautreau's unique and very contemporary exterior without creating such a defined focus that she becomes a satirical version of herself. Sargent's Old Master palette of blacks and browns contributes to this, creating crisp focus and alluring visual interest through simplicity and harmonization. She is the embodiment of Baudelaire's 'ideal self', an individuality that is very modern, with its cosmetics and corsets, but also timeless in its visual simplicity — a happy Baudelairean marriage of the modern and the timeless 'spirit' of its century.

Judith Gautier, who sat for a number of informal works by Sargent during this period, remarks in her review of the painting that there is a broader link between *Madame X* and this Baudelairean trope of feminine beauty:

> Is it a woman? A chimera? A figure of a unicorn rearing as on a heraldic coat of arms or perhaps the work of some oriental decorative artist to whom the human form is forbidden and who, wishing to be reminded of woman, has drawn this delicious arabesque [...].[30]

Though Gautier relegates the subject of the painting to an archetype as opposed to a living body, Sargent's translation of Gautreau into the medium of paint allows her figure to transcend the messiness of human form in a reverse Pygmalion process, achieving the status of spiritual 'chimera', one which Pater also addresses when he makes mention of sculpture's 'white light, purged from the angry, bloodlike stains of action and passion, [which] reveals, not what is accidental in man, but the god in him'.[31] The blank space of the white sculptural body, and the transformations that body goes through in its translation into art and literature, allows the aesthete to purify sexual attraction and desire into an ideal of aesthetic appreciation. It allows for the expression of a loftier purpose. If Sargent is presenting Gautreau in the guise of a type of classical beauty, it is possible that he is making a similar statement, negating the corporeal trappings that accompany work as a 'professional beauty' and transforming them into a more aesthetic appreciation of her provocative self-fashioning between historical and modern forms.[32]

On the one hand the body is the site of the senses, a place to cultivate experience and impressions, while on the other that body is to be transcended in order to reach pure enlightenment, revealing 'the god within'. Sargent's debt to Pater is clear. The critical responses to *Madame X* suggested this uncomfortable duality, where its subject is simultaneously likened to a 'corpse' and also pure spirit and ideal beauty, a tension articulated by juxtaposing Gautier's 'chimera' and Phillips's 'sculpturesque'.[33] Jane Thomas identifies this uncertainty as the innate struggle between two kinds of responses to the sculptural body; the 'kinesis of desire' and the 'stasis of the pure aesthetic response'. The former represents the bodily response to a sculpture or work of art — the visceral or emotional reaction it elicits — while the latter is a manifestation of one's potentially perverse desire to access a lost ideal beauty, or to 'stimulate longing for what can never be wholly realized in material form'.[34] Aestheticism's obsession with the sculptural form stimulated both the kinetic and the static; for Pater in *The Renaissance*, Winckelmann's discovery of Greek art presented a plastic embodiment of his reading of poetry and theory while simultaneously stirring his 'pulsation of sensuous life' and an 'enthusiasm that burned like lava within him'.[35] Baudelaire also speaks to the union of the historical and the modern, a kinesis reflected in the viewer's recognition of both the ephemerality and the timelessness present in the beauty of their own age. *Madame X* is a work that stimulates both the static and the kinetic for its viewer, evoking sensuality and beauty while also visually representing a lost classical ideal.

The Jamesian Juno

This struggle between the aesthetic and intellectual responses to the sculptural body may also have acted as a point of stimulus for other literary explorations on the topic in this period, specifically in the works of Sargent's lifelong friend, Henry James. James's tale 'The Last of the Valerii' (1874) also deals with the notion of the allure of the sculptural female form. Published first in *The Atlantic Monthly* in January 1874, and later as one of the short stories collected in *A Passionate Pilgrim and Other Tales* (1875), the tale makes use of a number of significantly Paterian themes, notably the idea of the female sculptural body and the fluidity between intellectual and sensual aesthetic responses. It is curious to note that this work appeared less than a year after James wrote to his brother that he had encountered Pater's newly published *The Renaissance* in a shop in Florence. In a letter dated 31 May 1873 James wrote that he was 'in flames' about buying it and that it 'treats of several things I know nothing about'.[36] 'Flames' is a provocative term, recalling Pater's renowned phrase in the book's conclusion 'to burn always with a hard, gem-like flame', but also in its similarities to Winckelmann's burning 'like lava' at his introduction to sculptural form.[37] The publication of a tale that deals with the nearly devastating magnetism of a sculptural body in such close proximity to his discovery of Pater implies a tantalizing thread of association between the works.

However, unlike Pater and more like Sargent in this case, James transferred his obsession with the aesthetics of sculpture onto a significantly *female* form. This may signify James's literary processing of a symbolic issue he saw in *The Renaissance* — the relationship between the statue and female beauty as sharing a symbiotic relationship that both gives life and inspiration to its viewer while also holding the potential to draw that viewer into a state of obsession, dissolution, and decay. Pater mentions this in his discussion of the *Mona Lisa* (1503–06), for she has

> a beauty wrought out from within upon the flesh, the deposit, little cell by cell, of strange thoughts and fantastic reveries and exquisite passions [...]. She is older than the rocks among which she sits; like the vampire she has been dead many times [...]. Certainly Lady Lisa might stand as an embodiment of the old fancy, the symbol of the modern ideal.[38]

The emasculating combination of power and beauty in vampiric women like Pater's *Mona Lisa* and *femmes fatales* like Judith and Salome is symbolized by the white skin of sculpturally posed women, frozen in time through paint. That Lady Lisa embodies both the 'old fancy' and its 'modern ideal' certainly carries through to *Madame X,* with Gautreau's crown of Diana and her corseted form. For Pater, the *Mona Lisa* represents a similar symbiosis between a living and an immortal beauty, first described in Pater's text as a 'living Florentine' who, through the medium of Leonardo's brush, has become an 'ideal lady' and a 'creature of his thought'.[39] The decadent, uncanny beauty of the female sculptural body is one that can pass fluidly between matter and form, and yet in James's tale, in a type of un-rendering of the aestheticization process that Pater explores with Lady Lisa, the reverse becomes true. Instead of translating hedonic female beauty into an immortal, and thus unnatural, point of desire by converting the human into the artistic object, in 'The Last of the Valerii' James instead transfigures the Juno statue from a sculpture to a living figure — an art form to a fleshly object — transformed through the obsession of one of the story's protagonists. J. Hillis Miller, in his *Versions of Pygmalion* (1990) explores James's story in terms of its Pygmalionism, but also in terms of its Paterian elements, particularly in relation to Pater's 'The Myth of Demeter and Persephone', published in the *Fortnightly Review* of 1876.[40] Despite its playful reversions of Pater in this respect, James still emphasizes here that it is unnatural or perverse *desire* that is both aroused by and instilled into art objects, uniting the static into the kinetic of aesthetic response through a body set (or turned) into stone. But what is also relevant is the tale's exploration of the restraint of the hidden aesthetic self. James uses the sculpture of the Juno to awaken the inner world of the senses. As Lene Østermark-Johansen comments, 'The notion of sculpture as a "dead art" connects the material with a dead past and a numbed audience in need of aesthetic stimuli.'[41]

In a brief overview, 'The Last of the Valerii' tells the story of the unnamed narrator's goddaughter Martha — a supreme example of sweet American womanhood with 'the air and almost habits of a princess' — and her early marriage to the emotionally and financially bankrupt Count Marco Valerio.[42] His only contribution to the marriage is his family's ancestral villa, which Martha's American fortune saves from the depths of ruin. Upon her arrival in Rome, Martha sets about to improve its grounds, directing workers to begin archaeological excavations in order to search for lost historical treasures. After some time, the grounds produce a magnificent statue of a Juno, which appears to the Count in a dream just as she appears out of the ground. Bewitched by her beauty, the Count secretes her away to an old garden Casino, where he keeps her under lock and key, much to the increasing neglect of his poor new wife. He frequently sneaks away to the statue, being caught at one point by the spying narrator to be 'lying flat on the pavement [in front of it] prostrate, apparently with devotion' (p. 165). Eventually the wife, harnessing her American bravado, is stirred to act against the increasing distance between herself and her husband. Recognizing the statue as the cause of her marital discord, she has the statue returned to her earthly grave. Her husband acquiesces, but keeps, in secret and as a reminder, the Juno's fragmented right hand.

James makes use of a number of Aesthetic themes in this story, but none more wholly relevant to this discussion than that of the intersection between the modern and the classical. At one point in the story the archaeologist who digs up the Juno states to the narrator that he is not surprised by the Count's reaction to the statue, for 'Ancient relics may work modern miracles. There's a pagan element in all of us [...] and the old gods have still their worshippers. The old spirit still throbs here and there [...]' (p. 167). The Juno's sculptural body makes light of the fact that the Juno does not convert the Count into a pagan, but that it rather awakens the deeper sensual and Aesthetic self, or the 'pagan' within him. The Juno unlocks a bizarre and perverse animalism; as the reading of Plato's *Symposium* did for the Oxford aesthetes, she validates secret inner sexual inversions by drawing forth innate attractions to unnatural things, in this case a desire for paganism and a relationship with a woman who is not one's wife. This contrast between social morality and the epicurean self is made more evident at the beginning of the story, when Martha claims that her love for the Count would inspire her to convert to Catholicism, while the Count dissuades her by claiming that he is a 'poor Catholic' as his nature leans more towards paganism (pp. 132–33). The Count accepts Christianity as the established ethical code in the society in which he moves, but he does not agree that it is the one that speaks to him personally. When the Juno appears, she brings forth his 'paganism' into the moonlight for all, or at least the narrator, to see, symbolically representing the nature of the struggle between one's private, inner aesthetic and decadent self and one's public, socially-acceptable identity.

The Count's wrestling with his own passions in the face of social respectability is not the only duality present here. Just as *Madame X* visually represents the conflation of the modern and classical beauty, so too do the female characters in James's story present conflicting representations of femininity. James presents the only female characters in the story, Martha and the Juno, as representative of typical contrasting tropes. Martha is the modern beauty and dutiful wife in every sense of the word — she is all sweetness and light, and lives only for the pleasure of her husband and his caresses. She is also decidedly monotheistic. The Juno, on the other hand, embodies all those feminine attributes considered wicked, decadent, and sinful. Paradoxically, though her body is made of stone, she represents corporeal pleasure and sensuality as evidenced by the idolatrous response she evokes from the Count. His relationship with the Juno is one of wine and worship, libation, and licentious implication. The relationship between these women, however, is strikingly co-dependent. Instead of making these female characters separate or anathema to each other, James presents them as a symbiotic pair who pull life and energy from each other, so much so that at one point the narrator cries that 'to rival the Juno she [the Contessa] is turning to marble herself!' while Martha indicates that 'His Juno's the reality; I'm the fiction!' (pp. 167 and 169). Though textually they exist in separate bodies, James's pairing of their reactions in this way indicates that they are actually a unified self, linked together by the love of the Count. This echoes Pater's *Mona Lisa* who embodies both feminine archetypes, as she represents the grace and beauty of a living Florentine as well as the 'strange thoughts and fantastic reveries and exquisite passions',[43] but also Baudelaire's understanding that 'beauty is always and inevitably of a double composition'.[44] Martha is the modern and ephemeral, the Juno the timeless and eternal. Together they combine to challenge the Count's fidelity to each of the conflicting halves of his inner and outer self.

At the end of the tale, however, it becomes obvious which half must win. In order to spur the story to conclusion, and to regain her power (and her husband), Martha finally acknowledges that 'We must smother her beauty in the dreadful earth! It makes me feel almost as if she were alive' (p. 174). Her actions reverse the process by which desire gives life to inanimate objects through the act of looking. By burying the statue back in the ground, the Juno is made invisible and thus no longer able to withdraw life from the Count. His adoring and life-giving gaze is now correctly transferred back to the more appropriate place for it — the hearth and home. In this process, the Juno is transformed from object to Pygmalion and back to object in one fell swoop, and as the Count preserves a small piece of the Juno in secret, so too does James indicate that the Aesthetic self is not a piece of human nature that is wont to be wholly and utterly buried. As Leon Edel summarizes in his review of the tale in *Stories of the Supernatural*, 'civilized man does well to keep the primitive side of his nature properly interred'.[45]

The visual relationship between James's Juno and Sargent's *Madame X* is one of the symbolic unification of these two seemingly contradictory halves of the feminine self. James divides them into two characters, while Sargent brings them together into one body in his combination of living flesh and sculptural form. Both writer and painter, however, emphasize that there is a spirit in the inanimate — a ghost in the machine — delineated by Gautier's 'chimera' and the narrator's viewing of the Juno's spirit in the moonlight. *Madame X* is a work that represents the fluidity between boundaries, between the living and the dead, between art and immorality, between flesh and sculpture. This synaesthetic nature of the portrait and its existence between worlds speaks to the idea of the image as one that transgresses borders. As Lynda Nead states:

> Danger does not lie in any given category but in transitional states; it is the process of belonging to neither one state nor another that is most threatening [...]. Objects or individuals which transgress these classifications challenge correct definition and right order.[46]

Both *Madame X* and James's Juno exist on the peripheries of feminine boundaries and as such their allure is both perverse and undeniable. For James's story, this boundary is exemplified by the pure representation of the Count's wife, whose actions attempt to 'correct' or 'rectify' the wicked behaviour aroused by the Juno. In this light it is also possible to return to Sargent's original intention for the dual exhibition of the portrait along with *Mrs. Henry White*. If *Madame X* can be seen as an archetype of Pater's view of the co-dependent relationship between the beautifying and degenerate aspects of female pulchritude, then it is possible to apply this wider duality to the contradictory messages offered by the intended presentation of these two portraits. If *Madame X* signifies the Aesthetic alignment between modern and classical beauty, decadent and graceful form, the painterly alongside the sculpturesque, then what exactly does Sargent say with *Mrs. Henry White?*

On the one hand we might argue that *Mrs. Henry White* was intended to embody all the traditional connotations the colour white had for wider Victorian society. Lee, in her discussion on the symbolism of the colour in her essay 'Beauty and Sanity' (from *Lauris Nobilis* in 1908), not only discusses what these 'acceptable' forms of whiteness represent, but in a discussion germane to this text, also contrasts this whiteness with the Aesthetic inversion of desire and how that can be explored through lived female experience. In her first description in the text, Lee explores how the colour white is conventionally associated with concepts of purity, domesticity, and cleanliness, and although the text does not explicitly state 'femininity', they can certainly be read as such with their descriptions of 'daintiness' and 'fairness':

> For the love of white has come to mean [...] strength, cleanness, and newness of sensation. [...] The love of white means [...] in human beings good health, and youth and fairness of life [...] care, order, daintiness of habits, leisure and affluence.[47]

And yet as an aesthete, or one who aligned herself with that unwholesome and decaying breed who 'invert' their sexuality and find passion in unnatural pleasure and pursuits, she finds she does not like such things: 'But what if we do not care for white? What if we are so constituted that its insipidity sickens us as much as the most poisonous and putrescent colours which Blake ever mixed to paint hell and sin?' Thus, in this estimation, those who do not like the purity of white are labelled 'abnormal, unwholesome, decaying; very good, then why should we not get pleasure in decaying, unwholesome and abnormal things?'[48] These words find an echo in Sargent's own thoughts, written to Lee while he worked on *Madame X*, where he stated with a palpable sense of glee:

> Do you object to people who are fardées to the extent of being uniform lavender or blotting paper colour all over? If so you would not care for my sitter. But she has the most beautiful lines and if the lavender or chlorate-of-potash lozenge colour be pretty in itself I shall be more than pleased.[49]

Sargent is clearly aligning himself with that 'abnormal' sect of Aesthetes who took no pleasure in the wholesomeness of whiteness, but rather revelled in its implications of a darker, dangerous beauty, fraught with hints of decay. But Lee posits that whiteness has this duality; for the 'normal' sects of society it is a colour of naturalness and purity, but for those with decadent inclinations it indicates something entirely different. Therefore, if Sargent intended to display two completely opposing representations of female bodily whiteness in his joint exhibition of *Madame X* and *Mrs. Henry White*, it is possible to consider that the works were intended to be a visual display of these symbolic attributes of whiteness as it intersects with the female form. For example, *Mrs. Henry White* certainly reflects these affirmations of 'good' whiteness — affluence, youth, vital health, and pure race — and as much was implied in the reviews of this piece. The *Art Journal* praised it for its 'freshness of youth, [with the] carriage of a graceful head', while R. A. M. Stevenson found it 'admirably filled' with 'quantities of tranquil space'.[50] *Madame X*'s whiteness was instead compared to a corpse and a chimera, with the less pejorative comments merely attributing her colouring to the 'sculpturesque'. Her whiteness, ensconced in a sculptural body, was an appropriate vehicle for Sargent to convey the decadent symbols and desires he found in the works of Baudelaire, Pater, and his relationships with fellow 'perverse' Aesthetes. It holds the potential for a vast amount of contradictions — a fleshly body in a frozen, hardened pose, a classical goddess under the guise of a contemporary beauty, the whiteness implied by moral purity negated by the indecent skin of a purportedly 'loose' woman. Everything that is white about this portrait is decidedly *not white* — even the whiteness implied by the sculptural body, with its Paterian evocations of immortality and deification are diminished by the image being an artistic 'impression' — a capturing of a mortal beauty eventually to fade.

However, one only has to consider the very tongue-in-cheek satirical nature of painting *Mrs. Henry White* in shades of white to ascertain which kind of 'whiteness' Sargent found more appropriate to his own tastes. For one critic, *Madame X* was 'Hogarthian [...] dictated by the impulse of painting a beauty *à la mode* in all the unbeautiful aspects of such a product of the art of society'.[51] But in light of the themes discussed in this chapter, it is perhaps more appropriate to see *Mrs. Henry White* as satire in its capturing of a beauty that was more 'traditional' in the face of *Madame X*'s decadent sculptural form. Both these images illuminate many late nineteenth-century preoccupations with the representation of the female body — the sculptural form as opposed to the fleshly one, feminine purity as opposed to decay, and the notion of the natural form versus Baudelaire's celebration of artifice. To return to Lee, who sums this up astutely for Aestheticism, and for Sargent's portraits of *Madame X* and *Mrs. Henry White* as well: 'As art is one of mankind's modes of expressing itself, why should we expect it to be the expression only of mankind's health and happiness? Since life has got two rhythms, why should art only have one?'[52]

Notes to Chapter 10

1. Evan Charteris, *John Sargent* (New York: Charles Scribner's and Sons, 1927), pp. 61–62.
2. 'Just one illegible line. This is the evening of the fatal sending in day & I have sent nothing in. Neither you nor the Gautreau were finished. I have been brushing away at both of you for the

last three weeks in a horrid state of anxiety. Your background has undergone several changes and is not good yet. Well the question is settled and I am broken. Your frame is charming. One consolation has been that I know you do not care a bit whether your portrait is exhibited or not. Is not that true? May I send it to the academy? P.S. I send the Boit children to the Salon.' Washington DC, Archives of American Art, Smithsonian Institution, John Singer Sargent Letters, Roll 647, Frame 856, John Singer Sargent to Mrs. Henry White, 15 March 1883.
3. For an exploration of the social and cultural circumstances relating to the production and reception of *Madame X*, more specifically how it plays with ideas of fashion, identity, and cosmetics, see Susan Sidlauskas, 'Painting Skin: John Singer Sargent's *Madame X*', *American Art*, 15 (Autumn 2001), 8–33.
4. Charles Baudelaire, 'Salon de 1859', in *Curiosités Ésthétiques* (Paris: Michel Lévy Frères, 1868), pp. 245–358 (p. 318).
5. Richard Ormond, 'John Singer Sargent and Vernon Lee', *Colby Quarterly*, 9 (September 1970), 154–78 (p. 168).
6. See Irene Cooper Willis, *Vernon Lee's Letters* (London: Privately Printed, 1937), pp. 78–80; pp. 152–55.
7. *Ibid.*, p. 144.
8. See Caroline De Costa and Francesca Miller, 'Sarah Bernhardt's "Doctor God": Samuel Jean Pozzi (1846–1918)', *Australian and New Zealand Journal of Obstetrics and Gynaecology*, 47 (2007), 352–56.
9. Andrew Stephenson, 'Precarious Poses: The Problem of Artistic Visibility and its Homosocial Performances in Late-Nineteenth-Century London', *Visual Culture in Britain*, 8 (Summer 2007), 73–103 (p. 93).
10. Claude Phillips, 'The Salon II', *The Academy*, 632 (14 June 1884), 427–28 (p. 427).
11. Margaret Bertha Wright, 'American Art at the Paris Salon', *The Art Amateur*, 9 (July 1883), 24–25 (p. 24).
12. Walter Pater, *The Renaissance: Studies in Art and Poetry* (New York: Macmillan, 1873), p. 139.
13. Michael Hatt, 'Thoughts and Things: Sculpture and the Victorian Nude', in *Exposed: The Victorian Nude*, ed. by Alison Smith (New York: Watson-Guptill, 2001), pp. 37–49 (p. 38).
14. Frank N. Turner, *The Greek Heritage in Victorian Britain* (West Hanover: Halliday Lithograph, 1981), p. 78.
15. *Ibid.*, pp. 77–78.
16. Pater, *The Renaissance*, p. xi.
17. John Addington Symonds, *Studies of the Greek Poets*, 2 vols (London: Smith, Elder & Co., 1877), I, p. 437.
18. Stefano Evangelista, '"Lovers and Philosophers at Once": Aesthetic Platonism in the Victorian Fin de Siècle', *The Yearbook of English Studies*, 36 (2006), 230–44 (pp. 231–32).
19. Linda Dowling, 'Ruskin's Pied Beauty and the Constitution of a "Homosexual" Code', *The Victorian Newsletter*, 75 (Spring 1989), 1–9 (p. 1).
20. Algernon Charles Swinburne, *The Swinburne Letters*, 2 vols, ed. by Cecil Y. Lang (New Haven: Yale University Press, 1959), II, p. 261; Dowling, 'Ruskin's Pied Beauty', p. 1.
21. See Catherine Maxwell, '"A Queer Sort of Interest": Vernon Lee's Homoerotic Allusion to John Singer Sargent and John Addington Symonds', in *Writing Women of the Fin de Siècle*, ed. by Adrienne E. Gavin and Carolyn W. De La L. Oulton (Basingstoke: Palgrave Macmillan, 2012), pp. 166–78.
22. Ormond, 'John Singer Sargent and Vernon Lee', p. 17.
23. Pater, *The Renaissance*, pp. 224–35.
24. This feature was also used by later sculptors, particularly in the eighteenth century, as in René Frémin's *A Companion of Diana* (1717) in the Louvre, and Jean-Louis Lemoyne's later version, now in the National Gallery of Art in Washington DC (1724).
25. Pater, *The Renaissance*, pp. 224–35.
26. Charles Baudelaire, *The Painter of Modern Life*, trans. by Jonathan Mayne (London: Phaidon, 1995), p. 37.
27. *Ibid.*, p. 12.
28. *Ibid.*, pp. 1–2.

29. Ibid.
30. Judith Gautier, 'Le Salon: Premier Article', *Le Rappel* (1 May 1884), 1. English translation taken from Richard Ormond and Elaine Kilmurray, *John Singer Sargent: The Early Portraits* (London: Yale University Press, 1998), p. 114.
31. Pater, *The Renaissance*, pp. 224–25.
32. Ibid., p. 37.
33. 'The flesh painting [...] has far too much blue in it, and [...] more resembles a dead rather than a living body'. William Sharp, 'The Paris Salon', *Art Journal* (June 1884), 179–80 (p. 180); see also Ralph Curtis's description of the sitter as 'decomposed' in a letter home to his parents in Charteris, *John Sargent*, pp. 61–62.
34. Jane Thomas, 'Icons of Desire: The Classical Statue in Later Victorian Literature', *The Yearbook of English Studies*, 40 (2010), 242–72 (p. 247).
35. Pater, *The Renaissance*, pp. 193–95.
36. Henry James to William James, 31 May 1873, in *Henry James Letters, Volume I: 1843–1875*, ed. by Leon Edel (Boston: Harvard University Press, 1974), pp. 390–92; quoted in Richard Ellmann, 'Henry James Amongst the Aesthetes', in *Henry James and Homo-Erotic Desire*, ed. by John. R. Bradley (Basingstoke: Macmillan, 1999), pp. 25–44 (p. 25).
37. Pater, *The Renaissance*, p. 250.
38. Ibid., pp. 129–30.
39. Ibid., p. 129.
40. See J. Hillis Miller, *Versions of Pygmalion* (Cambridge: Harvard University Press, 1990), pp. 211–42.
41. Lene Østermark-Johansen, *Walter Pater and the Language of Sculpture* (Farnham: Ashgate, 2011), p. 118.
42. Henry James, 'The Last of the Valerii', in *A Passionate Pilgrim and Other Tales* (Boston: James R. Osgood and Company, 1875), pp. 125–78 (pp. 127–28). Subsequent references to this text are given parenthetically.
43. Pater, *The Renaissance*, p. 129.
44. Baudelaire, *The Painter of Modern Life*, p. 3.
45. *Henry James: Stories of the Supernatural*, ed. by Leon Edel (New York: Taplinger, 1970), p. 70.
46. Lynda Nead, *Female Nude: Art, Obscenity and Sexuality* (London: Routledge, 1992), p. 31.
47. Vernon Lee, 'Beauty and Sanity', in *Lauris Nobilis: Chapters on Art and Life* (London: John Lane and the Bodley Head, 1908), pp. 115–60 (pp. 134–35).
48. Ibid.
49. Ormond and Kilmurray, *The Early Portraits*, p. 113.
50. 'The Exhibition of the Royal Academy', *Art Journal* (August 1884), 241–44 (p. 242); R. A. M. Stevenson, 'J. S. Sargent', *Art Journal* (March 1888), 65–69 (p. 68).
51. W. C. Brownell, 'The American Salon', *The Magazine of Art*, 7 (January 1884), 492–99 (p. 494).
52. Vernon Lee, 'Beauty and Sanity', p. 122.

CHAPTER 11

Sensory Nullification in the Poetry of Ernest Dowson

Alice Condé

Ernest Dowson (1867–1900) published his first collection of poetry in 1896. *Verses* is a slim volume with a front cover designed by Aubrey Beardsley, featuring a curved stylized 'Y' shape consisting of a thin double border containing three thin lines emerging from the bottom left corner with tiny curled leaf embellishments at their tips (Fig. 11.1).[1] The simplicity of Beardsley's design contrasts with the sensory excesses suggested by the embellishment and ornamentation in his other works from the *Savoy* period of 1896 such as the *Venus and Tannhäuser* illustrations, and complements the refinement of Dowson's verse.[2] As R. K. R. Thornton points out, the shape is 'a skeleton [...] of many of Beardsley's designs'.[3] Beardsley's skeletal, unadorned design is evocative of Dowson's poetry, which I suggest we might read as a dilution or weak reflection of Decadent themes. As evidenced within this volume, Decadent literature is characterized by a preoccupation with extreme sensations and sensory experiments. Dowson, however, presents the world as dull (grey and white are favoured colours in his verses), desire as unpleasantly painful, and he often expresses a wish for silent solitude or death as a respite from sensory stimulation.

Linda Dowling remarks that 'regret and resignation are [Dowson's] distinctive notes'.[4] Themes of finality, death, ennui and desolation characterize Dowson's verses composed during the final decade of the nineteenth century. Regret and resignation are often expressed by Dowson in association with the young girl as a figure of tension. In his two published poetry collections, *Verses* and *Decorations: In Verse and Prose* (1899), the girl is both an idealized image of youth and a painful reminder of the transience of youth. This was a personal obsession of Dowson's and an important motif running throughout his work from his early poetry to his final collection.[5] In this chapter I examine Dowson's move away from the bodily sensuality so celebrated by other Decadent writers by considering his treatment of female figures, with particular reference to his use of Catholic or devotional imagery in comparison with the earlier Decadent work of Algernon Charles Swinburne and Charles Baudelaire. The girls in Dowson's poetry resemble previous incarnations of cold and distant Decadent cruel women, but are described in terms of distance and longing. Rather than sensory excess in Dowson's poetry, I would suggest we find sensory nullification.

Fig. 11.1. Front cover of Ernest Dowson's *Verses* (1896) with design by Aubrey Beardsley. © The British Library Board, K.T.C.26.a.11 (front cover).

Arthur Symons compares Dowson's obsession with young girls to a sensory experience, the 'supreme sensation':

> Always, perhaps, a little consciously, but at least always sincerely, in search of new sensations, my friend found what was for him the supreme sensation in a very passionate and tender adoration of the most escaping of all ideals, the ideal of youth. Cherished, as I imagine, first only in the abstract, this search after the immature, the ripening graces which time can only spoil in the ripening, found itself at the journey's end, as some of his friends thought, a little prematurely. I was never of their opinion. [...] The situation seemed to me of the most exquisite and appropriate impossibility.[6]

The 'situation' Symons refers to is Dowson's love for Adelaide 'Missie' Foltinowicz. Dowson met Adelaide in November 1889 in her parents' restaurant, which he nicknamed 'Poland', in Soho's Sherwood Street. She was eleven years old. Adelaide came to represent the ideal of childhood, an obsession of Dowson's that predated their meeting as evidenced in the early 'Sonnets — Of a Little Girl' sequence (only one of which, 'Sonnet IV', was printed in *London Society* in November 1886). Adelaide, or the fantasy ideal she represented for Dowson, is a spectral and haunting figure in his introspective work, which is inspired by his own feelings and experiences. She rejected Dowson's proposal of marriage in April 1893 shortly before her fifteenth birthday and went on to marry a tailor, August Noelte, in 1897. Thus, she was cast as the eternal silent symbol of his unfulfilled desire and the ideal of childhood.

Decadence and masochism

In Decadent writing, the unattainable beloved is frequently constructed through corporeal imagery, in terms of the apparent physicality of female body combined with elements of statue-worship.[7] Masochistic sexuality features heavily; love and erotic desire are figured as painful and pleasurable, satisfying Decadent desires for paradox and perversity. Women are imagined as cold, unmoving objects of devotion, and yet these statue-like fantasies appear to be brought to life when they are the subjects of poetic address or when their torments are imagined as extremes of sensory experience leaving physical traces on their lovers' bodies. For example, in Swinburne's 'Dolores', from *Poems and Ballads, First Series* (1866) the speaker longs for the 'pangs and the kisses that rain | On the lips and the limbs of thy lovers' and 'the ravenous teeth that have smitten | Through the kisses that blossom and bud'.[8] As with 'Our Lady of Pain', the Decadent cruel woman is often rendered according to masochistic aesthetics, as a perverse idol or deity figure to be worshipped. Dowson shares the perennial Decadent fascination with religion, but for him the appeal is not the ostentatiousness and ritual of Catholic worship, nor the evocation of Christ's body as a veil for (homo)sexuality.[9] Dowson's poems on religious themes, such as 'Carthusians' and 'Nuns of the Perpetual Adoration', focus instead on the calmness and serenity that he perceived as the result of a life of solitude and devotion.

Dowson's poetry records the despair of unrequited love and the pain of the tormented individual who cannot escape his own desires. In *The Decadent Image: The Poetry of Wilde, Symons, and Dowson* (2015), Kostas Boyiopoulos conceives of Dowson as a poet who 'perpetually desires [...] desire itself'.[10] 'For Dowson', he states, 'sexual experience always remains in the domain of fantasy even when he is in close proximity with the girl of his fixation. This constitutes a Decadent desire that always returns to itself.'[11] The paradox of distant fantasy in spite of physical closeness informs Dowson's treatment of the sensory aspects of desire in his verses. His ultimate love object never responded to his advances, and yet he continued to visit Adelaide, prolonging his own torment. In his personal life he abandoned himself to drunkenness and degradation in vain efforts to shake off despair. Hopelessness manifested itself in later life in his dishevelled and unkempt appearance, neglect of personal hygiene (dental hygiene in particular — Jad Adams notes that Dowson's teeth blackened and caused him such pain that he had them periodically extracted),[12] and self-destructive behaviour, but his poems lack an emphasis on the sensory extremes of drunkenness and self-abuse. The futility of such pursuits is captured poetically in the Cynara poem in which Dowson focuses instead on distance and unfulfilled desire.

In nineteenth-century European Decadent writing, masochistic self-torment is frequently depicted in scenarios of female figures tormenting submissive male counterparts. We can trace the preoccupation back to Charles Baudelaire's *Les Fleurs du mal* [*Flowers of Evil*] (1857, revised 1861) in which women are often compared to serpents, vampires, and monsters, and Swinburne's *Poems and Ballads* with its sadomasochistic themes inspired by Baudelaire. The cold and cruel mistress Wanda in Leopold von Sacher-Masoch's *Venus im Pelz* [*Venus in Furs*] (1870) is the prototypical masochistic fantasy woman, and 'masochism' derives from Sacher-

Masoch's name. The invention of the term, and its earliest definition, is accredited to Richard Freiherr von Krafft-Ebing, and his 'medico-forensic study' *Psychopathia Sexualis* (1886). Krafft-Ebing explained, 'I feel justified in calling this sexual anomaly "Masochism," because the author Sacher-Masoch frequently made this perversion, which up to his time was quite unknown to the scientific world as such, the substratum of his writings.'[13] Other Decadent examples of cruel women include Jules-Amédée Barbey d'Aurevilly's collection of six short stories, *Les Diaboliques* [*The She-Devils*] (1874), each of which features a cruel or vengeful woman. In Rachilde's *Monsieur Vénus* (1886) the sadistic Raoule cruelly enacts sexualized violence upon the body of her feminized male lover. Octave Mirbeau's *Le Jardin des supplices* [*Torture Garden*] (1898) tells the story of a woman who is sexually aroused by scenes of gruesome torture. The cruelty of these women is a source of both pain and pleasure to their male counterparts, who adopt a masochistic position in relation to the seemingly strong and dominant women.

In English Decadent writing at the *fin de siècle* the cruel woman undergoes a transformation from active, seductive and fleshly, to cold, distant and ethereal. For example, in Oscar Wilde's *Salome* (1894) the fatal princess is reimagined as a ghostly 'shadow of a white rose in a mirror of silver'.[14] In Symons's *Silhouettes* (1892, revised 1896) and *London Nights* (1895, revised 1897), dancing girls are described as fleeting shadows, and the anatomized bodies of lovers are white and cold. Joseph Bristow notes in '"Sterile Ecstasies": The Perversity of the Decadent Movement' (1995) that the fragmented presentation of the woman in Symons's 'Bianca' sequence makes her an elusive figure: 'the impulse to anatomize the female body fails to produce the intensities that would seem to inform this [sexual] desire. The more he fetishizes each bodily part, the more her flesh dissolves before him.'[15] The synecdochic presentation of the female body renders it intangible to both reader and speaker.

Dowson is a figurehead of English Decadence; this is recognized by Adams who declares him to be the 'archetypal decadent poet',[16] and Thornton, who states that 'Dowson is at the heart of the Decadent movement. [...] The Decadent Dilemma runs through his whole work; it shapes his whole life'.[17] The English Decadent tradition, like Dowson himself, was short-lived, reaching a peak in 1895 and declining rapidly. The torment of desire is turned progressively inwards in late-Victorian Decadent literature, with Symons's quest to represent his own moods and sensations in poetry, and Dowson's verses addressed to unattainable young ideals reflecting his own anguish. Dowson was writing at a time when Decadence was giving way to other literary tendencies such as Symbolism and Modernism. Dowling recognizes this in her reflection on Dowson as an intermediary figure between Decadence and Modernism. She notes that he contracts the world according to his view of life as suffering:

> The weary speakers who in life 'sit and wait | For the dropt curtain and the closing gate' may find themselves after death loitering in precincts equally weary, in 'Hollow Lands' bordering Swinburne's classical underworld on one side and the wastelands of T. S. Eliot's Hollow Men on the other. [...] Dowson reduces the 'real' multitudinous Tennysonian world to a simpler sphere of roses, wine, desire, and death.[18]

A sense of exhaustion is symbolized by the figure of the girl in Dowson's poetry. The girl embodies his projected anxieties, appearing as a lifeless figure, a Pygmalion's statue that represents the poet's agony at the impossibility of possessing the object of his desires.

Thornton declares Decadence to be 'a literature of failure, and a record of a wistful mood of inadequacy in confronting man's impermanence in a world of appearances'.[19] This is the position Dowson occupies in literary Decadence; he records failure and inadequacy. Despite glimpses of happiness — a moment of tranquillity in 'Breton Afternoon' or a brief sunlit union with a child in 'Transition', for example — Dowson's verses fall back upon themes of pain and desolation. As the final lines of 'Transition' lament, 'The roses fall, the pale roses expire | Beneath the slow decadence of the sun'.[20] Decay is inevitable, and pleasure is marred by the knowledge of its transience.

Masochism and the female figure as idol

Masochism involves delighting in descent, and using this descent to achieve transcendence. Anita Phillips, in *A Defence of Masochism* (1998), puts it thus: 'Masochism is a movement which integrates the lowest impulses with the highest; it is a story about falling in order to ascend.'[21] Thornton frames the 'decadent dilemma' in similar terms of spiritual ascent versus worldly baseness in his essay ' "Decadence" in Later Nineteenth-Century England' (1979): 'The Decadent is a man caught between two opposite and apparently incompatible pulls: on the one hand he is drawn by the world, its necessities, and the attractive impressions he receives from it, while on the other hand he yearns towards the eternal, the ideal, and the unworldly.'[22] We find such a dilemma in Dowson's poetry, in which the eternal innocence represented by the girl is impossibly juxtaposed with her idolizer's sexual desire. His yearning to be free of earthly, carnal desires, results in an impulse towards the celestial repose of death. Within Decadent poetry and prose, masochism is deployed as a figurative trope to combine both impulses, towards the worldly and the unworldly, resulting in a tension that is either masochistically enjoyed, for example by Swinburne, or impossible to unify for Dowson. From a Decadent perspective Baudelaire suggests that the lower impulses are bodily, sexual, and natural, while the higher impulses involve refinement and a symbolic transcendence of the worldly to the artificial, the intellectual and the beautiful. In his confessional prose writings titled *Mon cœur mis à nu* [*My Heart Laid Bare*] (1864) Baudelaire proclaims that

> In every man, and at all times, there are two simultaneous yearnings — the one towards God, the other towards Satan. The invocation of God, or spirituality, is a desire to ascend a step; the invocation of Satan, or animality, is a delight in descending. To this latter one should relate one's enamourments with women, one's intimate conversations with animals — dogs, cats, etc.[23]

Phillips's and Baudelaire's statements about falling and ascending echo Christian mythology and the act of falling to one's knees in order to pray, and this is exploited in a subversive fashion by Decadent writers. Swinburne in particular combines the notion of devotional worship with masochistic submission. In 'Dolores' the agony of submission is written within the constraints of lyric poetry, as a kind of prayer or invocation of a goddess figure. The sentiment expressed in the poem is an impassioned plea for sexual gratification, and the pain it entails: 'Ah, feed me and fill me with pleasure, | Ere pain come in turn.'[24]

Swinburne invokes ritualized submission through an address to a female authority. 'Dolores' deliberately combines the notion of worship of a figure that is at once holy and devilish, with submission. Religious symbolism runs throughout the poem. She is simultaneously a 'high' virtuous, and 'low' sinful icon. She is called 'Our Lady' like the Catholic Virgin, but she is also nurtured on sin — 'What sins gave thee suck?' — and associated with hell and the devil.[25] Chris Snodgrass observes that 'As devouring as [Swinburne's] *femmes fatales* often seem, they are fundamentally passive.'[26] Dolores is imagined as a cold and immobile passive figure in the form of a blasphemous altarpiece. The opening lines invoke imagery of a statuesque figure:

> Cold eyelids that hide like a jewel
>   Hard eyes that grow soft for an hour;
> The heavy white limbs, and the cruel
>   Red mouth like a venomous flower [...].[27]

These cold eyelids, hard eyes like jewels, and heavy white limbs are all indicative of something not living, not quite real. Virginia M. Allen describes Dolores as an 'enamelled altarpiece'[28] which suggests that the speaker of the poem is on bended knee before her. The submissive stance that the masochist adopts, whether in reality or only symbolically, is ambiguous. It is an image suggestive of genuflection, humble supplication, or enforced subjugation.

This cold and distant female ideal resembles the Lady of medieval courtly love poetry before whom the troubadour poet symbolically prostrates himself. Slavoj Žižek and Jacques Lacan have acknowledged that this Lady is an insubstantial projection of male desire.[29] However, addressing a fantasy female image creates the illusion that she exists. This technique can be traced back to Robert Browning's dramatic monologue poems composed in the early Victorian era. In *The Female Sublime from Milton to Swinburne: Bearing Blindness* (2001), Catherine Maxwell examines Victorian poetry in terms of a crisis of gender identity, whereby male poets are feminized through their artistic endeavours. Observing a tendency for male poets to display pleasure in being dominated by female power, Maxwell suggests a compulsion towards submissiveness and self-feminization helps the poets to achieve vision. The striking factor in Maxwell's analysis is the observation that the male poet retains his dominance in a subtler manner than simply silencing and controlling women. The control is less obvious, because of the illusion of activity on the part of the woman, which gives the impression of independence. Maxwell compares the female images in Browning's poems to Pygmalion's idealized female image: 'Browning's male speakers typically invert Ovid's myth, reducing a woman, even through her death, to a composition of their own creating. They desire feminine simulacra, static art-objects, whose fixed value will reflect their self-estimation.'[30] Browning's women, such as Porphyria and the famous 'Last Duchess', reflect the insecurities of the poems' male speakers, who kill women into art in an attempt to control them. In order to (re)animate them, they must speak for them.

Rather than fatally manipulating women into submission, Swinburne's speakers celebrate cruel and dominating women. They masochistically direct their own torment and take pleasure in it. Swinburne's poetic monologues are often addressed to silent auditors who are reminiscent of Pygmalion's statue. His speakers adopt poses of subjection and genuflection before female figures that they conjure up as reflections of the pleasurable torment of sexual desire. 'Dolores' is spoken entirely by the voice of a male lover. This poem is written in a regular rhyme scheme and metre, and returns, like an incantation, to the refrain 'Our Lady of Pain' which ends every second stanza. However, the female centre of this poem is an imaginary one. She has no voice and no suggestion of an actual or stable identity. Dolores is conceived of in terms of coldness and immobility, adding to her passivity. She is formed according to Swinburne's Decadent desires.

As an image of the Virgin Mary, 'Our Lady of Seven Sorrows', Dolores recalls the similar invocation of the virgin mother in Baudelaire's 'À une Madone' [To a Madonna]. In this poem the speaker addresses a statue of the Madonna, imagining that he can adorn it with his own sorrows and desire:

> I'll cut your Cloak in the barbaric mode,
> Lined with Distrust, a heavy, stiff abode
> Emprisoning those charms I hold so dear;
> Brocaded not of Pearls, but of my Tears!
> My trembling Lust will do me for your Gown,
> Surging Desire that rises or sinks down.[31]

Baudelaire's speaker imagines piercing the Madonna's heart with daggers formed from the seven deadly sins. He will 'plant them all within your panting Heart, | Within your sobbing Heart, your streaming Heart!'[32] In *Desiring the Dead: Necrophilia and Nineteenth-Century French Literature* (2003), Lisa Downing observes that the speaker first fantasizes a statue then symbolically kills it. She speaks of the statue as a projection of desire and a figure animated in the poet's mind. She notes, 'In "À une Madone", a fantasized religious icon, a statue of Mary, is animated by the poetic imagination and finally killed by seven knives, representing the seven sins.'[33] It is Downing's view that Baudelaire enacts his death drives through this necrophiliac fantasy. She states that 'the woman's identity is borrowed to allow the game to be played: the poet is doing to her (the part of him that is split off as an other) what he cannot do to himself.'[34] The female image is therefore a fantasy that represents the poet's own self. She is imagined in highly sensory terms: she is symbolically enveloped within the speaker's trembling lust, elevated by his surging desire for her, and the climactic imagery of penetration of her panting, sobbing, streaming heart seems to mimic the speaker's own sexual ecstasies.

In a similar yet muted fashion, girls in Dowson's poetry represent his exhausted world-weary attitude. Rather than creating a sense of vitality and dominance, he speaks of girls as ghostly shadows and cold dead bodies. Like Baudelaire, he kills girls symbolically in his poems, in an expression of the desire to control them. 'You would have understood me, had you waited', published in *Verses*, is an address to a dead beloved combining the inaccessibility of the cruel woman with the idealized image of the corpse as a screen for the projection of the lover's desires. The speaker claims ownership of the woman after her death. As she is incapable of rejecting him, her inanimate state allows the speaker to feel that he has a greater claim to the woman than he did when she was living:

> I would not waken you: nay! this is fitter;
>   Death and the darkness give you unto me;
> Here we who loved so, were so cold and bitter,
>   Hardly can disagree.[35]

Her death gives her to him; he can finally take control over her without fear of rejection. The woman who was 'fated | Always to disagree' with the speaker, in a phrase which is repeated twice in the poem, is no longer able to disagree with him in death.[36] The poem closes with the speaker imagining a truce between them — they 'Hardly can disagree' because she can no longer speak, this is a perverse power he takes over her.[37] The sinister dynamic of Browning's 'My Last Duchess' and 'Porphyria's Lover' is evident here; the dead beloved is under the control of her lover, who now speaks for her.

In a similar vein 'The Dead Child', a poem from *Decorations*, imagines death as a means of arresting the development of innocence to maturity, preserving the child in an ideal state of youth before the transition to adulthood can take place. The dead child will never be 'defiled' by ageing and experience:

> Lie still, and be
>   For evermore a child!
> Not grudgingly,
>   Whom life has not defiled,
> I render thee.[38]

Unlike the speaker of 'You would have understood...', who takes comfort in his beloved's death because it enables him freely to project his desires on to her, this speaker is melancholy and wishes to die also. He is exhausted, and expresses desire to be dead with the child. He wishes 'To share thy sleep', and 'I want to come thy way, | And share thy rest.'[39] Death is a means of stopping time and achieving peace.

Dowson's deathly despair

Dowson seems to have enjoyed a reckless flirtation with dangerous behaviour, and his acquaintances remember him deliberately hurting or degrading himself and taking pleasure in his own pain. Robert Sherard, in whose house Dowson eventually died, acknowledged that Dowson 'hunted after suffering with the same eagerness with which most men pursue pleasure'.[40] William Rothenstein wrote 'Poor Dowson was a tragic figure. While we others amused ourselves, playing with fireworks, Dowson meant deliberately to hurt himself. [...] he punished and lacerated himself, as it were, through excess.'[41] The excessive aspect of the decadent lifestyle was painful for Dowson, and the pleasurable aspect of masochism is missing from his friends' accounts of his character. He seems to have abandoned himself to suffering, ceding control to his own perverse desires. His poems reflect pure despair, rather than the paradoxical pleasure/pain aspect of masochism. But while he punished himself physically 'through excess', in his poetry he renounces such excess, and concentrates on the inaccessibility of the object of desire.

As Thornton points out in his comparison of Dowson's 'Amor Umbratilis' to the masochistic oblations to deity figures in the poetry of Swinburne, 'If it derives from Swinburne, the passion is cooled, slowed down, made unassertive; it is a masochism of self-denial, not self-laceration.'[42] 'Amor Umbratilis' is one of the opening poems in *Verses*, and was first published in the *Century Guild Hobby Horse* in October 1891.[43] In the first stanza the speaker adopts a submissive position as he presents himself to his unresponsive beloved, 'To lay down at your unobservant feet, | Is all the gift I bear.'[44] He lowers and debases himself by kissing the ground on which she has trodden, 'I lay | My lips upon your trodden, daisied grass'.[45] The woman is a typical cold, disdainful character according to the speaker, who laments his unacknowledged position, 'I watch you pass and pass, | Serene and cold'.[46] Dowson turns the courtly love convention back upon itself. The troubadour poet usually pours words upon the disdainful woman, but Dowson's speaker promises silence instead. The poem opens with the line, 'A gift of Silence, sweet!' This self-silencing is remarked upon by Nick Freeman, who compares Dowson's 'attenuated' poetic vocabulary to Swinburne's. The admired lexis of Swinburne is evident in a diluted form in Dowson's poetry. Rather than revelling in the evocative potential of language, he limits his vocabulary to a selection of repeated terminology and imagery, and to demonstrate this Freeman has arranged Dowson's forty most frequently used words into an imagist-style poem:

> Delicate roses despair, mouth
> Grey, moon bitter.
> Sleep, dark love:
> Rest. Hair, sigh.
> Cold ghost, violet passion,
> Sick heart, tears.
> Old desire flowers.
> Red wine vanity.
> Night soul darkness, desolation.
> Ivory star vine,
> Sow lily white sun,
> Reap golden dew apples.[47]

While Freeman considers it 'fundamentally unfair to caricature him in this way',[48] this list clearly exposes Dowson's preference for muted tones and muted sensations — pallor, greyness, coldness, darkness, and death. Sensory nullification can be observed in Dowson's poetry, in which the pleasurable (and corporeal) aspect of corporal punishment is missing from the depiction of cruel girls. His figures are cold and distant or frozen statues.

The clearest example can be found in 'Epigram', a poem in which the Pygmalion myth is reversed. The poem can be read in two ways: as a fantastical transformation of a real woman to stone, or as a metaphor for his beloved turning cold and rejecting him:

> Because I am idolatrous and have besought,
> With grievous supplication and consuming prayer,
> The admirable image that my dreams have wrought
> Out of her swan's neck and her dark, abundant hair:
> The jealous gods, who brook no worship save their own,
> Turned my live idol marble and her heart to stone.[49]

The living woman (or girl) is the inspiration for the speaker's fantasy, the 'admirable image that my dreams have wrought'. He has been adopting a masochistic stance of supplication before the image of the woman, which he has created from his own dreams, but which is as inaccessible as a marble statue. Boyiopoulos explains,

> by turning into a frigid stone, she changes into the very idol fashioned by the poet-Pygmalion, a Pre-Raphaelite lady that is both cruel and controlled. The speaker's prayer and supplication in fact are returned: the image has turned into a *princesse lointaine* that both obstructs and encourages worship within a poetics of apartness.[50]

Rather than a statue being brought to life by the strength of her lover's desire, here the living object of desire is turned to stone in a divine retribution for the speaker's idolatrous ways.

Inaccessible ideals

The notion of punishment for romantic desire is a prominent theme in Dowson's work. To take one example, in 'Impenitentia Ultima' the girl is the object of worship, like the Virgin Mary idol.[51] She is not the agent of the speaker's pain but she is the cause of it nonetheless. The girl is a being so pure and beautiful that the speaker would accept the punishments meted out by an angry god in order to look at her for an hour. The speaker imagines that if he were granted one final grace from God 'Before my light goes out forever' he would ask to be able to see the girl he loves.[52] He begs to be able to serve his beloved who is cast in the role of mistress, even though this devotion will condemn him to the torments of hell:

> But once before the sand is run and the silver thread is broken,
>   Give me a grace and cast aside the veil of dolorous years,
> Grant me one hour of all mine hours, and let me see for a token
>   Her pure and pitiful eyes shine out, and bathe her feet with tears.[53]

The imagery of foot-bathing is reminiscent of the sinful woman in the biblical gospel of Luke 7.38, who washes Jesus's feet with tears and is forgiven. Dowson's speaker is the servant of his beloved woman, but she is not cast as cruel or commanding like Swinburne's Dolores. She is instead longed for as a benevolent and comforting presence at the end of the speaker's life, 'Her pitiful eyes should calm [...] And her eyes should be my light whilst the sun went out behind me, | And the viols in her voice be the last sound in mine ear.'[54] As penitence for his decision to be with her, he would endure the wrath of God and punishment of hell:

> Before the ruining waters fall and my life be carried under,
>   And Thine anger cleave me through as a child cuts down a flower,
> I will praise Thee, Lord, in Hell, while my limbs are racked asunder,
>   For the last sad sight of her face and the little grace of an hour.[55]

It is not the girl herself who is torturing him, but the torture is a result of his devotion to her. He sets her up as a benevolent Virgin Mary type, but this elevation is his own projection and the hell to which he consigns himself is a place away from her charms and 'grace'. In Dowson's poem we do not encounter the same sadistic death drives as Baudelaire's address to the Madonna, but frustration at the inaccessibility of the desired object.

The ultimate inaccessible ideal can be found in Dowson's 'Non sum qualis eram bonae sub regno Cynarae',[56] composed in February 1891 and subsequently revised several times.[57] It was published in Volume 6 of *The Century Guild Hobby Horse* in the same year, in the *Second Book of the Rhymers' Club* in 1894, and in *Verses* in 1896. The Cynara poem is a premature elegy for the Decadent movement, reflecting the exhausted mood of the end of the century and the impossibility of finding happiness through pleasure-seeking excess. Decadence is, of course, a self-conscious tradition that celebrates the very pain and languor that Dowson's speaker suffers from in the Cynara poem. However, this poem's tone is mournful, not celebratory. The word 'desolate' is repeated at least once in every stanza, establishing the poem as a lament.

In the opinion of Dowson's contemporary Holbrook Jackson, 'The whole attitude of the decadence is contained in Dowson's best known poem [...]. In that poem we have a sort of parable of the decadent soul. Cynara is a symbol of the unattained and perhaps unattainable joy and peace which is the eternal dream of man.'[58] However, the speaker's attitude *towards* decadence is at odds with the perversity, artificiality, egoism, and curiosity that Jackson establishes as the key characteristics of Decadent fiction.[59] Music, wine, dancing, feasting, and sex are lamented as inadequate distractions from Dowson's speaker's despair. He regrets the choice of roses (symbols of Decadence for Dowson) over lilies. Even though he has 'Flung roses, roses riotously with the throng' he has not been able to 'put thy pale, lost lilies out of mind'.[60] Dowson's speaker imagines Cynara as a projection of his own ideals, to which he has tried and failed to remain faithful.

Intoxication and the prostitute's purchased body are insufficient replacements for the intangible Cynara, who represents an ideal that cannot be bought as the prostitute can, nor attained by consuming mind-altering substances. The ideal is symbolized by the shadow that haunts the speaker while he desperately seeks to forget her:

> I cried for madder music and for stronger wine,
> But when the feast is finished and the lamps expire,
> Then falls thy shadow, Cynara! the night is thine;
> And I am desolate and sick of an old passion,
>   Yea hungry for the lips of my desire:
> I have been faithful to thee, Cynara! in my fashion.[61]

Unlike other Decadent writers who celebrate debauchery and the 'bought red mouth', Dowson exposes such hedonistic posturing as a distraction from the desire for an unattainable ideal.[62] For Dowson, Cynara is at odds with wickedness, wine and music. She is not part of it, as are Symons's dancing-girl lovers or Swinburne's idol-like goddess figures. Dowson looks beyond the decadent lifestyle, interrogating the motivations for such pleasure-seeking behaviour. His speaker is haunted by an inescapable desire for something else, which Jackson identifies as joy and peace. Cynara is a figment of the speaker's imagination, thus her distance is paradoxically described in terms of closeness since her origins are within his mind. She is a shadow which falls between the lips of the speaker and his bought lover: 'betwixt her lips and mine | There fell thy shadow, Cynara! thy breath was shed | Upon my soul between the kisses and the wine'.[63] Cynara's breath on the speaker's soul combines two intangible incorporeal images. She is purely a fantasy ideal that has long been yearned for.

Religious calm and sensory nullification

Dowson was painfully familiar with yearning for an ideal. His personal letters and his poems demonstrate an oscillation between taking comfort in desire for Adelaide as an ideal on one hand, and wishing for solitude and oblivion as an escape from desire on the other. To intensify the issue, the young girl herself exists in a transitional state, between innocence and maturity. Dowson laments the impermanence of youth and the inevitability of ageing.[64] Writing to Arthur Moore in 1890, he refers to the child being the only solace in his life, but also indicates his despair towards life:

> Children certainly reconcile one — (or at least in my case) more than anything else to one's life but on the whole I am more & more convinced each day that there is nothing really worth doing or having or saying. At least I can't fix on any tangible object or aim in life which seems so desirable as the having got it finally over — & the remaining *in perpetuo* without desire or aim or consciousness whatsoever.[65]

For Dowson the oblivion of death is regarded as an escape from the torment of being dissatisfied with life, as in 'The Dead Child'. He also fixates on a living escape in the form of religious retreat. Boyiopoulos compares Dowson to Symons, whose poetry evokes sensation,

> Whilst in Symons desire is pursued in the immersion through the senses, in Dowson, desire is pursued and sustained by deliberately abstaining from its fulfilment. [...] Catholicism is a trope through which Dowson's poetic personae are allowed to retreat into a monastic, sequestered and isolated world; they avert their gaze from the flux of the modern Victorian world.[66]

In Symons's poetry women appear to stir all his senses; they are associated with exotic colours, flowers, and perfume. Symons himself noted the disparity between his own love of the theatre as a synaesthetic paradise and Dowson's preference for taverns for taverns' sake:

> It was at the time when one or two of us sincerely worshipped the ballet; Dowson, alas! never. I could never get him to see that charm in harmonious and coloured movement, like bright shadows seen through the floating gauze of the music, which held me night after night at the two theatres which alone seemed to me to give an amusing colour to one's dreams. Neither the stage nor the stage-door had any attraction for him; but he came to the tavern because it was a tavern, and because he could meet his friends there.[67]

Symons captures dancers' movement and vivacity in the *London Nights* poems, creating a sense of kinesthetic vitality, as Katharina Herold examines in detail elsewhere in this volume. In contrast, Boyiopoulos notes, Dowson avoids the sensory in favour of abstinence and escape. Dowson is devoted to spiritual rather than earthly or fleshly pleasures. He desires religious calm and sensory nullification.

In 'Breton Afternoon', published in *Decorations*, we encounter a speaker in a peaceful place, presumably the Breton countryside.[68] He experiences a spiritual calm surrounded by nature away from the city. His surroundings are imbued with a religious atmosphere, where he can hear 'Only the faint breeze pass in a whisper like a prayer'.[69] The place seems unreal, a 'dream-land', in which calmness and clarity descend upon the speaker like a spell. In his trance he is at peace, 'Out of the tumult of angry tongues, in a land alone, apart, | In a perfumed dream-land set betwixt the bounds of life and death'.[70] The speaker's distance from the Babel of voices is beneficial to him. Alone in this liminal space his senses are awakened to the aromas of the countryside, an intersensorial paradise where the 'scented-gorse floats through the sun-stained air', and the sound of the angelus is 'rose-white'.[71] The description of the scent of the gorse is one of only a handful of references to fragrance in Dowson's poetry. In contrast to the Decadent poets who celebrate floral odours, Dowson rarely evokes the sense of smell. Flowers, especially roses and violets, are a particular obsession, but are described visually, in terms of colour. The speaker of 'Breton Afternoon' reproaches himself for his floral fixation, trivializing his past despair now that he is at peace: 'And the world fades into a dream and a spell is cast on me; | *And what was all the strife about, for the myrtle or the rose,* | *And why have I wept for a white girl's paleness passing ivory!*'[72] The girl is the pale marmoreal archetype of the Decadent cruel woman, and here Dowson's speaker renounces her. While alone and apart from the company of others he can distance himself from the situation, rationally dismissing his own desires. However, his peace is transient. Having located himself in a moment of spiritual fulfilment, it is ironic that he is disturbed by religion in the very place where he has found his peace. The sound of 'the rose-white angelus | Softly steals my way from the village' and wakes him.[73] He must face reality once again. The poem ends as the speaker echoes Catholic prayer: '*Mother of God, O Misericord, look down in pity on us,* | *The weak and blind who stand in our light and wreak ourselves such ill.*'[74] He returns to a state of sensory deprivation, symbolically blinded by his own blocking of the light.

While expressing a longing for isolation, 'Breton Afternoon' marks an unusual moment of positivity in Dowson's final collection (the following two poems, 'Venite Descendamus' and 'Transition', return to familiar Dowsonian themes of death, silence, and the impossibility of recapturing transient youth). It ends on an admission of the speaker's own complicity in his torment. He has shed tears of strife over a desired girl but this is an anguish of his own making. For Dowson religious devotion is pursued as an escape from desire. The speaker of 'Nuns of the Perpetual Adoration', one of the first poems in *Verses*, aspires to the meek and simple existence of a devoted order of nuns. They do not have to face an internal battle with desire and passion, since they are sequestered away from the lives of others: 'Outside, the world is wild and passionate; | Man's weary laughter and his sick despair'.[75] As in the Cynara poem, supposedly enjoyable pursuits — passion and laughter — are presented as empty and exhausting. The nuns have removed themselves from this existence.

> They saw the glory of the world displayed;
>   They saw the bitter of it, and the sweet;
> They knew the roses of the world should fade,
>   And be trod under by the hurrying feet.[76]

Dowson uses Sapphic sensory terminology of bitter and sweet (see Sarah Parker's chapter, pp. 121–40), and the contrast implies not simply that the sweetness is worth the bitterness, but that they are equally worthless. The speaker is envious of the nuns' ability to acknowledge the futility of such transient unpleasurable pleasures: 'Yea! for our roses fade, the world is wild; | But there, beside the altar, there, is rest.'[77] They are protected from the exhausting life doomed to decline outside the convent.

Decorations contains a similar poem, 'Carthusians'. Here, the speaker desires the peace of monks who exist in solitude. Dowson wrote to Moore on 3 April 1891 that he had spent a day at a Carthusian monastery, and he was enchanted by the silent solitude of its inhabitants.[78] The monks of 'Carthusians' are alone in a group, and described in a series of self-contradictory phrases. 'A cloistered company, they are companionless', 'They are but come together for more loneliness'.[79] Their isolation is ultimately rewarding as they achieve transcendence above the tedium of secular existence:

> Our viols cease, our wine is death, our roses fail:
> Pray for our heedlessness, O dwellers with the Christ!
> Though the world fall apart, surely ye shall prevail.[80]

Once again Dowson returns to wine and roses as negative motifs. He reverses the convention of the rose as a symbol of beauty, emphasizing instead its transience and inevitable decay. Those associated with Decadent roses are fated to failure and death, while the 'cloistered company' of monks achieves transcendence away from mortal failures.

In 'Extreme Unction', from *Verses*, Dowson celebrates the ritualistic anointing of the sick, one of the three sacraments — along with Viaticum and the Sacrament of Penance — that make up the last rites in the Catholic tradition.

> Upon the eyes, the lips, the feet,
>   On all the passages of sense,
> The atoning oil is spread with sweet
>   Renewal of lost innocence.
>
> The feet, that lately ran so fast
>   To meet desire, are soothly sealed;
> The eyes, that were so often cast
>   On vanity, are touched and healed.
>
> [...]
>
> Yet, when the walls of flesh grow weak,
>   In such an hour, it well may be,

> Through mist and darkness, light will break,
> And each anointed sense will see.

Dowson imagines the final healing as a 'renewal of lost innocence'. It is a return to the ideal state of innocent purity. Once again Dowson associates spirituality with the nullification of bodily sensation. The feet are 'sealed', the eyes and ears are 'From troublous sights and sounds set free'. The anointing symbolizes freedom from desire, and from vanity. The description of the body as 'walls of flesh' suggests a dualistic notion of body and soul, and hints at the soul being trapped within these walls. The living body, with its desires and sensations, is a prison. Healing the fleshly form by symbolically blocking the 'passages of sense' opens the soul to a new and perfect type of vision as the sensory parts of the body are freed from the impurity of desire.

Dowson's Decadent diminuendo

For Dowson, desire is associated with the senses, and the lack of sensory evocation in his poems represents the impossibility of fulfilling his desires. Romantic desire is a torment because its object forces him to face a paradox. He yearns for the ideal represented by the young girl, but knows his desire cannot be realized because that would signal the girl's maturity. Both desire and the ideal would be destroyed in the fulfilment. Decadent ennui, as Jackson notes in *The Eighteen Nineties*, arises because the easy gratification of desire leads not to satisfaction but to a new desire for a different sensation.[81] Dowson's fantasy of marriage to Adelaide never died because it was never fulfilled. Dowson returns compulsively to the ideal girl in his poems, where she appears dreamlike, intangible, inaccessible, just as he returned compulsively to 'Poland' to visit the girl who it was impossible for him to possess. First her age and then her refusal of his marriage proposal were obstacles to Dowson's obtaining the object of his desire. It is likely that Dowson would never have found complete satisfaction in romantic relationships, and we can speculate that his attraction to Adelaide would have waned as she advanced into womanhood. Symons attributed the 'exquisite impossibility' of the relationship to Dowson's knowledge that Adelaide would grow up and 'spoil in the ripening'. As the anonymous dedicatee of Dowson's *Verses*, Adelaide is cast as an unattainable beloved. In Wilde's *The Picture of Dorian Gray* (1891) Dorian's portrait absorbs his sins and ages for him, but in Adelaide's case her image in the poems remains pure, youthful and rosy while she herself lived out the sad and corrupted life, eventually dying in December 1903 from blood poisoning following an abortion.[82]

Verses opens with a declaration that 'They are not long, the days of wine and roses'.[83] Wine and roses in the Cynara poem are inadequate substitutes for a pure ideal of peace. Dowson acknowledges the eventual exhaustion of the pleasure-seeker through imagery of roses fading and withering. His published poems begin with a warning, and end with 'A Last Word', the final poem in *Decorations*. The speaker seems critical of the life lived as a Decadent:

> [...] we cannot understand
> Laughter or tears, for we have only known

> Surpassing vanity: vain things alone
> Have driven our perverse and aimless band.[84]

Dowson frequently makes use of the double meaning of 'vain' to refer to arrogance and futility. Both senses of the term are self-defeating: the ideal girl is a narcissistic self-reflection, and the pursuit of an impossible ideal *in vain* leads to disappointment. As in Dowson's other poems, death is welcomed as a liberating final freedom from the torment of love and desire. This 'last word' on Decadence embraces death as the ultimate release from the languor and ennui of a 'perverse and aimless' life. Dowson's poetry is an apt diminuendo for the end of the century, and we can observe an increasing pessimism in his later volume, an overall sense of submitting to death-driven thoughts. As Thornton points out, 'Almost every poem in *Decorations* ends on a note of disillusion, reaching nothing, silence'.[85]

Unlike Swinburne's poetry, in which the sensory excesses of pleasure and pain are celebrated, and Symons's poems, in which the figure of the dancer is a metaphor for the poet's struggle to represent the fleeting sensations of erotic experience, Dowson's verses are preoccupied with decline and death. His girls are antithetical to the pleasure-seeking aspects of Decadence. They are ideals of innocence, purity and youth that cannot be reached by the adult man. Dowson is a 'reverse Pygmalion' poet, who symbolically kills the image of the young girl into art. The girl is the unattainable statue that does not gratify its creator by coming to life. Dowson turns to sensory nullification rather than celebrating the pleasures of the flesh, and his poetry reflects his own self-tormenting masochism and longing to escape from desire into solitude and silence.

Notes to Chapter 11

1. Beardsley, who was disdainful of Dowson, joked that the letter 'Y' stood for '*Why* was this book ever written?' James G. Nelson, *Publisher to the Decadents: Leonard Smithers in the Careers of Beardsley, Wilde, Dowson* (University Park: Pennsylvania State University Press, 2000), p. 159, quoting Vincent O'Sullivan, *Aspects of Wilde* (London: Constable, 1936), p. 127.
2. Dowson admired the design, writing to the book's publisher Leonard Smithers that 'Beardsley's binding block is admirable — *simplex munditiis* ['elegant simplicity', from Horace's Ode I.V], & yet most sumptuous. I am only afraid the reviewers will think the contents unworthy of such display.' Letter to Leonard Smithers, c. 4 June 1896, in *The Letters of Ernest Dowson* collected and edited by Desmond Flower and Henry Maas (London: Cassell & Company, 1967), p. 365.
3. R. K. R. Thornton, *The Decadent Dilemma* (London: Edward Arnold, 1983), p. 177.
4. Linda Dowling, *Language and Decadence in the Victorian Fin de Siècle* (Princeton: Princeton University Press, 1986), p. 204.
5. Dowson's early poetry, which remained unpublished during his lifetime, is collected as *Poésie Schublade* in *Ernest Dowson: Collected Poems*, ed. by R. K. R. Thornton and Caroline Dowson (Birmingham: Birmingham University Press, 2003).
6. Arthur Symons, 'Ernest Dowson', in *The Poems of Ernest Dowson: Verses, The Pierrot of the Minute, Decorations in Verse and Prose* (Portland, ME: Thomas B. Mosher, 1902), p. xxiii.
7. Asti Hustvedt explores in interesting detail examples from French Decadent fiction of attempts to create the perfect artificial feminine image in sculptures and corpses, in a reversal of the Pygmalion model in which the ideal image is brought to life. See Asti Hustvedt, 'The Art of Death: French Fiction at the Fin de Siècle', in *The Decadent Reader: Fiction, Fantasy, and Perversion from Fin-de-Siècle France*, ed. by Hustvedt (New York: Zone, 1998).
8. A. C. Swinburne, 'Dolores', in *Poems and Ballads & Atalanta in Calydon*, ed. by Kenneth Haynes (1866; London: Penguin, 2000), p. 127, ll. 166–67; p. 126, ll. 113–14.

9. Elsewhere in this volume Sarah Parker and Matthew Brinton Tildesley discuss the use of Christian imagery in terms of lesbian sexuality in the poetry of Michael Field and gay sexuality in John Gray's poetry, respectively.
10. Boyiopoulos uses the example of 'Autumnal', a poem from *Verses*. Kostas Boyiopoulos, *The Decadent Image: The Poetry of Wilde, Symons, and Dowson* (Edinburgh: Edinburgh University Press, 2015), p. 138.
11. Boyiopoulos, *The Decadent Image*, p. 153.
12. See Jad Adams, *Madder Music, Stronger Wine: The Life of Ernest Dowson, Poet and Decadent* (London: I. B. Tauris, 2000), p. 123.
13. Richard Freiherr von Krafft-Ebing, *Psychopathia Sexualis*, 12th edn, trans. by Franklin S. Klaf (1903; New York: Arcade Publishing, 1998), p. 87. Gilles Deleuze's 1967 essay on masochism, 'Coldness and Cruelty', uses *Venus in Furs* as a template for masochism, noting the masochist is director of his own torment, and that the cruel mistress is often a cold and distant type. See Gilles Deleuze, 'Coldness and Cruelty', in *Masochism*, trans. by Jean McNeil (1967; New York: Zone Books, 1991).
14. Oscar Wilde, *Salome* (London: Elkin Matthews & John Lane, 1894), p. 3.
15. Joseph Bristow, '"Sterile Ecstasies": The Perversity of the Decadent Movement', in *Essays and Studies 1995: The Endings of Epochs*, ed. by Laurel Brake (Cambridge: D. S. Brewer, 1995), pp. 65–88 (p. 78).
16. Adams, *Madder Music, Stronger Wine*, p. ix.
17. Thornton, *The Decadent Dilemma*, p. 71.
18. Dowling, *Language and Decadence*, p. 205.
19. Thornton, *The Decadent Dilemma*, p. 190.
20. Ernest Dowson, 'Transition', in *Decorations: In Verse and Prose* (London: Leonard Smithers, 1899), p. 28.
21. Anita Phillips, *A Defence of Masochism* (London: Faber and Faber, 1998), p. 159.
22. R. K. R. Thornton, '"Decadence" in Later Nineteenth-Century England', in *Decadence and the 1890s*, ed. by Malcolm Bradbury and David Palmer (London: Edward Arnold, 1979), p. 26.
23. Charles Baudelaire, *My Heart Laid Bare and Other Prose Writings*, trans. by Norman Cameron (London: Soho Book Company, 1986), p. 181, quoted in Marie Lathers, *Bodies of Art: French Literary Realism and the Artist's Model* (London: University of Nebraska Press, 2001), p. 109.
24. Swinburne, 'Dolores', p. 123, ll. 31–32.
25. *Ibid.*, p. 123, l. 48.
26. Chris Snodgrass, 'Swinburne's Circle of Desire: A Decadent Theme', in *Decadence and the 1890s*, ed. by Ian Fletcher (New York: Holmes and Meier, 1980), pp. 60–87 (p. 73).
27. Swinburne, 'Dolores', p. 122, ll. 1–4.
28. Virginia M. Allen, *The Femme Fatale: Erotic Icon* (Troy, NY: Whitston Publishing Company, 1983), p. 118.
29. See Jacques Lacan, 'Courtly Love as Anamorphosis', in *The Ethics of Psychoanalysis 1959–1960: The Seminar of Jacques Lacan, Book VII*, trans. by Dennis Porter, ed. by Jacques-Alain Miller (London: Routledge, 2008), and Slavoj Žižek, 'Courtly Love, or, Woman as Thing', in *The Metastases of Enjoyment: On Women and Causality* (1994; London: Verso, 2005).
30. Catherine Maxwell, *The Female Sublime from Milton to Swinburne: Bearing Blindness* (Manchester: Manchester University Press, 2001), p. 153.
31. Charles Baudelaire, 'To a Madonna', in *The Flowers of Evil*, trans. by James McGowan (Oxford: Oxford University Press, 1998), p. 119.
32. *Ibid.*, p. 121.
33. Lisa Downing, *Desiring the Dead: Necrophilia and Nineteenth-Century French Literature* (Oxford: Legenda, 2003), p. 78.
34. *Ibid.*, p. 85.
35. Ernest Dowson, 'You would have understood me, had you waited', in *Verses* (London: Leonard Smithers, 1896), p. 26.
36. *Ibid.*, p. 25; p. 26.
37. *Ibid.*, p. 26.
38. Dowson, 'The Dead Child', in *Decorations*, p. 4.

39. *Ibid.*, p. 5.
40. Robert Harborough Sherard, *The Real Oscar Wilde* (London: T. Werner Laurie, 1916), p. 82.
41. William Rothenstein, *Men and Memories*, 2 vols (London, 1931), I, 238, quoted in Adams, *Madder Music, Stronger Wine*, pp. 103–04.
42. Thornton, *The Decadent Dilemma*, p. 90.
43. The word 'Umbratilis', meaning 'unworldly', is taken from Pater's *Marius the Epicurean*: 'Had the Romans a word for *unworldly*? The beautiful word *umbratilis* perhaps comes nearest to it'. Walter Pater, *Marius the Epicurean*, ed. by Michael Levey (1885; London: Penguin, 1985), p. 49. This unworldliness is consistent with one half of Thornton's 'decadent dilemma', and in this poem the speaker is trapped at the level of the worldly — literally prostrate on the earth — and unable to reach his unworldly ideal.
44. Dowson, 'Amor Umbratilis', in *Verses*, p. 7.
45. *Ibid.*
46. *Ibid.*
47. Nick Freeman, '"The Harem of Words": Attenuation and Excess in Decadent Poetry', in *Decadent Poetics: Literature and Form at the British Fin de Siècle*, ed. by Jason David Hall and Alex Murray (Basingstoke: Palgrave Macmillan, 2013), pp. 83–99 (p. 89).
48. *Ibid.*
49. Dowson, 'Epigram', in *Verses*, p. 54.
50. Boyiopoulos, *The Decadent Image*, p. 177.
51. The title translates as 'final impenitence'. The poem was published in *Verses* and first printed in *The Savoy* (January 1896).
52. Dowson, 'Impenitentia Ultima', in *Verses*, p. 47.
53. *Ibid.*, pp. 47–48.
54. *Ibid.*, p. 48.
55. *Ibid.*
56. The title is a quote from Horace, Ode IV.I, 'I'm not the man I was | in good Cinara's reign'. *The Complete Odes and Epodes*, trans. by David West (BC 23; Oxford: Oxford University Press, 2008), p. 112, ll. 3–4.
57. On 7 February 1891 Dowson sent a draft of the poem in a letter to Arthur Moore. See *The Letters of Ernest Dowson*, pp. 134–35.
58. Holbrook Jackson, *The Eighteen Nineties: A Review of Art and Ideas at the Close of the Nineteenth Century* (1913; Harmondsworth: Penguin, 1939), p. 59.
59. 'The chief characteristics of the decadence were (1) Perversity, (2) Artificiality, (3) Egoism and (4) Curiosity'. Jackson, *The Eighteen Nineties*, p. 58.
60. Dowson, 'Non sum qualis eram bonae sub regno Cynarae', in *Verses*, p. 17.
61. *Ibid.*, p. 18.
62. *Ibid.*, p. 17.
63. *Ibid.*
64. Dowson wrote to Arthur Moore of Adelaide, 'What a terrible, lamentable thing growth is! It "makes me mad" to think that in a year or two at most the most perfect exquisite relation I have ever succeeded in making must naturally end.' Ernest Dowson, letter to Arthur Moore, 5 March 1891, in *The Letters of Ernest Dowson*, p. 187.
65. Dowson, letter to Arthur Moore, 28 March 1890, in *The Letters of Ernest Dowson*, p. 144.
66. Boyiopoulos, *The Decadent Image*, p. 144.
67. Arthur Symons, 'Ernest Dowson', p. xxi.
68. First published in *The Savoy* (July 1896).
69. Dowson, 'Breton Afternoon', in *Decorations*, p. 25.
70. *Ibid.*
71. *Ibid.*
72. *Ibid.*
73. *Ibid.*, p. 26.
74. *Ibid.*
75. Dowson, 'Nuns of the Perpetual Adoration', in *Verses*, p. 2.
76. *Ibid.*

77. *Ibid.*
78. See Dowson's letter to Arthur Moore, 3 April 1891, in *The Letters of Ernest Dowson*, p. 191. He composed the poem the following month.
79. Dowson, 'Carthusians', in *Decorations*, p. 7.
80. *Ibid.*
81. 'To kill a desire, as you can, by satisfying it, is to create a new desire. The decadents always did that, with the result that they demanded of life not a repetition of old but opportunities for new experiences.' Jackson, *The Eighteen Nineties*, p. 59.
82. See Adams, *Madder Music, Stronger Wine*, p. 179.
83. Dowson, '*Vitae summa brevis spem nos vetat incohare longam*', in *Verses*, p. iii.
84. Dowson, 'A Last Word', in *Decorations*, p. 39.
85. Thornton, *The Decadent Dilemma*, p. 105.

CHAPTER 12

Afterword: Decadent Taste

David Weir

Decadence is like syphilis: you either get it or you don't. Unlike syphilis, however, the only way to 'get' decadence is by developing a taste for it. But what is decadent taste? One of the interesting things about this question is that the idea of taste is much easier to understand than the concept of decadence. The idea of aesthetic taste is based on the sense of taste, so taste makes sense because sense makes taste. Decadence, on the other hand, is hard to make sense of because the concept is attached to so many different ideas, attitudes, orientations, movements, histories, arts, artists, and so on. As I have noted elsewhere, before you can say what *decadence* is, you must first say what decadence *is*.[1] Is it racial degeneration, historical decline, philosophical pessimism, personal immorality, physical entropy, artistic imperfection, artistic innovation, or all of the above? The fact that decadence has been studied using the analytical procedures of such disparate disciplines as eugenics, history, philosophy, psychology, physics, and aesthetics illustrates just how polyvalent the concept of decadence is. But this very polyvalence might point to the possibility that decadence involves some kind of core concept after all, because a person with a certain, singular type of taste can appreciate, say, both the austere pessimism of Schopenhauer and the florid sexuality of Elagabalus. Such comprehensiveness argues that the taste for decadence is rather catholic: if you like Huysmans, chances are you will also like Wilde, even though Huysmans and Wilde are two rather different kinds of writers, when you think about it, yet our taste for the one easily accommodates the other. And does the reader exist who adores Baudelaire but abhors Verlaine? I remember my own sense of delight when I discovered Edgar Saltus: oh good, I thought, here is another one; likewise with Ben Hecht. I knew instantly that Saltus and Hecht were decadents because of my own developed taste for decadence. But, again, what is decadent taste?

This is an aesthetic question. Etymologists tell us that the Greek word αἰσθητικός (*aistheticos*) means both feeling and perception (*OED*), so aesthetics must then have to do with how we feel about what we perceive. It was not until the eighteenth century that aesthetics became established as a field of philosophical inquiry, but that historical fact also helped to expand aesthetics beyond the century of its birth. Classical thinkers, principally Plato, Aristotle, and Longinus, were retrospectively aligned with aesthetics after the German rationalist philosopher Alexander Gottlieb Baumgarten (1714–1762) developed the new science in the middle of the eighteenth century. But Plato, Aristotle, and Longinus provide little help in elucidating the question of decadent taste. The Platonic theories of *enthusiasmos* and *mimesis* — the first an account of how art is created (by inspiration) and the second an account of its ontological status (an imitation of something real) — are of little use to understanding how we feel about what we perceive when we read Baudelaire or look at Moreau, partly because the classical theories of inspiration and imitation are somewhat at odds with one another (inspiration implies a connection to truth, while imitation connotes falsity), and partly because decadent art often involves a confluence of both of them. That is, the decadent artist or writer often takes inspiration *from* imitation, as in the aforementioned case of Wilde and Huysmans, or the not-yet mentioned case of Wilde and Pater. So Plato's aesthetics does not take us very far toward an understanding of decadent taste, and neither does Aristotle's. It's good to know that tragedy is an imitation of an action, but with decadence there is so little action to imitate — think of Des Esseintes day-dreaming in his armchair — that the Aristotelian revision of Platonic mimesis is not so helpful either. Maybe we can say that decadence is less an imitation of an action than an imitation of an attitude, but such a formulation brings us no closer to the question of taste. Suppose decadence *is* an imitation of an attitude: why do we like it?

The idea of aesthetic taste originated by taking the physical sense of taste as an analogue for artistic judgment.[2] Unlike the other senses, taste provides instantaneous verification of goodness or badness. Our eyes may need to adjust to the light; our ears might not be able to discriminate a single voice in the cacophony of a crowded room; but our tongue reacts instantly with gusto or disgust to whatever finds itself inside our mouth, whether animal, vegetable, or genital. Moreover, with the other senses, touch included, we feel apart from the objects we apprehend. But taste is internal, like the mind, and it is our own, or so we think: we see and hear the same things other people see and hear, but have different tastes. The variability of individual tastes, however, paradoxically involves universality: we all *have* taste, however subjective it might be. This fact about the taste of sense underlies one of Immanuel Kant's key insights about the sense of taste. If I say, 'This is beautiful', that does not mean that you will agree with me; you might say, 'That is beautiful', but we agree in so far as we both understand that there is a category of beauty underlying our variable impressions of it. Kant calls this 'subjective universality', since the judgment of taste 'must claim validity for every man, without this universality depending on objects'.[3]

For Kant, questions of aesthetic judgment were limited to two categories, the beautiful and the sublime, but perhaps his thinking can be extended to the category of decadence. Indeed, the aforementioned conceptual polyvalence of decadence makes it an ideal candidate for an aesthetic category, since judgements of taste do not involve concepts, the domain of reason, but feelings, the domain of aesthetics. In other words, the conceptual difficulty that attaches to decadence might be an intellectual liability, but it is an aesthetic asset. That is, the conceptual vagueness of decadence might make it *like* beauty, or *like* the sublime, in so far that decadence, like the more familiar aesthetic categories, does not appeal so much to our rational capacities as it does to our imaginative proclivities. In addition, two more Kantian concepts might be invoked to clarify the question of decadent taste. First, Kant observes that the formal relations of a work of art make it seem as if it has a purpose even when it doesn't because it has been regulated 'according to the representation of a certain rule' (p. 294). This trick of perception, however, is the product merely of the formal design of a work that is nonetheless *not* designed for a particular end. Hence the work of art has 'purposiveness without purpose' (p. 294). And while 'art for art's sake' may not be identical with decadence, the dictum that 'All art is quite useless' does suggest a certain kinship between Kant and that Holy Trinity of useless Decadents, Gautier, Pater, and Wilde. Second, Kant says that since judgments of taste involve 'a subjective principle which determines what pleases or displeases only by feeling and not by concepts, but yet with universal validity, [...] such a principle [can] only be regarded as a *common sense*' (p. 302). The taste for decadence seems to work as Kant describes. It is clearly a subjective principle, and the determination of whether something qualifies as decadence is more a matter of sensibility than rationality. We know what decadence is without necessarily calling upon a clear concept of decadence: we know it when we read it, see it, or feel it. But since decadence is categorically different from beauty, why don't we call this subjective capacity not a 'common sense' but something more refined, an uncommon sense.

Traditionally, the aesthetic analogy likens beauty and ugliness to delight and disgust, but what happens when disgust delights? The taste for decadence involves precisely such delight in disgust, an uncommon sense that finds delight in things that people who have normal taste react to with revulsion. If *disgust* seems too strong a word, remember that the Latin *gustus* at the root of it simply means 'taste', so the uncommon sense of decadence involves a taste for the distasteful. This meaning might be compared to the taste for terror that emerged in the eighteenth century as the counterpart to the more sedate taste for beauty. The taste for terror originates in the late seventeenth century after the rediscovery and translation of the first century BCE treatise attributed to Longinus, titled *Peri Hypsos,* now known as *On the Sublime.* Granted, relating the sublime to decadence is a rather odd thought experiment, but I can think of at least two reasons for making the comparison. First, the taste for terror is like the taste for the distasteful in that both tastes involve an attraction to something that, for the sake of our health or well-being, we would not ordinarily be attracted to. As Edmund Burke put it in his much-read investigation into the sublime first published in 1757, 'Whatever is fitted in any sort to excite the ideas of pain, and danger, that is to say, whatever is in any sort terrible, or is conversant about terrible objects, or operates in a manner analogous to terror, is a source of the *sublime*.'[4] Given the importance of the taste for terror to the development of the Gothic novel in the eighteenth century, Oscar Wilde's *The Picture of Dorian Gray* might be advanced as a concrete case of decadent sublimity, since that novel is nothing if not neo-Gothic. Huysmans also provides reason for linking the sense of the sublime to the taste for decadence. In *À rebours,* Des Esseintes feels 'overwhelmed' by Moreau's representation of Salomé, 'petrified and hypnotized by terror'.[5] So the sublime taste for terror does find a partial analogue in the decadent canon, with the significant difference that the basis for the terror that the protagonist feels in both Wilde's novel and in Huysmans's is not nature — not the cataract or the glacier or the craggy Alps — but art: the mysterious portrait in the case of Dorian Gray, the painting of Salomé in the case of Des Esseintes.

Another reason for entertaining the comparison of the taste for terror and the taste for the distasteful lies in the idea that the effect of the sublime in art cannot be produced by following rules; ruggedness, not perfection, is the source of the sublime. In Chapter 14 of *À rebours,* when Des Esseintes contemplates the appeal of contemporary poets like Verlaine, he reflects that

> [i]mperfection itself pleased him, provided it was neither base nor parasitic, and it may be that there was a certain amount of truth in his theory that the minor writer of the decadence, the writer who is incomplete but nonetheless individual, distils a balm more irritant, more sudorific, more acid than the author of the same period who is truly great and truly perfect. (p. 170)

Whatever similitude there might be between sublimity and decadence, two points of difference assert themselves. First, the taste for terror mostly depends on nature: it is the lightning storm, the hurricane, or the raging sea that overwhelms and frightens us. The romantic sublime pits nature against us, while the decadent aesthetic pits us against nature. Second, the aesthetics of sublimity aligns greatness with imperfection, whereas the aesthetics of decadence opposes them. Indeed, the 'minor writer of the decadence' who practises imperfection pleases Des Esseintes because he is *not* great. Moreover, the satisfaction Des Esseintes takes in imperfection is a strange sort of satisfaction because it involves discomfort. The work of the minor writer is compared to a balm, or medicinal ointment, but this balm does not heal; rather, it irritates with its acid effect. Yet this is the aesthetic experience Des Esseintes prefers: he has a taste for something that is to some degree distasteful.

This kind of taste should be distinguished from a type of taste that may well have developed, at least in part, *because* of decadence but is not the same thing: namely, camp — 'the good taste of bad taste', as Susan Sontag defines it in her seminal essay of 1964.[6] Indeed, Sontag lists certain works 'which are part of the canon of Camp' which might also be listed among the canon of decadence, such as Max Beerbohm's *Zuleika Dobson* and Aubrey Beardsley's drawings (p. 277). But Beerbohm and Beardsley can also be considered secondary or derivative in relation to, say, Baudelaire and Huysmans, exemplars of 'high' Decadence, not the 'low' Decadence or 'decadent Decadence' that came after them.[7] Decadent taste and camp taste both lie outside the realm of normal or acceptable taste, but for different reasons. There is an ostentatious element to camp that suggests deliberate antagonism to the 'straight' tastes of the bourgeoisie. True, both the lover of camp and the aficionado of decadence are proud of their outsider taste. What Max Nordau said in *Entartung* [*Degeneration*] (1892) of the decadent sensibility might apply equally to camp: 'The ordinary man always seeks to think, to feel, and to do the same as the multitude; the decadent seeks exactly the contrary.'[8] But the connoisseurs of camp not only appreciate art that is at odds with established or acceptable taste — they also make a show of doing so. Decadents, by contrast, keep to themselves and have no need to set their taste against that of the crowd. More important, a taste for the distasteful is not bad taste; on the contrary, it is highly refined, unusual, exotic, even unlikely.

The taste for the distasteful is the product of a particularly acute, elevated sensibility attuned to nuances that the ordinary mortal has no chance of appreciating.

An acute taste for the distasteful, or something like it, appears in all the classic nineteenth-century texts of decadence. Gautier describes Baudelaire's style as like that of 'the Lower Empire, [...] veined with the greenish streaking of decomposition', that is, with gangrene.[9] Such corruption is, paradoxically, a sign of refinement. Gautier reminds us that normal physical taste is instinctive; therefore, it is animalistic. Only human beings can develop perverse tastes and take delight in disgust. As Gautier also says, depravity is a sign of humanity: it is impossible for animals to 'break [...] away from the normal type' because they 'are helplessly directed by unchanging instinct' (p. 55). Maintaining a depraved distance from normality, then, is not only human — it is civilized. Indeed, the removal from both normality and need is the mark of a highly refined civilization, one in which 'la vie factice' replaces 'la vie naturelle'.[10] The maintenance of the artificial life, unlike the natural one, requires satisfaction of hitherto unknown needs. The reader of Baudelaire's poetry will encounter references to nicotine, alcohol, and opium, none of which are particularly nutritious, so the person who leads 'la vie naturelle' does not need them; but the person who leads 'la vie factice' does because complicating and enriching existence is much more interesting than simply sustaining it.

The taste for civilized depravity, for vices that do nothing to sustain our animal nature, is analogous to an aesthetic taste for art and literature that does nothing to improve our moral nature. If nicotine, alcohol, and opium are not good for us, then neither are Baudelaire, Huysmans, and Wilde, and it is because these things are not good for us that we like them so much. It really is unfortunate that self-destruction has somehow acquired a bad name, because there is no denying its appeal. Gautier seems to have known this in making his assessment of Baudelaire, and so did Arthur Symons when he described Decadence as a kind of desirable illness, 'a new and beautiful and interesting disease'. He mentions *la névrose,* the 'pet malady' of the Goncourt brothers, whose style Huysmans describes — 'with delight' — as 'high-flavoured and spotted with corruption'.[11] The French phrase Symons quotes — 'tacheté et faisandé' — is also said to be key to Huysmans's own style. The latter word, especially, appears in *À rebours* whenever Huysmans describes Late Latin literature or the poetry of his contemporaries Verlaine and Mallarmé. Art that has the quality of *faisandage* is specifically, generically decadent.

The word *faisandage* is derived from *faisan*, 'pheasant', and the adjective *faisandé* derived from the noun means 'gamey'. So the aesthetic taste Des Esseintes has for late Latin literature and for his *symboliste* contemporaries has as its analogue the physical taste for a particular type of food, namely, the sort of game served on the tables of aristocratic estates: pheasant and deer. The simple fact that such food is aristocratic fare, inaccessible to the hated bourgeois class, is part of its appeal, so it follows that literature with the gamey flavour of pheasant or venison would also satisfy aristocratic tastes. This is part of Huysmans's meaning in *À rebours,* but Des Esseintes's rarefied taste in literature also has an analogue in another nineteenth-century food fact. Because commercial refrigeration was not available on a large aristocratic estate in the days of Des Esseintes,[12] pheasant and venison would have been preserved by salting; the meat would also have required heavy seasoning to disguise the taste of incipient decay. In *À rebours,* the metaphor of tainted game — *faisandage* — is used to describe Latin literature of the fourth century, 'as it decomposed like venison, dropping to pieces at the same time as the civilization of the Ancient World, falling apart while the Empires succumbed to the barbarian onslaught and the accumulated pus of ages' (p. 33). The metaphor likening late Latin literature to decaying meat continues, with Des Esseintes maintaining his interest in it even after 'it was rotten through and through and hung like a decaying carcass, losing its limbs, oozing pus, barely keeping, in the general corruption of its body, a few sound parts, which the Christians removed in order to preserve them in the pickling brine of their new idiom' (p. 35). Here, Christianity is the salt that makes the rotten language palatable, but no Christian brine allays the decadence of Des Esseintes's modern, secular contemporaries. Verlaine and Mallarmé both write in 'le style faisandé', while the brothers Goncourt employ 'le style tacheté' — a style spotted or mottled like tainted meat: not rotten exactly, but starting to decay.[13] Decadent taste, in short, involves a taste for decay: this tautology is not so simple as it sounds, because such taste must be developed, the senses must be educated to accept something that the person of normal taste would not find appealing.

Decadent taste, then, involves a paradox that does not attach to the taste for beauty, since the sense of taste in that typical aesthetic case is truly like the taste of sense. Just as we know instantly whether the taste of food delights or disgusts, so we know immediately whether a work of art or the face of one's friend is beautiful or ugly. But the uncommon sense of decadent taste seems to be something that requires cultivation. The senses, in short, need to be educated. The education of the senses in the direction of decadence is one of the subjects of *The Picture of Dorian Gray,* if we read the novel as an *Unbildungsroman* of Dorian's undoing. Early on, the highly refined, corrupt aristocrat Lord Henry Wotton hints at the reciprocal relationship of refinement and corruption when he declares to his soon-to-be protégé Dorian Gray, after he sees the younger man 'drinking [the] perfume' of lilac-blossoms 'as if it had been wine': 'You are quite right to do that. [...] Nothing can cure the soul but the senses, just as nothing can cure the senses but the soul.'[14] The meaning here is a touch ambiguous, since *cure* can mean either 'heal' or 'preserve', as when meat is cured or preserved by salting it. Possibly, Lord Henry means 'preserve', but Dorian clearly takes *cure* to mean 'heal'. The former is actually more consistent with the original Conclusion to Pater's *Studies in the History of the Renaissance* (1873), which Wilde echoes in various ways throughout the novel. In that celebrated conclusion, Pater describes the reciprocity of sensuous experience and sensible reflection on that experience as a source of instability and dissatisfaction that can only be — or best be — alleviated by making the object of experience 'art and song'.[15] In Pater's system, the senses preserve the soul and the soul preserves the senses. But Dorian does not think that *cure* means 'preserve'; he thinks *cure* means 'heal'. As he makes his way to the opium dens late in the novel, Dorian reflects on Lord Henry's words: '"To cure the soul by means of the senses, and the senses by means of the soul!" How the words rang in his ears! His soul, certainly, was sick to death. Was it true that the senses could cure it?' (p. 179) Pater offers the assurance that 'art comes to you professing frankly to give nothing but the highest quality to your moments as they pass, and simply for those moments' sake' (p. 121). Wilde has Dorian echo Pater's claim that the 'wisest' among us spend the brief interval of our life 'in art and song' (Pater, p. 120) when he thinks that

> [u]gliness was the one reality. The coarse brawl, the loathsome den, the crude violence of disordered life, the very vileness of thief and outcast, were more vivid, in their intense actuality of impression, than all the gracious shapes of Art, the dreamy shadows of Song [...] (p. 181)

What Dorian describes is degradation rather than decadence; nevertheless, this perversion of Pater still preserves what is most Paterian about the relationship of the soul to the senses, or of sensibility to experience: 'intense actuality of impression'. But what does this taste for degradation have to do with the taste for decadence? Is it simply decadent taste in a lower register? I wonder if degradation really is the opposite of decadence, and I wonder because of the word *ugliness*: 'Ugliness was the one reality.' Clearly, Dorian's delight in degradation would not be magically transformed into delight in decadence simply by changing *ugliness* to *beauty,* or by transposing any of the other terms in Dorian's series into their opposites. Make beauty the one reality, change 'the coarse brawl' into 'the reasoned argument', 'the loathsome den' into 'the civilized salon', 'the crude violence of disordered life' into 'the gentle peace of ordered existence', and so on, and what you wind up with is at an even further remove from decadence than the degradation Dorian finds in the opium dens of Blue Gate Fields.

Possibly, the concord of decadence and degradation — different as they seem to be at first glance — is one form of correspondence, where decadence is to degradation as sensuousness is to sensuality. The doctrine of correspondences is suggested by Lord Henry's observation that Dorian drinks the perfume of lilac-blossoms as if it had been wine, thereby pointing out the correspondence of the sense of smell with the sense of taste. This little synaesthetic moment is proof that the great transformation in the doctrine of the correspondences wrought by Baudelaire in the middle of the nineteenth century had become a thoroughly received tradition by the end. Originally, the Swedish mystic Emanuel Swedenborg (1688–1772) devised the doctrine to explain how the spiritual world interpenetrates the natural world: 'all things that exist in nature, from the least to the greatest, are correspondences. That they are correspondences is because the natural world with all things in it, exists and subsists from the spiritual world, and both worlds from the Divine.'[16] Baudelaire inherited the Swedenborgian system of correspondences that made sensuous impressions symbols of divine things and transformed it into a synaesthetic system that turned sensuous impressions into symbols of other sensuous impressions: 'There are perfumes fresh as the flesh of children, soft as the sound of oboes, and green as the grass of prairies.'[17] What this and other synaesthetic experiences — 'corrupt, rich, triumphant' — do for us is *expand* our experience to the point that we understand just how infinite that experience really is: infinite odours like 'amber, musk, benjamin, and incense' sing to us and make us realize that the correspondence that counts is the one within, between the mind and the senses, not the one between the mind and some divine realm that, Swedenborg-style, is merely mediated by the senses. Now if the Baudelairean point of the senses is to experience the transports of this infinity within, maybe Dorian's opium works quite as well as Pater's art after all. And maybe that is all art is anyway: the opium of the elite.

The sensuous sublime of echoing odours and reverberating colours certainly enlivens the taste of sense and complicates the sense of taste. Indeed, such sense now seems so uncommon that only someone with a truly select sensibility can have the synaesthetic experience: only the seer can see how soft the sound of lavender is or hear how green those prairies are. At first glance, or first whiff, this elevated Baudelairean state of the senses does not seem quite the same as the taste for decay, but they are both distasteful — if we concentrate for a moment on the initial morpheme of that word, which implies 'removal, aversion, negation, reversal' (*OED*). If decadent taste does involve a taste for the distasteful, such taste includes removal from, aversion to, negation and reversal of aesthetic and social conventions that are validated by people with normal tastes. When his doctor tells Des Esseintes that he must return to Paris for his health, 'lead a normal life again', and 'above all to try and enjoy the same pleasures as other people', the Decadent exclaims, 'But I just don't enjoy the pleasures other people enjoy!' (p. 196) Other people do not enjoy listening to the taste of music, gazing on real flowers that look like fakes, likening literature to a decaying carcass, or making decay itself the pattern of all artifice. Likewise, the Finnish pessimist Joel Lehtonen (1881–1934) has the Nietzschean narrator of his novel *Mataleena* (1905) express the perverse wish for illness when he says that 'if everyone else flaunts their good health, [I] want to be decadent'.[18] The Goncourt brothers, too, found confirmation of their superior aesthetic taste in their neurasthenia, caused, they thought, by the historical accident that forced them to live among the crass, bourgeois society of the Second Empire. We now know, of course, that the brothers' sickness — Jules's anyway — was more likely the result of syphilis, not the new and interesting disease of decadence that Symons described.[19]

But still, decadence is a bit like syphilis after all. You either get it or you don't, and in order to get it, it must be communicated to you. Communication of both disease and aesthetic taste occurs within communities, and it does seem to be true that decadents — as Matthew Potolsky has argued — form a 'self-selected community of taste'. Moreover, the Decadents of the nineteenth century may well have been the first to make 'the association of subcultural affiliation with taste'.[20] The curious thing about this subcultural community of elites who call themselves Decadents is that it is so completely based on taste that taste itself is often what the decadent text is *about*. Verlaine's poem 'Langueur', for example, details the speaker's stylistic taste for 'indolent acrostics' ('des acrostiches indolents') and his sexual taste for neglectful slaves ('un esclave un peu coureur qui vous néglige').[21] And Huysmans's *À rebours* is almost entirely about the refined aesthetic preferences of its mostly inert protagonist. Decadent taste, in other words, operates not only as the basis for the aesthetic appreciation of the reader but also as the creative impetus for the author, whose creation — the decadent hero — is distinguished mainly by his decadent taste. Author, audience, and character, in other words, are all members of the same taste-based community, all motivated by their common appreciation of the uncommon sense of decadence. While it may seem strange to contemplate such kinship between twenty-first-century readers and nineteenth-century authors (and their characters), they all seem to share the central symptom of decadent taste: the transformation of the natural process of decay into an artificial path to aesthetic satisfaction.

Notes to Chapter 12

1. David Weir, *Decadent Culture in the United States: Art and Literature against the American Grain, 1890–1926* (Albany: State University of New York Press, 2008), p. xiii.
2. Monroe C. Beardsley, *Aesthetics: From Classical Greece to the Present: A Short History* (Tuscaloosa and London: University of Alabama Press, 1966), p. 180.
3. Immanuel Kant, *Critique of Judgment*, ed. by Albert Hofstadter and Richard Kuhns, *Philosophies of Art and Beauty: Selected Readings in Aesthetics from Plato to Heidegger* (Chicago: University of Chicago Press, 1976), p. 286. Further references to this edition are cited parenthetically in the text.
4. Edmund Burke, *A Philosophical Enquiry into the Sublime and the Beautiful*, ed. by James T. Bolton (New York: Routledge, 2008), p. 39.
5. Joris-Karl Huysmans, *Against Nature*, trans. by Robert Baldick (New York: Penguin, 2003), p. 55. Further references to this edition are cited parenthetically in the text.
6. Susan Sontag, 'Notes on Camp', in *Against Interpretation and Other Essays* (New York: Picador, 1966), p. 291. Further references to this edition are cited parenthetically in the text.
7. For this formulation, see George C. Schoolfield, *A Baedeker of Decadence: Charting a Literary Fashion* (New Haven and London: Yale University Press, 2003), p. 372, and Weir, *Decadent Culture in the United States*, pp. xvi-xvii.
8. Max Nordau, *Degeneration* (Lincoln: University of Nebraska Press, 1993), p. 306.
9. Théophile Gautier, 'Charles Baudelaire', in *The Works of Théophile Gautier*, ed. and trans. by F. C. de Sumichrast, 24 vols (New York: Sproul, 1903), xxiii, 40. Further references are cited parenthetically in the text.
10. Claud-Marie Senninger, *Baudelaire par Théophile Gautier* (Paris: Klincksieck, 1986), p. 125.
11. Arthur Symons, 'The Decadent Movement in Literature', in *Decadence: An Annotated Anthology*, ed. by Jane Desmarais and Chris Baldick (Manchester and New York: Manchester University Press, 2012), p. 252.
12. See Ivan T. Berend, *A Economic History of Nineteenth-Century Europe: Diversity and Industrialization* (Cambridge: Cambridge University Press, 2013), p. 234, n. 37.
13. Joris-Karl Huysmans, *À rebours*, ed. by Pierre Waldner (Paris: Garnier-Flammarion, 1978), p. 223.
14. Oscar Wilde, *The Picture of Dorian Gray* (New York: Penguin, 2010), p. 23. Further references to this edition are cited parenthetically in the text.
15. Walter Pater, *Studies in the History of the Renaissance*, ed. by Matthew Beaumont (Oxford: Oxford University Press, 2010), p. 120. Further references to this edition are cited parenthetically in the text.
16. Emanuel Swedenborg, *Heaven and Its Wonders and Hell: From Things Heard and Seen* (Boston and New York: Houghton, Mifflin, 1907), p. 63.
17. For the French text of Baudelaire's poem 'Correspondances', see *The Flowers of Evil*, trans. by James McGowan (Oxford: Oxford University Press, 1993), p. 18. Translation mine.
18. Quoted by Pirjo Lyytikäinen, 'Decadent Tropologies of Sickness', in *Decadence, Degeneration and the End: Studies in the European Fin de Siècle*, ed. by Marja Härmänmaa and Christopher Nissen (New York: Palgrave Macmillan, 2014), p. 85. For a sketch of Lehtonen's literary career, see Kai Laitenen, 'The Rise of Finnish Language Literature, 1860–1916', in *A History of Finland's Literature*, ed. by George C. Schoolfield (Lincoln: University of Nebraska Press, 1998), pp. 133–35.

19. According to Roger L. Williams, the nature of Jules de Goncourt's fatal illness 'is absolutely clear: its etiology (syphilis) was established in 1913; and proof that Jules had been syphilitic was published in 1957.' See *The Horror of Life* (Chicago: University of Chicago Press, 1980), p. 108. Edmond de Goncourt (1822–96) survived his younger brother Jules (1830–70) by a quarter-century, dying at the age of 74, not, evidently, a victim of syphilis.
20. Matthew Potolsky, *The Decadent Republic of Letters: Taste, Politics, and Cosmopolitan Community from Baudelaire to Beardsley* (Philadelphia: University of Pennsylvania Press, 2013), pp. 11, 8.
21. Paul Verlaine, *One Hundred and One Poems: A Bilingual Edition*, trans. by Norman R. Shapiro (Chicago: University of Chicago Press, 1999), p. 134.

APPENDIX

Carnal Flowers, Charnel Flowers: Perfume in the Decadent Imagination

Selected by Catherine Maxwell

1. Tuberose and Meadowsweet

Mark André Raffalovich*

Of tuberose I sing and meadowsweet:
One flower much whiter than the fervent dove,
Whose scent in living pulses seems to beat:
Magnetic ardour, drowsy scent of love,
O memory, O presence odorous,
Thy life's perfume, my perfect tuberose!

O meadowsweet, my passion's purity,
O distant echo, faintness rapt and fresh,
That means my soul to thee, and thine to me,
O symbols flowersoft of soul and flesh,
My hands on my love's knees, and my love's feet,
Of tuberose I sing and meadowsweet.

I sing for one we love, my rhymes and I,
Who loves my song for me, me for my song,
    One whom we love we know well why,
        My song and I.
O love do you love us for short, for long,
        Me and my song?
Of meadowsweet I sing, of meadowsweet!

    O mine, my meadowsweet,
      O slender grace to me,
    O fairness made to meet
      With slimness loftily,
    And white but rose-delighted,
    And pink but pale-affrighted,

---

* From *Tuberose and Meadowsweet* (London: David Bogue, 1885), pp. 37–43.

With gazing unreserved
    On love's most steep abysses!
Spreading smiles many curved!
    Soft dreamful skin and kisses,
O mouth not meant to speak
The riddle of thy cheek!
What can be whispered lower,
    Hardly with words to-day,
(But flower-leaf touching flower)
    O do not stir to say.
Silence, for silence knows best.
Be mute: the amorous best!

Of meadowsweet I sing, of meadowsweet.
Slender and sweet, like honey, like thy hair,
O like my words to thee, like meadowsweet,
    Stainless and tender, tall and fair,
    Fair like thy hair,
Tender and sweet like grasses to thy feet,
    Like meadowsweet,
Of meadowsweet I sing, of meadowsweet!

O flower, O love, most mystical and fresh,
Whose breath can thrill us with a breath most sweet,
As with the touch of warm seraphic flesh,
Of meadowsweet I sing, of meadowsweet!

Of tuberose, O love, of tuberose,
I sing of tuberose, of tuberose!
It may be summer in the woods to-day,
Or winter with the trees, or spring, who knows?
It may be pleasant on the new-mown hay
Or near the sea-rock where the wet wind goes,
And happy lovers find their kisses salt.
It may be summer in the woods to-day
Or spring unfolding such a perfect rose
That it would not be fairer for a fault;
If you have me, and I have you, then say
What should we do, who love with empty shows?
It may be summer in the woods to-day,
Or winter with the trees, or spring, who knows?
Of tuberose I sing, of tuberose!

Behind the soft green curtains half undone,
The fluttering paleness, is it morn or eve,

To-day that ends, to-morrow that's begun?
While through the cream white muslin like a sieve,
Some precious light is shed like powdered amber
Between the soft green curtains half undone,
Enough of light to see you nor to grieve–
Glimpses and whispers outside of our chamber,
Inadequate beneath a useless sun,
What sight or sound can one of us receive?
Behind the soft green curtains half undone
The fluttering paleness, is it morn or eve?

Here in the vague and close confined room
All senses are as one acutely blent,
When speechless, touching not, in silent gloom
We yearn and languish with a single scent,
Relentlessly and subtly odorous.
Here in the vague and close confined room
And of Lethean pleasures redolent,
The strong inevitable tuberose
Surrounds irradiating to a tomb,
Where half-unconsciousness is well content.
Here in the vague and close confined room
All senses are as one acutely blent.

If this be death, then we are dead indeed!
O do not stir lest we find life again:
What should we have of life? There is no need
For us to fill the hollow hours in vain
Or lengthen out the sobbing of our breath.
If this be death, then we are dead indeed,
Or waiting for the whole of life to wane,
After the last sigh, love, the first kiss, death!
I think that on some battlefield we bleed,
And I would live once more to be so slain.
If this be death, then we are dead indeed.
O do not stir lest we find life again!

Of tuberose I sing, of tuberose!
O love, O flower, whose name I may not tell
Save unto one alone who is not here,
But who perhaps like me remembers well
One flower, one scent, one hour and one called dear.
For this perfume since then a grave profound,
Wherein is laid of life the perfect whole,
Has undivided from desire been wound

About the inmost longings of my soul.
And when I sicken of my living now
This wizard flower brings back again thy breath,
Touches my mouth and hands: how far art thou?
For I do feel thee like delight or death,
Thy shoulders and thy arms, thy shadowed hair,
Thy speechless lips and thy unaltered stare.
Of tuberose, desirous tuberose,
Of tuberose I sing, of tuberose,
Of tuberose I sing and meadowsweet.

Too much has my desire been heard to moan
Within the narrow cavity of rhyme,
And made poor music in a place of stone,
For loved henceforth or unbeloved, time
No longer may deny for all his wrong,
One worth my rapture, rapture worth my song.
And if my kisses have been strangely red
You must ask meadowsweet and tuberose,
Or pale like them and mutely sung instead;
If each flower cannot tell, at least each knows,
And either scent remembers, white and strong,
One worth my kisses, kisses worth my song.

Give me thy voice, thy breath, thy lids, thy presence,
Thy arm, thy neck, and much too sweet, thy breast;
And bruise my life until thou find its essence,
Love's deepest poppy for my soul's dear guest.
Let them be crushed beneath thy darling feet,
Darling, my tuberose and meadowsweet!

2. Tuberoses

A. Mary F. Robinson*

I.

The Tuberose you left me yesterday
   Leans yellowing in the glass we set it in;
It could not live when you were gone away,
   Poor spike of withering sweetness changed and thin.

And all the fragrance of the dying flower
   Is grown too faint and poisoned at the source,
Like passion that survives a guilty hour,
   To find its sweetness heavy with remorse.

What shall we do, my dear, with dying roses?
   Shut them in weighty tomes where none will look
— To wonder when the unfrequent page uncloses
   Who shut the wither'd blossoms in the book? —

What shall we do, my dear, with things that perish,
   Memory, roses, love we feel and cherish?

II.

Alive and white, we praised the Tuberose,
   So sweet it fill'd the garden with its breath
A spike of waxy bloom that grows and grows
   Until at length it blooms itself to death.

Everything dies that lives — everything dies;
   How shall we keep the flower we lov'd so long?
O press to death the transient thing we prize,
   Crush it, and shut the elixir in a song.

A song is neither live nor sweet nor white.
   It hath no heavenly blossom tall and pure,
No fragrance can it breathe for our delight,
   It grows not, neither lives; it may endure.

Sweet Tuberose, adieu! you fade too fast!
   Only a dream, only a thought, can last.

*From *Songs, Ballads and a Garden Play*
(London: T. Fisher Unwin, 1888), pp. 22–24.

III.

Who'd stay to muse if Death could never wither?
   Who dream a dream if Passion did not pass?
But, once deceived, poor mortals, hasten hither
   To watch the world in Fancy's magic glass.

Truly your city, O men, hath no abiding!
   Built on the sand it crumbles, as it must;
And as you build, above your praise and chiding,
   The columns fall to crush you to the dust.

But fashion'd in the mirage of a dream,
   Having nor life nor sense, a bubble of nought,
The enchanted City of the Things that seem
   Keeps till the end of time the eternal Thought.

Forswear to-day, forswearing joy and sorrow,
Forswear to-day, O man, and take to-morrow.

3. Tuberose

Theodore Wratislaw*

Cool flower! that to my heated lips
Hast clung through half an amorous hour,
I love thee and thy honey drips!
White, languid, heady-scented flower!

My mistress plucked thee from the lulled
Heat of her odorous alcove.
I know the smooth white hands that culled
Thy stem, white messenger of love!

But ah! what missive comes with thee,
My tender bloom, my welcome guest?
In secret dost thou bear to me
The languid fragrance of her breast?

Haply among thy honeyed whirls
A fervent kiss alone abides:
And yet in these enchanted curls
Perchance some traitor poison hides.

Dear poison, send thy deadliest breath
Subtly about me as I lie,
That none may part from me in death
The murderous flower by whom I die!

---

* From *Orchids* (London: Leonard Smithers, 1896), p. 30.

SELECT BIBLIOGRAPHY

BARTHES, ROLAND, *The Pleasure of the Text*, trans. by Richard Miller (New York: Hill and Wang, 1998)
BOYIOPOULOS, KOSTAS, *The Decadent Image: The Poetry of Wilde, Symons and Dowson* (Edinburgh: Edinburgh University Press, 2015)
BRADBURY, MALCOLM and DAVID PALMER (eds.), *Decadence and the 1890s* (London: Edward Arnold, 1979)
BRADSTREET, CHRISTINA, 'Scented Visions: the Nineteenth-century Olfactory Imagination' (unpublished PhD thesis, Birkbeck, University of London, 2008)
BRANT, CLARE, 'Fume and Perfume: Some Eighteenth-Century Uses of Smell', *Journal of British Studies*, 40 (2004), 444–63
BURR, CHANDLER, *The Emperor of Scent: A Story of Perfume, Obsession, and the Last Mystery of the Senses* (London: Arrow Books, 2004)
CYTOWIC, RICHARD E., DAVID M. EAGLEMAN and DMITRI NABOKOV, *Wednesday is Indigo Blue: Discovering the Brain of Synesthesia* (Cambridge, MA: MIT Press, 2009)
DESMARAIS, JANE, 'Perfume Clouds: Olfaction, Memory and Desire in Arthur Symons's *London Nights* (1895)', in *Economies of Desire at the Victorian Fin de Siècle: Libidinal Lives*, ed. by Jane Ford, Kim Edwards Keates and Patricia Pulham (Oxford: Routledge, 2016), pp. 62–79
DESMARAIS, JANE and CHRIS BALDICK (eds.), *Decadence: An Annotated Anthology* (Manchester: Manchester University Press, 2012)
DOWLING, LINDA, *Language and Decadence in the Victorian Fin de Siècle* (Princeton: Princeton University Press, 1986)
GORDON, JAN B., 'The Danse Macabre of Arthur Symons's *London Nights*', *Victorian Poetry*, 9 (1971), 429–43
HALL, JASON DAVID and ALEX MURRAY (eds), *Decadent Poetics: Literature and Form at the British Fin de Siècle* (Basingstoke: Palgrave Macmillan, 2013)
HANSON, ELLIS, *Decadence and Catholicism* (Cambridge, MA: Harvard University Press, 1997)
HOWES, DAVID, *Empire of the Senses: The Sensual Culture Reader* (Oxford: Berg, 2005)
HOWES, DAVID and CONSTANCE CLASSEN, *Ways of Sensing: Understanding Senses in Society* (Oxford: Routledge, 2014)
HUSTVEDT, ASTI (ed.), *The Decadent Reader: Fiction, Fantasy, and Perversion from Fin-de-Siècle France* (New York: Zone, 1998)
KERMODE, FRANK, *The Romantic Image* (London: Routledge and Kegan Paul, 1957)
MARCOVITCH, HEATHER, 'Dance, Ritual, and Arthur Symons's *London Nights*', *English Literature in Transition, 1880–1920*, 56 (2013), 462–82
MAXWELL, CATHERINE, 'Whistlerian Impressionism and the Venetian Variations of Vernon Lee, John Addington Symonds, and Arthur Symons', *Yearbook of English Studies*, 40 (2010), 217–45
—— *Second Sight: The Visionary Imagination in Late Victorian Literature* (Manchester: Manchester University Press, 2011)
—— 'Paterian Flair: Walter Pater and Scent', *The Pater Newsletter*, 61/62 (Spring/Fall 2012), 21–42

—— 'Scents and Sensibility: The Fragrance of Decadence', in *Decadent Poetics: Literature and Form at the British Fin de Siècle*, ed. by Jason David Hall and Alex Murray (Basingstoke: Palgrave, 2013), pp. 201–25

ØSTERMARK-JOHANSEN, LENE, *Walter Pater and the Language of Sculpture* (Farnham: Ashgate, 2011)

POTOLSKY, MATTHEW, *The Decadent Republic of Letters: Taste, Politics, and Cosmopolitan Community from Baudelaire to Beardsley* (Philadelphia: University of Pennsylvania Press, 2013)

SCOTT, CLIVE, 'Symbolism, Decadence and Impressionism', in *Modernism: A Guide to European Literature 1890–1930*, ed. by Malcolm Bradbury and James McFarlane (London: Penguin, 1991), 206–27

THORNTON, R. K. R., *The Decadent Dilemma* (London: Edward Arnold, 1983)

TOWHEED, SHAFQUAT, 'Containing the Poisonous Text: Decadent Readers, Reading Decadence', in *Decadences: Morality and Aesthetics in British Literature*, ed. by Paul Fox (Stuttgart: Ibidem, 2006), 1–32

WEIR, DAVID, *Decadence and the Making of Modernism* (Amherst: University of Massachusetts Press, 1995)

—— *Decadent Culture in the United States: Art and Literature against the American Grain, 1890–1926* (Albany: State University of New York Press, 2008)

INDEX

Adams, Jad 202–03
Aestheticism 4, 164, 184, 186–89, 192
Allen, Grant 74
Allen, Virginia M. 205
anatomical Venus 53, 63 n. 3
androgyny 61, 93
d'Annunzio, Gabriele 15
Antosh, Ruth 76
appetite 3, 6, 70–72
Athenæum, The 83, 86, 88, 90, 91
Avril, Jane 150
Aztecs 35

Barbey d'Aurevilly, Jules-Amédée 203
Barthes, Roland:
  A Lover's Discourse 118
  The Pleasure of the Text 85–86, 102, 107, 110–11
Baudelaire, Charles 1–3, 6–7, 9, 12, 24, 36–37, 45, 55, 58, 69–70, 72–74, 182, 184, 186, 190–92, 195, 197, 200, 202, 204, 206, 219, 222–23, 225–26
  Les Fleurs du mal 2, 6, 7, 37, 69, 72, 73, 115, 202
    'À une Madone' 206, 210
    'Le Balcon' 69
    'Chanson d'après-midi' 6–7
    'Correspondances' 72–73, 225
    'L'Ennemi' 73
    'Le Flacon' 2
    'L'Irréparable' 69
    'Le Soleil' 109
  Mon cœur mis à nu 204
  The Painter of Modern Life 190–91, 195
  Le Spleen de Paris, Petits poèmes en Prose:
    'Anywhere Out of the World' 73–74
Beardsley, Aubrey 19, 22–24, 60, 104, 168, 174, 178, 200–01, 222
  The Fat Woman 23
  The Rape of the Lock 23
Beaulieu, Denyse 35
Beaumont, Avril 85
Beckett, Samuel Joshua 143
Beckson, Karl 19
Beerbohm, Max 222
Benjamin, Walter 71
Bennett, Paula 134
Bernhardt, Sarah 15, 58, 184
Bersani, Leo 145
Betjeman, John 1
Blain, Virginia 130–31

body 5, 13, 105, 165, 168, 178
  as art 57, 60, 61, 95, 107, 166
  Christ's 177, 202
  female 11, 12, 46, 63, 94, 106, 108, 129, 130, 131, 133, 137, 142, 144, 149, 177, 202, 210
  moving 148, 150
  parts 52, 141, 151, 173
  sculptural 11, 182–97
  sexual 33, 34, 39, 46, 111–12, 122, 128, 134, 152, 170, 172, 173, 174, 203
  textual 86, 102–06, 107, 110, 114, 115, 116, 118, 130, 224
books 7–10, 56–57, 69, 72, 80, 83–86, 95–98, 101–18
Borrow, George 90–91
Bourget, Paul 102–03
Boyiopoulos, Kostas 202, 209, 211–12
Bradley, Katharine:
  see Field, Michael
  The New Minnesinger 126–27
Bradstreet, Christina 4
Bresdin, Rodolphe 68
Bristow, Joseph 203
Broadbent, Muriel 168
Broumas, Olga 136
Brown, Ford Madox 87
Browning, Robert 20, 123, 205, 207
Bryher (Annie Winifred Ellerman) 135
Burke, Edmund 221
Burton, Richard 104, 118, 171

Cage, John 146
Caine, Hall 88
Carew, Thomas 105–06
Carpenter, Mary Wilson 133
Carson, Anne 126
Carter, Alexandra 151
Carter, Alfred 69
Catholicism 11, 54, 78, 110, 116, 132, 134, 166, 169–71, 176–78, 194, 212, 213–14
censorship 54, 58, 63 n. 2, 167
Century Guild Hobby Horse, The 164–68, 208, 210
Cevasco, George 70
Chameleon, The 178
Chant, Laura Ormiston 164
Chesterton, G. K. 26
Circe 131–32
Classen, Constance 3–4

Coburn, Alvin Langdon 25–28
    Fountain Court 26, 27
    London 26
    Men of Mark 25–26
Collecott, Diana 126, 136
colour 7, 19, 20, 21, 22, 60, 69, 72, 74, 81 n. 20, 112, 124, 150–51, 189, 196–97, 200, 211–12, 226
Conrad, Joseph 15, 16
Cooley, Arnold J. 5
Cooper, Edith:
    'Circe at Circaeum' 131
    see Field, Michael
Corbin, Alain 3–4
Crackanthorpe, Hubert 166–67
criminality 8, 40–41, 46–47, 57, 122
Cunningham, Merce 146
Custance, Olive 110

dance 10, 107, 141–58
dandyism 18–19, 71
D'Arcy, Ella 168
De Bury, Richard 103
Decadence:
    and the body 1, 5–6, 9, 11–13, 57, 60, 101–18, 162–79, 186–97, 214
    and celebrity 18, 83–98
    and correspondences 7, 9, 72–74, 186, 225
    in England 12, 203
    and food 3, 6, 70, 132–37, 223–24
    in France 51
    and illness 1, 36, 67–68, 72, 74–78, 80, 223, 226
    and objects 9, 52–54, 60–61, 66, 68–70, 95, 97, 104–05, 115
    Roman 3
    and sensuality 2, 51, 60–62, 89, 162–79
    and space 45, 66–80, 109, 146–49, 151, 212
    women in 5, 10, 12, 51–63, 77, 105–08, 121–37, 152
Degas, Edgar 21, 25
Descartes, René 68
Dial, The 11, 23, 166, 168–76, 178
Dierkes-Thrun, Petra 152
disgust 1–3, 6, 12–13, 79, 131, 162, 219–27
Donne, John 106
Douglas, Alfred 169
Dove, Roja 33
Dowling, Linda 57, 102, 111, 188–89, 200, 203–04
Downing, Lisa 206
Dowson, Ernest 1, 5, 11–13, 108, 164, 200–15
    Decorations: In Verse and Prose 12, 200, 207, 212
        'Breton Afternoon' 204, 212
        'Carthusians' 213
        'The Dead Child' 207, 211
        'A Last Word' 214–15
        'Transition' 204, 212
        'Venite Descendamus' 212
    and Foltinowicz, Adelaide 12, 108, 201–02, 211, 214
    'Sonnets — Of a Little Girl' 201
    Verses 11–12, 200, 206, 208, 214
        'Amor Umbratilis' 208
        'Epigram' 12, 208–09
        'Extreme Unction' 213–14
        'Flos Lunae' 108
        'Impenitentia Ultima' 209
        'Non sum qualis eram bonae sub regno Cynarae' 13, 202, 210–11, 213–14
        'Nuns of the Perpetual Adoration' 212–13
        'Preface: For Adelaide' 108
        'Villanelle of His Lady's Treasures' 108
        'You would have understood me, had you waited' 206–07
dream 7, 45, 64 n. 14, 69, 72, 76–79, 115–16, 133, 155, 176, 177, 194, 209, 212, 214
Dujardin, Édouard 102
Dunn, Henry Treffry 95, 97
Duplan, Pierre 148
Duse, Eleonora 15
Dyer, Alfred Sayce 163

Edel, Leon 195
Eliot, T. S. 15, 157, 203
    'The Perfect Critic' 15
Ellena, Jean-Claude 47
Ellis, Havelock 10, 41, 122, 167, 178
    Studies in the Psychology of Sex 122
Ellmann, Richard 55–56
enfleurage 35, 44
eroticism, *see* sexuality

faisandage 223–24
Fassbinder, Rainer Werner 137
feminism 63 n. 6
femme fatale 45–46, 122, 144, 150, 152, 156, 193, 205
Field, Michael 5, 10–11, 38, 121–37, 176
    Callirrhoë 121
    Long Ago 10, 121, 123, 125–27, 129–30, 133, 135
        'Poem I' 129
        'Poem III' 125, 134
        'Poem XIII' 131
        'Poem XVII' 125
        'Poem XXVIII' 126
        'Poem LII' 129
        'Poem LXII' 126
    Mystic Trees 134
    Poems of Adoration 134
        'After Anointing' 134–35
        'That He Should Taste Death For Every Man' 134
    Sight and Song 131
    Underneath the Bough:
        'Why are Women Silent?' 133
    Wild Honey from Various Thyme 10, 132–33
        'Cherry Song' 133

'The Feeding of Apollo' 132
'The Feeding of Bacchus' 132
'Festa' 132–33
Works and Days 121
fin de siècle 1, 3, 12–13, 15, 22, 102, 104, 122, 124, 141, 157, 203
Flaubert, Gustave:
  L'Éducation sentimentale 108
  'Hérodias' 144
  Le Tentation de Saint Antoine 104, 107
flowers 7–8, 32–50, 74–79, 125, 129–31
  Amorphophallus 75, 77
  Anthurium 75
  Caladium 74
  garland-weaving 129–31
  language of 8, 34, 37
  meadowsweet 38–39
  orchid 7, 32–33
    Cattleya 75–77
  poisonous 32, 33, 43, 46–47, 125
  tuberose 7, 33–47
Fontenay-aux-Roses 68
Ford, Ford Madox 17
Fort, Paul 58
fragrance, *see* smell
Freeman, Nick 208
Fuller, Loïe 142–43, 157

Gallienne, Richard Le 88
Gantz, Katherine 53
Gass, William H. 101, 103
Gautier, Judith 184, 191
Gautier, Théophile 16, 42, 110, 112, 184, 221, 223
Gautreau, Virginie 182, 189–93
Gordon, Jan B. 149, 155
Gray, John 11, 168–71, 176–78
  'The Barber' 116
  'Les Goncourts' 166, 169
  'A Hymn Translated from the Italian of Saint Francis of Assisi' 170–71
  'Leda and the Swan' 171
  'Light' 176–78
  'Parsifal, after Verlaine' 169
  'The Redemption of Durtal' 169
Greenaway, Peter:
  The Pillow Book 9–10, 102, 112–18
Guilbert, Yvette 15

Hankey, Frederick 104, 118
Hanson, Ellis 109–10, 134
Harland, Henry 168
Hatt, Michael 187
Hawthorne, Melanie 54–55, 58, 60–61
Hawthorne, Nathaniel 46
H.D. 124, 135
hearing, *see* music
Hecht, Ben 219

hedonism 2, 11, 162, 169, 184, 188
Helleu, Paul 184
Hemans, Felicia 123
Hersey, George L. 5
Highsmith, Patricia 137
Holdsworth, Roger 150
Holmes, Diana 58
Hopman, Marianne Govers 131
Horne, Herbert Percy 164
Horsley, John Calcott 162–63
hothouse 9, 23, 31, 37, 69–70, 74, 78–80, 81 n. 19 and 27
Hunt, Holman 19–20
Hutchinson, Ben 102
Huysmans, Joris-Karl 1, 6–7, 9, 15, 52, 55–57, 58, 66–80, 110, 144, 176, 184, 219–24, 226
  À rebours 6–7, 9, 52–57, 66–80, 103–04, 107, 111, 122, 144, 176, 184, 219–24, 226
  En rade 78–79
  Là-bas 79
hysteria 67–68, 178

Image, Selwyn 164–67
impressionism 7, 16–17, 20–22, 24, 28 n. 9, 149
Ingram, John 34
intersensoriality 2–3, 91, 98, 150, 174, 212
Irvine, Susan 47

Jackson, Holbrook 16, 103, 118, 210–11, 214
James, Henry 184
  'The Last of the Valerii' 11, 192–96
Jerome, Jerome K. 163
Johnson, Lionel 16–17, 121

Kant, Immanuel 220–21
Kelmscott Manor 95
Kermode, Frank 3, 141
Kernahan, Coulson 87–88
kinesthetics 11, 141–58
Krafft-Ebing, Richard Freiherr von 121, 178, 203
Kravis, Judy 148

Laban, Rudolf 156
Lacan, Jacques 205
La Charité, Virginia 149
Laforgue, Jules 15
Lane, John 168
Latham, Sean 85–86
Lawless, Alex 33
Lee, Vernon (Violet Paget) 11, 41–42, 184, 186, 189, 196–97
  Miss Brown 85–87, 89
Lehtonen, Joel 226
Leigh, Arran (Katharine Bradley) 123–24
Leighton, Frederick 168
L. E. L. (Letitia Elizabeth Landon) 123
Lippincott's Monthly Magazine 23, 55, 178

Lloyd's Weekly Newspaper 90
Longinus 221
Lorrain, Jean 57
love, *see* triangle
Louÿs, Pierre 171
Lowell, Amy 135–36
Lugné-Poë, Aurélien-Marie 58
Luyken, Jan 68

Machen, Arthur 9–10, 108–12
   The Hill of Dreams 10, 101–03, 108–12, 114
Mackmurdo, Arthur Heygate 164
Madden, Ed 37
Mallarmé, Stéphane 7, 10–11, 15, 51, 58, 104, 141–52, 157, 223–24
   'Autre étude de danse' 142
   'Ballets' 151–52
   Un coup de Dés jamais n'abolira le Hasard 10, 141, 146–49, 157
   'Crayonné au théâtre' 142–43
   'Crise de vers' 142
   Hérodiade 141, 143–46, 151, 157
   'Le Livre' 149
Mann, Thomas 102
Martin, Violet Florence 135
Maxwell, Catherine 5, 84, 90, 126, 189, 205
memory 45, 71, 74–78, 176
Mendès, Catulle 55
Mercure de France 52, 55, 60
Miller, J. Hillis 193
Mirbeau, Octave 6, 203
mirror 8, 11, 58–60, 65 n. 25, 144, 150, 157, 172, 174, 203
Mitton, Matthew 127
Modernism 15, 85, 104, 124, 135–36, 156–57, 179, 203
Montesquiou-Fezensac, Robert de 71–72, 184
Moore, Arthur 211, 213
Moore, George 103, 105, 107, 109
Moore, Thomas 34
Moore, Thomas Sturge 11, 168, 172–73
Morris, May 95–96
Morris, William 95
Munro, John M. 21
music 20–21, 25, 64 n. 31, 69, 116, 121, 150
music-hall 107, 164, 168
   Alhambra 16, 149, 177
   Empire 149, 164
   Moulin Rouge 150

Nead, Lynda 195
Nisard, Désiré 3
Nordau, Max 122, 222

olfaction 4, 69
   see also smell
Østermark-Johansen, Lene 193
Ovid 123–24

Pachmann, Vladimir de 15
paganism 134, 135, 188, 194
Pageant, The 11, 176–78
Paglia, Camille 78
Pall Mall Gazette 19
Pater, Walter 7, 11, 19–20, 22, 25, 32, 36–37, 56, 86, 101–02, 121, 128–29, 150, 164, 167, 177–78, 182, 186–90, 192–93, 195, 197, 220–21, 224–26
   Appreciations, with an Essay on Style 101
   'An English Poet' 36
   Gaston de Latour 103
   Greek Studies 128
   Marius the Epicurean 56
   'The Myth of Demeter and Persephone' 193
   Studies in the History of the Renaissance 20, 25, 32, 37, 56, 102–03, 167, 177–78, 187–90, 192–93, 195, 224–25
Patti, Guesch 116
Peace Rhind, Jennifer 38
Pease, Alison 122
perfume 2, 5, 33, 47, 69
   see also smell
perversity 12, 32, 51, 57, 70, 93, 118, 122, 202, 210, 223, 226
Phillips, Anita 204
Phillips, Claude 187, 192
Piesse's Art of Perfumery 33, 35, 46
Plato 188–89, 193, 219–20
pornography 54, 104, 107, 173
Potolsky, Matthew 8, 57, 226
Poucher, William A. 34
Pound, Ezra 157
Powell, Kerry 152
Poynter, Edward J. 163
Pozzi, Samuel Jean 184
Prettejohn, Elizabeth 127
Prins, Yopie 130
Proust, Marcel 76, 184
puritanism 162, 164, 165, 168, 169, 178–79
Pygmalion 5, 10, 11, 12, 52, 53, 109, 116, 186, 191, 193, 195, 204–06, 208–09, 215 and 215 n. 7

queer, *see* love
Quincey, Thomas de 176

Rachilde (Marguerite Eymery) 1, 5, 8, 51–63, 203
   L'Araignée de cristal 8, 51, 58–60, 62
   La Jongleuse 51, 60–63
   Madame la Mort 51
   La Marquise de Sade 51, 55
   Monsieur Vénus 8, 51, 52–57, 203
   La Voix du sang 51
Raffalovich, Mark André 36–41, 55
   Tuberose and Meadowsweet 8, 37–41, 229–32
Redon, Odilon 57, 68, 78
religion 6, 11, 41, 65, 71, 73, 78–80, 90, 94, 104, 109–11, 124, 132–35, 162–79, 202, 205, 209–14

Reynolds, Dee 146, 148
Reynolds, Margaret 123
Rich, Adrienne 136–37
Ricketts, Charles 121, 168–69, 173–74, 176
Rilke, Rainer Maria 102
Robinson, Agnes Mary Frances 5, 7–8, 38, 41–45
   'Tuberoses' 42–45, 233–34
Robinson, Mabel 42
roman-à-clef 9, 83–98
Romany 84–85, 90–91
Rossetti, Christina 133
Rossetti, Dante Gabriel 43, 83–98, 106–07
Rossetti, William Michael 19, 88, 89
Rothenstein, William 207
Rothko, Mark 23
Ruskin, John 18, 20
   see also Whistler, libel trial
Russell, Ada Dwyer 136

Sacher-Masoch, Leopold von 202–03
Saltus, Edgar 219
Sappho 10, 38, 121–37, 173, 213
Sargent, John Singer 11, 155, 182–93
   Fumée d'Ambre Gris 186
   Heads and Faces of Javanese Dancers 153–55
   Madame X 11, 182–87, 189–97
   Mrs. Henry White 11, 182, 184–85, 196–97
   Oyster Gatherers at Cancale 186
   Portraits d'enfants (*The Daughters of Edward Darley Boit*) 187
Sarton, May 137
Savage, Reginald 169
Savoy, The 15, 19, 20, 21, 167–68, 178, 200
Schwob, Marcel 51, 58
Scott, Clive 17
sculpture 11–12, 144, 182–97, 205
sensorium 3, 4, 9, 12, 69, 92, 94, 97
sensory studies 3–4
sexuality:
   chastity 11, 60–61
   eroticism 6, 8, 43, 60–62, 75, 103, 110, 114, 121–37
   fetishism 52–53, 98, 110–11, 118
   homosexuality 8, 11, 37, 40–41, 52–53, 56, 92–93, 121–22, 128, 169–71, 186, 188–89, 202
   lesbianism 41, 55, 121–37
   masochism 12, 111, 118, 202–10, 215
   necrophilia 118, 206
   sadism 128, 203
   sadomasochism 47, 51–54, 62, 137, 202
Shakespeare, William 44
Shannon, Charles 11, 121, 168–69, 173–76
Shaw, Bernard 151
Shelley, Percy 35–37
Sherard, Robert 207
Shiel, M. P. 110
Shikibu, Murasaki 112
Shirley, James 106

Shōnagon, Sei 112, 114, 115
Siddal, Elizabeth 94
sight, *see* vision
Silverman, Willa Z. 72
skin 5, 10, 36, 46, 77, 112, 114, 117, 118, 184, 187, 193, 197, 198 n. 3
smell 4–5, 7, 12, 13 n. 4, 16, 31–50, 68–69, 75–76, 79
   body odour 45–46
   of flowers 15–31, 68, 75–76, 79
   hyperosmia 76
   incense 79–80
   olfactory recall 45, 75
   perfume 2, 31–50, 44–47, 69, 75–76, 79, 101, 133, 212
Smith, Alison 163
Smithers, Leonard 22, 171
Snodgrass, Chris 205
Snyder, Jane McIntosh 124, 129
Solomon, Simeon 128, 189
Somerville, Edith 135
Sontag, Susan 102, 120, 222
Staël, Madame de 123
Stephenson, Andrew 186
Stevenson, R. A. M. 197
Süskind, Patrick 112
Swedenborg, Emanuel 72–73, 225–26
Swinburne, Algernon Charles 1, 10, 12, 19, 37–39, 41, 46, 84, 87–88, 104, 122–23, 127–28, 130, 133, 189, 200, 202, 204–06, 208–10, 215
   'Charles Baudelaire' 37
   Poems and Ballads:
      'Anactoria' 10, 41, 122, 127–28, 130, 133
      'Dolores' 202, 204–06, 209
      'Fragoletta' 127
      'Hermaphroditus' 122
      'Laus Veneris' 39
Symbolism 8, 10–11, 16, 24, 51, 57–59, 78, 141–42, 144, 146, 149–51, 155–57, 186, 203
Symonds, John Addington 36, 130, 188–89
Symons, Arthur 5, 7, 10, 12, 15–28, 52, 80, 92, 121, 141–42, 149–57, 164, 168, 201, 203, 210–12, 214–15, 223, 226
   'At the Alhambra: Impressions and Sensations' 168
   Cities 21, 26
   Cities and Sea-Coasts and Islands 26
   Cities of Italy 21
   'The Decadent Movement in Literature' 15, 16, 17, 92–93, 156, 223, 226
   'Ernest Dowson' 201, 211
   The Fool of the World 24
   From Toulouse-Lautrec to Rodin 17
   Images of Good and Evil 24, 142, 150
      'The Dance of the Daughters of Herodias' 10, 156–57
   'Impressionistic Writing' 21, 24
   Knave of Hearts 24
      'The Brother of a Weed' 16

London: A Book of Aspects 20, 25, 26
London Nights 15, 19, 21, 142, 150, 203, 212
    'At the Foresters' 107
    'Bianca' 203
    'La Mélinite: Moulin Rouge' 150, 152
    'Leves Amores' 22
    'On the Stage' 151–52
    'Stella Maris' 22
    'To A Dancer' 152
    'White Heliotrope' 106
    and *The Savoy* 19, 20
Silhouettes 15, 16, 20, 24, 142, 150, 203
    'Javanese Dancers' 155–56
Spiritual Adventures:
    'An Autumn City' 18
    'The Death of Peter Waydelin' 7, 22–23
    'A Prelude to Life' 28
Studies in Seven Arts 25
    'The Painting of the Nineteenth Century' 22
The Symbolist Movement in Literature 15, 24, 149, 156
William Blake 24
    'The World as Ballet' 149
synaesthesia 2, 3, 9, 39, 69, 72–73, 111, 121–22, 150, 187, 225–26

taste 10, 12, 121–37, 213, 219
    aesthetic 22, 219–27
    flavour 10, 12, 122, 124–37
texts, *see* books
Thain, Marion 132
Thomas, Jane 192
Thornton, R. K. R. 200, 203–04, 208, 215
Times, The 11, 18, 83, 162–67
tongue 10, 36, 123, 124, 125, 128, 134, 135, 136, 138 n. 19
touch 5–6, 11, 39, 61, 68, 83, 85, 91–92, 95, 97, 105, 116, 135, 144, 146, 173, 176–77, 187, 220
Toulouse-Lautrec, Henri de 15
Towheed, Shafquat 86
triangle, *see* queer
Turner, Frank 188

Ulrichs, Karl Heinrich 121
Uzanne, Octave 104

Valéry, Paul 102
Vallette, Alfred 51, 58
venereal disease 54, 74, 77–78

ventriloquism 84, 104, 107
Verlaine, Paul 15, 20, 102, 169, 219, 223–24, 226
Vintschgau, Maximilian von 124–25
violence 44, 51, 53, 61–62, 203
vision 7, 10, 15–28
voyeurism 61, 172–75

Wainewright, Thomas Griffiths 103
Waterhouse, William 4
Waters, Sarah 137
Watts-Dunton, Theodore 5, 9, 19, 83–98
Weinfield, Henry 148
Weir, David 66
Wells, H. G. 32
Wharton, Henry Thornton 123, 125, 130, 173
Whistler, Beatrice 24
Whistler, James McNeill 7, 17–28, 179 n. 2
    Arrangement in Black 21
    Caprice in Purple and Gold 19
    The Gentle Art of Making Enemies 18, 22
    Nocturne — Blue and Gold — Old Battersea Bridge 22
    libel trial with Ruskin 18–19, 22, 24, 29 n. 20
    'The Ten O'Clock Lecture' 26
White, J. W. Gleeson 176
white[ness] 12, 45, 108, 114, 182, 184, 186–90, 196–97, 200
    and homosexuality 186, 188–89
Wilde, Oscar 1–3, 12, 18, 21, 24, 32, 37, 51–63, 79, 86, 101, 110, 121, 144, 164, 169, 172, 178, 188, 203, 214, 219–22, 224–26
    'A Bevy of Poets' 37
    'The Decay of Lying: An Observation' 21
    The Importance of Being Earnest 24
    and Lorrain, Jean 57
    The Picture of Dorian Gray 2, 7–8, 32, 55–57, 79–80, 101, 115, 118, 161, 164–65, 169, 178, 214, 221–22, 224–26
    Salomé 8, 58, 60–63, 144, 203
Wind, Edgar 126
Wratislaw, Theodore 7–8, 45–47
    'Tuberose' 8, 45, 235
Wright, M. B. 187

Yeats, W. B. 15, 44, 157
Yellow Book, The 15, 166–68, 178

Žižek, Slavoj 205

www.ingramcontent.com/pod-product-compliance
Lightning Source LLC
LaVergne TN
LVHW061250060426
835507LV00017B/1991